1978

Mental retardation

SOCIAL AND EDUCATIONAL PERSPECTIVES

Mental retardation
SOCIAL AND EDUCATIONAL PERSPECTIVES

CLIFFORD J. DREW
Assistant Dean,
Graduate School of Education,
University of Utah,
Salt Lake City, Utah

MICHAEL L. HARDMAN
Assistant Professor,
Department of Special Education,
University of Utah,
Salt Lake City, Utah

HARRY P. BLUHM
Associate Professor,
Department of Educational Psychology,
University of Utah,
Salt Lake City, Utah

With a foreword by
BURTON BLATT
Director and Professor,
Division of Special Education and Rehabilitation,
Syracuse University, Syracuse, New York

The C. V. Mosby Company
Saint Louis   1977

Copyright © 1977 by The C. V. Mosby Company

All rights reserved. No part of this book may be reproduced
in any manner without written permission of the publisher.

Printed in the United States of America

Distributed in Great Britain by Henry Kimpton, London

Library of Congress Cataloging in Publication Data

Main entry under title:

Mental retardation.

    Includes bibliographical references and index.
    1. Mentally handicapped children. 2. Mentally
handicapped children—Education. 3. Mentally
handicapped—Employment. I. Drew, Clifford J.,
1943-   II. Hardman, Michael L. III. Bluhm,
Harry P.
HV891.M44   362.3   76-26680
ISBN 0-8016-1462-7

GW/M/M 9 8 7 6 5 4 3 2 1

CONTRIBUTORS

MICHAEL J. BEGAB

National Institute of Child Health and
    Human Development,
Bethesda, Maryland

BURTON BLATT

Director and Professor,
Division of Special Education and
    Rehabilitation,
Syracuse University,
Syracuse, New York

HARRY P. BLUHM

Associate Professor,
Department of Educational Psychology,
University of Utah,
Salt Lake City, Utah

DONN BROLIN

Department of Counseling and
    Personnel Services,
University of Missouri at Columbia,
Columbia, Missouri

PHILIP J. BURKE

Division of Personal Preparation,
Bureau of Education for the Handicapped,
U.S. Office of Education,
Washington, D.C.

ROBERT A. BURT

Professor of Law,
College of Law,
The University of Michigan,
Ann Arbor, Michigan

FLORENCE CHRISTOPLOS

Division of Graduate Studies,
Bowie State College,
Bowie, Maryland

ELEANOR COLEMAN

Supervisor, Girls' Physical Education,
Duval County,
Jacksonville, Florida

DAVID M. CONGDON

HIP Coordinator and Psychologist,
Lincoln State School,
Lincoln, Illinois

MATILDA F. de BOOR

Waisman Center,
University of Wisconsin at Madison,
Madison, Wisconsin

VICTOR EISSLER

Institute of Contemporary Corrections and
    Behavioral Sciences,
Sam Houston State University,
Huntsville, Texas

WALTER F. ERSING

Department of Physical Education,
Ohio State University,
Columbus, Ohio

CHARLES M. FRIEL

Institute of Contemporary Corrections and
    Behavioral Sciences,
Sam Houston State University,
Huntsville, Texas

KATHRYN A. GORHAM

Director, Montgomery County Association for
    Retarded Citizens' Family and Community Services,
Silver Springs, Maryland

CAROL GRAHAM

Virginia Association for Children with
    Learning Disabilities
Blacksburg, Virginia

BOBBY G. GREER

Department of Special Education and
  Rehabilitation,
College of Education,
Memphis State University,
Memphis, Tennessee

FRANCES KAPLAN GROSSMAN

Department of Psychology,
Boston University,
Boston, Massachusetts

ROBERT HARTH

Assistant Professor,
Department of Special Education,
University of Missouri at Columbia,
Columbia, Missouri

JUNE B. JORDAN

Assistant Director,
Council for Exceptional Children
  Information Center,
Reston, Virginia

MERLE B. KARNES

Institute for Research on
  Exceptional Children,
Department of Special Education,
University of Illinois, Urbana-Champaign,
Urbana, Illinois

CHARLES KOKASKA

Department of Education,
California State University at Long Beach,
Long Beach, California

OLIVER P. KOLSTOE

School of Social Education and
  Rehabilitation,
University of Northern Colorado,
Greeley, Colorado

PETER G. KRAMER

Director of Physical Education,
Golden Hills Academy,
Ocala, Florida

E. L. LOSCHEN

Department of Psychiatry,
Southern Illinois University School
  of Medicine,
Springfield, Illinois

DONALD L. MacMILLAN

College of Education,
University of California at Riverside,
Riverside, California

ROBERT L. MARSH

Department of Criminal Justice,
Boise State University,
Boise, Idaho

STEVEN MAURER

Special Education Division,
University of Northern Iowa,
Cedar Falls, Iowa

JANE R. MERCER

Professor and Chairperson,
Department of Sociology,
University of California at Riverside,
Riverside, California

ELIZABETH OGG

Public Affairs Committee,
New York, New York

JOHN OSTANSKI

Department of Special Education,
University of New Orleans,
New Orleans, Louisiana

ROBERT PERSKE

Institute for Development of
  Human Resources,
Random House,
New York, New York

PHILIP ROOS

Executive Director,
National Association for Retarded Citizens,
Arlington, Texas

DAVID A. SABATINO

Department of Special Education,
Northern Illinois University,
De Kalb, Illinois

R. C. SCHEERENBERGER

Central Wisconsin Colony and Training School,
Madison, Wisconsin

ED SKARNULIS

Department of Family Practice,
College of Medicine,
University of Nebraska,
Omaha, Nebraska

MARYLANE Y. SOEFFING

Education Specialist,
Council for Exceptional Children
  Information Center,
Reston, Virginia

ED SONTAG

Division of Innovation and Development,
Bureau of Education for the Handicapped,
U.S. Office of Education,
Washington, D.C.

SUSAN STAINBACK

Special Education Division,
University of Northern Iowa,
Cedar Falls, Iowa

WILLIAM STAINBACK

Special Education Division,
University of Northern Iowa,
Cedar Falls, Iowa

HAROLD W. STUBBLEFIELD

VPI and SUI,
College of Education,
Blacksburg, Virginia

JAMES A. TESKA

Department of Special Education,
Southern Illinois University,
Carbondale, Illinois

PETER VALLETUTTI

Director of Special Education,
Coppin State College,
Baltimore, Maryland

ROBERT YORK

Department of Studies in Behavioral
  Disabilities,
University of Wisconsin at Madison,
Madison, Wisconsin

R. REID ZEHRBACH

Institute for Research on Exceptional Children,
Department of Special Education,
University of Illinois, Urbana-Champaign,
Urbana, Illinois

FOREWORD

The temptation is to write about the compelling issues in this collection. Also, I think it would be enjoyable to write about the authors, several of whom I know, and of the others whose works I know. I must still those motivations, because if I don't there may be the pull to write about myself, and that would surely be immodest and probably uninteresting. Besides, the editors write very effectively about the issues and the authors in their succinct section introductions. Why repeat needlessly?

Therefore, I have decided to concentrate on two themes: what I seek in a book, any book; and why I conclude that this book deserves the attention of people concerned with the so-called mentally retarded.

As in any other situation, a person must always deal with limited resources. The university has limited resources; the public school has limited resources; the individual has limited resources. And for so many of us, aside from the seemingly perennial grind of trying to make ends meet in a world seemingly gone haywire, time itself is among the scarcest commodities—in spite of my observation elsewhere that too many people appear to have very little to do. So we must select our books with care, not an easy decision given the flood of paper that assaults us in this era of "publish or perish," "read or be labeled ignorant" (even if thinking itself is suspect in certain quarters). Then why this book? That's a question whose answer, at least my answer, comes later.

I look for a book that will teach me not only about the technical aspects of a problem but the reason for its importance. Certainly, elementary teachers must read books about the teaching of reading. Yet in some sense, those books must also be connected with what someone should read as well as how someone reads.

I look for commitment of the authors when I peruse a book. I remember that Socrates was put to death because of his alleged corruption of youth. He was killed because the people didn't like what he taught. Teaching once held this importance, and I expect books about teaching to have a seriousness of purpose that can overcome different values and opinions between the author and the reader, or even an author's "mistakes."

I look for maturity in those who would have the courage to write books. Don't misunderstand, and that usually is an invitation to misunderstand, but I think there may be something "wrong" with the role-models that teachers and professors present to their students. This is my way of suggesting that students sometimes gain the impression that their teachers have little to do except to play with or entertain students. There is the suggestion here that people who don't *have* to teach may be the ones who should be encouraged to teach. And I feel somewhat the same way about writers. That is, writers should be competent to do something else, such as carpentry, fishing, farming, working with children, advocacy—you name it, but something else. And their books and papers should reflect those outside lives. At least I'd appreciate that.

Last, my kind of book is one that attempts to enlarge our lives, not in the physical or materialistic sense but in spiritual and personal ways. So many of the things that are made supposedly for people that are huckstered in our open markets accomplish little more than to make people useless. The electric can opener and pencil sharpener don't do the job better than the old-fashioned tools, while they make the human being stand around and wait for the can or pencil to drop. We have too many rowing machines that don't move and bicycles that go nowhere and television sets that destroy conversation. Let a book bring us closer together or let it bring a human being together inside.

I now return to the earlier question: Why this book? The issues in this book are clearly laid out, and those are the important issues in our field: the family, evaluation, social issues, legal issues, the curriculum, the teacher, vocations, and physical education. There appears to be a thoughtful order to the sections, the chapters, and the discussion questions. It is good that Clif Drew, Mike Hardman, and Harry Bluhm began with attitudes and perspectives from those who really know, the brothers, sisters, and families of the so-called mentally retarded. This is an honest book, each chapter chosen with apparent care, not a book to salve the temporary irritation or to pander to the immediate fad but more so a volume to have and to return to.

There it is, what I like to have in books that I read and why I found that this measures well.

Burton Blatt

PREFACE

Mental retardation has been an area of interest to many for a considerable length of time. Even disregarding very early recorded descriptions (dating several hundred years B.C.), mental retardation has a history that predates many of the current areas of concern in special education. In spite of this long record of attention, it is only in relatively recent times that serious consideration has been given to the broader perspectives of this complex problem. The realization that social and educational influences are vitally intertwined has emphasized the fact that no single perspective or facet of the problem is pure. It is virtually impossible, and certainly imprecise, to view a given behavioral phenomenon in a simplistic, single-focus manner. This is certainly the case with mental retardation, a phenomenon that has a dramatic impact on and is affected by all of society from nearly every vantage point.

The purpose of the present volume is to examine the social and educational perspectives of mental retardation, the impact of societal and educational institutions upon the mentally retarded individual, and, in turn, the impact of mental retardation on these institutions.

The book consists of two major parts, Social Issues and Educational and Vocational Issues. The first part is divided into four sections that address different but related social aspects of the mental retardation problem: family relationships, assessment, clinical-societal issues, and legal issues. Part Two, Educational and Vocational Issues, also contains four sections. These sections examine delivery patterns and instruction, implications for teacher preparation, vocational considerations, and physical and recreational education. Each of these areas could easily constitute an entire volume by itself and, in some cases, has. In many cases, however, these topics are only emerging as serious foci of attention.

We have drawn on the most recent literature in an attempt to present the current issues relating to social and educational perspectives of mental retardation. A conscious effort has been made to select articles that present the intended message in highly readable form. In many cases the message is controversial. This too is intentional since the problems of mental retardation are themselves embroiled in controversy. It is hoped that the reader will find this volume thought provoking and will be inclined to ponder the many complexities of mental retardation. The most serious attention and best thinking possible must be brought to bear if effective solutions are to be found for the problem of mental retardation.

Clifford J. Drew
Michael L. Hardman
Harry P. Bluhm

CONTENTS

PART I

SOCIAL ISSUES

FAMILY RELATIONSHIPS AND RETARDATION

Nowhere is the impact of mental retardation in the form of trauma, shame, distress, frustration, anger, and fatigue so keenly felt as in the family. These terms and numerous others are used in attempts to describe the experience of having a mentally retarded child in the family, yet no words can capture the complete essence of mental retardation. Words are inadequate in breadth and intensity to fully portray the problems involved. Language remains, however, the primary means of communicating or obtaining knowledge, and in the articles in this section various dimensions of family issues as they are influenced by the presence of a mentally retarded individual in the family are explored. Attitudes of significant others play an important role in many aspects of behavior. Consequently, it is necessary to have some idea concerning attitudes toward mental retardation in order to better understand the problem fully. Robert Harth's article provides an interesting overview of what the literature has to say about the attitudes of four groups concerning mental retardation—professionals, institutional employees, parents of retarded children, and retarded children themselves. This is followed by an article by Kathryn A. Gorham, with a more direct focus on parents of the retarded. This article discusses in a uniquely objective and yet

empathetic manner the frustrations of being a parent of a mentally retarded child, based on 13 years of experience. This perspective, which is difficult to achieve, is presented with a delicate balance of parental emotion and insightful advice to professionals. The articles by Matilda F. de Boor and Bobby G. Greer, which follow, represent brief vignettes of family perspectives with different but powerful messages; these are statements that must be read, pondered, and digested. Their depth is deceptive and emphasizes the viewpoint that length does not necessarily connote substance.

The impact of a retarded child on siblings has often been discussed informally but has been rarely journalized in any systematic fashion. The article by Frances Kaplan Grossman presents some fascinating insights into the world of brothers and sisters of retarded children. The techniques used for data collection are comprehensive, the questions asked are penetrating, and the results complex. This article serves to reemphasize the multifaceted nature of mental retardation, particularly when viewed in a societal context. The societal context would not be complete without a discussion of an institution of longstanding influence, religion. Harold W. Stubblefield's article on religion, parents, and mental retardation addresses this important area from a number of standpoints.

Families of retarded children can and should become more than reactors to their environment. This has become increasingly evident as knowledge and practice have progressed over the years. However, the nature and success of family involvement has varied greatly throughout the country. The final article in this section, by Merle B. Karnes, R. Reid Zehrbach, and James A. Teska, presents an exciting model for parental involvement. This model is particularly refreshing because it provides a much needed conceptualization of a highly complex area.

CHAPTER 1

"Attitudes and mental retardation: review of the literature"

ROBERT HARTH

University of Missouri at Columbia

ABSTRACT: *The following paper is a review of recent literature on attitudes toward mental retardation. There are two sections to the paper. The first discusses the attitudes of various population groups towards mental retardation. The second section is a discussion of attitude change research.*

The purpose of this paper is to present a review of the research done during the past decade on attitudes toward mental retardation. Attitudes, according to Osgood, Succi, and Tannenbaum (1957) act as predispositions toward behavior. They represent a verbal statement about how one feels toward a particular construct. Whether or not a person behaves toward that construct in a manner consistent with his stated attitude is another question. Other variables determine behavior besides verbal attitudes. However, attitudes are one contributor of a final behavioral act.

As we shall see from this review, people hold rather strong and divergent attitudes about mental retardation. And if these attitudes are one determinant of behavior towards people who are mentally retarded, then we must begin to look at the nature of these attitudes and how they can be modified.

Reprinted from the Training School Bulletin **69**:150-164, 1972, with permission.
Robert Harth, Ed.D., Assistant Professor, Department of Special Education, University of Missouri, Columbia, Mo.

The paper is divided into two basic sections. The first discusses the attitudes various population groups have about mental retardation. The second section deals with attempts to change attitudes towards mental retardation.

ATTITUDES OF VARIOUS POPULATION GROUPS

In this section, the attitudes of four population groups will be discussed. These groups are: a) professionals, b) institutional employees, c) parents of retarded children, and d) retarded children.

Attitudes of professionals

The major portion of this section will deal with attitudes of pediatricians and teachers. This is because they represent the most numerous studies appearing in the literature. Attitudes of other professional groups (e.g. nurses, physicians, social workers, psychologists) receive considerably less attention. One study, Babow and Johnson (1969) did study the attitudes of these and other professionals. However, this study will be more appropriately discussed in the next section on "Attitudes of Institutional Employees."

The first group of professionals to consider are pediatricians. These physicians are often the first professionals to become aware that a child is mentally retarded. Since they also often become the first professionals to help parents adjust to the birth as well as to help them make future plans, their attitudes are crucial. This is particularly true in the instance of helping parents make a decision about institutionalization or home care. Olshansky and Sternfeld (1962) addressed themselves to this issue. They were concerned with whether or not pediatricians trained before the recent public concern about mental retardation would reflect modern attitudes toward institutionalization. The subjects were 30 established pediatricians (13 had 20 or more years experience, six had between 10 and 19 years, 11 had between one and nine years). The results were rather discouraging. They indicated that few of the pediatricians had any well developed perspective to guide their interactions with parents of retarded children.

As a follow-up to the above study, Olshansky and Kettell (1963) attempted to study attitudes towards institutionalization of pediatricians still in training. Since these pediatricians were still in school they should show more modern views. The results did indicate that these pediatricians tended to hold the newer views of preferring home care over institutionalization. However, the results also indicated that these pediatricians had limited knowledge, training and interest in the area of mental retardation. Similar results were reported by Fishler, Koch, Sands and Bills (1968). Using fourth year medical students they found that home care was preferred over institutionalization. They also found a lack of knowledge and interest in mental retardation.

These few studies point out that medical education programs are generally deficient with regards to mental retardation. There is some evidence from these studies that medical schools now are encouraging pediatricians to suggest home care over institutionaliza-

tion. However, these studies also indicate that medical schools do not teach much about the nature of mental retardation, nor do they encourage medical students to specialize in this area of service or research. This is an unfortunate state of affairs when we realize that physicians are often the first professionals to face parents with the fact that they have a retarded child.

Equally important in the problems of mental retardation are teachers. Teachers probably spend more time with retarded children than do most other professionals. Kingsley (1967) studied the attitudes of prospective teachers toward exceptional children. It is interesting to note that these students had an adequate understanding of the general purpose of special education. This is consistent with Olshansky and Kettell (1963) as well as with Fishler, Koch, Sands and Bills (1968). However, when these students were asked to rank the exceptional child they would most and least like to teach, they indicated the most preferred to be the gifted and the least preferred to be the severely retarded. Further, they felt that the severely retarded needed to be institutionalized as opposed to being provided educational services. Bergan and Smith (1966) also investigated the attitudes of prospective teachers toward mental retardation. They found that retarded children of higher socioeconomic status were regarded more favorably than retarded children of lower socioeconomic status.

Harth (1971) compared the attitudes of special education students and regular education students towards mental retardation. He found that overall, special education students had more favorable attitudes towards mental retardation than did general education students. Using a scale that measures five dimensions of attitudes he found that special education students were: 1) more willing to decrease social distance between themselves and the mentally retarded, and 2) more positive about the private rights of the mentally retarded, i.e., feeling that the mentally retarded have individual rights of free association in playgrounds, schools, housing, etc.

In considering the attitudes of teachers, Fine (1967) expressed concern over the relationship between attitudes and behavior. This concern stemmed from an investigation of the attitudes of elementary special and regular class teachers. He found that not only do special class teachers place greater emphasis on personal and social adjustment than do regular class teachers, but they also make less demands upon lower ability students to try harder. Schmidt and Nelson (1969) reported the same results with secondary level teachers.

The concern here is that special class teachers may be underestimating the ability of their students. This is reminiscent of Dunn's (1968) classic paper. In reviewing the research on the efficacy of special classes for the educable mentally retarded, Dunn concluded that the academic achievement of these students was lower in special classes than in regular classes. Thus, the notion of teachers contributing to the lower achievement of their students gains support.

Further support for this notion came from the work of Rosenthal and Jacobson (1968). It will be recalled that these authors found that when teachers were told to expect great achievement from randomly selected students, these students actually did show some improvement. If this notion of expectancy works to increase achievement, one would expect that it could work to hinder achievement.

Thus there appears to be a need for concern about the attitudes of professionals. The present review indicated that these attitudes appear to affect performance of retarded children. The evidence for this, however, is indirect. Independent research would have to take it beyond the suggestive stage. If attitudes do indeed affect behavior, it is apparent that greater stress needs to be placed in professional training programs. Many of the studies cited suggested this.

Warren and Turner (1966) have added a caution to the studies of the attitudes of professionals. The concern here was with the finding that the severely retarded appear to be the least preferred type of exceptional child. This tends to give the impression that there is something about severely retarded children that makes them distasteful to professionals. In studying the attitudes of a variety of professionals, these authors found that their subjects least preferred working with the severely retarded and their university programs stressed this area of exceptionality least. Thus, there is some suggestion that the least preferred status of the severely retarded may be more a function of lack of familiarity and knowledge than an actual distaste for these people.

Attitudes of institutional employees

Employees in institutions for the retarded have also been studied. As with teachers, many of these employees spend considerable time with mentally retarded people. Babow and Johnson (1969) studied the attitudes of 760 such employees (513 psychiatric technicians, 127 nurses, 50 physicians, 28 social workers, 14 rehabilitation therapists, 10 psychologists, and 18 of unreported occupations). Using Tyron's 0 analysis they were able to identify five clusters of employees, each representing a different attitude picture. Cluster One employees (called humanistic) were highly motivated for change and were in positions to do something about it. Cluster Two employees (called negative custodials) had a negative orientation to mental retardation and a sociotherapeutic orientation. They were also high on authoritarianism, on anomie, and on a somatotherapeutic orientation. Unfortunately, 91 percent of these people were involved in direct patient care. The largest cluster of people were intermediate in most measures and were called "middle of the roaders." Cluster Four individuals were intermediate on mental retardation orientation, on anomie, on somatotherapeutic orientation and on sociotherapeutic orientation. However, they were high on authoritarianism. Unlike Cluster Two, these individuals were called "benevolent custodials." Cluster Five individuals were called "ideological inconsistency" being contradictory and inconsistent in their responses.

One often hears the statement that it is

difficult to change institutional practices. Perhaps some of this difficulty can be explained by different attitude orientations in institutional employees. The study above indicated that people in power were highly motivated to make the institution more humanistic. The problem is that many of the employees in direct patient care held opposing attitudes. One is led to wonder, for instance, if plans for change are sabotaged by patient care workers.

Bozarth and Daly (1969) similarly reported differences in attitudes among institutional employees. This study differed in approach from the previous one in that comparisons were made between occupational groups. They reported that work supervisors tended to view residents as significantly better than either educators and activity employees. There is suggestion here that institutional variables may account for these differences. The performance requirements at work are quite different than performance requirements in school. Whereas the retarded child may perform adequately on the job he probably does not do as well in school.

Polonsky (1961), in fact, cautions that differing attitudes may be the result of specific situational variables in the institution. His study on the opinions of psychiatric technicians concerning mental retardation suggested two processes responsible for these beliefs. The first, an external pressure, appears to result from environmental pressures and events. This is what Bozarth and Daly (1969) seemed to be suggesting. The second process he called pressure from within. There was some evidence to support the notion that opinions about mental retardation were related to the ways technicians regarded people in general, reflecting a general philosophy of human nature. Polansky noted that in studying attitudes, it is necessary to study the interaction of beliefs and attitudes with specific situational variables.

One thing appears to be quite apparent when talking about the attitudes of institutional employees towards mental retardation. This is that there are more than one set of attitudes operating in institutions. Further,

and perhaps even more importantly, these are often competing attitudes that could interfere with the running of the institution. It would appear that the most effective attitude change procedures should be incorporated into in-service and pre-service institutional education programs. Attitude change research will be discussed in more detail in the next major section of this paper.

Attitudes of parents

The literature on attitudes of parents of retarded children indicates that these attitudes may be quite potent. Eyman, Dingman, and Sabagh (1966) demonstrated that parents' attitudes, along with education and socioeconomic status were more important in determining speed of institutionalization than was the child's handicap or his behavioral problem. Ohlson (1968) found that maternal resistance to placement of her child in a special class for EMR children was positively related to his performance in arithmetic, to his total arithmetic test score, to a high behavior rating and to a composite criterion variable which indicated good performance in both achievement and behavior. Finally, Sundstrom (1968) reported a significant positive correlation between mothers' attitudes and reading achievement of their retarded children.

Thus, there appears to be some justification for studying these attitudes. There are numerous studies that attempted to describe the attitudes of parents of retarded children. Blumberg (1965) found that parents of educable and trainable retarded children had more favorable attitudes towards their children than they did towards educable and trainable children in general. They saw their children as possessing more adequate personal and social skills than non-institutionalized children.

Dingman, Eyman and Windle (1963) found that mothers of mildly retarded children had more protective child-rearing attitudes than parents of severely retarded children. Another study on child rearing attitudes (Klausner, 1961) indicated differences between parents of noninstitutionalized and institutionalized retarded children. Parents of non-institutionalized children tended to be more agreeing with domineering statements (as measured by the Shoben Parent Attitude Survey); showed more restrictive and negative child-rearing practices; and indicated less feelings of depression and fewer signs of immaturity. Finally, Worchel and Worchel (1961) demonstrated that parents were rejecting of their retarded children. It is interesting to note that thus far this is the only study to report rejecting attitudes. However this is also the only study that compared the attitudes of parents towards both retarded and nonretarded children. Thus, looking only at attitudes of parents towards their retarded children may present a completely different picture than when attitudes toward retarded and nonretarded are compared.

While there is a value in looking at parental attitudes per se, it may be more valuable to look at the conditions under which these attitudes vary. Barber (1963) found that attitudes of parents of retarded children were not influenced by the sex of the retarded child. They were, however, influenced by the intellectual capacity of the child and by the socioeconomic status of the family. The author noted that parents from lower socioeconomic classes tended to have child rearing attitudes associated with defensiveness, aggressiveness, dominance, authoritarianism and rejection of their children. The question, of course, is whether these attitudes preceded the retarded child. The author noted the same basic attitude structure with normal children. However, these attitudes were more intense with a retarded child. Thus, one would hypothesize these attitudes preceding the child, but becoming more intense with the birth of a retarded child.

Takeguchi (1967) also reported on a study relating socioeconomic status and parental attitudes. He found that parents of educable and trainable retarded children had similar conceptions of "mental retardation," "educable mentally retarded," and "my own child," regardless of social class. However, he found that the concept "trainable mentally retarded" was influenced by socioeconomic status. Low socioeconomic status parents rated this concept significantly lower than parents of higher socioeconomic status.

Another variable correlating with parental attitude is parental religion. Zuk, Miller, Bartram, and Kling (1961) reported on the relationship between religious belief and maternal acceptance of retarded children. The authors reported a low but positive correlation between these two variables. Mothers who rated themselves more intense in religious practice tended to express attitudes that were more accepting of retarded children. The authors further noted that the most intensely religious parents were Catholic. They further related this to the notion of guilt. Catholicism says that parents should not blame themselves, thus, there is less associated guilt with the birth of a retarded child. This, in turn, allows the parents to be more accepting of a retarded child.

Hoffman (1965) lent support to the Zuk et al. study. He reported that Catholic families tended to be more accepting of their retarded child. Instead of relating this finding to guilt he related it to the Catholic notion that suffering, though painful, is a part of life. He then reported on the attitudes of different religious groups. Christian Scientists tended to deny the diagnosis and seek magical cures, while Fundamental Protestants were characterized by guilt, stemming from the belief that retardation is an ascription for the "sin of the father . . . visited on the children."

While both socioeconomic status and religious belief appear to be relevant factors in the attitudes of parents of retarded children, the nature of the relationship is unclear. The research here is quite sketchy, suggesting the need for a more detailed delineation of variables. Both socioeconomic status and religious belief are rather broad variables. There are important concomitants of each that could account for these differences. For instance, are attitude differences a result of guilt or religious belief? Are the socioeconomic differences the result of the increased stress of low socioeconomic environments or socioeconomic status itself? If it is guilt and stress (or any of a number of other variables) then similar attitudes should occur where we find guilt and stress. We need research that systematically partials out of the concomitants of socioeconomic status and religious belief and begins to specify the variables more precisely.

Somewhat related to the idea of parental attitudes is the idea of attitudes of adolescents towards a retarded sibling. Adams (1966) studied this problem. Although showing that, in general, siblings of mentally retarded children living at home are not adversely affected by this, he did show some interesting differences, particularly with regard to religion. Protestant siblings of retarded children showed poorer home interpersonal relationships than did Protestant siblings of normals. The opposite was true of Catholic siblings. Thus, religious belief shows up again as a relevant variable, operating in much the same manner as it did with parents.

Self attitudes of retarded children

Thus far we've considered only the attitudes of various groups of people towards the mentally retarded. In this section, we will consider the self attitudes of retarded children. Ringness (1961) compared the self-concepts of children of low, average, and high intelligence. He found that retardates had the least realistic self-concepts. However, of even more importance, he found that retardates did not have one attitude about themselves. Self concept varied depending upon the situation the child was in (school, playground, etc.). It would appear that, as Bozarth and Daly (1969) reported, attitudes of institutional employees are somewhat dependent upon the situation in which they observe the child, so are the self attitudes of retarded children a function of the activity in which they find themselves.

Meyerowitz (1962) compared the self-attitudes of retarded children in regular and special classes. He found that educable retarded children in special classes had poorer self concepts than educable retarded children in regular classes. One would be tempted to criticize the study on the basis of selec-

tive placement. That is, retarded children with more problems are placed in special classes, thus the expected poorer self concept. Meyerowitz, however, controlled for this by constituting the special and regular class students on a random assignment basis. This study, along with Fine's (1967) cited earlier, suggests a rather interesting phenomenon. It will be recalled that Fine found special class teachers to expect less of retarded children than do regular class teachers. Add to this the self-derogation reported by Meyerowitz, and Dunn's (1968) findings that retarded children perform at a lower level in special classes, and you have the suggestion of a vicious cycle leading to poor performance.

Mayer (1967) studied only special class retarded children. He attempted to find a relationship between self concept, sociometric ratings, and socioeconomic status. Sociometric rating was not correlated with self concept. A low correlation, however, did suggest a relationship between self-concept and socioeconomic status.

The finding that sociometric status is not related to self-concept is a bit puzzling. It seems to suggest that retarded children are not responding to social cues from peers. Peers seem to have no effect upon self-concept. Two events could explain this. The first relates to this lack of awareness. It will be recalled that Ringness (1961) found that retarded children were unrealistic in their self-concepts. This suggests a lack of responding to environmental cues. One wonders whether this is an actual phenomenon. The second is a measurement problem. Ringness also noted that the retarded child's self ratings tended to be somewhat unreliable. This could produce spurious scores and cautions one to be wary of such ratings.

Knight (1968) reported on a self attitude study. She was able to show reliable measurement instruments, which should tend to answer one of the events mentioned above. She compared negro retarded boys in special classes, negro retarded boys in regular classes, and white retarded boys in special classes. Results of the study supported the notion of self derogation among negro retarded boys in special classes.

Unlike the other studies reported, Knight found that her retarded subjects tended to have realistic self concepts. Also, unlike some of the other studies, this study reported the use of a reliable measurement instrument. This tends to lend some support to the measurement issue mentioned on the preceding page. Perhaps some of these findings were a function of measurement problems. Knight's study would tend to suggest this.

Further support for this comes from McAfee and Cleland (1965). It will be recalled that earlier studies suggested that retarded children were unresponsive to peers in developing a self concept. Cleland and McAfee suggested just the opposite. They found that retarded males used normal peers as ideal self-models, indicating a high responsiveness to peer relations. Again, this lends further support to the measurement question.

The idea is beginning to emerge that peer interaction may be a variable in the self-concept of retardates. The relationship of other variables with self-concept is also discussed in the literature. Ringness (1961) suggested situational factors. Gorlow, Butler, and Guthrie (1963) found self-concept to be related to I.Q., school achievement, success in institutional programs, and success on parole. Kniss, Butler, Gorlow, and Guthrie (1962) looked not at self-concept, but on ideal self-concept. They found this unrelated to age, I.Q., and length of institutionalization.

Summary

The research reported in this section is rather illuminating. Several major points seem to be emerging. The first relates to those factors that contribute to an attitude picture. Polonsky's (1961) conception of both internal and external factors involved in a person's attitudes seems to be a useful paradigm. He noted, in talking about internal factors, that one's general philosophy of life is related to one's attitude about mental retardation. One sees support for this in the studies on religious belief (Zuk, Miller,

Bartram, and Kling, 1961; Hoffman, 1965; Adams, 1966).

Polonsky (1961) also suggested external pressures operating on the attitudes of retarded children. One sees this as operating in his study. One also sees that external, or situational variables, also contribute to a retarded child's own self attitudes (Ringness, 1961; Meyerowitz, 1962).

Although we've dichotomized these two pressures (external and internal) Polonsky actually postulates an interaction process. The study by Barber demonstrated that lower socioeconomic parents start with an attitude towards children and child rearing (internal). With the birth of a retarded child these attitudes, though basically the same, become more intensified (external). Thus we end up with an interaction of external and internal processes working to develop an attitude towards retarded children.

Another point that has emerged from this section relates to the effects of attitudes on the behavior of children. We start with the work of Rosenthal and Jacobson (1968) who demonstrated the effect of teacher expectancy on achievement. We move next to Fine's (1967) paper that showed special class teachers expect less of retarded children than do regular class teachers. This leads us to Meyerowitz's (1962) study that indicated the educable retarded children in special classes demonstrated more self derogatory attitudes than do educable mentally retarded children in regular classes. Finally, we have Dunn's (1968) review of the literature on the efficacy of special classes for retarded children. He indicated that special class retarded children achieved less than regular class retarded children. The end product appears to be a cycle of attitudes leading to behavior, leading to incompetence. Although this appears to be a quite logical conception one would feel more comfortable if the interaction of these variables were incorporated into one study. Combining the results of independent investigations into a chain of events is always a dangerous enterprise. However, these studies do suggest a profitable direction for further study.

A final point should be made about this section. This relates to implications for training. There is concern that attitudes among professionals may be, at least partly a function of formal training. Several studies reported a relationship between low acceptance of the retarded and lack of exposure to mental retardation in formal training programs (Olshansky and Kettell, 1963; Fishler, Koch, Sands and Bills, 1968; Kingsley, 1967; Warren and Turner, 1966). If we feel that it is important for pediatricians, teachers, and other professionals to be concerned with the problems of mental retardation, then we must increase training experiences for these professionals.

ATTITUDE CHANGE

One of the major justifications for studying attitudes towards any group of people is to begin to bring about changes in attitudes. It will be recalled that Osgood, Succi, and Tannenbaum (1957) talked about attitudes as predispositions towards behavior. They may not account for all of the variance involved in a decision towards particular behavior, but they do account for some. As such, they become one aspect of planning behavioral change of particular groups.

The literature on attitudes towards the mentally retarded reflects the use of several independent variables as possible correlates of changes in measured attitudes. For purposes of this review they were divided into the following three categories: a) social contact, b) informational procedures, and c) other procedures.

Social contact

The notion behind this research strategy is that the more contact a person has had with retarded people the greater the probability of having favorable attitudes. Supposedly, social contact would help a person see a retarded person as a person, rather than a series of stereotypes, most of which are negative.

Strauch (1970) attempted to study the expressed attitudes of normal adolescents who had social contact with EMR adolescents through special subjects in school. This group was compared with another group of normal adolescents who had not had such contact. Results indicated that contact per se was not sufficient to produce more positive attitudes towards EMR pupils. It was suggested that such social contact would have an opposite effect. It could produce negative attitudes. The author did feel, however, that if social contact were to be successful, it would have to involve cooperative types of activities. Activities where retarded and non-retarded pupils worked together on some particular task.

Chennault (1967) attempted this. In this study, attempts were made to improve peer acceptance of unpopular children (Negro, I.Q. 50-79, C.A. 10-16) in eight classes. Both popular and unpopular children participated in organized cooperative group activities. Results, as measured by prepost sociometrics, indicated that unpopular children participating in the experimental treatment improved significantly in peer acceptance and in their perceived peer acceptance. This could not be said for unpopular children in the control condition.

It would appear, then, that mere social contact is not sufficient to bring about attitude change. More direct and organized procedures appear to be appropriate. Jaffe (1967) added a caution. Performing a study similar to Strauch's he was able to show that although high school students having had contact with a mentally retarded person assigned more favorable traits to the concept of "the mentally retarded person" than a non-contact group, they did not show any differences on an affective dimension. Thus it would appear that social contact may produce a cognitive acceptance but not necessarily an affective acceptance. Like Strauch's research, the study did not involve cooperative group activities. To be answered yet is the issue of whether cooperative group activities could produce affective as well as cognitive attitude changes.

Jaffe's work is important for another reason. He indicated that attitudes are multidimensional. This means that there may be several attitudes towards mental retardation. Thus various intervention procedures may produce changes in different dimensions.

A variant to the social contact strategy is the use of tours of institutions for the retarded as producers of attitude change. Cleland and Cochran (1961) attempted to assess the stress-producing aspects of a tour to produce attitude changes in high school seniors. The tours were varied by having the subjects tour the institution in different sequences of most shocking to least shocking wards. The results produced no significant attitude changes. Kimbrell and Luckey (1964) also used tours to produce attitude change in adults. Using the same measurement instrument as Cleland and Cochran (1961) the authors were able to demonstrate positive attitude change. This, of course, is difficult to reconcile with the Cleland and Cochran study. One could hypothesize the differences as being due to the differences in ages of the subjects. However, this is speculation at this time. There is no empirical evidence to support this.

Informational procedures

Another method used to produce attitude changes is through the use of informational procedures. The idea behind this procedure is to provide subjects with information about mental retardation in the hopes of changing attitudes. Quay, Bartlett, Wrightsman, and Catron (1961) used three methods of introducing information (lecture, discussion, booklet) to attendants in institutions for the retarded. Results indicated the lecture group to be the only group to produce positive changes in attitude. The discussion groups produced the least change. The authors interpreted the results to indicate that authoritative methods are most effective, particularly with the particular subject population used in the study. Lectures represent the most direct, authoritative approach, with a booklet being less direct but still authoritative. Discussion groups probably represent the least authoritative approach, incorporating democratic principles and free exchange of ideas. Bitter (1963) lent support to this

idea. He attempted to change the attitudes of parents of trainable retarded children and reported inconclusive results.

Begab (1969) presented evidence on the potency of social contact as opposed to informational procedures in producing attitude change. Results of this study indicated that knowledge through direct contact with mentally retarded people has greater impact on attitude change than knowledge alone. Thus, support continues for the notion that the more direct the procedure, the greater the probability for producing attitude change.

Other procedures

A rather interesting approach to attitude change was presented by Mandel (1968). The notion here was to use socially disadvantaged children to produce attitude change in their parents and teachers. Mothers and teachers rated their children's behavior on the Head Start Behavior Inventory at the beginning of the study. The mothers also made estimates as to how well their children would perform on a set of tasks from the Caldwell Preschool Inventory. Children were then tested on the tasks. For the next five weeks the children brought home a bag of fruit and a toy with a note from the teacher saying how well they had done. Posttesting followed this procedure. Results indicated no differences between rewarded and non-rewarded children on mothers' behavior ratings, although Mexican-American mothers' estimates of change in their children were more accurate than those of mothers of negro children.

Finally, Mann (1968) attempted to change the self-attitudes of educable retarded boys through counseling. Using an experimental-control group design the author found that counseling did produce changes in self-attitudes. Reduction in anxiety was also noted in the experimental group.

Summary

Several points begin to emerge with respect to attitude change. First, it appears that bringing about significant positive changes in attitudes is not a simple matter. The research seems to indicate that rather direct, well organized procedures are required (Strauch, 1970; Chennault, 1967; Quay, et al., 1961; Begab, 1969). Mere exposure to retarded people or telling people about mental retardation does not appear to be sufficient.

Perhaps one of the reasons that institutional tours fail to produce positive attitude change relates to the discussion of the attitudes of institutional employees. It will be recalled that Bozarth and Daly (1969) found situational variables related to attitudes. Situations that showed the retarded person as a poor performer (e.g. school) tended to be associated with more negative attitudes. Institutional tours tend not to be attractive. The image presented is usually one of incompetence, particularly if the tour involves visits to the wards housing the most severely retarded. If this is the case, to be consistent with Bozarth and Daly one would hardly expect positive attitudes to follow such tours.

On the other hand, those procedures that get the retarded person actively involved and productive tend to be conducive to the production of positive attitude changes (Chennault, 1967). Perhaps, rather than tours, we should get visitors and residents actively involved in projects.

There is also evidence that attitudes toward mental retardation are multidimensional and intervention procedures may differentially affect different components of attitudes (Jaffe, 1967). Further, there are suggestions that attitude change may be differentially affected for different ethnic groups (Mandel, 1968) and by age of subjects (Cleland and Cochran, 1961; Kimbrell and Luckey, 1964). It should be noted that this last statement is made rather tentatively. There is not direct evidence to support this notion. However, the issue is empirical and thus available to systematic study.

A final statement should be made about the research itself. One point that is evident is that there is no organization to the research. The reports are relatively scattered and there does not seem to be a consistent line of research. Further, attitude change research in mental retardation seems to have no theoretical base. A recent book on attitude change (Kiesler, Collins and Miller, 1969) presented numerous well developed theories of attitude change. It is interesting to note that tests of these theories do not appear in mental retardation literature. This is not surprising since the authors noted that much attitude change literature does not represent tests of these theories. It would appear that one means of developing a consistent program of attitude change research might be to test the effectiveness of competing theories.

REFERENCES

Adams, F. K. Comparison of attitudes of adolescents toward normal and toward retarded brothers. *Dissertation Abstracts*, 1966, 27, (1-A), 662-663.

Babow, I. & Johnson, A. C. Staff attitudes in a mental hospital which established a mental retardation unit. *American Journal of Mental Deficiency*, 1969, 74, 116-124.

Barber, B. A study of the attitudes of mothers of mentally retarded children as influenced by socioeconomic status. *Dissertation Abstracts*, 1963, 24, 415.

Begab, M. J. The effect of differences in curricula and experiences on social work student attitudes and knowledge about mental retardation. *Dissertation Abstracts*, 1969, 29, (11-A), 4111-4112.

Bergan, J. R. & Smith, J. O. Effects of socio-economic status and sex on prospective teachers' judgments. *Mental Retardation*, 1966, 4, 13-15.

Bitter, J. A. Attitude change by parents of trainable mentally retarded children as a result of group discussion. *Exceptional Children*, 1963, 30, 173-177.

Blumberg, A. A comparison of the conceptions and attitudes of parents of children in regular classes and parents of mentally retarded children concerning the subgroups of mental retardation. *Dissertation Abstracts*, 1965, 25, (11-A), 6407.

Bozarth, J. D. & Daly, W. C. Three occupational groups and their perceptions of mental retardates. *Mental Retardation*, 1969, 7, (6), 10-12.

Chennault, M. Improving the social acceptance of unpopular educable mentally retarded pupils in special classes. *American Journal of Mental Deficiency*, 1967, 72, 455-458.

Cleland, C. C. & Cochran, I. L. The effect of institutional tours on attitudes of high school seniors. *American Journal of Mental Deficiency*, 1961, 65, 473-481.

Dingman, H. F., Eyman, R. K. & Windle, C. D. An investigation of some child-rearing attitudes of mothers with retarded children. *American Journal of Mental Deficiency*, 1963, 67, 899-908.

Dunn, L. M. Special education for the mildly retarded: Is much of it justifiable? *Exceptional Children*, 1968, 35, 5-22.

Eyman, R. K., Dingman, H. F. & Sabagh, G. Association of characteristics of retarded patients and their families with speed of institutionalization. *American Journal of Mental Deficiency*, 1966, 71, 93-99.

Fine, M. J. Attitudes of regular and special class teachers toward the educable mentally retarded child. *Exceptional Children*, 1967, 33, 429-430.

Fishler, K., Koch, R., Sands, R. & Bills, J. Attitudes of medical students toward mental retardation: a preliminary study. *Journal of Medical Education*, 1968, 43, 64-68.

Gorlow, L., Butler, A., & Guthrie, G. M. Correlates of self-attitudes of retardates. *American Journal of Mental Deficiency*, 1963, 67, 549-555.

Harth, R. Attitudes towards minority groups as a construct in assessing attitudes towards the mentally retarded. *Education and Training of the Mentally Retarded*, 1971, 6, 142-147.

Hoffman, J. L. Mental retardation, religious values, and psychiatric universals. *American Journal of Psychiatry*, 1965, 121, 885-889.

Jaffe, J. Attitudes and interpersonal contact: relationships between contact with the mentally retarded and dimensions of attitudes. *Journal of Counseling Psychology*, 1967, 14, 482-484.

Kiesler, C. A., Collins, B. E. & Miller, N. *Attitude change*. New York, Wiley, 1969.

Kimbrell, D. L. & Luckey, R. E. Attitude change resulting from open house guided tours in a state school for mental retardates. *American Journal of Mental Deficiency*, 1964, 69, 21-22.

Kingsley, R. F. Prevailing attitudes toward exceptional children. *Education*, 1967, 87, 426-430.

Klausner, M. The attitudes of mothers toward institutionalized and non-institutionalized retarded children. *Dissertation Abstracts*, 1961, 22(3), 915-916.

Knight, O. B. The self concept of educable mentally retarded children in special and regular classes. *Dissertation Abstracts*, 1968, 28 (11-A), 4483.

Kniss, J. T., Butler, A., Gorlow, L. & Guthrie, G. M. Ideal self patterns of female retardates. *American Journal of Mental Deficiency*, 1962, 67, 245-249.

Mandel, D. M. Influencing attitudes of parents and teachers through rewarding children. *Dissertation Abstracts*, 1968, 28 (10-A), 4004.

Mann, P. H. The effect of group counseling on educable mentally retarded boys' concepts of themselves in school. *Dissertation Abstracts*, 1968, 28 (9-A), 3467.

Mayer, C. L. Relationships of self-concepts and social variables in retarded children. *American Journal of Mental Deficiency*, 1967, 72, 267-271.

McAfee, R. O. & Cleland, C. C. The discrepancy between self-concept and ideal-self as a measure of psychological adjustment in educable mentally retarded males. *American Journal of Mental Deficiency*, 1965, 70, 63-68.

Meyerowitz, J. H. Self-derogations in young retardates and special class placement. *Child Development*, 1962, 33, 443-451.

Ohlson, G. A. The effects of maternal attitudes on self concept and classroom performance in pre-adolescent educable retardates. *Dissertation Abstracts*, 1968, 28 (12-A), 4913.

Olshansky, S. & Kettell, M. Attitudes of some interns and first-year residents toward the institutionalization of mentally retarded children. *Training School Bulletin*, 1963, 59 (4), 116-120.

Olshansky, S. & Sternfeld, L. Attitudes of some pediatricians toward the institutionalization of mentally retarded children. *Training School Bulletin*, 1962, 59 (3), 67-73.

Osgood, C. E., Succi, G. T., & Tannenbaum, P. H. *The measurement of meaning*. Urbana, Illinois: University of Illinois Press, 1957.

Polonsky, D. Beliefs and opinions concerning mental deficiency. *American Journal of Mental Deficiency*, 1961, 66, 12-17.

Quay, L. C., Bartlett, C. J., Wrightsman. L. S., Jr. & Catron, D. Attitude change in attendant employees. *Journal of Social Psychology*, 1961, 55, 27-31.

Ringness, T. A. Self concept of children of low, average, and high intelligence. *American Journal of Mental Deficiency*, 1961, 65, 453-461.

Rosenthal, R., & Jacobson, L. *Pygmalion in the classroom*. New York: Holt, Rinehart & Winston, 1968.

Schmidt, L. J. & Nelson, C. C. The affective/cognitive attitude dimension of teachers of educable mentally retarded minors. *Exceptional Children*, 1969, 35, 695-701.

Strauch, J. D. Social contact as a variable in the expressed attitudes of normal adolescents toward EMR pupils. *Exceptional Children*, 1970, 36, 495-500.

Sundstrom, D. A. The influence of parental attitudes and child-parent interaction upon remedial reading progress: a re-examination. *Dissertation Abstracts*, 1968, 28 (7-A), 2571-2572.

Takeguchi, S. L. A. A comparison of the conceptions and attitudes of parents of mentally retarded children concerning the subgroups of mental retardation as influenced by socio-economic status. *Dissertation Abstracts*, 1967, 27 (12-A), 4342-4343.

Warren, S. A. & Turner, D. R. Attitudes of professionals and students toward exceptional children. *Training School Bulletin*, 1966, 62 (4), 136-144.

Worchel, T. L. & Worchel, P. The parental concept of the mentally retarded child. *American Journal of Mental Deficiency*, 1961, 65, 782-788.

Zuk, G. H., Miller, R. L., Bartram, J. B. & Kling, F. Maternal acceptance of retarded children: a questionnaire study of attitudes and religious background. *Child Development*, 1961, 32, 525-540.

CHAPTER 2

A lost generation of parents

KATHRYN A. GORHAM

*Montgomery County Association for Retarded Citizens' Family and
Community Services*

Beckie, the fifth of my five children, is profoundly retarded. The 13 years since she was born have been enlightening ones for me. I have learned enough about other parents and their experiences with professionals, about parent organizations, and about the service system for "exceptional" children to be able to pass as a professional myself and get paid for doing what I used to do as a volunteer. Although I have learned much, I am clearly one of the lost generation of parents of handicapped children. We are parents who are either intimidated by professionals or angry with them, or both; parents who are unreasonably awed by them; parents who intuitively know that *we* know our children better than the experts of any discipline and yet we persistently assume that the professionals know best; parents who carry so much attitudinal and emotional baggage around with us that we are unable to engage in any real dialogue with professionals—teachers, principals, physicians, or psychologists—about our children.

Between birth and the age of 13 Beckie has seen 11 physicians representing 5 special-

ties. She has also been referred to an audiologist, an occupational therapist, an optometrist, physical therapists, psychologists, and speech pathologists. In answer to the common accusation that parents "shop" for professionals who will give them a less painful diagnosis, I would suggest that most, like myself, see large numbers of professionals because the complexity or severity of the child's condition requires periodic reevaluation from a variety of viewpoints. One-stop diagnostic centers did not exist when our children were growing up; few exist now, so we have been "referred" from one diagnostician to another.

THE CLOSED FILES

Seeing so many diagnosticians and evaluators presents a problem. Not many parents are fortunate enough to have a pediatrician or family physician who will coordinate all the information for them. People move and change doctors. Some doctors are unwilling to be coordinators in the first place. What happens to the reports? They are collected in manila folders that follow the child from clinic to clinic and school to school. This would be fine if one master folder containing copies of all the information were in the hands of the parents. However, few parents are given copies of these reports. Strangers are permitted to read the contents of the child's records; the parents generally are not.

Reprinted from Exceptional Children 41:521-525, 1975, with permission.
Kathryn A. Gorham is Director, Montgomery County Association for Retarded Citizens' Family and Community Services, Silver Springs, Maryland. Portions of this article appeared in *The Futures of Children* by Nicholas Hobbs, San Francisco CA: Jossey-Bass, 1975.

When we parents fill out the application forms for a school, we sign a release form which says that the school may collect information about out child from past diagnosticians and schools. We usually do not ask to *see* the information which is being collected or sent. But we sign our names and give access to people whom neither we nor our children have met, who may read the records, mull over them, and make vital decisions about the education or treatment of our children on the basis of what they read.

Beckie has accumulated a thick folder in her 13 year pilgrimage from professional to professional. I have heard countless "interpretations" of its contents by social workers, but I have only read the accumulation once—last year. I did so then with feelings of guilt, because my access to them came as a professional on the staff of the organization which runs her training program, not as her parent. I found nothing in them that I could not understand, or ask someone about if I did not, and nothing that could not have been discussed freely and openly with the person who wrote it. And I suspect that my cause is typical rather than atypical. Sometimes the record collection process meant delays of 2 or 3 months before interviews for application to a school were granted. How much simpler it would have been if I had been able to carry her records with me.

THE IRONIES

Anyone who has lived with a handicapped child during the last decade or two will be able to construct a list of ironies that he has learned to live with. The following ones are derived from my Beckie notebook, as well as from talks with other parents.

1. The responsibility for monitoring our children's progress through the fragmented service system has been ours, but the array of physicians and other professionals we have seen have assumed that we could not possibly understand the complexities of their trade or that it would take too much of their time to explain them to us. We have had the responsibility, but educating and equipping us to do

the job better was generally not considered a part of the diagnostic obligation.

2. A parent who thinks something is developmentally wrong with his child usually turns to a physician who has probably only had minimal exposure to the total needs of the handicapped child and his family. Physicians are notoriously unschooled about nonmedical services and often cannot tell the parent what schools are available for handicapped children, or even *if* schools are available.

3. The more specialized the diagnostician is, the less concerned he is to give information to the parents and the less willing he is to deal with the parents' situation and feelings. Referral of the mother for counseling has been a common and comfortable solution for the physician or other diagnostician; but when parents are repeatedly forced to ignore many of their concerns, they are never free of them.

4. Some of us are told repeatedly by professionals that we should institutionalize our children, but we find institutions to be places that are the least equipped to help children.

5. We could release information about our children to professionals, but we have not been allowed to read it ourselves.

6. Now, we are often told that the best place for our children is in the community, in a neighborhood, with his family or a substitute family. Yet there are not enough group homes to begin to meet this demand, and foster homes are equally hard to come by. That leaves, as before, our own homes with respite care and home-support services, still only a possibility in most communities.

7. It is now commonly accepted that our children have a constitutional right to a free education, but extra appropriations to make the classrooms materialize have not yet followed the legislation and litigation. We are told again to inform our legislators of the need. Why must we tell them *again?*

8. In the past we were made to feel guilty when we did not institutionalize our chil-

dren, and now, under the new normalization principle, we are made to feel guilty if we do.

THE EFFECTS

So much for the ironies of our past experiences and our current dilemmas. We have learned to live with them, but not without accumulating some scars which clearly mark us as members of the "lost generation":

- We are angry. We have gone to the helping professions and have received too little help.
- We are still in awe of specialists and intimidated by their expertise.
- We are unduly grateful to principals or school directors for merely accepting our children in their programs. The spectre of 24 hour a day, 7 day a week care at home, with the state institution as an alternative, had made us too humbly thankful.
- We demonstrate a certain indifference to the latest bandwagon on which the mental retardation experts are riding. Mixed messages have been so much a part of our history that, rather than join the parades, we tend to listen politely, then do what we think best for our child. We are often, therefore, accused of apathy.
- Many of us have concluded that it is best not to worry about next year (or tomorrow) because things might be better then (or worse). Certainly it seems impossible to "plan for the future" as most of us are so frequently admonished to do. Generally I have found that those who wanted me to plan for Beckie's future were suggesting that I place her on the roster for permanent residence in the state institution. That is, in fact, the only option available at present. In Maryland I cannot even provide for her future by putting money aside and setting up an inheritance. If I die, and she must enter an institution, the state's general fund becomes heir to her belongings, and the money saved could go for something as remote to her well being as highway construction. So we worry about the future, but planning for it is not yet really a fruitful activity.

- We are tired. We have kept our children at home and raised them ourselves, with all the extra demands on time and energy which that implies—often without much help from the community, neighborhood, professionals, friends, or relatives, and in fact commonly against their well intentioned advice. We have founded parent groups and schools, run them ourselves, held fund raising events to pay teachers and keep our little special schools afloat, organized baby sitting groups, and summer play groups. We have built and repaired special playground equipment for our children's use at home and at school. We have painted classrooms and buildings; we have written legislators and educated them about our children's needs and rights. We have collated and stapled hundreds of newsletters, attended school board meetings, lobbied at the state legislature for better legislation for handicapped children, informed newspaper reporters about inhumane conditions in institutions, and written letters to editors. All this we have done for a decade or more.

Small wonder that so many professionals would often prefer *not* to deal with parents. Few of these qualities encourage the kind of open, frank, informative dialogue that the professional wants—possibly as much as the parent *should* want it.

Changing habits of communication cannot happen without efforts from both parents and professionals. Here are some suggestions for achieving the dialogue that could be so helpful to the parent, the professional, and most importantly, to the child.

SUGGESTIONS FOR PROFESSIONALS

Let the parent be involved every step of the way. The dialogue established may be the most important thing you accomplish. If the parent's presence is an obstacle to testing because the child will not "cooperate" in his presence, the setup should include a complete review of the testing procedure with the parent. (Remote video viewing or one-way windows are great if you are richly endowed.)

Make a realistic management plan part of the assessment outcome. Give the parents suggestions for how to live with the problem on a day to day basis, considering the needs of the child, the capacities of the family, and the resources of the community. Let the parents know that you will suggest modifications if any aspect of the management plan does not work.

Inform yourself about community resources. Give the parents advice on how to go about getting what they need. Steer them to the local parent organization. Wherever possible, make the parent a team member in the actual diagnostic, treatment, or educational procedures. It will give you a chance to observe how the parent and child interact.

Write your reports in clear and understandable language. Professional terminology is a useful shortcut for your own notes, and you can always use it to communicate with others of your discipline. But in situations involving the parent, it becomes an obstacle to understanding. Keep in mind that it is the parent who must live with the child, help him along, shop for services to meet his needs, support his ego, and give him guidance. You cannot be there to do it for him, so the parent *must* be as well informed as you can make him. Information that he does not understand is not useful to him. The goal is a parent who understands his child well enough to help him handle his problems.

Give copies of the reports to parents. They will need them to digest and understand the information in them, to share the information with other people close to the child, and to avoid the weeks or months of record gathering which every application to a new program in the future will otherwise entail.

Be sure the parent understands that there is no such thing as a one shot, final, and unchanging diagnosis. Make sure he understands that whatever label you give his child (if a label must be given) is merely a device for communicating and one which may have all kinds of repercussions, many of them undesirable. Make sure he understands that it says very little about the child at present and even less about the child of the future. Cau-

tion him about using that label to "explain" his child's conditions to other people.

Help the parent to think of life with this child in the same terms as life with his other children. It is an ongoing, problem solving process. Assure him that he is capable of that problem solving and that you will be there to help him with it.

Be sure that the parent understands his child's abilities and assets as well as his disabilities and deficiencies. What the child *can* do is far more important than what he cannot do, and the parent's goal thereafter is to look for, anticipate, expect, and welcome new abilities and to welcome them with joy when they appear. Urge him to be honest with his child. Tell him that the most important job he has is to respect his child, as well as love him, and to help him "feel good about himself." Tell him that blame, either self blame on the part of the child must be avoided [sic].

Warn the parent about service insufficiencies. Equip him with advice on how to make his way through the system of "helping" services. Warn him that they are not always helpful. Tell him that his child has a *right* to services. Tell him to insist on being a part of all decisions about his child.

Explain to him that some people with whom he talks (teachers, doctors, professionals of any kind, or other parents) may emphasize the negative. Help train the parent not only to think positively but to teach the other people important in his child's life to do so.

SUGGESTIONS FOR PARENTS

You are the primary helper, monitor, coordinator, observer, record keeper, and decision maker for your child. Insist that you be treated as such. It is your right to understand your child's diagnoses and the reasons for treatment recommendations and for educational placement. No changes in his treatment or educational placement should take place without consultation with you.

Your success in getting as well informed as you will need to be in order to monitor your child's progress depends on your ability to work with the people who work with your child. You may encounter resistance to the idea of being included in the various diagnostic and decision making processes. The way you handle that resistance is important. Your best tool is not anger. Some of your job will include the gentler art of persuasion. Stay confident and cool about your own abilities and intuitions. You know your child better than anyone else; you are a vital member of the team of experts.

Try to find a person who can help you coordinate the various diagnostic visits and results. Pick the person with whom you have the best relationship, someone who understands your role as the principal monitor of your child's progress throughout life and who will help you become a good one.

Learn to keep records. As soon as you know that you have a child with a problem, start a notebook. Make entries of names, addresses, phone numbers, dates of visits, the persons present during the visits, and as much of what was said as you can remember. Record the questions you asked and the answers you received. Record any recommendations made. Make records of phone calls too; include the dates, the purpose, and the result. It is best to make important requests by letter. Keep a copy for your notebook. Such documentation for every step of your efforts to get your child the service he needs can be the evidence which finally persuades a program director to give him what he needs. Without concise records of whom you spoke to, when you spoke to him, what he promised, and how long you waited between the request and the response, you will be handicapped. No one can be held accountable for conversations or meetings with persons whose names and titles you do not remember, on dates you cannot recall, or about topics which you cannot clearly discuss.

Understand the terminology used by the professional. Ask him to translate his terms into lay language. Ask him to give examples of what he means. Do not leave his office until you are sure you understand what he has said so well that you can go to your child's

teacher, for instance, and explain it in clear, understandable language. Write down the professional terms too. Knowing them might be useful some time.

Ask for copies of your child's records. Don't just try to remember what was said in conferences. Learn as much as you can about your child's problem by reading. Don't believe everything you read. Remember: Books are like people. They might present only one side of the story.

Talk freely and openly with as many professionals as you can find. Talk with other parents. Join a parent organization. By talking with people who "have been through it already," you can gain a perspective on your particular problems. You will also receive moral support and will not feel quite so alone. Get information from parent organizations about available services and about their quality. Remember that a particular program might not help your child even though it has proved helpful for another child. Visit programs if you have the time and energy to do so. There is no substitute for firsthand views.

Stay in close touch with your child's teacher. Make sure you know what is being done in the classroom so that you can follow through at home. Share what you have read with the teacher. Ask for advice and suggestions. The two of you are a team, working for the same goals. Make your child a part of that team whenever possible. He might have some great ideas.

Listen to your child. Only he can give you his point of view. Let him know that being different is fine. Your child will learn most from your example. Help him to think of problems as things that can be solved if people work on them together.

CHANGES AND THE FUTURE

The new parent today faces a world which is fortunately improved in many ways. The fact that his child has a legal right to education and training does not surprise this parent, and he *expects* programs to be provided. Consequently his attitude toward his school system and the people in it is different. He expects the vital services to be provided. He is not asking for services as if they were charity nor is he left with no option other than the institution if the few existing public or private special classes refuse his children.

Some things have not changed, however, and will not, unless we make them. The diagnostic experience is often still traumatic to many parents who receive little counsel, encouragement, or on-the-spot information about where to go for more support and help. Obviously such experiences and the damage they do will simply repeat themselves with another generation of parents unless the individuals involved take deliberate steps such as the ones outlined here to avoid that possibility.

CHAPTER 3

What is to become of Katherine?

MATILDA F. de BOOR

The following account, written by a graduate student interning at the Waisman Center in Madison, Wisconsin, is based on the records of one of her clients.

During the more than 20 years of her life, Katherine Jamieson has been diagnosed as retarded, borderline retarded, borderline, borderline normal, and every possible gradation in between. Her IQ has tested between 70 and 90 over the years, and as the AAMD definition of retardation fluctuated, so did the diagnosis. She has been in special classrooms, in sheltered workshops for adult retarded, in various types of training programs, in the mental hospital, and in a residential facility—the list is endless. The pile of material collected by her father is remarkable for what it includes. Perhaps more remarkable is that it exists at all.

The material Mr. Jamieson has collected falls into several categories. There are the myriad little pieces of paper with lists of places and telephone numbers, presumably places that Mr. or Mrs. Jamieson called in an effort to find placement for Katherine. When I gave up counting, I had deciphered 20. There are many letters received over a period of years from counselors, therapists, and supervisors giving reports on Katherine's

Reprinted from Exceptional Children 41:517-518, 1975, with permission.
Editor's note: The fact that this has been written is proof enough that problems of communication between families and the system still exist. Great strides have been made, but there is still far to go. JNN

progress or, usually, the lack of it. At one point there is a letter to Katherine from her father, full of anguish and rage. "What will you do if you don't make it here? There is nowhere else for you to go; we have tried everything. Do what they tell you." Between the lines is the unwritten note, "Do it for us. We can't do any more for you." At the end of the file there is a series of letters from a workshop. The letters say things such as "On the bottle washing detail Katherine was unable to apply herself, likewise on the dishwashing detail, but she has done adequate or above adequate work in some other detail." There is the reply from her father, "Thank you for your nice letter. It was so good to hear something positive about Katherine for a change."

There are letters from Katherine, long (13 pages) at times, barely legible, but coherent—letters home from a growing girl. Invitations designed for a spring party but never filled out and never mailed. A drawing, a long story. Notebooks with her algebra assignments and doodles. Signs of a girl growing up. Postcards to her brothers. Shoes put on layaway and never paid for.

Then there are all the bills, bills that every parent has (dentists, orthodontists) and bills that only Katherine's parents have. Mental health bills from psychologists and statements from the state hospital. Coupled with these are insurance forms, long letters to various agencies and insurance companies about forms that must be filled out. A statement from the state that Katherine is not qualified for disabled aid. A long letter to a state agency about the fact that the Jamiesons really cannot pay all these bills because they have other children who must not be deprived because of Katherine. The underlying message is clear; she is not their fault.

There are reports from many agencies. "Katherine is retarded." "Katherine will never be able to live alone." "We can't help her any more." "She's untrainable and always has been." A school for the retarded wants extensive information before they will even consider Katherine. Could the parents go and look at the facility before they once again do all the work involved in collecting files? No, says the school, only afterward when it is possible that she will be admitted will they be allowed to look. So they do all the paperwork and the school turns them down.

An indication of the impotent rage appears in a letter to a bus company demanding refund for a ticket purchased for Katherine but never used. Mr. Jamieson has asked for this before but was sent a long form. He writes back an enraged letter about their "stupid form" and their "stupid rules" and says that if he does not get his money back he will go higher. When one is dealing with important questions, it is the little annoyances that really do one in.

When Katherine was evaluated this week at our facility, the conclusion was that she is not retarded at all. So what is she? Is she the victim of growing up in the 1950's when *learning disability* was just a word? Could she have been helped had she been born in 1970? Possibly. But instead there is Mr. Jamieson and his file, which he marched in with and deposited.

The fact that this file exists says a great deal. Many of us have files on our children, but we do not save every scrap of paper on which we have scribbled notes to call so and so, arrange this or that. Mr. Jamieson did.

Most of us with children have doctor bills of all sorts, but we do not put them in a file marked with the child's name. Mr. Jamieson did. Most of us do not make copies of the letters we send to our children, or the notes we send to teachers, or the insurance forms we file when our child breaks his arm. Mr. Jamieson did, and the question is why?

I think it is a matter of quantity. Katherine Jamieson had a problem that became evident at the age of 2. Presumably with confidence, the Jamiesons went to the first professional for help and were told something negative such as "She is retarded," but they were not told what to do about it. Perhaps they were told "There's nothing to do; it's very sad."

This file picks up the last 4 or 5 years, by which time everyone the Jamiesons talked to was telling them (a) "We will only look at your child after you have filed 47 forms and let us look at everything concerned with Katherine, down to and including whether her grandmother had five toes or six," and then (b) either "Yes we will look at her" and "She is retarded and there is nothing to do" (not "We don't know what to do"), or "No, we will not look at her." By this time Mr. Jamieson has started to keep a file. At least he will have that to show for all his labors, since his daughter has not benefited by them. He reaches the point where he exchanges notes with the state hospital about the wording of the records. This is after he has decided that he will keep the records himself so that he can send them out to each agency instead of always going through the red tape of release forms.

The final impression gained from this file is that here is a father for whom the system has become the adversary. Rather than helping him and Katherine, the system is at war with them. If the time comes for the trial of the system against Katherine, Mr. Jamieson will have the evidence in his file. And he also has Katherine, now 21, unable to hold a job, promiscuous, unstable, happy only with her guitar. And the question which the Jamiesons asked 15 years ago is still unanswered: What is to become of Katherine?

CHAPTER 4

On being the parent of a handicapped child

BOBBY G. GREER

Memphis State University

Many of the basic problems with which parents of handicapped children have to deal come directly from society. Such problems originate in society's perpetration of certain myths or frauds, to put it bluntly. We are especially susceptible to these myths as we are growing up. One myth encouraged by the romance magazines that teenagers read is that marriage is "eternal bliss." Another more pertinent myth is that out of this eternal blissful union will come children who are both physically and mentally beautiful and perfect. Therefore, the parents of a handicapped child have not lived up to the "ideal" and have produced an imperfect replica of themselves. This may cause much unconscious, if not conscious, guilt, as well as feelings of inferiority. At the same time, if parents are unfortunate enough to have a handicapped child (which society says subtly they are not supposed to do), society then hypocritically says they must be *superparents*. They must supply enormous additional amounts of care, love, and attention to their child. They must do this, additionally, on a 24 hour a day, 365 day a year basis; otherwise, they are *superbad*.

As a professional evaluating a child's progress, I can be the most patient, empathetic person on earth for half an hour or an hour. I can look critically at the impatient, harried parent. Unfortunately many professionals encountered by parents of handicapped children do not take the 24 hour, 365 day a year responsibilities of parents into account in their evaluation of the parent.

In the back of parents' minds, then, is a vague awareness that society is looking over their shoulders and judging if they are carrying out their prescribed duties, giving much love, attention, and devotion, not missing any treatment appointments, providing the best available care, etc. This is a "goldfish bowl" type of existence which eventually takes its toll in energy, strength, and courage.

Parents of handicapped children must realize that fleeting moments of resentment and rejection of the burdens presented by a handicapped child are natural and are not indicative that they are bad parents. They need to seek help in solving their practical day to day problems. The best help can be found in interaction with parents who have experienced and solved such problems. Even though every family's situation is unique and what works for one family may not work for another, having someone with common prob-

Reprinted from Exceptional Children 41:519, 1975, with permission.

This article is part of an address given on April 6, 1974, to the Parent Involvement Program, sponsored by the Department of Special Education and Rehabilitation, College of Education, Memphis State University, Memphis, Tennessee. **Bobby G. Greer**, Associate Professor of Special Education and Rehabilitation at Memphis State University, is handicapped himself, and is the father of a handicapped baby girl.

23

lems with whom to interact is in itself therapeutic.

Parents must realize also that only by banding together can they bring about the changes in society which are needed. Legislators and other government leaders listen to groups when they might not listen to individuals. Therefore, in order to exercise their "clout," parents of the handicapped must unite and seek common goals to alleviate society's barriers to their children's welfare.

CHAPTER 5

Brothers and sisters of retarded children

FRANCES KAPLAN GROSSMAN
Boston University

The young man spoke calmly and with a degree of objectivity about his retarded younger brother: "It's taught me to be tolerant. I mean from a very early age I've learned people are different, and you have responsibilities to other people. I've always been geared to just being aware of prejudice and misconception. James is different, but he's not *that* different. That's one thing it's undoubtedly taught me, that there are not only normal people and crazy people but there are shades, and it's just getting used to that fact."

Here was a college student who clearly had benefited from the experience of growing up with a brother who had Down's syndrome, Mongolism. He regarded the experience as beneficial, and my co-workers and I agreed with him. He had culled from his life with James an important and enduring lesson about prejudice and compassion. Moreover, we found no evidence that this young man had been limited or harmed in other ways by his close contact with a retarded sibling.

This account runs across the grain—the dominant attitude toward mental retardation in our culture is that it always has tragic implications not only for the retarded person but for the family as well. Retardation is considered traumatic and heavily burdensome to the family and neighbors of the afflicted family.

Reprinted from Psychology Today 5(11):82-84, 102-104, 1972, with permission.

James's older brother, and many of our other subjects, effectively disputed this attitude. But there were others whose experiences with retarded siblings were dramatically different. Here is a young woman, also a college student, who is speaking of the difficult life she led while she was home from school on vacation: "I'm the only normal adolescent that she's known and she idolizes me, and she thinks it's really neat all the things that I do when I go out. If I take her shopping with me, which my mother likes for me to do, she'll follow so closely behind me that if I stop she would step on my heels. And if I bend over to touch a sweater, she'll touch it exactly the same spot at the same time! She just mimics me!

"It's very strange to be thrown suddenly back into this suburban home life with a sister like that, who is not normal, who you can't talk to. And I realize it could just as easily have been me, and I just feel terribly sorry for her. But I do usually lose my temper an awful lot; it drives me crazy the way she idolizes me! She drools down my neck and it makes me a complete nervous wreck, and I just have to control myself every minute! It's terribly hard for me!"

It is clear that this young woman, unfortunately, had been harmed by her life with a retarded sister.

These two students typified the variation we discovered in the way our subjects were affected by living under the influence of a retarded sibling.

We were not surprised to find subjects who had benefited from the experience. Our preliminary hypothesis, confirmed by our experimental results, was that many of the problems associated with mental retardation are not inevitable. Nor can they be located primarily in the defective child's head. Our research reveals that the social and psychological reactions of siblings, parents and friends to the retarded child exert influence on whether the traditional problems will arise.

SAMPLE

We became interested in studying brothers and sisters as an important aspect of the social system that is affected by a retarded child.

We recruited 83 college-student volunteers, each of whom had a retarded brother or sister. Our control group was a matched sample of students with normal brothers and sisters. We interviewed each student individually and in depth about his experiences. Several written tests followed. We taped interviews, transcribed them, and then scored each student on 50 different measures relating to his experience.

Most retarded siblings of our subjects had organic defects. They ranged in handicap from mild to severe retardation, and from no demonstrable physical defect to major defect. About 25 percent were mongoloid.

STATUS

To isolate the differences that might be anticipated as a result of social and cultural variations among our subjects, we selected half from a highly competitive, expensive Eastern college (Private U) and half from a much less expensive local college (Community U).

We rejected the term "socioeconomic status" when we started to describe the differences between the families in our research population who had enrolled their sons and daughters in the private university and the families whose sons or daughters were students at the community college. We felt the term reflected little else than the father's level of education and his job description. Instead, we drew up a list of additional points that included the family's interest in educating the children and its cultural and social expectations for them. We labeled this the "sociocultural status" (SCS).

SPLIT

Our final tabulations revealed a number of subjects who appeared to have benefited from the experience of growing up with handicapped siblings. Just as clearly, we identified a number who had been harmed. The ones who benefited appeared to us to be more tolerant, more compassionate, more knowing about prejudice and its consequences and they were often, but not always, more certain about their own futures, about personal and vocational goals, than comparable young adults who had not had such experiences.

The ones we judged to have been harmed often manifested bitter resentfulness of their families' situations, guilt about the rage they had felt at their parents and at the retarded sibling, and fear that they themselves might be defective. Often they had been deprived of attention that they needed to help them develop, simply because so much family time and energy had been given to the handicapped children.

LIFE-STYLE

In comparing the control group with the experimental subjects we found few general differences in personality characteristics that clearly could be attributed to the presence or nonpresence of a retarded child in the family. The siblings of the retarded children are not different as a group on general measures of adaptation and functioning.

We acknowledge, of course, that we had isolated a highly select group of siblings of retarded children: those who had made it to college and were comfortable enough about their family situations to volunteer to discuss them in a research setting. We conclude that, for such a group, having a retarded sibling does not in itself determine the ability to function or to adapt.

We were unable to get meaningful data on the proportion of siblings of retarded children who had benefited from the experience as opposed to those who had not. Our sample was not meant to provide such a comparison, for it was heavily biased in favor of well-adjusted siblings. To be successful, the experiment had to pinpoint the *reasons* for the differences in adjustment, to provide meaningful data on, for example, the relation between affluence or sex or education or male-female parent dominance and the ability of normal children to adjust to a retarded sibling.

And, in fact, the strongest and most impressive finding of the study was that differences in the life-styles of the families affected, to an extraordinary degree, the way each of our subjects described his experiences with a retarded brother or sister.

FAVORED

The families of Private-U students, whom we called upper-SCS, all had fathers with high-educational status, holding jobs that are generally notable for high income or for the unusual training or ability they require, or for both.

These families are a highly favored group. They have considerable advantages of money and education. The members of such a family often are psychologically close; they create an intense atmosphere in which family relationships assume great importance. The development of children to their highest potential is a major goal in such a family, and the goal heightens the intensity of parent-child ties.

These characteristics have a profound influence on the way a retarded child is regarded and treated. Such families have money for the services they want for the child, including private residential placement, if it is desired, and fine medical care. The mother can hire domestic help to free her for the time-consuming care of the retarded child. Without such help, her attention to her other children might be severely limited. Or, if the mother wants to lead a normal social life, she can have professionals nurse the handicapped child in the home.

In our sample, many of the upper-SCS families made determined, successful efforts to protect their normal children from all the inconveniences and deprivations that the presence of a retarded child can occasion.

SONS

Oddly enough, the sex factor appeared to be as important in the upper-SCS families as in the lower-SCS families. Possibly because they have high education-career hopes for their normal sons, upper-SCS families exempt their sons from the demanding duty of caring for retarded children. They do not as extensively exempt their daughters from this duty.

In many cases the upper-SCS retarded children live most of their lives away from home, a practice made possible by the families' greater income.

One Private-U student commented upon the manner in which the family protected him from the difficulties caused by the occasional presence of his retarded younger brother: "I get a kick out of him, I really do. He's a lot of fun. Maybe it's because I have all the privileges of him without the real responsibility. I remember one vacation, I had bunk beds in my bedroom and so he slept with me. And one night he got sick or something during the night, and Mom came. And I ended up in her bedroom and she cleaned it up. This was the type of thing that happened. Mom always took care of him, so I just got the really good side of him."

In such a family, when a sibling is shielded from the impact of a retarded child's physical or mental handicap, family attitudes are more important than the degree of handicap, and the effects on the sibling are primarily psychological. The normal child's development and adjustment depend, in such a setting, on the meanings and explanations the family provides for itself regarding the handicap. These verbalizations, in turn, directly affect the family's self-image. The fact that such a family is preeminently aware of the potential of its children, of their goals and accomplishments, heights the impact of a child with a limited capacity to develop. The family sometimes compensates by expecting much more of the normal child.

BOTHERING

The upper-SCS family, with its intense (positive or negative) relationships between parents and children and among the siblings, may greatly magnify its subtle feelings and reactions towards a retarded member. These parental feelings and reactions—that is, the extent to which the parents appeared to accept the retarded child and his handicap— were the strongest single factor affecting the ability of the normal upper-SCS youngsters to cope on their own.

One Private-U man had a retarded older brother who had been living in an institution for many years. There had been little direct contact between them. From our interviews and written tests we judged this young man to have been harmed by his relationship to the retarded brother. We asked him what effect having a retarded brother had had on him: "I don't know, probably just thinking about him is slightly depressing and slightly bothering. I mean, just thinking about him in that state, thinking about what kind of life he's leading and how it affects my parents, and how it affected their behavior towards their other children."

We asked him what he told his friends about his brother: "Well, that he exists, basically. That I do have a brother, mentally retarded. Not much that we can carry on conversationally. It makes other people feel uncomfortable, usually, to hear you talk about a family tragedy."

MOTHER

In the upper-SCS families, when a family had been open and comfortable in talking about the handicap, the normal sibling was more curious and asked more questions, and was more able to deal with the facts. It is the mother, in her close contact with the children, who most subtly and clearly conveys to the normal children her attitude toward the retarded child, whether it is loving or resentful or fearful or guilty.

There was a clear relationship between the upper-SCS family's acceptance of the retarded child and the openness and curiosity that the normal siblings remembered when they talked with us. Their acceptance was not related to the severity of the handicap or to the physical condition of the handicapped child.

AWAY

Not surprisingly, among these upper-SCS families, the more-severely retarded children tended to be put into institutions more often and to stay longer than less-severely retarded children. The popular view, as we noted before, is that such frequent and prolonged absence of a retarded child relieves normal siblings of anxieties regarding the child. But, in striking contrast to this view, our study shows that for these upper-SCS students, no matter how handicapped the child, his presence at home helped his siblings to adapt to his retardation, and had a very positive effect on their liking for him and on their response to him as a fellow himan being with feelings, as a person much like themselves.

Gail is a retarded child, upper-SCS, who was sent directly to an institution from the hospital at which she was born. The following remarks by her older brother (number five in a family of 11), illustrate sadly and clearly the enormous guilt and discomfort that can be aroused in a child when his retarded sibling is sent away, and the resulting dehumanization of that child in the eyes of the normal brother. We first asked what he thought was important for us to understand about his sister.

"Uh, I think the retarded sibling has been institutionalized since birth, a few days after she was born or something, and she's never been home, which I think is very good. With lots of other kids in the family, it would just be impossible for her to have any self-esteem when she reached the stage where she should have any. I don't see how it could possibly be sensible to have somebody who is definitely handicapped and could not possibly keep pace with someone a year younger around the house."

We asked him what Gail was like:

"Well, she's Mongoloid. I feel rather uninterested in her. I mean, you know, I'm interested in her progress, but I don't really enjoy going to see her. I don't enjoy it. Obviously, it's not very pleasant."

EFFECT

Later we asked what he thought the effect on him had been:

"I don't think she's affected me except, well, you run into the question of euthanasia. And just arguing about justified abortion, such as, if you know a kid is going to be Mongoloid, is it right to have her exist like that for as long as she lives? I mean, it's certain she won't live very long; she's six now, but that's rather old for a Mongoloid, actually. It's just a certain bother with everyone involved. But just in terms of herself, is it worth bringing someone into the world and sticking them with that?"

We asked, "Do you remember when you first learned Gail was retarded and what you thought?"

"I was kind of surprised, but I don't really know if it destroyed anything. I feel, I feel definitely that it's the only solution, unless it's an only child, it's not feasible to have her at home at all."

We asked him if he ever talked to friends about Gail.

"Well, I have, but it's not exactly my favorite topic."

"Have you ever told a girl friend?" we asked.

"Oh, come on. On a date?"

HARMED

The defensive quality of this young man's efforts to rationalize Gail's residential placement is obvious. We were certain this youth had a much greater involvement with Gail—positive or negative—than his remarks indicated on the surface. The fact that he was willing to participate in the research indicated this interest. It was obvious, too, that he desperately wished Gail had never been born or that she would die soon. (His conviction that children with Down's syndrome usually do not survive childhood is

erroneous.) We judged him to have been harmed by the experience of having a retarded sibling.

We eventually realized that the major impact upon these upper-SCS families of sending a child to an institution was not predictable on the basis of such factors as the nature of the institution, its expense, the frequency of visits, etc. Instead, the impact depends in great part on the psychological reactions of all concerned to the exclusion of a family member. It was clearly true that for these families there were sufficient resources for relieving the normal children of the burdensome care of the handicapped child. But the price was often guilt, overidentification with the handicapped child, fear on the part of the normal sibling that he or she might also be eliminated from the family and elaborate fantasies regarding the retarded sibling that build up in the absence of day-to-day contact. These effects played a major role in the normal children's adjustment to the situation.

CONTRAST

The families of the Community-U students stand in startling contrast. These families, which were of lower-middle socioeconomic status, had one or more children attending a local college. The students were bent on surpassing their parents in earnings and careers. Lack of money often was a serious limitation for these families; it inevitably affected their manner of caring for retarded children. The parents were poorly educated and, in the eyes of their children, were inept at coping with the burden of retarded children. The primary goal of many of these families was simple survival as financially viable, coherent family units. Parental guidance toward the fullest development of each child was a luxury, out of the question. Rather, as each child became old enough to help out, he was expected to share the burdens of family life.

The energy thus preempted left little for intense family involvement. These families appeared to be loosely knit, their members relatively uninvolved with one another. By the time they reached college age, lower-SCS students appeared to feel free to disregard their parents' views, partly because the students' own upward mobility made their parents less useful as models. Consequently, their parents' reactions towards retarded children had little impact on their own current thoughts and feelings about the retarded members of the families.

The striking difference between lower-SCS families and upper-SCS families is found in the primary impact of a retarded child. In an upper-SCS family, the major impact can be seen in the interactions of family members over their attitudes toward the handicapped child. In a lower-SCS family, the primary impact is seen quite simply in the degree and kind of hardship inflicted upon the family by the retarded child.

SISTERS

We discovered a significant sex difference in the lower-SCS families, as we had among the upper-SCS families. The lower-SCS young women in our sample had been expected, from the time they were quite young, to assume a major share of responsibility for handicapped siblings. They spent enormous amounts of time with the children. The ability of these young women to cope with life was directly affected by the seriousness of the siblings' mental and physical handicaps, which was not true of the upper-SCS women students. The young women from larger families coped better, probably because they had normal sisters and brothers who helped them.

We can see in the following excerpt from an interview with a young woman from Community U the enormous burden she bore, partly because her mother was incompetent. The young woman, whom we will call Elizabeth, is the oldest of three; the youngest, Mary, is a mildly retarded girl. Elizabeth discussed Mary's handicap matter-of-factly and also spoke easily of her own resentful feelings towards the retarded sibling. "I love her just like my other sister, and sometimes it's a lot easier to love her. But there have been times when I resented the responsibility for her."

Elizabeth told of having to oversee Mary's school work, when it became evident to her father that her mother was doing an inadequate job of it. "So I took over then, and I went to see the teacher all the time, and I found out what Mary had to do and everything. I don't regret anything other than the fact that I did lose quite a bit of my privacy, because Mary just attached herself right to me. Mary is very attached to my mother and myself, so as long as one of us is around, she's not bad. But she can be very upset when neither of us is around."

Elizabeth told us dispassionately that their mother had had enormous difficulty in accepting the fact that Mary was handicapped, and that she should be treated as normally as possible, not overprotected. "But my mother can't, isn't going to, face that completely. And she's gotten 100 percent better than when Mary was younger, but she's got a long way to go yet." We judged Elizabeth to have benefited overall from her experience.

CHRIS

One can see, in an excerpt from our interview with another young woman at Community U, a casual attitude toward other family members, including the retarded child, and the psychological distance at which the family members are held. This young woman had a retarded brother seven years younger than she. We asked how she felt toward him. "Well, um, I love him very much, and I don't resent him anymore, but when I was younger, I think I did."

When we asked how much time she had spent caring for him, she replied: "Well, I've babysat for him, from nine to five during the summer, and during the school year, until five o'clock."

"Did you ever wish Chris weren't around when your friends were there?"

"Oh, definitely. I remember, this is really strange, one time when I was about 12 we were in the pool, and I tried to drown him! It was really horrible, my mother almost flipped! Oh, I don't know, I guess it was a horrible thing to do, but I didn't know what I was doing. I just knew, I guess, that I had to babysit for him all the time, and he was just a bother to me." We asked what she felt the effect had been on her father. "My father is of very low intelligence. I think he kind of resents my brother in a way, because my mother gives him all the attention. And my mother, you know, it takes up all her time. She was completely nervous. When she found out that he was retarded, I think she sort of had a breakdown, and now she won't admit that he is retarded." We judged that the net effect of the experience was neutral for this young woman.

PARODY

The young Community-U men were not as psychologically involved with their families as the young men and women from upper-SCS families were, nor were they expected to help care for the handicapped siblings the way the young lower-SCS women were. Of all our subjects these young men appear to be least affected by the experience of living with a retarded sibling. They are also least knowledgeable about their siblings' handicaps.

One interview with a young Community-U man is almost a parody of uninvolvement. This young man, whom we will call Robert, was the oldest of three boys. Doug, the youngest, was mildly retarded. Robert told us he did not know what was wrong with Doug, that his parents had never told him. We asked if he could find out for us, and he was not sure that his parents would tell him. (This was the only instance we encountered, in working with 83 subjects, where a sibling didn't have a good idea of the diagnosis.)

We asked how Robert thought Doug viewed himself. "I don't know. I haven't given it much thought lately." We asked how he felt Doug's handicap had affected him. "Well, I don't know, I've been thinking about that since I got your letter. I really don't know how it affected me. My parents were very strange about this thing. They never really, really talk to me about it. So I don't really know how it affected me." We asked later if he had spent a lot of time with

Doug. "I guess not, I babysat occasionally."

RATIO

Among lower-SCS students, as among upper-SCS students, there was a favorable ratio between open and comfortable family discussion of retardation and the student's own acceptance of the retarded child.

Very few lower-SCS families in our study had placed retarded children in institutions. Many had sought such placement and some certainly would have benefited from it. This inability to obtain placements and the caretaking burden it placed on normal siblings was a definite factor in the degree to which our young Community-U subjects had adjusted to their handicapped brothers and sisters.

This research demonstrates once again that in our culture, sociocultural status has far-reaching consequences on the families of retarded children.

It is heartening to see changes in professional attitudes toward putting retarded children into institutions. Until recently, such placement was almost universally advised; all too frequently the advice was based on the belief that a handicapped person always "contaminated" the family and generated great psychological burdens. Our findings that the reactions of other family members are not inevitably determined by the nature and degree of the handicap itself cut through this mistaken belief.

It is the family's definition of the problem that most directly affects the ability of individual members of the family to adjust to a retarded child. The presence of a retarded child can enhance a family's normal development, or at least not hinder it.

The recent shift away from institutions is only partly due to this realization. Other influences are the rising costs of placement, increased awareness of the harshness of the institutions, and growing sensitivity to the negative effects that placement and separation have on the whole family.

CHAPTER 6

Religion, parents and mental retardation

HAROLD W. STUBBLEFIELD

Clover Bottom Hospital and School
Donelson, Tennessee

ABSTRACT: *The role of religion in the parental acceptance of a retarded child is receiving increasing attention. It has been demonstrated that religious faith affects the response to a retarded child and that the birth of a retarded child also affects religious faith. This article interprets the relation of religion to parental acceptance, suggests specific areas for future research, and calls for interdisciplinary collaboration between clergymen and professional workers in mental retardation.*

The role of religion in the parental acceptance of a retarded child is frequently acknowledged in the literature on parent counseling. One study (Michaels & Schueman, 1962) observed that while the religious faith of parents may serve as a constructive, supportive force, religion, in too many instances, is used in a negative fashion, impeding a realistic handling of the problem.

Such specific religious factors as religious affiliation and religious interpretations of illness influence the parents' response. These are noted by Eaton and Weil (1955), Farber (1959), and Zuk, Miller, Bartram and Kling (1961). Other studies (Murray, 1959; Stubblefield, 1964, 1965) demonstrate that the birth of a retarded child may precipitate a theological crisis for the parents. Furthermore, particular emotional reactions have distinct religious meanings. Zuk (1959) suggestively explored the problem of guilt in relation to Catholic theology, while Lynd

(1958) related the feeling of shame to parental attitudes toward defective children.

Unfortunately these insights have resulted in neither controlled depth studies into the religious aspects of the parents' experience nor systematic organization of these data. This article is an attempt to organize these data into a meaningful pattern, to interpret the role of religion in the parents' response to a retarded child, and to suggest specific areas for future research. Such a perspective should prove helpful to counselors in dealing with parents' religious concerns and should also demonstrate that this is a fruitful area for scientific investigation.

RETARDATION AS A THEOLOGICAL CRISIS

When research findings are analyzed, two definite patterns of relationship between religion and parental acceptance are apparent. The first pattern is that the birth of a retarded child preciptates a theological crisis for many parents.

The emotional impact upon some parents

Reprinted from Mental Retardation, 8-11, August 1965, with permission.

is severe enough to shatter their religious faith. One mother (Murray, 1959) of a retarded child contends that having a child who will remain a mental cripple for his entire life places parents, at least in their feelings, outside the province of God's mercy and justice, if they can still believe that there is a God. This mother further charges that these theological problems are almost always ignored by professional workers.

Moreover, a survey (Stubblefield, 1964) of 220 Protestant and Catholic clergymen disclosed that 15 percent of these ministers believed that having a retarded child had caused doubt about the goodness of God in the parents known to them, and 13 percent had observed reactions of guilt. Failure to resolve this conflict, they noted, often resulted in attitudes of chronic bitterness, resentment, or apathy.

Another dimension of the theological crisis is the belief that the retarded condition is the punishment of God. Involved here, of course, is the problem of sin, guilt and forgiveness. In some instances, such a belief represents man's persistent need to affix responsibility and to believe that God visits the sins of the fathers upon the sons (Oates, 1957). It may simply reflect the religious training which the parents received as children.

Attributing mental retardation to God's judgment is not always the result of faulty religious instruction. Guilt also operates at a deeper, more unconscious level where direct confrontation and re-education are not sufficient. For some parents this belief is a way to preserve self-esteem in the face of an irrevocable tragedy. Feeling punished for sins may be more tolerable than to believe that this event has no meaning and is unrelated to one's personal identity. It reflects "a universal human tendency to avoid the anxiety of feeling helpless in the hands of what seems to be an impersonal, irrational fate (Thornton, 1964)."

Feelings of punishment also result from the sense of social isolation which parents of retarded children experience in our culture. Guilt caused by alienation from social relationships is thus interpreted as alienation from God.

A distinction, however, must be drawn between a sense of guilt and genuine guilt. Belief that one is being punished is often realistically related to concrete deeds for which forgiveness is needed. For instance, in conversation with a minister, the mother of a retarded son stated that she could not understand why God was punishing her. When the minister explored why she felt this way, the mother reported having attempted an abortion during the pregnancy because she did not want any more children. Now the mother was literally attempting to make "atonement" by overprotecting the child, even to the extent of refusing to let other family members care for him.

A further distinction should be noted between shame and guilt. In guilt feelings, the person feels that he has committed sin or transgression, that he is no good, and that atonement must be made. In feelings of shame, the person feels that he has failed to live up to his highest aspirations, that he is inadequate or inferior. One aspect of the experience of shame with particular religious interest is what Lynd (1958) calls the "threat to trust." This experience so contradicts what one has been led to expect that he questions his own adequacy or the values of the world of reality. Lynd further contends that feelings of shame for one's children become codified as a parental defect. Thus what is frequently interpreted as guilt may be closer to a sense of shame.

While the theological crisis is most often interpreted negatively, in terms of guilt and punishment, some positive effects may result. Nothing here is to be construed to mean that mental retardation is a "positive blessing in disguise" as some theologians and even parents have indicated. Nevertheless, as the Judaeo-Christian tradition has rightly emphasized, suffering is redemptive as well as destructive. Through suffering, religious faith can be deepened, strengthened, and one's ultimate beliefs and values clarified.

In the survey of clergymen, 41 percent had observed that a retarded child stimulated greater faith in the parents known to them, while 28 percent had observed families who were brought closer to the church as a result of this experience. Parents themselves have testified that as a result of their experience they were turned "from the superficialities of life to those things that really matter"; that they learned the deeper meanings of patience, humility and gratitude; and that they developed a "strange kind of courage" because in one sense they had borne "the ultimate that life has to offer in sorrow and pain (Murray, 1959)." These positive effects, when they exist, need to be accepted by the counselor and assimilated by the parents as a legitimate response to a retarded child.

To set this crisis in its proper context involves a longitudinal perspective as well as a cross-sectional one. The process of discovering, accepting and planning for a retarded child is similar to a grief process. What is appropriate and healthy at one stage is inappropriate at another. The health or pathology of the theological crisis is partly determined by the time factor. For parents, initially, to feel anger and bitterness toward God and to project blame on God is quite natural and can be dealt with sympathically and reflectively. For these same feelings to be strongly expressed six years later, as in the mother who wondered why God was punishing her, may indicate severe emotional disturbance, requiring more intensive treatment.

RELIGIOUS FACTORS IN PARENT'S RESPONSE

Thus mental retardation as a theological crisis is best understood in relation to the religious history of the parents. Not only does the birth of a retarded child affect religious faith, but religious faith also affects the parents' response to this event. This is the second pattern of relationship between religion and parental acceptance. At least three religious factors have been recognized as formative influences.

One is the religious affiliation of the parents. Two recent studies disclosed that Catholic parents tend to be more accepting of a retarded child than either Protestant or Jewish parents. Farber (1959) found that removing a retarded boy from a Catholic home had little effect on the marital integration, but that non-Catholics seemed to be benefited when the retarded boy was institutionalized. In Zuk's questionnaire study (1961) of 72 mothers, the Catholic mothers, on three items, more frequently reflected greater acceptance of the child and indicated greater intensity in religious practices of prayer and church attendance.

In accounting for these differences, Farber suggested "that participation in the Catholic church and/or Catholic definitions of home and family life were supportive." Similarly, Zuk believed that the Catholic mothers' greater acceptance resulted from the Catholic doctrine that parents should not feel guilty for bearing a retarded child. Instead, they should accept the child as the gift of God. Neither Protestant or Jewish teachings are this explicit. The rationale underlying these conclusions seems to be that the greater acceptance of the Catholic parents results from different attitudes toward homemaking and children in general. Some studies (Lenski, 1963; Masland, Sarason, & Gladwin, 1958) support this conclusion. Religious affiliation, however, "is but one aspect of broader subcultural differences which are at work." It should not be used as an independent variable without qualification.

A second factor is the religious interpretation of the cause of illness. Contrast the results of these two interpretations. In a study of the Hutterite community, a close knit, communal, religious group, Eaton and Weil (1955) found considerable social acceptance of the retarded. This acceptance apparently stemmed from two sources. First, genetic reasons were usually advanced to explain the prevalence of 51 cases of mental retardation. No moral or social stigma was attached. Second, the care of handicapped persons was considered to be a religious obligation. In this atmosphere, retardation is accepted matter-of-factly. When retardation is recognized, the person is taken to the doctor to determine if there is any medical remedy. The community provides the family with additional care if needed. Other children are punished if they ridicule or take advantage of the afflicted child. Retardates who reach adulthood are encouraged to work.

In contrast, belief that retardation is the punishment of God creates extreme guilt and prevents parents from realistically planning for a retarded child. Mr. Tucker, the father of a six-year-old retarded son, remarked to a minister at an evaluation clinic that if he and his wife had been "the kind of persons that God wants us to be, it wouldn't have happened." Moreover, he believed that if they now become the kind of persons God wants them to be, their son would be cured. So strongly did he believe this that he sent his son's name to Oral Roberts for prayer. Mr. Tucker refused to accept the limitations of his son. Instead, the child became the center of the family, and the needs of the other son and the mother were sacrificed in the care of the retarded child.

A third factor is the religious teachings regarding the expression of feeling. Every religion and culture structures acceptable patterns for the expression of emotions and reaction to such crucial events as illness and death. Moral values are even attached to the kinds of intensity of emotions permitted to be expressed.

When a religious group interprets mental retardation as a sign of God's disfavor, and this interpretation is accepted, as in Mr. Tucker's case, guilt tends to be the dominant emotion expressed. When parents, however, cannot accept the interpretation of the religious community, they either suppress their deeper feelings or reject the community's interpretation. Mr. Tucker's wife, for instance, openly disagreed with his viewpoint. Instead of feeling guilt for producing a retarded child, she felt hostility toward God for allowing this to happen. She could not understand why they of all people had a retarded child. As she said, they were as good as most people, and many other persons could have endured this crisis better than she.

With other parents, negative and socially unacceptable feelings are suppressed, as Winburn Davis (1962) noted. These unex-

pressable feelings included guilt, disappointment, fear of the future, failure, shame, repulsion of the child, and hopelessness. Many of the parents that Davis, a social worker, interviewed reported that they stopped crying after the birth of their retarded child. Their feelings were "frozen." Only after freedom to honestly acknowledge their emotions in the presence of an accepting person were they able to cry again.

AREAS OF RESEARCH AND COLLABORATION

Emerging from this discussion are several areas in which exploratory research is needed. These are: (1) the effect that the birth of a retarded child has on the religious faith of parents; (2) the teachings of religious groups regarding attitudes toward children, their beliefs about acceptable responses to crucial life events, and how parents use religious beliefs to structure their response to a retarded child; (3) the distinction between a healthy or pathological use of religion; (4) the process through which parents move, over a long period of time, in interpreting retardation in light of their religious faith; and (5) a comparison of the degree of acceptance of retardation by "religious" persons and "nonreligious" persons.

At the present stage of knowledge, observation and exploration on a descriptive level needs to be done before research limited to a formal design is undertaken. There is still need to ask questions and explore "hunches" for which no research instruments may be available. However, testable hypotheses should emerge that can be explored in formal studies.

Two procedures are indicated. The first is the collection of clinical data. This includes surveying existing clinical records of parent interviews and encouraging parent counselors to record interviews in which religious concerns are expressed. Questionnaire studies are needed to furnish comparative data as Zuk (1959) and Farber (1959) found in relation to religious affiliation and parental acceptance. Further studies, however, should inquire directly into religious matters and elicit the parents' interpretation rather than the interpretation being superimposed by the investigator. Personal interviews with parents would also yield valuable data. These would be depth interviews, with a minimum of structure, in which parents are encouraged to discuss freely the religious concerns associated with their retarded child.

A second procedure involves historical and theological studies. Some topics are suggested in the following questions: What are the teachings of the Catholic, Jewish, and Protestant faiths on sin and guilt, providence and predestination? To what degree do these teachings make parents feel responsible for a condition such as mental retardation? What are the teachings of these groups on marriage, the family and children which structure the parental response to a retarded child?

What is being suggested here is that clinical data cannot be rightly interpreted apart from the perspective of the disciplines of theology, sociology of religion and psychology of religion. The role of religion in parental acceptance cannot be adequately appreciated apart from an understanding of the function of religion in the "life-economy" of persons and the theological teachings of the religious community to which they belong. Attention must be given to the belief systems which give meaning, order and purpose to life and to the uses which these beliefs are put in meeting actual life situations.

To this end, collaboration with clinically trained clergymen, hospital chaplains, and professors of pastoral counseling is imperative. A maximum level of collaboration would be to use such a person as a theological consultant. In a clinical setting, a theological consultant could render such services as counseling with parents when the minister's role is appropriate, interpreting the religious concerns of parents and the beliefs of specific religious communities to staff members, and participating in research. Two of the illustrations in this paper were taken from parent interviews of such a theological consultant, functioning as a member of the diagnostic team in the evaluation clinic of a children's hospital. To some degree, such collaboration is occurring in a few state hospitals.

A less formal level of collaboration involves bringing together a group of carefully selected community pastors to share and reflect on their ministry and experiences with parents, with specific reference to religious concerns. The survey of clergymen, previously cited, demonstrated that almost every minister, at sometime in his ministry, has contact with retarded persons and their parents. Many of these ministers provided a variety of pastoral services and had observed that religion was frequently dynamically involved in the nature of the parents' reaction.

"A man's religion," says Gordon Allport (1950, p. 142), "is the audacious bid he makes to bind himself to creation and to the Creator. It is his ultimate attempt to enlarge and to complete his own personality by finding the supreme context in which he rightly belongs." Thus the parents' search to find meaning and peace through religion is one of the unexplored frontiers of mental retardation. It presents a unique opportunity for creative interdisciplinary collaboration and research.

REFERENCES

Allport, G. *The Individual and His Religion.* New York: Macmillan, 1950.

Davis, W. Emotional Acceptance of Mental Retardation. Paper read at Southern Baptist Conference on Guidance and Counseling, Nashville, Tennessee, September 25, 1962.

Eaton, J. W. & Weil, R. J. *Culture and Mental Disorders: A Comparative Study of the Hutterites and Other Populations.* Glencoe, Illinois: The Free Press, 1955.

Farber, B. Effects of a Severely Mentally Retarded Child on Family Integration. Monograph, *Society for Research in Child Development.* Antioch Press, 1959.

Lenski, G. *The Religious Factor.* Anchor Books edition. Garden City, New York: Doubleday and Co., Inc., 1963.

Lynd, H. M. *On Shame and the Search for Identity.* New York: Harcourt, Brace and Co., 1958.

Masland, R., Sarason, S. B., & Gladwin, T. *Mental Subnormality: Biological, Psychological, and Cultural Factors.* New York: Basic Books, Inc., 1958.

Michaels, J., & Schueman, H. Observations on the Psychodynamics of Parents of Retarded Children. *American Journal of Mental Deficiency,* 1962, *66*, 568-573.

Murray, Mrs. M. A. Needs of Parents of Mentally Retarded Children, *American Journal of Mental Deficiency,* 1959, *63*, 1078-1088.

Oates, W. E. *The Religious Dimensions of Personality.* New York: Association Press, 1957.

Stubblefield, H. W. The Ministry and Mental Retardation. *Journal of Religion and Health,* 1964, *3*, 136-147.

Stubblefield, H. W. *The Church's Ministry in Mental Retardation.* Nashville, Tenn.: Broadman Press, 1965.

Thornton, E. E. *Theology and Pastoral Counseling.* Englewood Cliffs, N.J.: Prentice-Hall, Inc., 1964.

Zuk, G. H. The Religious Factor and the Role of Guilt in Parental Acceptance of the Retarded Child. *American Journal of Mental Deficiency,* 1959, *64,* 139-147.

Zuk, G. H., Miller, R. L., Bartram, J. B., & Kling, F. Maternal Acceptance of Retarded Children: A Questionnaire Study of Attitudes and Religious Background. *Child Development,* 1961, *32,* 525-540.

CHAPTER 7

Involving families of handicapped children

MERLE B. KARNES
R. REID ZEHRBACH
Institute for Research on Exceptional Children
Department of Special Education
University of Illinois, Urbana-Champaign

JAMES A. TESKA
Department of Special Education
Southern Illinois University
Carbondale, Illinois

Parental involvement in programs for handicapped children has long been an important aspect of a quality program for these children. Unfortunately, with few exceptions, most efforts have met with little or no success. Two basic factors seem to be associated with this lack of success—attitudes of professional personnel and their lack of skills in working with parents. These two factors are so closely interwoven that it is difficult to determine cause and effect relationships. For example, the attitude that the professional person is an "expert" and must impart knowledge, as reflected in parent-teacher conferences and to a large extent in Parent Teacher Association (PTA) meetings, prevents his listening to parents, an essential ingredient for working with them.

A programmatic research-based effort involving family members of handicapped and disadvantaged children has enabled the authors to delineate a set of assumptions leading to the development of a model for family involvement in an education program (Karnes et al., 1968, 1969, 1970, 1971). According to these assumptions, family members:

1. Are interested in the growth of their child and would like to improve their interaction with him.
2. Can be helped to improve their skills necessary for interaction.
3. Can work in a classroom setting, including one in which their own child is participating.
4. Will find the time to become involved if the involvement is meaningful.
5. Will learn most effectively when their training is specific and has direct application.
6. Are easiest to involve when their goals and values are congruent with those of the school and most difficult when there is a great discrepancy in the "match."[1]

Reprinted from Theory into Practice, College of Education, The Ohio State University, 11(3):150-156, 1972, with permission.

[1]The concept of the "match" is derived from J. McV. Hunt, *Intelligence and Experience* (New York: Ronald Press, 1961) but refers to the amount of agreement or disagreement between the goals of the school and the goals of the family.

7. Will require the greatest flexibility in programming when there is a wide discrepancy in the "match."
8. Will become involved to the extent to which they participate in decision making.
9. Will involve themselves most when feedback exists and is positive.
10. Will involve themselves most when professional personnel show a genuine respect for the family members as individuals.
11. Will involve themselves most when served by professional personnel who have been trained to work with family members in divergent, appropriate ways.
12. Will involve themselves most when the approach is highly individualized.
13. Will be able to apply new knowledge to other family members, particularly other children.

14. Will develop more positive attitudes when the involvement is successful.
15. Will need less help and support from professional staff as they acquire more effective knowledge and skills.
16. May acquire sufficient skills to work with family members of other families.

The above set of assumptions has been delineated to help clarify the basis on which programs for family members might be established. Implementation of these ideas may be difficult because of the breadth of the assumptions and the magnitude of problems. A model that demonstrates these beliefs is therefore proposed to help professional persons implement the program (Fig. 1).

Since any program to involve family members must be flexible, the model that helps professionals develop plans and procedures for meeting the needs of family members with highly individualized sets of problems must also be flexible. Therefore, the basic

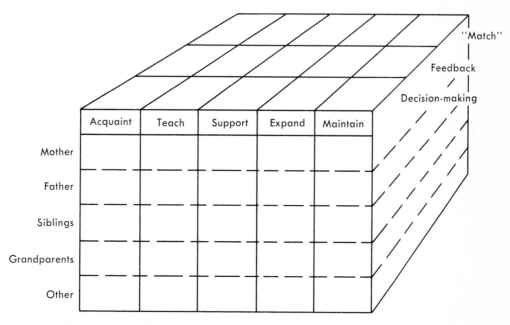

Fig. 1. The ATSEM Model for Parent Involvement.
Procedures used to implement ATSEM dimension:
1. Home visit
   a. Observe parent-child interaction
   b. Demonstrate teaching behavior
2. School
   a. Parent observe child
   b. Parent teach child
3. Parent discussion groups
4. Personal interview
5. Therapy
6. Cassette tapes
7. Toy library

dimension of the proposed model is a longitudinal process dimension called ATSEM. It derives its label from the initials which stand for the five main areas: *Acquaint, Teach, Support, Expand,* and *Maintain.*

The *Acquaint* phase describes the *process* of involving the family member in activities that maximize the growth of the child, both at home and at school. The end of the *Acquaint* phase is signaled when the professionals are able to state rather clearly that the family member has committed himself (herself) to work with others to facilitate the child's growth. The attainment of this goal is often indicated subtly. Moreover, some family members never seem to reach the goal, although, in the process, they may significantly improve the way they cope with their child's problems.

The *Teach* phase is also viewed as a process. During the process, the family member learns a set of techniques, skills, and attitudes that helps him teach the child new knowledge and behaviors. Many of these skills are attained by providing the family member with concrete tasks to teach the child until the parent learns how to teach concepts without help. The family member has completed the *Teach* phase when he (she) has shown the ability to approach the child and teach him new concepts and ideas with little direction from others. Obviously there are considerable individual differences among family members with regard to their ability to teach the child. Consequently, the goals of the *Teach* process for various family members differ, so goal attainment must be, in part, described in terms of the family member's potential for learning new ideas, attitudes, and skills (i.e., the goals for a family member who, himself, is intellectually, socially, or emotionally limited will differ from those for the family member who is more able).

The third phase of the model, the *Support* phase, is defined as that time during which the family member requires special emotional, social, or economic support. Thus, support may help the parent learn how to obtain services from the Division of Services

for Crippled Children, to complete high school via a General Education Development Test (G.E.D.), to seek additional help from Aid to Dependent Children (A.D.C.), to seek help from a mental health facility. Regardless of the need, professional or paraprofessional individuals implementing the ATSEM Model are encouraged to do all they can to help the family members obtain the needed support.

One of the limitations inherent in the model is that it implies that the support activities occur after the *Teach* phase. With family members from low income backgrounds, this order often holds true (i.e., the low-income family member often needs help to learn specific, concrete techniques for working with his child before he develops the confidence in staff members that allows him to seek help concerning other, more personal, problems). For example, the mother on A.D.C. may hide some facts that are causing her difficulties with the bureaucracy until she trusts a staff member enough to share her problems and obtain aid in their resolution.

On the other hand, many family members will require support before, or along with, participation in other project activities. The mother who has a multi-handicapped child and is too insecure to leave her home may require many home visits before she can feel secure enough to leave the home and observe the child functioning in the classroom. It may be that she must observe her child functioning in the classroom before she can truly feel comfortable in trying to teach her child a new activity. Thus, the model might be alternately described as the ASTEM model.

The *Support* phase terminates when the family members indicate that they are able to function without the need for additional supportive service help. Again, the goals must be individualized because some may attain a high degree of personal integrity while others may only make modest improvements because they lack the intellectual, social, emotional, or other abilities to become fully productive.

The parents enter the *Expand* stage when they feel emotionally and socially secure and are able to expand their horizons with the child. For example, the parent taking her child into the supermarket for the first time without fearing that the child will throw a temper tantrum or otherwise embarrass the family member may indicate such growth. Termination of the *Expand* phase of the model is difficult to define because theoretically a parent should never cease to attempt to expand his child's horizons and development of knowledge. Yet, once a family demonstrates through day-to-day behavior that they consistently expand the child's knowledge and skills, it seems appropriate to focus on procedures that will maintain such behavior.

The *Maintain* phase of the model is multifaceted. Some individuals in this phase have made considerable progress in working with their children, but require continued reinforcement to maintain this higher level of functioning. Another aspect of the *Maintain* phase is that it is often used to help parents *Acquaint* other parents with the program. It would seem that providing family members with the opportunity to help others understand the program is one way of assisting the *helping* person learn and reinforce previous learnings. For example, if a parent has difficulty accepting fully the handicap of his child, then explicating this feeling to a newly entering parent may help each parent clarify his feelings.

In summary, the ATSEM model is a process-oriented model that focuses on bringing family members into contact with a program and then involving them actively in the program. As originally conceived, the model was essentially unidimensional with the major focus on the mother. It soon became apparent that the model should be expanded to include all family members. The expansion became almost mandatory when it became apparent that fathers could and *should* be involved with the program. Similarly, earlier studies (Karnes, Zehrbach, and Teska, 1971) had suggested that the older siblings could successfully assist in the development of younger children. A second dimension of the ATSEM model, then, would seem to be that all family members should be involved.

Another limitation of the model is that it does not help implementers make decisions as to which family member(s) should be involved. Such a decision must be derived from a careful study of the total family and the potentials for involvement of each family member or clusters of family members. Thus, it may be fruitful to involve only a mother in one family, a father in a second, and the mother, father, and grandmother in a third. Contingencies such as working hours, financial conditions, and basic emotional adjustment are all factors that play a part in the decision. This facet of the model should help remind the implementors that all family members should be considered as potential candidates for involvement during the planning and implementation stages.

The third dimension in the model considers how parents are involved as participants in the on-going process. To date, three areas have been identified as pertinent—"Decision-Making," "Feedback," and the "Match" between family and school goals. The concept of parental involvement in the decision-making process is somewhat foreign to school personnel because, until recently, most decisions were based on the belief that school personnel were in the best position to make such decisions. Recently it has become apparent that parents may hold different, yet valid, goals as compared with those of school personnel. Therefore, when establishing a program for family involvement, serious consideration needs to be given to how each family member can participate in the decision-making process.

A second area of this dimension, "Feedback," has received even less consideration. Once a parent starts to function within the decision-making process, he must have information as to the effectiveness of his decisions. We have yet to devise a fully effective system for feedback. Parent conferences can be more effective communicators than report cards, yet, most school personnel lack the ability to conduct a truly effective parent conference. Some literature is beginning to develop in which parents gather their own information and make their own observations (Lindsley, 1968). All that can be said to date, however, is that meaningful feedback systems for parents must be established.

Much has been written recently about the need to establish an appropriate "Match" between the cognitive development of the child and the curriculum in which he functions. Much less has been said, except from a polemic point of view, about the need to establish programs for parents that develop a "Match" between the parental values and goals and those of the school. This "Match" should be a primary consideration factor in the development of a family involvement program.

A fourth dimension is that of "Procedures." After the professional staff decides which family member or members to involve, they must decide how to approach him. Home visits with a variety of foci for a visit, group discussion, observation at school, teaching in the classroom at school, coordination with other agencies to obtain specific help, working with other parents, fathers' programs have been useful procedures.

Each of these activities can help achieve certain goals. Not all are, or should be, used with every family. Typically, the procedures will change as progress is made. For example, a home visitor or parent makes a series of home visits to establish rapport with parents that allows them to participate in (become *acquainted* with) the project. Then, the parents may come to the school and observe the child in the classroom to learn some techniques for *teaching* the child. Later, as feelings are aroused, the parents might join a parent group and gain *support* from other parents who are facing similar problems. Finally, the home visitor may start a series of visits to the home to help the parents as they *expand* their horizons for the child. And, finally, the parent may return to the parent groups as he *maintains* his growth by helping other parents enter the process.

The preceding brief overview reveals how various types of activities can be involved in the ATSEM process. Following is a discussion in greater depth of some implications of these activities.

OBSERVATIONAL HOME VISITS

The home visit can fulfill a variety of extremely useful functions, from gathering information to supporting parents. Typically, the first home visit is made by a trained home visitor, paraprofessional, or professional. Subsequently, a parent who has been involved in the program might make a follow-up visit to establish greater rapport. Specific visits to observe parent-child interaction, conditions in the home—economic, social, emotional—might then be made. Once information has been gathered and some initial plans outlined, the home visits may be curtailed as the parent becomes involved in other aspects of the program.

HOME TEACHING VISITS

Since the purpose of the program is to help parents learn to cope with and teach their child, assistance with these activities in the home is of paramount importance. Many parents can teach successfully in the classroom under the supervision and guidance of a teacher, but when they face the same task at home, they are less successful. Observation in the home by a paraprofessional or professional may identify specific difficulties and procedures for improvement. In other instances, the parent may need emotional and social support. For example, a parent may come to parent meetings and seemingly understand his problems, then inadvertently reinforce the child for temper tantrums. Again, a visit in the home may be fruitful.

DISCUSSION GROUP

One effective technique is a parents' discussion group. Bringing together certain selected, but not all, parents to discuss mutual child-oriented problems in the context of what one can do to positively help children has been extremely useful. Verbal parents help the nonverbal parents identify their problems, while the nonverbal parents provide a sounding board that helps verbal parents understand what is being said. To be productive, the discussion subjects must be ones the parents feel are important rather than those arbitrarily chosen by the professionals. Also role playing by these parent groups is usually an effective technique.

Classroom observation is also a very useful technique. A parent may say, "My child is a finicky eater," and then see the child eat "disliked" foods in the classroom and even ask for more. Similarly, the child who has temper tantrums at home may manifest appropriate behavior at school. Further, the child may show in school that he has learned although he may not exhibit his learning at home. Such observations may help a parent understand that the problems do not reside in the child.

Classroom teaching is also extremely beneficial to a parent. Observation of a child in action, followed by the parent successfully teaching the child similar material can make a parent more confident in his ability to teach the child.

NEWSLETTERS

A newsletter written by parents for circulation among parents of children in the program conveys information about the program. A newsletter also interprets the program for others. When parents express and share their ideas in writing, they also clarify their thinking. Further, parents of handicapped children can often convey ideas and feelings to parents of other handicapped children more effectively than can professionals.

CASSETTE TAPES

A library of cassette tapes on subjects of interest to family members can be most helpful. A family member can listen to a tape while doing other things in the home. Some family members find listening to a tape an easier way of learning than reading the material.

Cassette tapes can also stimulate discussions. A five-minute tape on a subject chosen by the family members can stimulate a half-hour of group discussion. These tapes

may be made by professionals and/or by the parents.

TOY LENDING LIBRARY

The toy lending library (Karnes et al., 1968) used in previous projects has been helpful in this program. Family members check out toys, books, and puzzles to use with their handicapped child. They often solicit the help of the professional in selecting the appropriate item. During small group meetings the parents discuss the effectiveness of the toys and the ways in which they encouraged the use of the toys. During such group meetings, professionals often demonstrate use of the toys to achieve certain ameliorative or remedial objectives.

Making instructional materials from readily available and inexpensive materials has proved interesting and valuable in soliciting the involvement of family members in the education of the handicapped child (e.g., egg cartons for sorting, cardboard pictures for classifying, puzzles made of pictures pasted on cardboard, etc.). Parents gain a better understanding of activities appropriate for achieving objectives promoted by the school. They learn specifically what activities foster confidence in working with a handicapped child.

An illustrative case study of family involvement of a multi-handicapped child implementing the ATSEM model follows.

Tim, a four-year-old mentally retarded, hyperactive child with delayed speech patterns, entered the multi-handicapped program after being dismissed from a preschool for normal children because of "inability to adjust and participate." Tim's father, a university student, cared for Tim while his mother worked full-time outside the home. A local mental health clinic referred Tim's parents to the model program for the multi-handicapped at the University of Illinois.

After an initial, brief interview to determine Tim's eligibility for the project, he was referred to a project psychologist for extensive study. Then a social worker obtained additional information about the home and the development of the child from the parents and social agency records. The project admissions committee reviewed this information and found Tim eligible for the project.

Project personnel established goals and objectives for working with the parents. It was apparent that highly individualized objectives would be necessary for working with each parent. The father was permissive, yet concerned about the welfare of the boy. The staff thought he might quickly progress from the "Acquaint" to the "Teach" stage. They expected him to reveal this growth through consistent completion of all tasks asked of him by project personnel.

The mother, in contrast to the father, was a reluctant participant in the project. She appeared overly firm, almost to the point of punitiveness in handling the child. She showed little warmth toward him and had a defeatist attitude regarding his potential for growth. These feelings seemed to be based, in part, on the pressures of reality, such as holding a full-time job, and keeping the household running as smoothly as possible. These pressures, coupled with Tim's dismissal from a local preschool program, made the mother feel frustrated and guilty for having produced such a child.

The staff attempted to allay the mother's feelings of guilt and to help her develop the confidence and skills necessary to teach her child. She was encouraged to attend weekly parent meetings, and to express her feelings toward her handicapped child in small group meetings with other parents of young handicapped children. A parent in the "Maintain" stage acted as her confidant and supporter and provided her with basic information about the project. She viewed video tapes of Tim engaged in productive activities in the classroom. Professional personnel were assigned to help guide her observations. The staff invited the mother to observe Tim in the classroom when her work schedule would permit absences of one to two hours.

The father progressed through the "Acquaint" phase as anticipated and he rapidly moved into the second stage of the parent involvement model, the "Teach" stage. Since he had demonstrated his interest in his child's growth and had displayed an aptitude for teaching him, project staff involved the father in deciding how best he could become involved in the project. He decided to improve his teaching skills by participating in actual classroom teaching for two hours daily for a week (such a goal seems reasonable and attainable regardless of the father's occupation). In addition, the father decided to reinforce school learnings by working with Tim at home during the evening and weekends. The classroom teachers recommended various activities to the father. Also, groups of parents met with staff and learned how to teach certain knowledge and skills through role playing, demonstration, and discussion.

The father made rapid progress and contributed greatly to the child's growth, but the involvement of the mother proceeded slowly, yet in a positive direction. Almost four months of effort by project personnel and other parents were required to help the mother fully accept the program and understand and tentatively accept the child's strengths and weaknesses. At this point it was felt that she could attain positive satisfaction from engaging in basic teaching skill activities. She would work with the child, using a picture story from the toy lending library, before his bedtime. Both the activity and time of day were carefully selected to assure a positive relationship between mother and child. Teachers demonstrated how to use such a book with the child. Very gradually, the mother indicated that she was successful in these and more complex activities. She volunteered to come to school and teach in the classroom and asked to be assigned to the story period.

After a year in the project, the parents expanded their activities by taking the child on field trips to local stores and to visit relatives, and even on a short vacation. Previously these activities had been impossible because of the child's hyperactivity and obvious slowness in learning, and because of disagreements between the parents on the handling of the child.

After a year in the program, the mother referred a parent of a handicapped child to the project. Further, the father was elected by the parents to be a member of the advisory board of the program. The progress of the parents was not without problems. On several occasions, the mother became very distressed and threatened to withdraw from the program. She was overhead to say, "I don't know what I am doing here. I'm not helping Tim or anyone else." Nevertheless, through the efforts of professional personnel and other parents, this family was able to progress. The grandparents, who lived in the vicinity, also visited the program. They understood the objectives established for Tim and learned appropriate activities for reinforcing these efforts. Mary, Tim's seven-year-old sister, learned to help the parents with Tim by playing simple games encouraging language and motor development with him. Care was taken to ensure that Mary also received her share of attention so that she did not feel ignored.

In summary, this article has proposed a model for conceptualizing family involvement in an educational program for young children. Heuristic value of the model has been demonstrated through a discussion of the various components. Further, practical suggestions and problems in implementation have been delineated and illustrated in a case study involving a family with a multi-handicapped child.

REFERENCES

Hunt, J. McV. *Intelligence and Experience.* New York: Ronald Press, 1961.

Karnes, Merle B., Studley, W. M., Wright, W. R. and Hodgins, A. S. "An Approach for Working with Mothers of Disadvantaged Preschool Children." *Merrill-Palmer Quarterly* 14 (1968): 174-184.

Karnes, Merle B., Hodgins, A. S. and Teska, J. A. *Investigations of Classroom and At-Home Interventions.* Vol. I. *Research and Development Program on Preschool Disadvantaged Children.* Final Report. Bethesda, Md.: ERIC Document Reproduction Service (ED 036 663), 1969.

Karnes, Merle B., Teska, J. A. and Hodgins, A. S. "The Successful Implementation of a Highly Specific Preschool Instructional Program by Paraprofessional Teachers." *Journal of Special Education* 4 (1970):68-80.

Karnes, Merle B., Zehrbach, R. R. and Teska, J. A. "A New Professional Role in Early Childhood Education." *Interchange* 2 (1971):89-105.

Lindsley, O. R. "Training Parents and Teachers to Precisely Manage Children's Behavior." Paper read at C. S. Mott Foundation, Compendium of Presentations of Special Education Colloquium Series, June, 1968.

SECTION ONE

Discussion questions

1. What attitudes discussed by Harth seem to be facilitating services to mentally retarded individuals? Which are influencing services in a negative manner? How might attitudes be altered?

2. How do parents contribute or serve to dispel the perceptions of mentally retarded individuals typically held by the lay public?

3. Do you see ways in which the parental involvement model presented by Karnes and associates could be implemented in settings you have known about? Describe and discuss problems that might be encountered.

ASSESSMENT OF THE RETARDED INDIVIDUAL
Issues and Implications

Assessment, perhaps more than any other single area, has presented perplexing problems to those studying mental retardation. Throughout the history of assessment in mental retardation there have been a series of controversies concerning both what to measure and how this measurement should be accomplished. Although current definitions of mental retardation often include multiple areas of assessment (for example, adaptive behavior), much of the controversy has paralleled the issues involved in intelligence and its measurement. The controversies surrounding the development and measurement of intelligence have traditionally been heated and emotional. They have penetrated the very core of problems in mental retardation. It is therefore not only appropriate but essential that issues relating to assessment be examined in a volume concerned with social and educational perspectives of mental retardation. That is the purpose of this section.

The literature on intelligence and its development and measurement spans several decades and would fill many volumes. One has only to review small segments of this vast literature to come away confused and fully convinced that this is a complex and controversial area. The first two articles in this section present interviews with Drs. Burton Blatt and Jane R. Mercer, two eminent professionals who have examined the controversies and conducted extensive investigation in this area. Blatt's interview explores intelligence in the context of education and society in general. He presents some extremely provocative questions and issues for those involved in mental retardation. Mercer's interview addresses the very difficult problem of assessment in mental retardation and how this relates to culturally different children. She further discusses her extensive research, which has been aimed at developing more appropriate assessment techniques than have been used previously.

The impact of labeling a child has received considerable attention over the years and has become a priority concern for many educators in recent years (for example, Beery, 1972). The process and dilemmas of labeling are discussed by both Blatt and Mercer. The third article in this section presents a different and complementary perspective of labeling. In this selection Carol Graham details the story of a young boy and his life as he progresses through a series of diagnoses and labels. Told through the eyes of his parents, this article portrays vividly the confusion and frustration of diagnostic imprecision and labeling. This selection also functions as an important preface for the subsequent article by E. L. Loschen, which discusses issues and problems of diagnosis and treatment failures.

The final article in this section, by David M. Congdon, presents a brief but powerful philosophical challenge to the manner in which mentally retarded children are frequently viewed. This selection provides a thought provoking conceptual question that haunts the memories of most workers in mental retardation as well as laymen who have been involved in the area. It supplies a postscript to this section on assessment, an issue of significant proportions.

REFERENCE

Berry, K., editor: Models for mainstreaming, Sioux
  Falls, South Dakota, 1972, ADAPT Press.

CHAPTER 8

On the educability of intelligence and related issues —a conversation with Burton Blatt

JUNE B. JORDAN

Assistant Director, Council for Exceptional Children Information Center

Dr. Blatt, for a number of years you have been concerned with the human rights, educational opportunities, and adequate care and understanding of the mentally retarded. What do you see as the primary issues and problems facing the special education community today?

Dr. Blatt: If we would come to some understanding of this whole field of special education as being embedded in metaphors and politics and economics, rather than in science and data, then we can see where the issues are. The issues have to do with what people's rights are—not with what privileges we're going to give them. The issues are not tied to methodological or pedagogical problems or with "let's develop a better curriculum for the mentally retarded" or "let's develop a better method," but really, with when we shall free people. Let's found a world where people are free.

Now to focus on the primary issue, the one that I singularly devoted my own professional career to, concerns what I call the "educability hypothesis"—the hypothesis that intelligence is educable and that development is a function of practice and training. Also, in re-

lation to this issue is the need to better understand the discrepancy between what we say and what we do. That is, on the one hand we speak, write, make pronouncements, and even pass legislation as if society believes that people can change—that retarded children can be helped to become less retarded, or disabled people can become less disabled. On the other hand, we allocate resources and engage in practices which clearly illustrate we don't believe that people can change.

Let's be clear now on the educability hypothesis. Is intelligence educable? Can people change? Can we prevent subnormality? Can we reverse disability?

If one reads the literature, he would come away confused. You have Herrnstein, Jensen, Shockley on one hand, and you have Rick Heber, Ira Gordon, and Susan Gray, some others, Sarason, myself, maybe some others, on the other hand. And you ask, well, can people change? It's an open question. Although there is *little scientific evidence* that permits some definitive answers to this so called nature-nurture question, there is a lot of *clinical evidence*—in enormous amounts—that intelligence is educable. The story of the wild boy of Aveyron, Mae Seagoe's *Yesterday Was Tuesday, All Day and All Night*, the autobiography of Helen Keller—all of these, and so many more cases that have been published provide truly co-

Reprinted from Education and Training of the Mentally Retarded 8:219-227, 1973, with permission.
Burton Blatt is Director and Professor, Division of Special Education and Rehabilitation, Syracuse University.

gent testimony in support of the hypothesis —at least in support of the idea—that our clinical mission is not to make a decision whether somebody can or can't change, but to make it come true that somebody can change.

Now from the question whether people can change, there are some others. What is a human being? Now, that sounds like an awfully simple question, but it isn't simple. In the old days just being born determined whether you were a human being or not, but today the question isn't answered that easily. We have a legislator in one state who proposed legislation to legalize euthanasia, not only for the so called elderly, terminally ill, but also for the very severely defective. And so we do have very important problems that the culture faces.

Do people understand for themselves what a human being is, and secondly, are they agreed on what human beings are entitled to because they are human beings. Those questions are the fundamental questions to me. Whether children are "mainstreamed" or not, whether you improve institutions, or evacuate them, or knock them down, those questions can't be answered until we come to some agreement on the educability issue. Can people change?

You stated earlier, related to this issue, that there was a discrepancy between what we say and what we do. Can you give some examples of that?

Dr. Blatt: Sure. I'll give you several examples. In one state, whose mental health budget I recently examined for the current year, the division of mental retardation in their Department of Mental Health has a budget of approximately $235 million. Of those $235 million, $233 million are allocated for institutional care. In one of the largest states in the country, there is no more than $2 million provided for community programing for the mentally retarded, and $233 million to support institutional programing! In that same state they doubled the number of group homes during the past year. But in a state that has a population of 15 or 16 or 17 million,

they doubled the number of group homes from 12 or 13 to about 22 or 23. It's hardly anything in a state of that size! And, at the same time, they are now completing a half billion dollar building program for institutions.

In another city that I visited recently I asked if I could see what facilities and programs they had for the retarded in that community. They took me to a beautiful halfway home. The adults who were living there were working in the community. Later I found out that this is the only such home in the state sponsored by the Department of Mental Health!

How many, I'll ask you, how many of the almost 1 million children who are called mentally retarded in the nation's public schools are in truly integrated settings? I would say very few. Very few. Very few have opportunities to be engaged in more integrated kinds of programs with resource teachers or all the other kinds of new programs that we read about but we don't implement. And I can go on.

Why have we so segregated people? Why? And why don't we take seriously the idea that the community is where people belong? I think it's related to this hypothesis of educability.

You mentioned integrated settings in the public schools. I get the impression that the mainstreaming activity is not as widespread as some of us think it is.

Dr. Blatt: That's right.

In interviews with leadership people throughout the country, we're getting expressions of concern that "mainstreaming" is occurring without adequate preparation, programs, and personnel, and some criticism of "spokesmen" who are promoting the concept. Would you comment on this?

Dr. Blatt: I very much agree with them. I'm glad you've called me on this question because I don't want to be misunderstood. Of the retarded children in the public schools, I'd say those who are truly integrated are literally a handful. There have been some who have been identified as retarded and nothing done for them. The great majority who have been identified as retarded, have been put in segregated classes. There are others who are identified as retarded who are now supposedly mainstreamed but they're not. They're dumped back in regular classrooms, ordinary classrooms, without any special help.

I just learned while attending a leadership meeting about an enormously expensive mainstreaming project. Well, anyway, 99 percent of the funds that went into it never really affected the child in the regular program. Most of the money went to diagnosis and evaluation of the child, and the rest went to administrative costs. Only 1 percent went into backing up that child's expenses in the regular class.

So I quite agree with the critics. Another factor is that there is no money in the Department of Mental Health for mainstreaming. Most of the monies still go to the institutions. Institutions don't have to justify themselves, as they continue to get funds year after year. There's no accountability in institutions. And so after all of the institutions and state schools get their money, there's precious little remaining for community programing. And that little which is remaining, so it appears, seems to go into evaluation of kids and administrative costs, and conferences on mainstreaming, but not into the mainstreaming effort itself. There's very little of it. So those who are dismayed with mainstreaming are not dismayed by the effects of mainstreaming. They're dismayed at the discrepancy between the rhetoric and the practice. There is no mainstreaming. We've never really tried to make it work.

The people in our field are still hung up on some kind of alchemy. If we can only find the better method, or the better curriculum, we're going to solve the problems of the handicapped. That won't do anything to solve the problems. It will just contribute a small fraction to the variants in their lives. The real source of variance comes from what's in our heads about priorities—about the value of freedom, as contrasted to our need to protect.

It's not going to be scientists who are going to move the field ahead for people. It's going to be historians who can in some way recreate for us what has happened to people—historians who have been trained, and who can describe the world as it was and as it is, and maybe how it might be. Poets view the world differently; they aren't bound by the tradition of one's science, and one's literalness, and can say, "You know, I have a view of the world which says maybe things can be different for people." And that takes a poet, you see, not a scientist.

I think our culture has been hung up on a reverence for life. We revere life; and we revere protection. We want to protect people. We want to protect the disabled, and we put them in convalescent homes. We put people in special schools for the trainable because we don't want them to be ridiculed. We want to protect her, we want to shield her. So we revere life, and also we want to protect people. That's all a part of our reverence for life.

We also revere competence. These two reverences for freedom are in some way dissonant one from the other. On the one hand, we say we want to protect people, we want them to live long, long lives. We revere life.

On the other hand, we can only respect the competent person. If you're competent you go to college; you're respected if you're the president, or the governor, or the senator, or the professor, or the doctor. You're not respected if you're the attendant at the state school, or the dishwasher, or if you're not bright, or if you're not educated.

I'm suggesting something else. I'm suggesting that somewhere between the founding of this country, at the expense of other people's freedom, and today we lost a most important concept, the cornerstone of the founding of this country, one that we should revere more than even life and competency. That's the reverence for freedom.

We have relegated freedom as a low third priority. We build institutions; we design segregated classes; we put old people in convalescent homes to protect their lives and also to shield the competent from the incompetent. We do not revere freedom as the primary ideal. I want to live my life in a free environment. That's more important than even life. And that, to me, is really a most critical issue.

What did you mean when you said this field of special education is embedded in metaphors? Are you talking about what we mean by special education, mental retardation?

Dr. Blatt: You see, these are metaphorical words, and the field itself is a metaphor. You're dealing here with values and prejudices and ideals and little of that is related to science. *Epidemiology* is an awfully scientific word itself, and deals with some very scientific questions, but the epidemiological research suggests that mental retardation does not have integrity in and of itself. That this thing we call mental retardation, or this thing we call special education, is intimately bound to values and prejudices and politics and toleration of communities. To think of this field in purely scientific or scholarly terms is to mislead oneself so drastically as to become almost helpless insofar as practice is concerned.

Look at the life of Helen Keller, which is my favorite example. On one hand you admit that, yes, she was not mentally retarded, she was truly a brilliant person, but before she *wasn't* mentally retarded, she *was* mentally retarded. And that's the point. That the term *mental retardation* is a metaphor. It's an administrative term. It doesn't have the scientific validity and integrity that we assumed it had. And that's the second point. That's the hopeful point. We still don't take seriously enough the hypothesis of educability, but people, people in our field, are beginning to better understand that these terms are metaphors.

Look at the recent AAMD nomenclature change. Prior to 1959, mental retardation was considered a constitutional condition of the central nervous system. It existed from birth or early age, incurable, irremediable.

Then in 1959, the so-called Heber manual taught us that it may not be a constitutional condition. We learned something about mental retardation. We learned something about what we call "cultural familial mental retardation." And so the definition was changed. The definition, I think, would make Alfred Binet happy, because this was the kind of definition he proposed 75 years ago. A functional one. It said, essentially, that mental retardation refers to subaverage intellectual functioning, associated with impaired adaptive behavior.

Now in 1973, the definition was changed. If people don't read this revision very, very carefully, they'll miss a very significant change that illustrates the essential metaphorical and political nature of this condition. Since 1959, until this past spring, subaverage intellectual functioning was defined as more than *one* standard deviation on the wrong side of the mean—that is, psychometric retardation was said to be less than an 85 IQ associated with this impaired adaptive behavior. The current definition says, no it isn't *one* standard deviation on the wrong side of the mean, it's *two* standard deviations. And so in one fell swoop of the chairman's pen, this committee *has cured* more mental retardation than all clinicians and scientists since the beginning of time! They reduced the incidence, or the theoretical incidence, or the psychometric incidence, from 16 percent to 3 percent. Just by changing the definition! Well, you can't do this with leprosy, you can't do this with syphilis, and you can't do this with pregnancy. You can't do this with any objective disease. But you can do it with mental retardation, you can do it with mental illness, you can do it with phobias, and you can do it with what is agedness. What is the definition of a feeble person, or the aged, or the mentally retarded? They are metaphors. We're beginning to understand this now.

I assume you feel this practice of labeling children, putting them into a category and calling them mentally retarded, is not appropriate, but yet you use the term yourself.

Dr. Blatt: Because I too am victimized in the same way you are. You know we create an insane problem? We've labeled, we've categorized, we've labeled more, and we've said all of this is science and scientific. Now, in order to communicate I must use these terms.

I recommend to you and our readers Thomas Szasz's new book, *The Second Sin.* Everybody knows that the first sin was when Adam and Eve ate the apple and they lost their innocence, and God was displeased when they lost their innocence because He didn't want them to know wrong. That was when He banished them.

But there was the second sin, when human beings developed a language that was so clear and precise there was no misunderstanding. They could communicate with each other. This, too, displeased God, because if they could communicate clearly, eloquently, and precisely with each other, they might even invent a new God. They might even disavow this God. That was when He caused them to create the Tower of Babel, and so they went all over the face of the earth with their different tongues. And ever since human beings have been unable to adequately and clearly communicate with one another. And it's nowhere more apparent than in this field we call special education or mental retardation.

How do you see teacher training programs responding to the issues and needs of the field? Is the trend toward competency based teaching a hopeful sign?

Dr. Blatt: We're beginning to understand, I think, something John Dewey said many years ago—that teachers also own the schools, and that teachers should be a part of the creation of the schools, and that teacher training programs must change, not in the tired ways we've spoken about change. It's not enough to say that we're interested in competency based teaching. We must change teacher training, as the schools must change, where the role of the teacher shifts from that of being a technician who delivers services and implements programs or uses methods that others have developed, to a creator of environments.

The teacher preparation program must become not so much training, but education, in a way where teachers can unfold, can learn about themselves, can learn about the process of child-adult interaction, and can have some experience in creating environments for children and for themselves. As John Dewey said, the schools must be a place for teachers to learn as well as for children to learn. And that's good.

Just in recent years we are more and more appreciating this wisdom of Dewey. Schools must be places for *the teacher* to grow and learn. A truly active, inviting, lively, educational environment cannot be developed without the teacher being part of the liveliness and the activism of the environment. She should not be only a technician or an implementer.

We've also learned from our studies, that there is little independent variation to be found in either curricula, or methods, or organizational designs of schools. We have not been able to demonstrate the effectiveness of either special curricula, or special methods, or special kinds of designs, open schools, closed schools, segregated schools, integrated schools, special classes, regular classes, Cuisenaire Rods, Minnesota math, Frostig, Kephart, precision teaching, etc. These are grist for the mill and they're important.

But . . .! What I'm saying is that they're important in that they're part of history. We should learn about methods, curricula, and designs whether they're administrative designs or whether they're methodological designs, for the same reason we learn other history, so that we do not repeat our errors. Unfortunately, the only thing we've learned from history is that we learn nothing from history. But, nevertheless, we should try to learn more about the past, about the ways other people have confronted problems with disabled children—how they've tried to design strategies to deal with the problems and help children to learn and to grow.

We should not learn curricula and methods for prescriptive purposes. We should learn these methods, these curricula, and these different ways of organizing programs so that we understand better how other people have tried to deal with the problem. Then we can design environments with our children and with our clients that will best fit our needs. That will take a different kind of teacher—not a technician, but a creator.

How would you design, or what elements would you include, in this "lively" curriculum for a creator type teacher?

Dr. Blatt: There are some ingredients that I would like to include. I can't train or work with teachers without children around—without children coming regularly to a place where university students are. That's why we have our psychoeducational clinic. I had a similar type of clinic in Boston, and in New Haven almost 20 years ago. I've always had children around, because I've learned that you can't look at a group of children for more than a few minutes without having questions about their interactions. If you look at such a group over a period of months, you literally see every pedagogical problem that one can ever encounter. How you deal with these problems, how you discuss them, how you try to understand them, and how you try to relate those problems with the theoretical courses and didactic work that one gets in the university, are all part of an inductive approach to learning about pedagogy and strategies of teaching.

Then there is the central skill to help somebody who wants to be a teacher, or a psychologist, or a social worker, or a doctor, which is to describe behavior; that's the start. How to separate the description of behavior from an analysis of what it might mean. And that's not easy. It's not easy to describe behavior. It's impossible to precisely describe behavior. It's even impossible for you and your camera to precisely describe a complex human setting because the camera is guided by somebody's hand and brain, and there are things that will be missed that are terribly important.

The professional literature reports many various successful instructional approaches and techniques. What advice would you give the creative teacher with problem children in his or her class? Should the teacher sample all to try for "the best fit"?

Dr. Blatt: No, because that's impossible. I would say that she should collaborate with another teacher or two in the school. They ought to observe each other and they ought to develop among the three or two or four of them a pact that, "I will observe you, and after the observation we'll talk about it. The one thing we'll have in common is you and your children, and the one way I'll be different is that I've taken distance. I've observed you while you've been enmeshed, so possibly I could see things that you haven't seen, and you will see things in my room that I haven't seen. But we will try to trust each other. We'll develop what I call a friendship relationship. We will trust enough so we'll be able to say anything to each other, and with each other."

Then possibly every week or so there should be a staffing. Somebody will present a child to the three or four of the school team, and each staffing will include such questions: What's the presenting problem? Second, what did you try to do about the problem? Third, what happened? And fourth, if you had to do it all over, what would you do differently, or what have you learned from this? Hopefully, the principal might be involved at times. They'd share materials with each other. They'd share exciting papers. They'd share ideas. "We're going to learn something. We're going to learn from our observations, we're going to learn from the children, and we're going to work. We're going to do our work together and separately, and we'll respect each other for it." To me that is a lively place!

When I taught school that's just what I did with two or three teachers. We studied kids together. We had seminars, and we tried to understand what all of this is about. When we couldn't understand it among ourselves, we brought somebody in to help us, or we read a book. When we saw something that was appealing and made sense in the book, we shared it with our colleagues.

Let us talk a bit about your writing. Your three unique books, *Christmas in Purgatory*, *Exodus from Pandemonium*, and *Souls in Extremis* are powerful, moving pieces of work. Did you have an audience in mind when you wrote these books? Who do you hope will read them?

Dr. Blatt: That's hard to say. I write about my agenda. I write what I must write. I think the work itself, my work, and anyone's work, if it rings honestly, that is if the person tries to write honestly, the work leads to the author. So, in a way, somebody who reads my work might learn something about me.

The problems that I speak about in these books are not problems that I think are indigenous only to our field, to special education or to mental retardation. I think they're the problems that get at the very core of the question—what is a human being? And what is a human being entitled to, because he is a human being? And how do I conceptualize humanity? And not only humanity in general, but my own humanity.

Now you ask, who do I want to read the book. I want anybody who's interested in his own evolution as a human being, who asks the question what have we become as people, what have I become as a human being, what could I be? You know you always hear that a reader is lucky when he finds a good book or a good writer. Well, the writer is lucky to find a good reader. Just as lucky. By a good reader, I mean somebody who will enter the reading experience with some intelligence and be prepared to work, prepared to engage oneself in an experience, in a give and take, even though you never or hardly ever see the writer.

Somebody once said that discovery consists of seeing what everybody has seen, but thinking what nobody else has thought. And that's the job of the writer and scholar, and the person who spends some time trying to analyze himself and the world. So I write books because I want to express myself. I write books, I write papers, and I write criticism, so I can better understand what I'm trying to learn. I don't write to get on paper what I've already learned. If others are interested in what I write, fine. That pleases me. If they like what I write, that pleases me even more. But the thing that pleases me most of all is that they take me seriously, even more than that they like me, or what I write. If they take me seriously, I'm very grateful.

I'm sure many readers take your messages seriously and want to take some positive action. Do they write to you or talk to you, and what do you reply?

Dr. Blatt: Sure, sure. And what I say is, you've got to change, like I have to change. What else can one do? Before you try to change the world and enjoin others to tear down the institutions, or mainstream the children, or change the law, or what, *you* have to change. It's in the Talmud, before you try to change the world, you have got to change. It starts with you—with me. That's the beginning context. And how do you change? That's what you've got to struggle with, you have to analyze things, you have to analyze yourself, you have to understand where you are, you have to try to unravel your prejudices, you have to try to unravel your sense of things, and that takes time, that takes effort. You have to try to understand what you should do. Now that's where I had to begin, and that's why I selected the road I've taken, and I think that's where each of us might begin.

CHAPTER 9

New assessment techniques for mentally retarded and culturally different children—a conversation with Jane R. Mercer

MARYLANE Y. SOEFFING

Education Specialist, Council for Exceptional Children Information Center

Assessment, labeling, and placement of children have long been issues of concern for special educators. Today, there is a renewal of efforts to develop valid assessment techniques, terminate detrimental labeling practices, and insure educational placements in the best interests of individual children. In the following interview Jane R. Mercer, a distinguished sociologist, provides the new perspective of a related discipline to assessment and placement issues. Dr. Mercer is Professor of Sociology at the University of California, Riverside, and was previously Research Specialist at Pacific State Hospital, Pomona, California.

Dr. Mercer discusses major findings of her research on the epidemiology of mental retardation and on labeling practices. She explains the inadequacies of standardized intelligence test norms for culturally different children and describes new measurement instruments and statistical techniques she is developing to more accurately measure the learning potentials of black and Mexican American children. Implications for the field of special education are noted.

Dr. Mercer, you were the field director of an 8 year research project, which studied the epidemiology of mental retardation in the community of Riverside, California. Would you give an overview of that project as it relates to your current work?

Dr. Mercer: The study was conducted at Pacific State Hospital and codirected by Dr.

George Tarjan and the late Dr. Harvey F. Dingman (Tarjan et al., 1973). We studied the epidemiology of the community of Riverside to determine the prevalence rates of mental retardation. Two approaches were used. In one approach we did a household survey of a representative 10% sample of the population of the entire community. We screened approximately 7,000 persons under the age of 50 for symptoms of mental retardation. We used as our definition subnormal IQ and subnormal adaptive behavior which follows the American Association for Mental

Reprinted from Education and Training of the Mentally Retarded **10:**110-116, 1975, with permission.

Jane R. Mercer is Professor and Chairperson, Dept. of Sociology, University of California, Riverside.

Deficiency (AAMD) definition of mental retardation. During the household survey we also contacted all community agencies which served the mentally retarded and developed a case register of those persons labeled mentally retarded. We contacted over 241 community agencies and eventually developed a register of approximately 800 names.

We found that there was a disproportionately large number of black persons and Mexican American persons labeled mentally retarded by community agencies. There were about 100% more blacks, about 300% more Mexican Americans, and about half as many Anglo Americans labeled mentally retarded as could be expected based on their respective proportions in the population. We also discovered that the schools were the chief labelers; over half of the persons labeled mentally retarded were people who had been labeled by the schools. Lower class people were more likely to be identified and labeled mentally retarded than people of other social classes. Also, more males were labeled mentally retarded. From these and other findings we came to three conclusions.

Our first major conclusion was that the clinicians, psychologists, and medical doctors in the community were not measuring adaptive behavior as called for by the AAMD definition. They were not measuring adaptive behavior primarily because there were no adaptive behavior scales available for them to use. Thus most definitions of mental retardation in the community were being made by clinicians almost entirely on the basis of an IQ test score. Medical doctors might also give a medical examination, and in some cases there were physical anomalies. However, there were many persons labeled mentally retarded who did not have any physical anomalies. We concluded that an adaptive behavior scale needed to be developed and that clinicians should begin to systematically measure adaptive behavior, as well as use IQ tests. We found many people in our study who had low IQ scores, but appeared to have normal adaptive behavior. They were filling a normal complement of social roles and a label of mental retardation was inappropriate for them.

The second major conclusion had to do with the cutoff level for defining someone as mentally subnormal. When we were first starting the study, we discovered that there were three different cutoff levels that were typically used by people in the field. The American Association for Mental Deficiency recommended that anyone more than one standard deviation below the mean on a standard IQ test should be considered subnormal. This would include the approximately 16% of the total population that has an IQ score of 85 or below. The public schools on the other hand were for the most part using a cutoff of IQ 79 or below, which would be approximately the bottom 9% of the population. In the testbooks written by the people who developed IQ tests, men such as Wechsler and Terman, a person was defined as subnormal only if he was in the bottom 3% of the population, or two standard deviations and more below the mean. We found all three of these definitions being used simultaneously. I found nothing in the literature which discussed which of these three cutoffs was the appropriate cutoff to use or even addressed this as an issue. When we analyzed our findings, we concluded that the traditional cutoff of 3% or below was the cutoff that was least likely to label a person as mentally retarded who was regarded as normal by persons in his family and neighborhood and other areas of life. It was least likely to label someone as subnormal who was fulfilling his social roles appropriately, that is, had normal adaptive behavior. So we recommended that clinicians use a 3% cutoff. In their new nomenclature AAMD now uses the 3% cutoff. They no longer are using the 16% cutoff that they had at the time of our study.

In making the third major conclusion, we rediscovered and were greatly impressed by something that was already known. Tremendous cultural biases exist in the IQ test, and the test is not appropriate when used with many lower class persons and certainly when used with many Mexican Americans and black persons who do not share the same cultural traditions as the dominant Anglo American society. The IQ test is simply not a valid measure of their biological potential because they have not had similar opportunities to learn what is in the test. In looking at our statistics we concluded that the large disproportionate rates of identifying blacks and Mexican Americans as subnormal was primarily due to the invalidity of the IQ test when used on culturally different persons. So our third conclusion recognized that a system needed to be developed that would somehow correct for cultural biases in the IQ test and make it a more valid measure of the potential of persons who were not from the dominant Anglo culture.

What research have you initiated to develop improved assessment procedures for culturally different children?

Dr. Mercer: Some of my colleagues were interested in the possibility of developing a set of instruments or assessment procedures which would fulfill the recommendations of my original study. We submitted a proposal to the National Institute of Mental Health and were funded in 1970 to develop a System of Multicultural Pluralistic Assessment (SOMPA). We are calling it pluralistic assessment because we feel that in evaluating a child many different aspects of his performance should be taken into account. No single measure should become the determining factor. The use of an IQ test and no other measure was one factor which produced many of the discrepancies that we discovered in our original study. SOMPA is pluralistic because it contains multiple measures. We are focusing specifically on developing practical screening instruments that can be used by schools and clinics. Our battery is designed for children 5 through 11 years of age because these are the critical years when children are most likely to be diagnosed, assessed, and labeled.

We are standardizing these measures on a representative sample of the public school population of the state of California. The sample includes 700 black children, 700 Chicano/Latino surname children (Mexican American, Latino, Puerto Rican, and Cuban), and 700 Anglo children. All together we have 2,100 children and their mothers.

Would you describe the individual measurement instruments which comprise the System of Multicultural Pluralistic Assessment?

Dr. Mercer: SOMPA will require an interview with the child's mother or principal caretaker and two test sessions with the child. When we interview the mother, we ask questions for three scales. The first scale, the Sociocultural Modality Index, is a series of structured questions about family background, including occupation of head of household, education of parents, whether they were reared in an urban or a rural setting, whether they were reared in the United States or a foreign country, size of the family, family structure, who is living in the family, size of the dwelling place, and whether it is overcrowded. There are about 25 questions that deal with the sociocultural environment. We also have included some questions about the family value system that we found were quite highly correlated with other sociocultural characteristics and were very good predictors of cultural difference. We have factor analyzed those questions and have reduced the sociocultural measures to nine specific submeasures. The scale is now developed and is very easy to score.

The second kind of information that we get from the mother concerns adaptive behavior. The Adaptive Behavior Inventory for Children is a series of age graded questions which measure the child's role performance in the family, his adaptive behavior in the neighborhood, his behavior as an earner and a consumer, his nonacademic role in school, his skill at interpersonal relations with peers and adults, and his ability to care for his own physical and health needs. We have standardized the Adaptive Behavior Inventory on our sample and we are in the process of developing the final forms for plotting profiles for children on the scales. This Inventory fulfills one of the recommendations from the earlier study—that the child's competence in noncognitive areas should be measured. We found that there were many children who were quite competent in their social roles in the family and community who might not be doing well on an IQ test. They were not comprehensively subnormal or mentally retarded according to the AAMD definition because they were able to cope intelligently with problems in social relations and social roles.

In addition to getting the sociocultural information and the adaptive behavior information from the mother, we also ask her a set of questions that deals with the child's health history. The Health History and Impairment Inventory is a series of questions about the pregnancy, birth history, early childhood diseases, accidents, falls, operations, and so forth. We are still in the process of scaling this Inventory. When we finish, we expect to have a set of coded, highly structured questions that can identify children who have a suspicious health history and who may be high risk children in terms of having suffered serious childhood ailments, operations, or diseases. We included this in the battery because we discovered that typically the public school does not have any kind of good systematic health history on children. We will be standardizing this Inventory and will develop a system so that school or clinic personnel will be able to identify children who have a suspicious health history and thus should be given a careful medical workup. We are trying to identify children who may need to be examined by a medical doctor before any decisions are made about their final treatment either in school or otherwise.

The other components of the battery are administered to individual children. One measure is a set of simple manual dexterity tasks called the Physical Dexterity Battery. We included tasks that had to do with the dexterity of hands and arms, with balancing, and with use of the feet. The performances on all of these tasks were subjected to factor analysis. We now have nine subtests as part of the Physical Dexterity Battery, which we have standardized so that any clinician who uses this set of measures and does it in the standardized way will be able to determine exactly where any individual child falls on the distribution that we secured. Children scoring in the low percentiles would be a high risk population and should be given medical examinations.

Another measure that we use in the clinical test situation is the Bender Gestalt, which is a measure of visual motor skills. The child draws a standard set of figures, which we score according to the scoring scheme that was developed by Koppitz. We also administer a revised version of the Wechsler Intelligence Scale for Children called the WISC-R.

SOMPA is a battery of six measures which should be used as a system of assessment. Single subtests or measures should not be used individually.

How do you interpret scores on the WISC-R so that they are meaningful for culturally different children?

Dr. Mercer: It is my contention that IQ tests measure what a child has learned about the dominant Anglo culture and, consequently, are a good measure of the child's current functioning level in relation to the culture of the traditional public school. If the child has an IQ score of 70 on the standard norms, this gives us a very accurate indication that the child's current functioning level, in terms of the culture of the school, is low. We would predict that that child will have difficulty coping with the cognitive tasks presented by the school and probably will need additional help of some kind. We do not interpret the child's score on the standard norms as a measure of biological potential or genetic potential, but simply as an indicator of his current functioning level in relation to the culture of the school. We need to get some estimate of the child's probable learning potential, but we cannot use the standard norms for all children since standard norms are not appropriate for children who have been reared in another cultural milieu.

Consequently, we have used a statistical technique which is called multiple regression to correlate the child's IQ score on the standard norms with the nine characteristics of the home as determined from the Sociocultural Modality Index. We have done this separately for each ethnic group. We have calculated three regression equations—one for predicting the IQ score of Chicano/Latino children from the cultural background of their families, another for predicting the IQ of black children from the cultural background of their families, and a third for predicting the IQ of Anglo children from the cultural background of their families.

We can now insert the scores for the cultural background of any child into the equation for his ethnic group, multiply those scores by the appropriate weights which are in this regression equation, add this all up, and get the average IQ score that you would expect for a child from that cultural background. In other words, for every child it is possible to determine, on the basis of the information gained from the mother about the family background, what the average IQ would be for a child from precisely his background. Then we can compare the individual child's score with the average score that we would expect from someone from his cultural background and see whether he is above or below expectation for his group. By this method we are able to control for the sociocultural difference and secure a better estimate of the child's probable learning potential.

For example, Juan, a 7 year old Mexican American boy in our sample, scored 113 on the standard norms for the WISC-R. Thus his current functioning level in terms of the dominant culture of the school would be above average. He probably would succeed in the regular program of the school without supplementary help. He would be an above average student and might even be successful in a college program. We next estimated Juan's learning potential by plugging into the Chicano/Latino regression equation the characteristics of Juan's family background. Juan was raised in a poverty stricken Mexican American home where Spanish was spoken most of the time. When we used the regression equation, we found that the average score from Juan's sociocultural modality was 91.6. His score was 22½ points higher than the average for his appropriate normative group. He was about 1.8 standard errors

above what would be expected or actually at about the 96th percentile. Juan was an outstanding child to have learned as much as he had of the content in an IQ test, given the fact that he was from a family background where he had had relatively little opportunity to learn the sorts of material in the test. Of course, there are also children who are scoring in the bottom 3% of the standard norms but in fact would be in the normal range once one took into account their cultural background.

In our pluralistic assessment system, the child would be evaluated not only in terms of the standard norms which would give his current level of functioning but in terms of his socioculturally appropriate norms which would give his estimated learning potential. The picture might be quite different depending on which set of norms are being interpreted. For most Anglo children, of course, the current level of functioning and the estimated learning potential will be identical. The norms of the test are appropriate for them because they come from the standard middle class mainstream Anglo cultural background. For most children there will not be any difference between the interpretation on the pluralistic norms and the interpretation on the standard norms. The clinician will be able to determine for every child whether the standard norms are appropriate. If the standard norms are not appropriate, the clinician will be able to determine on an individual basis within what normative framework the scores should be interpreted.

What use is being made of the information you have obtained from testing the children in your project?

Dr. Mercer: Basically, we are developing a set of profiles on children on the basis of the various SOMPA batteries. We are still in the process of doing this so I cannot tell you exactly what the basic types are, although we have a pretty good idea what they will be. We are quite certain that we will be able to identify a set of children, for example, who appear to have some type of biological or organic damage. These would be children who are low on the physical dexterity battery, who have a suspicious health history, and who therefore should be seen for a medical diagnosis for possible organic damage. These children may or may not have high or low adaptive behavior.

We anticipate that we will identify another group consisting of culturally different children. These children would have low scores on the standard norms for the IQ test, but score in the normal range using the culturally appropriate norms. They would have normal adaptive behavior, normal manual dexterity, and no suspicious health history. They would be children who are primarily culturally different, and thus the tests are not appropriate for them. They do not appear to be subnormal, except on the standard norms for the WISC-R. Their educational problems are problems of cultural difference.

Once we have identified statistically the major types of profiles that we get with this system then I think we will be able to sketch out, in broad outline form, the types of interventions which would seem to be appropriate for children who fall into different profile patterns. We strongly suspect that many of the minority children who may seem to be subnormal when the standard norms on the WISC-R are used may, in fact, prove to be mainly culturally different or generally in the normal range on adaptive behavior. Therefore, some treatment other than classes for the mentally retarded would be much more appropriate as an educational intervention.

What are the implications of your work with SOMPA for the field of special education?

Dr. Mercer: I think that there are several implications. The major hope that has motivated me from the very beginning is that SOMPA might be a method for correcting for the cultural biases in the standard measures of IQ so that clinicians can make a more valid assessment of children who are culturally different and of children who are from lower class or disadvantaged backgrounds.

I think SOMPA will be appropriate for most black, Chicano/Latino, and Anglo children. A similar approach could be used to develop appropriate equations and norms for other cultural groups. There are some people in Arizona who are experimenting with this system for Indian children. When SOMPA is published, other people will try to use it elsewhere and we will soon know how far we can generalize from our California data. I hope that it will at least be a beginning.

A second implication is that there will be many children who formerly were diagnosed as educable mentally retarded by an IQ test exclusively who will now be viewed primarily as children who come from culturally different backgrounds. The need will be to develop treatment programs that deal specifically with their cultural difference. In the case of Mexican American children, programs that deal specifically with helping them become acquainted with the culture of the schools and with the English language will be needed. This simply has not been done in the past, and while in the last 4 or 5 years there has been some movement in that direction, there still has been relatively little done to help Mexican American children bridge the cultural gap. They are simply dumped into the public schools on sort of a sink or swim basis. There are no carefully designed programs in most school systems to assist them, and many of them end up being defined as mentally retarded. This is also true of black children whose families are just recently out of the rural South and who come from a very difficult culture. They come from essentially a peasant culture and are thrown in the middle of an urban ghetto and into public school situations that they cannot cope with. It is not because they are mentally retarded or because they cannot learn but because the schools do not have any program to assist them to bridge this gap.

I am hoping that we will follow up on the program and determine its implications when it is actually used in a school system. I certainly will be interested in working with people who are interested in trying to develop appropriate curricular programs for children with different types of profiles, especially those with clearly sociocultural differences. Once we have defined the groups and described the characteristics and educational needs of the children, my hope would be that there will be educators who can then develop programs to meet those needs.

REFERENCE

The myth of the 3% prevalence. In G. Tarjan et al. (Ed.) *Sociobehavioral Studies in Mental Retardation: In Honor of Harvey F. Dingman* (Monograph No. 1). Washington, D.C.: American Association on Mental Deficiency, 1973.

CHAPTER 10

From label to child

CAROL GRAHAM

Once upon a time there was a very small boy named Timmy. And one day he turned into a label (actually several labels).

From infancy he is an extremely difficult child to live with. By eighteen months he is on tranquilizers to try to help him deal with what he considers a very terrifying world.

At three years, we his parents take him to a cerebral palsy clinic looking for help. Not only is he exaggerated in all of his reactions to his environment; he is unable to use his hands effectively. There he receives his first psychological testing. And his first label:

Timothy is a child who is presently functioning approximately one year below his chronological age. This moderate retardation is complicated by extreme anxiety and inability to identify satisfactorily with his contemporaries. It is the opinion of the examiner that the IQ of 72 on the Binet represents a maximum level of ability for this child. It is unlikely that he will be able to function consistently at this level because of the bizarre pattern of activity. . . . He is very easily disoriented and appears to lose sight of what he is doing or where he is without any apparent interruptions. The basis of his action seems to be subjective attitudes, ambivalence, and frequent shifts of ideas. . . . He has difficulty in projecting his abstract ideas. . . . We wish there could be something more that we could do for Timmy and his mother.

Reprinted from Academic Therapy 8:277-284, 1973, with permission.
Carol Graham, mother of six children, has been active for many years with the Virginia Association for Children with Learning Disabilities.

Help with coordination and behavior was requested—a label received.

The next year he is tested at a county evaluation clinic. We are still trying to understand this highly unpredictable child. And the clinic has this to report:

He comes on a little bit wise for a pre-school child. He is in perpetual motion. He is hyperdistractible, hyperactive, hypercurious, and hypoattentive. . . . He seemed to alternately enjoy and dislike the testing, and I could determine no particular pattern for this. . . . He has a vocabulary which is at least at his age level and perhaps a little higher . . . doesn't have any concept of form at all . . . fails to copy a circle at year III level . . . poor memory for the immediate, but he has a tenacious grasp on things that catch his fancy, no matter how much time has gone by. . . . At the general staff meeting it was the feeling of those present that "Timmy is retarded and the specific etiology of this retardation is unknown."

Now the stage is set—here is an educable retarded child. Rather unusual, but the label should hide any discrepancies. All further testing over the next few years will follow the same pattern.

Almost five years old. We place him in nursery school, where he learns to sit still in a classroom situation. Progress.

Almost six. Tim is withdrawn from a regular kindergarten program because his inability to handle pencil and crayon work makes the program too frustrating for him.

Same year. We enroll him in a private

school for the retarded. He is placed with the nine- and ten-year-olds who are functioning on his level. Within a month he is coloring very well and printing very poorly—but printing. By the end of the year he has some sight vocabulary in reading.

Almost seven. We apply for placement in an educable class in the public school system for the following school year. The reply:

We have received a report from "A" clinic in regard to your son Timothy. For the time being his name has been placed on the waiting list for the training center program. After we receive the evaluation from the "B" clinic we can be more definite regarding placement.

"B" clinic will not test Tim until a year after "A" clinic has tested him. The school system will not make a definite placement.

School starts. We go to the local school to see about placement in an ungraded primary program while the Office of Special Education decides where to place him. The principal is concerned. Timmy is placed in an educable class within two weeks.

A year passes. Timmy is doing well in class. The teacher assures us he is learning. Just *what* he is learning, we aren't sure, but he is happy and likes school.

Almost eight. He still hasn't learned to zip or tie or use his hands very well. We take Tim to a doctor of physical medicine at the local hospital to see if therapy can help him. Then the world is turned upside down. We are told: "This child is not retarded! Don't you ever call him that again. Take him to a neurologist and have him tested. This boy has soft neurological signs of brain injury."

The library is searched for information on brain-injured children. The book *The Other Child* is read. All of a sudden Timmy makes sense to his parents. Here are some answers to the questions we have been asking.

His teacher is questioned. Does Timmy really belong in her class? Well, now that we've asked, no.

The supervisor of special education is called. Does Timmy belong in an educable class? No, but it's the best available. Okay. Something is better than nothing.

He is tested by a neurologist and, on her recommendation, by a psychologist. Everything is confirmed. Soft signs of brain injury, perceptual problems, everything. Including retardation.

What about school? We have become active in a newly formed organization, the Virginia Association for Brain-Injured Children (now the Virginia Association for Children with Learning Disabilities), and have become more informed on what our local school system has to offer in the way of special education classes. Yes, he needs the type of program offered in the special learning problems class—but he wouldn't fit in an SLP class, you see. His IQ score is too low. He's retarded. The supervisor of special education has this to say:

Timothy's school placement was thoroughly reviewed at the admissions committee. It was felt that the class in Parklawn (EMR) is the best possible placement at this time.

Almost eight. The year passes with teacher and parents researching books to find methods to help Timmy learn. That summer he learns to read. All at once written words mean something to him. In one summer he goes from pre-primer to fifth-grade level in reading.

Almost nine. Teacher and parents both request that Timmy be placed in an SLP class. That spring he is retested by a school psychologist with the usual result: IQ 65, retarded. But group achievement tests given in school show he is functioning at grade level or above in every subject but math. Unfortunately, however, he has a label. And labels can't be disregarded.

That summer I meet a clinical psychologist who tests Tim and breaks the mold Tim has been cast in:

This most unusual child was seen today for the purpose of evaluating his potential and recommending school management. . . . He is slow in his reactions; however, if given time, he frequently ends up with the proper response. Anyone applying a test too rigorously might fail to credit him with the understanding that he really has . . . has had insufficient opportunity to do for himself so that he has made more progress with words than with action . . . there is not enough teaching in this boy's life. . . . On the Wide Range Achievement Test, he earned a grade of 2.2 on arithmetic, 4.2 on spelling, and 7.1 on reading. . . . Placement for this child is difficult because of the great unevenness in his development. There is a reluctance to categorize him as a slow-learner because it may very well be that the lack of learning is due to mismanagement. The concept of retardation appears inappropriate. At least an extremely small number of retarded 9 year olds recognize words at the seventh grade level. . . . It appears to this examiner that an effort ought to be made to give this child at least a trial placement in a regular class.

The result? Here is the coordinator of special education's report:

We have received a report from Dr. X on Timothy with such positive findings in comparison with previous test results. I am sure this information is only what you, as his mother, have been trying to communicate to us for some time.

Now Timmy is in an SLP class. Three years too late. The educable label is finally gone, but now he has a new one—"learning disabilities." He is given a program of putting together puzzles, connecting dots, and other types of nonacademic activities in an effort to fill in his developmental gaps. He needs academics. He has developed some sort of compensatory system for getting along in spite of the gaps. By May the teacher finally understands more about Timmy and starts a crash program of acquainting him with workbooks and other trappings of a regular classroom program. She realizes he doesn't fit in *this* class either. Here is part of her final report:

I do feel that Tim needs the experience of a regular classroom; that is, exposure to more children, to a more realistic setting, and to broader subject matter. . . . I am concerned about Tim's lack of ability to automatically absorb and be aware of the things going on around him without having them pointed out to him specifically. . . . Tim has not been able to overcome a concrete type of thinking. Despite all . . . he may receive what he needs—great support and no degrading. He questions his ability enough.

Age ten. Timmy is placed in the summer school program whose purpose is for each child to work at his own level. At the end of the summer program, we are called for a conference. The area supervisor of special education, the school psychologist, the teacher, the diagnostic-prescriptive teacher—all are present. The consensus: the regular classroom is where Tim belongs . . . much slower children than Tim in classes . . . unbelievable that he was ever placed in special education. . . .

Almost eleven. Tim is placed in the third grade. Because he has not been exposed to phonics, science, social studies, or spelling, the third grade seems to be about as high as he can be placed. He likes school better than ever before. He is eager to learn. As he expresses it so well (after four years in special classes): "You mean I won't have to go to kindergarten again? I can go to real school?"

When he is retested in December of that year his achievement scores are ninth grade in reading, fifth grade in spelling, and mid-first grade in arithmetic. And the health department psychologists have this to say:

The WISC was administered and Timothy achieved a verbal scale IQ score of 72, performance IQ score of 57, and a full-scale score of 63 . . . but this is not a complete picture of Timothy's abilities. It is apparent from an analysis of his achievement on the Wide Range Achievement Test and observations of his behavior that his academic and social verbal skills are at least average. . . . Data from projective materials indicate personality factors which are contributing to his decrements in intellectual function. In short, Timothy has at least average intelligence, but due to organic and psychological factors, he currently functions at the borderline level of mental retardation. Concerning school placement, Timothy would fit best in an ungraded classroom, ideally. If this is not available, then Timothy should remain in the regular academic program with some special tutoring in arithmetic, spatial, and perceptual skills.

Tim will be almost twelve when he enters the fourth grade. He still won't be in exactly the right place. But with the wide range of abilities and disabilities he now shows, there may never be the proper place for my son. At least he is now a *child* who reads extremely well and is poor in math. He is a *child* with problems in learning—but he is being given the chance to learn what he can from a wide and varied curriculum. He is no longer confined by a label to what he is offered and what he can learn. What the outcome will be, nobody knows. Nor will anyone try to predict. But there is the determination by the school he attends that he will be given a chance to learn without preset limitations.

Tim has been in the EMR program, the SLP program, and now the regular program. His class placement has often been unfortunate. When he was in the EMR classes he needed the type of training offered by an SLP class. But he was refused admittance because of an IQ score and a label of retardation. When he was in the SLP program he was placed, due to his seemingly severe visual-perception problems, with the younger group in an intensive readiness program. But Tim has already been halfway through a regular fifth-grade reading program and needs an intensive academic program to try to level out his abilities.

My son was the victim of a system that puts too much emphasis on IQ scores and labels. It forgets the child. Labels can be useful, but not when they are used to cover up inadequacies in a school system or to explain the unexplainable. The public school's awareness of the need for individualization in the school program grows all the time. If they can remember that this same type of individualization is also needed by special education children there will be no more stories like Tim's.

The following was written when it became evident that regular class placement without supportive help, and two grade levels below his peer group, was detrimental to Tim.

For most of his life, Tim has been treated as an academic entity. Whenever we discussed, planned, or thought about his future, it was relative to his academic life. He is also a social being, however—at school and in the outside world. But most important, he is an emerging personality with thoughts of his own regarding his rightful place in the world. We his parents and the school system should

be equally concerned about the Tim *he* sees. Let's take a quick look at what Tim thinks of the Academic Tim:

When he left special education two years ago and went to Glen Forest, his reaction was "You mean I don't have to go to kindergarten again?" He was overjoyed. By about midterm he was starting to question his placement. "The other kids in the class don't believe I'm eleven. They say if I'm really eleven, I must have failed. What grades did I fail?" Tim's glow about school was beginning to fade.

By May Tim was having frequent stomach-aches after lunch and someone from school would call because he needed to come home. Finally he had an upper GI series and, sure enough, there was an irritation of the duodenal cap. Medication kept that problem under control until the end of the school year. The summer vacation completed the cure.

During that year Tim didn't complain much about the Academic Tim. He seemed reasonably happy at home and school.

Now he is twelve and in the fourth grade. The school is doing what it can and he has a truly talented teacher. This year it took until February for the Nonacademic Tim to reveal himself. On Monday he had a "stomach-ache." Every child should be allowed a "stomach-ache day" occasionally. Tuesday he had a bad headache and stomach-ache. I thought that maybe he really was sick. By Tuesday afternoon there was no question in my mind: "You are going to school tomorrow, period!" He went Wednesday, and Thursday. Thursday morning he had a dizzy spell during opening exercises. This was real. He was frightened by this experience and was upset for quite a while after we got home. During a quiet time in the afternoon Tim was asked, "Please, tell me why you don't want to go to school."

Tim really let loose. "When I have to stay in from recess because I didn't finish my work, the others who had to stay in start whispering to each other and calling me names." "What kind of names?" "Retarded." "Are you retarded?" There was a long pause and then a soft, hopeful, and timid "No?"

We discussed what the word *retardation* means.

Then Tim said, "But soon I'll be a teenager and I should be going to Glasgow." (He has a sister, a year older, who goes to Glasgow.) Finally, "Couldn't I stay home from school for a week? Then I'll go back." The answer was "No."

Friday morning I went down to see why he hadn't come to breakfast. He was curled up in bed. No stomach-ache or other excuses. Just tears rolling down his face and the plea, "Please don't make me go today."

We have now reached the stage where he is "sick" every morning. He would rather stay home, be restricted to the house, clean his room, take a nap—anything rather than having to go to school. I believe once he is in school he is all right. The problem is getting him there.

Now let's look at some other facets of Tim in relation to the Academic Tim. We'll start with the family. He has a thirteen-year-old sister in the eighth grade. Tim is twelve and in the fourth. Where does that leave Tim? He has a ten-year-old brother in the fifth grade. Tim can read and spell better than Mike. What does this make Tim? He has a nine-year-old brother in the third grade. What about twelve-year-old Tim in the fourth grade?

Tim is emotionally and socially immature. Granted. But for the last three years his school contact has been with children two or three years younger; he is the next to oldest at home; the children his age in the neigh-borhood go to Glasgow. There is no common ground. I wonder why Tim isn't maturing faster?

Let's face the fact squarely. Timmy is different. He may never fit in socially with other children. He is a loner either by choice or because he is different. Keeping him with younger children will never teach him how his peers act. Being with his peers may not do it either. But the most important thing is it may help Tim feel better about himself. After five years of silence he is beginning to question the justice of his place in the academic world.

I feel this coming year should be the time to put Tim with his peers. Now is the time to place his social development and self-image at the same level of importance as his academic development. We need to remember that Tim will not always be in an academic world.

I believe Tim could make it in some sort of fashion at Glasgow next year. He may not fit in at Glasgow. But in his eyes he doesn't fit in at Glen Forest either. Try to put yourself in his place. If you were Tim, which would you prefer—being thirteen and struggling in the fifth grade, or being thirteen and struggling in the seventh grade?

"What grades have I failed?" Tim has not failed. Is it we—his parents, the school, the community—who have failed him through ignorance, misdiagnosis, lack of learning opportunities?

Let's stop making Tim pay for our mistakes.

CHAPTER 11

Failures in diagnosis and treatment in mental retardation[1]

E. L. LOSCHEN
Southern Illinois University

ABSTRACT: *Failures of individual treatment programs occur for various reasons. Failures due to inadequacies of diagnosis and/or planning may be prevented, at least in part, by utilizing care and thoroughness; however, vigilance is required to make sure that when difficult treatment problems arise, there is no interruption or prevention of the therapeutic trial.*

When clients do not respond to an MR treatment program, numerous factors may be responsible for the failure—perhaps there was inadequate political and social action (i.e., insufficient funding), diagnostic errors may have been made, or errors and inadequacies in planning intervention approaches may be the cause. Attempts to examine the latter two causes of failure will be presented in this paper.

DIAGNOSTIC EVALUATION

The vital nature of the diagnostic process has been noted by Bialer (1970), who points out that differential diagnosis must attempt to isolate and identify all relevant factors in the case of a given mentally retarded individual so that the most effective treatment for that individual can take place.

[1]This paper was presented in part at the AAMD Region 8 Conference, Fargo, North Dakota, October 9, 1973. Reprinted from Mental Retardation 13:29-31, 1975, with permission.
Author: E. L. Loschen, M.D., Assistant Professor of Psychiatry, Southern Illinois University School of Medicine, Springfield, Illinois 62708.

Likewise, Webster (1970) states that assessments of etiology, nervous system functioning, intellectual capacities, and emotional development should be included in any evaluation of the mentally retarded individual. All of this information is needed by the professional to accurately and comprehensively evaluate both the strengths and incapacities of the client.

Subtle physical disabilities including partial loss of vision, loss of hearing, or musculo-skeletal problems can be overlooked during evaluation. A 14-year-old young man who had been a resident of a large institution for about 10 years was referred to a community program. He was observed to function on a moderately retarded level, but notably was without meaningful speech. The referring institution also noted the young man suffered from a slight limp. Initial evaluation showed moderate autistic behavior including self-stimulation, some combativeness, and unwillingness to follow directions. He was particularly difficult to manage when it was necessary for him to negotiate the stairways in the 3-story building which housed the program. Consultation was requested in anticipation of returning this young man to the institution. Referral to specialists confirmed suspicions that the client had a moderate hearing loss and leg deformity which made it difficult for him to use the stairs in the new program. Both physical disabilities appeared to have played significant roles in his poor institutional record and in the inital poor adjustment to the community program; however, progress was rapid and sustained after a hearing aid and orthopedic shoes were acquired.

A second diagnostic pitfall can occur if the emotional attributes and problems of the client are not adequately assessed. Omission of this evaluation can lead to massive disruption of a program or even to refusal to carry out the treatment plan. In one instance, an emergency consultation was requested by a community facility because a 15-year-old boy had begun to destroy furniture two days previously; his performance level had been dropping steadily for two weeks. A review of his history showed that he had been placed in the program from a large institution. Initial evaluation at the community facility had been brief and had focused on his degree of retardation, which showed moderate mental retardation with marked amounts of self-stimulatory behavior and no speech. When the boy entered the program, he was on anticonvulsant medications and moderate doses of a phenothiazine drug. Since no information was requested from the institution about the reason for using antipsychotic medication, it was discontinued because of excessive sedation. A month later the client's behavior was observed to be attention-seeking and provocative, and his behavior was also disorganized, unpatterned, and agitated. Restitution of the psychotropic drug program demonstrated a return to previous functioning levels. Later, a review of previous records revealed a similar pattern had developed in the institution where the drug program had originally been implemented. A thorough evaluation should have included a review of past records.

In another case, a 19-year-old female was admitted to a psychiatric hospital after failing in a placement in a sheltered workshop and crisis group home. She had been accepted into the program by referral from her grandmother who had taken her home from a state mental hospital. Evaluation had consisted of a physical examination and an assessment of behavioral skills, which placed her in a mildly retarded range of functioning. Although she was maintained on high doses of phenothiazine medication, her behavior became progressively more antagonistic and disruptive at the sheltered workshop, eventually necessitating her admission to the crisis group home. Her behavior improved at the home, but promptly deteriorated upon return to the workshop. This led to her admission to a psychiatric hospital. During psychiatric evaluation in the hospital it was learned that her familial home was marked with frequent crisis and arguments with which she could not cope. Upon dismissal from the hospital the girl was placed in a structured living situation outside of the familial home, which resulted in improved performance in the workshop.

Sometimes, however, a thorough evaluation can prove to be inconclusive. A 9-year-old boy who had been seen by various agencies and professionals since age four had been diagnosed as suffering from infantile autism, childhood schizophrenia, or moderate mental retardation, and had received both psychotherapy and drug therapy in the course of two hospitalizations in psychiatric facilities. Upon observation, the boy's level of functioning was at about the 2-year-old level during these periods. Almost every day he would have episodes of violent behavior (spitting, encopresis, and fire setting) towards staff and other patients. During the year he was in the program he was maintained on a high level of antipsychotic medication and several behavioral programs were developed for him, but no changes in his behavior were demonstrated. After one year he was transferred to a state institution for the mentally retarded for long-term treatment and possible custodial care. Throughout his numerous evaluations, no clear concept of the young man's difficulties or behavior could ever be formulated, and therefore, adequate treatment planning could not be accomplished. This ultimately led to failure of the program to benefit the client.

PLANNING APPROACHES

Once skillful diagnosis has been formulated, an adequate and comprehensive treatment-management plan must be developed. Programs may fail or not even be implemented for a mentally retarded client because of errors at this level. These errors give rise to planning which (a) is inappropriate for the diagnosis, (b) is inappropriate for that program, or (c) includes inappropriate referral to other programs.

To be comprehensive, the plan must take into consideration physical, emotional, family and social aspects, as well as the degree of developmental retardation experienced by the individual. In the case of the 19-year-old girl previously mentioned, temporary placement out of the familial home into a crisis group home was not adequate planning for the degree of family dysfunction which she was experiencing. In this instance, reformulating her overall plan of pre-vocational training to include placement in a long-term structured living situation outside the familial home resulted in a marked change in both her behavior and general functioning in her training program.

Planning must include an awareness of the environment of the program or the absence of needed services in the program. One 20-year-old young man with a diagnosis of schizophrenia and mild mental retardation was referred to a sheltered workshop for prevocational training. Upon referral he was noted to be easily irritated by noise and disturbances between people. He could, however, function well in a protected hospital environment and had shown ability to use tools in meaningful work. The workshop was constructed so as to not allow him to be readily isolated from noise or other clients. Subsequently he suffered two acute psychotic episodes and continues to function at levels below expectations for his degree of impair-

ment. In this instance the environment of the program actively interfered with his progress.

In another case, a 15-year-old moderately retarded young man was referred for prevocational training. Since he had no meaningful speech, speech therapy was an integral part of the treatment plan. However, speech therapy was available at the prevocational program on a consultation basis only, and his deficits in speech and cognition were so severe that he had to be returned to his previous program. In this case, the program failed because it did not take into consideration individual treatment plans.

Another problem encountered in planning is inappropriate referral arising out of misconceptions about the program to which the client is to be sent. This arises most often when an individual who is chronically psychotic (but not developmentally retarded) is referred to programs for the mentally retarded because of the functional deficits the individual possesses. One 21-year-old woman with a diagnosis of chronic undifferentiated schizophrenia and an IQ of 110 was referred to a pre-vocational program because she was not motivated and would not hold a job for more than a few days. Adequate information was not available at the time of the referral. The referral source had visualized the program as one which developed motivation through positive reinforcement in a protected environment, when in reality the program focued on alleviating developmental deficits in areas such as motor skills needed for work placement, and on correcting and improving rudimentary social skills. This young lady was very unhappy with the placement and has not functioned adequately during the 3 years of her stay in the program. In this instance, the referral was not only destructive to the clinet, but also eliminated a place in the program for some other more appropriate referral.

CONCLUSION

Two important areas of concern in treatment and habilitation of mentally retarded clients are (a) thorough diagnosis and

(b) comprehensive individual planning. The diagnostic process should include evaluations of developmental retardation, physical status, emotional attributes, family structure, and the surrounding social-community factors. Individual prescriptive treatment must include a comprehensive set of actions for each of the problems identified in any of these areas, in addition to an adequate concept of the program to which the client is referred. The data gained from the diagnostic evaluation must be integrated with pertinent information about available treatment facilities if the best individual treatment program is to be achieved and continued treatment failure prevented.

A rational approach to diagnosis and planning must include care and concern with a goal of placement in the optimum program, but must also leave room for instituting the best program available when the optimum does not presently exist. In the case of individuals with multiple handicaps, adjustment in existing programs is more desirable than ignoring deficits or not even attempting intervention because the person does not meet the admission criteria of the program. To deny such intervention may cost the client the only change he had for improvement.

REFERENCES

Bialer, I. Emotional disturbance and mental retardation: Etiologic and conceptual relationships. In F. J. Menolascino (Ed.), *Psychiatric approaches to mental retardation*. New York: Basic Books, 1970.

Webster, T. G. Unique aspects of emotional development in mentally retarded children. In F. J. Menolascino (Ed.), *Psychiatric approaches to mental retardation*. New York: Basic Books, 1970.

CHAPTER 12

Croak of incompetence: exhibitionism

DAVID M. CONGDON

"Don't they sing well for the mentally retarded." The label "mentally retarded" is often objected to in the sense of diagnosis, but there is also an injustice when the labeling is provided to make exception or to discriminate. Such use is contrary to the philosophy of normalization. Institutions and agencies providing programs and activities for the mentally retarded must help the public move through a phase of awareness and exploitation to acceptance by doing away with overprotective as well as derogatory labeling. Probably because of failures in training and inappropriate placement, people are too ready to wave the banner of "special case" and exception.

According to the principle of normalization the life pattern of the mentally retarded should approximate that of the normal individual. The notion of placement by Adaptive Behavior functioning demands that the individual be placed in a setting which matches the abilities and needs of the individual. It could be suggested that there are certain quality standards of societies of normal individuals which should be maintained. If the quality of singing, workmanship, and social interaction is not sufficient to meet the societal standard for that situation without the special pleading case of "mental retarda-

tion," then the mentally retarded should not participate in that situation in that manner.

It can be argued that the mentally retarded are being exploited in an exhibitionistic and inhuman manner when special case and label "made by" or "performed by" the mentally retarded are attached. Sheltered workshops must therefore be able to deliver a product which has comparable value to any in the normal society. A lesser product should receive less money. Pleas on the part of sheltered workshop administrators to industries to "help the handicapped" imply that the quality of the product is not of par value.

In a home living or social situation when an abnormal social performance is excused on the basis of mental retardation, the educational failure is overlooked. By acceptance of less than an adequate performance, incompetence is encouraged. The limitations of the mentally retarded must be accepted but they need not be emphasized, exploited, and encouraged.

Many institutions and agencies have groups of mentally retarded or otherwise handicapped individuals who perform in one way or another for public groups. The moment bizarre behavior or an inadequate performance by normal standards needs to be explained by the knowledge that the group is handicapped is the moment of exploitation and exhibitionism. Great amounts of energy in training the handicapped individuals to perform are expended, and it is a point well taken that it is amazing the handicapped in-

Reprinted from Mental Retardation 12:29, 1974, with permission.
Author: **David M. Congdon**, M.A., is the HIP Coordinator and Psychologist at Lincoln State School, Lincoln, Illinois 62856.

dividual "does so well," but that group should not compete. The handicapped individual may enjoy the activity, but performances should be in private or for special interest groups. (Mothers have always thought their children sing well no matter how poorly.) Flaunting a poor quality performance does not lead to acceptance of an individual in a normal society. Demonstrating failure may expand failure into new areas and discourage the development of satisfactory skills.

The alternative to accepting a "mentally retarded performance" is training the mentally retarded to perform at an acceptable level in some area which is functional to the individual and the society. If the energy devoted to training a poor singing performance into a blind retardate were expended on removing the blindisms, that blind retardate would be much more normal. There are techniques for intensive training. The behavior modification strategies currently applied to programs provide some powerful means of

achieving acceptable levels of performance in domestic, communication, and social skills. An improved methodology of teaching tasks in a sheltered workshop produces work skills which far exceed the previous levels of competence. An extension of this philosophy suggests that unless prepared with the skills to adapt readily, the mentally retarded person should not be rushed into an area of functioning or placement which is inappropriate to his present ability. Lower the standard of quality of performance only when training to reach that acceptable standard has failed and the situation is necessary to the individual and fair to society. This would suggest that we should not rush into unrealistic placements or at the very least we should insure that community placement includes some further training to help the retarded individual adapt to the demands of the placement. The mentally retarded should not have to suffer the indignities and the loss of human rights when they are forced to emit the "croak of incompetence."

SECTION TWO

Discussion questions

1. How do some of the issues discussed by Blatt relate to the research being pursued by Mercer?
2. After reading Graham's article, do you see any particular changes that need to be made in our diagnostic and service pro-

cedures? What about philosophical changes or examinations?
3. What thoughts and feelings were generated when you read Congdon's article? Do you agree with his basic position? Why or why not?

CLINICAL-SOCIETAL ISSUES IN MENTAL RETARDATION

Historically certain types of mental retardation, certain areas of study, and issues related to both have been viewed as representing the "clinical" aspects of mental retardation. Over the years the problems and solutions related to these areas have received attention from a particular segment of professionals (for example, physicians, geneticists, biochemists) who were somewhat isolated from others working in mental retardation. Often professional factions developed that further interfered with communication and collaborative efforts on a broad scale.

Considerable progress has been made in identifying causes and treatment of those types of mental retardation that have traditionally been termed clinical. Medical research on such problems as PKU and hypoparathyroidism has made it possible to significantly diminish or even prevent mental retardation in some cases. Despite such important developments it became increasingly clear that the broad problem of mental retardation could not be addressed effectively with isolated foci of attention.

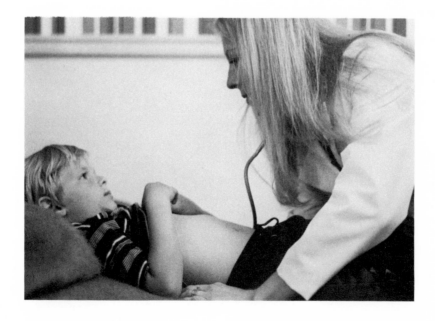

Clinical issues and problems simply had to be viewed in the broader context of the society in which they existed. The societal context is becoming a recurring theme. Such a viewpoint was introduced in Section One, it will be paramount in the issues presented in Section Four, and it provides a backdrop for nearly every area discussed throughout this book. The present section addresses certain clinical dimensions of mental retardation and the societal implications and considerations that accompany them.

The first article in this section emphasizes dramatically the societal implications of nearly every dimension of the mental retardation problem. Michael J. Begab discusses the status of clinical knowledge and technology related to mental retardation and then asks some very difficult questions concerning failures in this area. From this article it becomes very clear that knowledge in the absence of social considerations and planning will not solve the complex problems associated with mental retardation.

The residential institution has long played an important role in services to the mentally retarded. It has also, however, been one of the more controversial delivery patterns with debates being heated and complex. R. C. Scheerenberger's article explores various facets of deinstitutionalization. This paper is an appropriate sequel to the article by Begab since both are launched from the same point—challenges that have not been effectively met. Scheerenberger presents a model for deinstitutionalization that clearly illustrates the many social and clinical considerations requiring attention.

The final article in this section epitomizes the interaction between clinical practices and societal concerns. Philip Roos examines an extremely volatile issue—human rights and behavior modification. Although the present context is mental retardation, the reader will recognize this last issue as one with broad societal ramifications.

CHAPTER 13

The major dilemma of mental retardation: shall we prevent it? (some social implications of research in mental retardation)[1]

MICHAEL J. BEGAB

National Institute of Child Health and Human Development

We have made great strides in the past decade in ameliorating the consequences of mental retardation and its impact on family life. Many retarded persons have, as a result, realized a higher degree of independence, social usefulness, and self-fulfillment. We must continue and intensify our efforts to help the handicapped among us. Yet if we are to win the battle against mental retardation, we must seek out its causes and devise means for its prevention. This is our ultimate goal.

INCIDENCE AND PREVALENCE

Little more than ten years ago the President's Panel on Mental Retardation stated firmly that this goal was within our grasp. If we could apply all the knowledge about mental retardation already in hand, one-half of all new cases could be prevented; if we accelerated our research efforts, our preventive capabilities could be significantly greater. Toward this end, they proposed the construction of research centers on mental retardation to assist in finding its causes and

means of prevention and for the amelioration of its effects.

How far along the road to prevention have we traveled since this not yet prophetic pronouncement? What is our state of knowledge? The sophistication of our technology? What known preventive measures have we failed to apply? And what are some of the reasons for these failures? These questions form the theme of my address to you today.

Mental retardation is developmental in origin and bidimensional in character. No longer do we consider an individual retarded on the basis of subaverage general intelligence alone. To satisfy current definitions, he must have a coexisting impairment in adaptive behavior as well.

Both criteria are modifiable. Drastic changes in a child's life experiences can alter IQ, up or down, and adaptive behavior is even more malleable. The individual's capacity to cope with the demands of his environment is determined at least in part by socially defined age-specific norms. For this reason, a significant number of mildly retarded persons are recognized and function as impaired only during their school-age years. Changing expectations by age account for the phenomenon of the "disappearing retardate." Except for special education, this

[1]Presidential address delivered at the 97th Annual Meeting of the American Association on Mental Deficiency, Atlanta, May 1973. Reprinted from the American Journal of Mental Deficiency **78**:519-529, 1974, with permission.

behavioral adaptation takes place for the large majority without benefit of specific training for work or social skills. Could many more be helped to "disappear," to be integrated more effectively into the mainstream of community life? Would programs to improve adaptive behavior prove more effective than traditional efforts to raise IQ? To the extent that either intellectual function or behavioral adaptation can be accelerated before performance is impaired, we have reduced the incidence of the symptom. Given the same changes later in life, we have reduced its prevalence.

The dynamic nature of mental retardation denies the long-cherished bromide of "once retarded, always retarded." Failure to induce change early in life and thus prevent retardation in its primary sense need not doom an individual to a lifetime of maladaptation. For certain categories, particularly the so-called cultural-familial group, "cure" through behavior change is possible.

Let us return now to an examination of our progress in preventing mental retardation. Any effort to do this "by the numbers" is clearly not possible. While there are some fairly reliable data on the incidence of certain biologically based conditions such as Down's syndrome, genetic disorders, and inborn errors of metabolism, such data were not collected at specific points in time to allow for comparisons. Other agents such as teratogens, radiation, infectious diseases, and some forms of prematurity may result more frequently in anomalies other than mental retardation. Baseline data on these conditions are difficult to obtain.

The "numbers game" is even more complex when psychosocial or cultural-familial forms of retardation are embraced. Older studies on prevalence are confounded by variations in definition and the application of the single criterion of IQ. Where an upper limit of 70 IQ—or two standard deviations below the mean—is applied, there is some support in these studies for the widely used estimate of 3 percent of the general population. (Birch, Richardson, Baird, Horobin, & Illsley, 1970), but the range varies immensely, depending on methods of study and the age group studied.

If the single criterion of IQ yields such vastly divergent rates of mental retardation, how much more complex is the task when adaptive behavior is added? Existing measures of adaptive behavior, in fact, are not suited to prevalence studies because they were standardized on institutional populations (Adaptive Behavior Scales, Nihira, Foster, Shellhaas, & Leland, 1969). Scales for community-based groups are still being formulated. Thus, the finding in a recent study (Mercer, in press) and the speculation (Tarjan, Wright, Eyman & Keeran, 1973) that two-thirds of mildly retarded adolescents or young adults lose this label needs to be confirmed through empirical study and validated instrumentation. Such research will help resolve the issue of whether 2 million or 6 million persons in this country are retarded. The implications for program planning hardly need elaboration.

Despite these caveats, some observations can be made on factors that affect the incidence of mental retardation and inferences can be drawn regarding our progress in prevention. First, let us examine briefly some of the factors that may *increase* incidence, both in the United States and elsewhere around the world.

Biological determinants

In addition to enormous benefits, science and technology have also produced hazards to the public's health. At the current state of knowledge, some of the by-products of technological development and social change are only suspect, while others are more certain.

Among suspect agents are some of the addictive drugs and other pharmaceutical substances. In today's drug culture, many pregnant women addicted to heroin are giving birth to infants who show marked physiological withdrawal symptoms. The effect of this trauma on the central nervous system is unknown and will be difficult to isolate from the adverse social experiences that addicted mothers are apt to provide for their infants.

The relationship of such practices to mental retardation requires a closer look. Drugs such as LSD (lysergic acid diethylamide) may be even more suspect. They have been observed to induce meiotic chromosome damage and damage to human leukocytes. Chromosomal abnormalities, in turn, underlie some types of mental retardation.

The potential impact on fetal development could conceivably extend to some everyday over-the-counter drugs. Some investigators have demonstrated, for example, that large doses of aspirin in pregnant rats produce malformations of the central nervous system, internal organs, and skeleton. At subteratogenic dose levels, the newborn animals manifest behavioral impairments and possible brain damage. When such findings from animal research are coupled with studies of human newborns which show an incidence of over 2 percent born with major defects and nearly 15 percent with at least one minor anomaly, there is reason for pause. While there is no conclusive proof that drugs cause mental retardation, we cannot ignore the thalidomide tragedy and the potential consequences of increased drug abuse and drug use by pregnant women.

Pollution of the water we drink, the food we eat, and the air we breathe is widely recognized as hazardous to health, but seldom regarded seriously as a factor in mental retardation. We are all aware that infants who eat the crumbling paint from the walls of their slum homes can develop lead encephalopathy and mental retardation (Byers, 1959). There is also evidence that persons living near expressways have elevated levels of lead in their blood (Thomas, Milmore, Heidbreder, & Kagan, 1967). Is this hazardous to pregnant women and the mental development of young children? We do not know, but it could be.

Mercury, an industrial waste product and element in certain pesticides, is another proven cause of mental retardation. Children born to Japanese women who habitually ate shellfish from mercury-polluted waters during pregnancy were affected by cerebral palsy and mental retardation (Takeuchi & Matsumoto, 1969).

One more chemical agent of the many that could be identified deserved mention—smoking. The risks for cancer and heart disease are too well known to be elaborated here. The case against smoking as a contributing cause of mental retardation is perhaps less conclusive, but compelling nevertheless. According to some studies, smoking during pregnancy reduces mean birth weight and increases infant mortality (Frazier, Davis, Goldstein, & Goldberg, 1961; Simpson, 1957; Yerushalmy, 1964). The independent role of smoking in those adverse outcomes is supported by animal studies showing that the chemicals in cigarette smoke can retard fetal growth or cause stillbirths.

It is perhaps ironic that one of the great boons to medical diagnosis and treatment—the use of radiation—could have deleterious effects on the unborn child. The strongest evidence, of course, derives from the nuclear holocaust of World War II (Stein & Susser, 1971), with consequent cases of mental retardation, microcephaly, and leukemia. The critical fetal age for sensitivity to radiation appeared to be between 7 and 15 weeks of pregnancy. Such children suffered intellectual disability.

One could argue cogently that the radiation dosage of a nuclear bomb bears little resemblance to what occurs routinely in medical practice. Yet, the effects of diagnostic, fluoroscopic, and therapeutic radiation on pregnant women should not be summarily dismissed. In one case study of Down's syndrome children and controls matched for maternal age, any one form of exposure more than doubled the risk. For mothers exposed to all of these processes, the risk was seven times as great (Sigler, Lilienfeld, Cohen, & Westlake, 1965). The story about radiation is not yet fully told, but with technological advances and the atomic power plants of the future, in the absence of safe-guards, women may be subjected to cumulative dosages of harmful radiation well beyond the confines of the doctor's office or hospital.

The contribution of obstetric practice to incidence is not altogether clear. Improved techniques of delivery and neonatal care clearly expose fewer infants to brain-damaging experiences. However, among the damaged, a larger proportion tend to survive and their life expectancy is also greatly enhanced, thus increasing prevalence rates. As presently applied, prenatal care can modify certain conditions but not others. So far, the capacity to prolong life may exceed our skills in insuring that the newborn are physiologically well born.

Though these factors contribute adversely to the problem, on the whole some positive gains have been made. Infection, never a significant force quantitatively in the etiology of mental retardation, has been reduced even further. Such diseases as syphilis, bacterial meningitis, and rubella have yielded to techniques of prevention and treatment. As other viral agents are identified through continued research, still more progress can be anticipated.

The major factors affecting mental retardation among the poor are social/environmental in nature. Forces for social change, in fact, work in both directions. On the one hand, industrialization and the increasing complexity of urban living impose greater stress on adaptive capacities than the less demanding environment of an agrarian economy. Social roles today are more exacting than in years past and higher levels of education are demanded than are actually necessary to fulfill these roles. Thus, during World War II, one-third of the nation's youth were considered ineligible for the armed services because of mental unfitness. The army has subsequently learned that, with training, many marginally retarded youth can be successfully integrated into the armed forces.

For the most part, social change has benefited disadvantaged groups and alleviated some of the conditions associated with mental retardation. While much remains to be done to improve the economic status and living conditions of millions of Americans, the situation is nonetheless better than 30 to 40 years ago. The poor are better nourished, have greater access to health services, and more opportunities for higher education and meaningful employment. Health disorders and infant mortality and morbidity have declined significantly in many countries.

The impact of preschool day care centers, Head Start and Follow Through programs, compensatory education and other Great Society innovations also cannot be discounted. Evaluation of these activities suggests that we have not been remarkably successful in raising and sustaining mental performance over time. It is quite possible, however, that we have been looking at the wrong outcome variable and that many of these children have become better socialized, more highly motivated toward achievement, and thus better prepared for adult living. These potential gains remain to be documented.

On balance it would seem that social gains exceed social losses and that the incidence and prevalence of mental retardation may have declined somewhat over the past decade. This conclusion may be debatable. What is perfectly clear, however, is that the Panel's goal of a 50 percent reduction has not been even remotely approached.

Let us turn now to the second and third of my questions. What do we know about mental retardation that is not being applied? Are existing techniques and technology equal to the implementation task?

THE STATE OF KNOWLEDGE AND TECHNOLOGY

Global questions of this sort are far easier to formulate than answer, but certain categories of mental retardation contribute disproportionately to the total, and if we concentrate on these, a meaningful response is possible. I have chosen, therefore, to discuss four areas: (*a*) genetic disorders and inborn errors of metabolism; (*b*) prematurity and low birth weight; (*c*) malnutrition and undernutrition; and (*d*) psychosocial and environmental influences.

Genetic disease constitutes an appreciable fraction of pediatric practice. Of the patients sick enough to require hospitalization in children's facilities, about 20 percent have gene-related diseases. Among institution-alized retarded persons, one in ten has a genetically based condition. The incidence, almost twice as high for the more severely handicapped, still grossly understates the problem because of the many disorders such as Tay-Sachs disease that cause early death. Clearly, a successful attack on genetic disease would contribute significantly to the prevention of mental retardation.

The dramatic breakthroughs in recent years regarding cell structure and function and the transmission of genetic material have stimulated much research in this area and opened the door to new discoveries and promising therapies. One form of thera-apy is dietary manipulation of biochemical abnormalities resulting from single gene defects (Goodman, 1972). The phenylketon-uria (PKU) story, well known to most of you, is still not fully told. The success of dietary treatment when initiated during the first year of life is already fairly well documented, though uncertainty exists about the possi-bility of minor residual damage. Equally important is the knowledge that after 5 years of age, when myelination is complete and damage to the central nervous system less likely, the treatment can be discontinued without ill effects. But there are still unwrit-ten chapters of the PKU story. The accumu-lation of phenylalanine can result in an indi-vidual without the clinical condition of PKU. In these cases, an overly restrictive diet can produce malnutrition, too much intake, the loss of biochemical control.

For other metabolic abnormalities, this approach to treatment is as yet less effective. The considerable cost of the diet and the po-tential loss of biochemical control during in-fectious episodes and consequent brain dam-age casts much doubt on the long-range efficacy of this form of treatment. Dietary re-striction seems appropriate only in condi-tions in which the compounds involved can-not be synthesized by the body. Many disor-ders fall outside this criterion. Nevertheless, until new approaches are devised, we have no alternatives for the treatments of such conditions. Failure to intervene means death

or severe brain damage and lifelong depen-dency.

Certain genetic disorders are related to the absence or decreased activity of an enzyme. One way to correct the latter form of enzyma-tic deficiency is through cofactor sup-plementation. At least ten conditions are treatable in this manner. What works in some cases, however, does not work in others. In cases of a primary genetic defect in liver or kidney, organ transplantation offers more obvious but technically difficult so-lutions. Despite the problems of rejection, this therapeutic approach has been used with some success in cases of Cystinosis and Wil-son's disease. At our current stage of technology, however, the cure may be more hazardous than the disease. Ways to provide active enzyme other than through whole organ transplant are clearly needed. Where the enzyme must be transported across the "blood-brain barrier" (as in Tay-Sachs), the task is inherently more difficult.

One other approach that may come in for greater study in the treatment of single-gene defects is the use of viruses to supply missing genetic information. Viruses are seldom thought of in positive terms, but the DNA virus can affect RNA and protein synthe-sis and, if nonpathogenic, can result in sim-ple, long-lasting therapy. This technique is clearly far less dangerous than organ trans-plantation. Furthermore, if the virus entered the germ cells and became incorporated into the genome of the patient, the geno-type would be affected and future genera-tions safeguarded from the disorder. Some early studies suggest that this technology has potential, but much research will need to be undertaken before it can be widely applied as a therapeutic measure. At this date, these varied approaches to prevention are still some years away from implemen-tation.

Of more immediate application in the pre-vention of genetic disease is the use of ge-netic counseling and the detection of fetal disorders with the view of therapeutic abor-tion.

Genetic counseling consists of advising

parents of the statistical risks of giving birth to defective children and of alternative ways for satisfying parenthood needs. A major limitation in genetic counseling is that it can be applied only to parents who have already given birth to a defective child. In certain conditions, such as Tay-Sachs disease, galactosemia, and tuberous sclerosis, diagnosis is relatively simple and can be made from characteristic physical findings. In others, sophisticated laboratory studies are required, but here progress has been remarkably rapid. More than 40 inborn errors of metabolism, unrecognized as recently as 10 years ago, can now be identified early in life and some of them *in utero*.

The identification of the carriers of genetic disease must be simple and inexpensive to warrant mass scale screening. The genes for even rare disorders such as PKU and other inborn errors are carried by a significant 3 percent of the general population. Moreover, certain disorders such as Tay-Sachs disease occur most commonly in specific population groups—in this instance the Jews of Eastern European descent. To the extent that groups of women vulnerable to genetic disease can be identified, screening becomes feasible and prevention possible.

The best example of a vulnerable group are pregnant women over the age of 35. The incidence of gross chromosomal malformations in children born to these women is 1 to 2 percent (Lubs & Ruddle, 1970). Down's syndrome children are, of course, the most prevalent among these. Although women over 35 account for little more than 13 percent of all pregnancies, they produce half of the infants with trisomy-21. The application of antenatal diagnostic procedures and therapeutic abortion, where indicated, to this group alone could reduce the incidence of Down's syndrome by 50 percent. This condition represents the largest single category of organic etiology in mental retardation. Its prevention—well within the realm of modern technology—could result in enormous economic benefits to society and the avoidance of human tragedy.

Some problems in amniocentesis remain to be resolved, but they are of no great consequence and the procedure will be perfected even more with experience. Hazards to the fetus or mother as early as the twelfth week of pregnancy are minimal. Spontaneous abortion, maternal hemorrhage, or premature labor occurs no more frequently in these cases than in other pregnancies. A more complicated aspect of this procedure deals with the tests, including cell culture, performed on the amniotic fluid itself. Because these tests determine whether the pregnancy should be terminated, they must be performed with great precision. Only laboratories with considerable experience in this field can be relied on to avoid diagnostic errors. In the right hands, antenatal diagnosis and abortion, coupled with an effective public education program to reach vulnerable women, is a powerful tool for the prevention of mental retardation.

Prematurity and low birth weight

Another factor highly associated with mental retardation and related neurologic and behavior disorders is low birth weight and prematurity. The problem has become even more acute in recent years because of the notable increase in the survival rate for infants of very low birth weight (Hardy & Pauls, 1959; Nesbitt, 1959). Such infants are especially susceptible to disability or deficit. Many pose special problems to public health, welfare, and educational institutions.

Studies on the consequences of low birth weight suffer from variations in definition, design, and methodology, and there is increasing evidence that such children are not a homogeneous group and have different outcomes (Drillien, 1964). Some infants are born at term to mothers of small stature, other full-term infants may be malnourished *in utero*, while still others are born prematurely, after a short gestation period. The first group may be due to genetic influences; they have relatively low morbidity rates. The second group—the "small for dates" babies—tend to show retarded fetal growth and later sequelae distinct from those of low gestational age. These findings suggest that birth weight should be considered in conjunction with other variables, such as gestational age.

The strong correlation of low birth weight with race, socioeconomic status, and complications of pregnancy tends to confound the causal role of birth weight *per se* in mental retardation. Indeed, all of these latter factors correlate independently with low intelligence and in some studies seem to exert an even more influential role than birth weight (Baltimore Study). Nevertheless, the independent contribution of birth weight is well documented. That it may have an interactional effect with poverty and its corollaries, depressing even further the mental development of the premature disadvantaged child, is highly logical and is, in fact, supported by research (Douglas, 1956; Drillien, 1964). If children who are well born physiologically can become retarded, how much greater is the risk for the poorly born?

A compehensive review of the literature (Caputo & Mandell, 1970) indicates that very low birth weight individuals, and to a lesser extent the heavier prematures, are overrepresented in institutions for retarded persons or in special classes. They also evidence a greater frequency of hyperkinetic, disorganized behavior, autism, and maladaptation. Language development, reading, and academic skills are retarded and deficits in physical growth, motor behavior, and neurologic functioning are commmon.

The importance of this problem as an etiological agent in mental retardation should be self-evident. Can we prevent low birth weight? Failing this, can we prevent or at least minimize its detrimental consequences?

While low birth weight and prematurity can result in a a range of neurological sequellae, they are in turn caused by a similarly wide range of factors. Infectious diseases in mothers who may be malnourished and medically indigent, can stunt fetal growth. Toxemia and other complications of pregnancy can do likewise. The young teenage mother and the mother who has her children in quick succession also run a greater risk in this regard.

The prevention of these outcomes would seem straightforward. The medical care technology is certainly available, but the lack of social engineering has limited its application. Prenatal care as currently practiced has not been especially effective in the prevention of prematurity in the uneventful pregnancy, but newly developed techniques could help. For example, measurements of the estriol hormone, which reflects the blood supply to the uterus is one index to normal fetal development. Such potential disorders can be detected and treated by the obstetrician.

The problem of the young mother—often unmarried—poses different issues. With the range of contraceptive measures available today, unwanted pregnancies need hardly occur. Making birth control information and technical aids available to those who need them most, and motivating these people to use them, is a matter of public education, attitudes, and social values. The shift toward greater sexual permissiveness in our society could exacerbate this problem greatly, but may well be offset at least in part by the liberalization of the abortion laws. In any event, many of the causes of low birth weight can be eliminated. We need only the will to do so; the way is clear.

Where primary prevention of prematurity fails, children need not be doomed to later retarded development. Even without intervention, the majority "catch up" and show no discernible negative outcomes. This is suggestive evidence that the number of children showing damaging effects can be significantly reduced. On the premise that the sterile incubator, the hospital environment, and lack of early maternal handling offer less stimulation to premature than normal infants, investigators have provided compensatory handling for the infant during his hospital stay. These infants exhibit better conditioning performance than their unhandled peers. Undamaged animals in enriched environments (handling) show improvement in brain development, behavioral function, and emotional control. If it works with animals, why not with humans?

Malnutrition

Of the various factors associated with low birth weight and mental performance, malnutriton in the pregnant mother and the young infant may be the most significant and widespread. In developing countries, 3 percent of the children, or 11 million, suffer from severe protein-calorie deficiencies. Moderate malnutriton embraces another 76 million. The blacks in our urban ghettos, the Indians, other minority groups, and the children of migrant farm workers are part of this population.

The independent role of malnutrition in the mental retardation of humans is not yet fully understood. From animal research, however, the evidence is quite compelling. The off-spring of animals experimentally malnourished during critical periods of brain growth show permanent deficits in cell size and number, reduction in protein synthesis and severe neurochemical (RNA-DNA), electrical, and morphological changes in the brain. Intellectual behavior in these animals is more difficult to measure and document, but reactions of apathy, lassitude, appetite loss, and other behaviors are commonly noted. The effect on physical and brain development persists across generations even when the offspring of a malnourished mother is in turn well fed.

Some experts argue that the embryo is a complete parasite, obtaining from the mother's body all the nutrients it requires. But women unable to support a pregnancy are less likely to conceive and more likely to abort. Thus, when food shortages were severe in Leningrad during World War II, the stillbirth and prematurity rates were abnormally high (5.6 and 41.2 percent), many children died during the first 6 months of life (21 percent), and among survivors morbidity was high (32 percent) (Antonov, 1947).

Follow-up during adulthood of male survivors born during the famine in Holland did not show a higher rate of mental retardation (Stein, Susser, Saenger, & Marolla, 1972).

Selective survival is one possible explanation, and the high death rate observed in the mentally retarded early in life supports this view. It is also possible, as the authors suggest, that postnatal experience in the middle class families of these individuals compensated for presumed insult *in utero.*

The interactive role of nutrition with other psychosocial phenomena can best be understood through controlled field trials where these variables can be manipulated, or at least isolated and measured. Two large scale studies currently underway provide nutritional supplementation to pregnant women. Birth weight and later intellectual development are the outcomes being evaluated. Preliminary data suggest that birth weight can be raised in this manner, but the effect on intelligence remains to be determined.

The long-term effects of acute malnutrition in infants as represented by symptoms of kwashiorkor or marasmus are fairly well substantiated. Such children do not suffer sudden episodes of malnutrition, but probably require hospitalization because of infections, dehydration, or other conditions which aggravate their chronic undernourished state. Studies in Jamaica (Richardson, Birch, Grabic, & Yoder, 1972) and Uganda (Hoorweg & Stanfeld, 1972) indicate that these children later in life are shorter, less intelligent, poorer in school performance and motor coordination, and less socially competent than their classmates.

Social environmental factors

In the final analysis, any significant gains in the prevention of retardation depends on the effectiveness of measures to reduce mild retardation. Clearly, the optimistic projections of the President's Panel that the problem could be reduced by one-half was based on the belief that such measures could indeed be developed and applied.

The etiological basis for mild retardation, uncomplicated by demonstrable central nervous system pathology, remains a controversial issue. Most authorities accept an interactionist theory, recognizing that genetics and social environmental forces both impinge on intelligence. How much each contributes to the variance between individuals, however, is a matter of quite diverse opinion. The nature-nurture controversy rages on even today, but is far too complex to consider in the time remaining. Suffice to say that the role of environmental factors is of sufficient magnitude that dramatic changes in a child's daily living experiences can alter his intellectual status. Even where significant IQ changes are not achieved, providing the child with more acceptable adult models to emulate, improving his skills in interpersonal relationships, and promoting his sense of social values can forestall impaired adaptive behavior.

A number of experiments throughout the world support this view. Children raised in the kibbutz system of Israel, for example, while demonstrating individual variations in intelligence, rarely function at a retarded level. Significant numbers of these children are the products of many generations of poverty-ridden, functionally illiterate parents, not unlike the victims of our own slum culture. Apparently, early stimulation, group socialization processes, and substitute parenting can overcome familial deficits. There is even evidence from another project in Israel, that intervention as late as adolescence can effect intellectual performance (R. Feuerstein, personal communication, 1972). Through a structured program of instrumental enrichment, these adolescents made significant gains. Surprisingly, in the light of this country's growing disenchantment with residential care, the adolescents in this type of living arrangement did better than their peers in day-care settings. Manipulation of the child's total daily life experience seems to offer greater opportunity to stimulate, enrich, and motivate behavior.

Many of you are already aware of the early intervention project in Milwaukee conducted under the guidance of Rick Heber and reported at our last convention and at many other conferences (Heber, 1972). No single study can be looked to as proof positive when so many other intervention studies have failed to demonstrate sustained intellectual gains. Nevertheless, the potential social significance of this work and its relevance to the theme of this address, merits some detailed description here.

The initial step in this project involved a series of surveys of a residential section of Milwaukee having the lowest median family income, greatest population density per living unit, and highest rate of dilapidated housing in the city. In the first survey, all families in this slum area with a newborn infant and at least one other child of the age of 6 were selected for study. The major finding was that maternal intelligence proved to be the best single predictor of intellectual development in the children. Mothers with IQs under 80, though constituting less than one-half of the total group, accounted for four-fifths of the children with IQs under 80. Furthermore, the offspring of the relatively "brighter" mothers remained at a constant IQ level over time, whereas the others declined progressively with age. A later survey indicated a similar, but not as striking, congruence to the IQ of the father. This data strongly supports the conclusion many clinicians in the field have commonly observed, that mild retardation is not randomly distributed among the poor, but is heavily concentrated in clusters of families with intellectually subnormal parents.

The implications of this relationship between maternal-child IQ for prevention is self-evident. It matters not whether one views this as a prepotency of hereditary factors or the inability of the subnormal mother to create a satisfactory learning environment for her child's development. Effective family planning to reduce the size of these families would prevent the birth of children often destined by unfortunate happenstance to become retarded. It is also conceivable that these marginal parents, already overburdened in their struggle for social survival, would be less marginal if they had fewer children to care for.

The marginally intelligent mother is generally known to public welfare agencies and other social institutions and is likely to deliver her baby in a municipal hospital. The likelihood is great, despite the prevailing views of opponents to public welfare, that many of these pregnancies are not only unplanned, but unwanted. Failure to provide these women with birth control information, contraceptive devices, and the opportunity for voluntary family planning is a distinct disservice to them in the fulfillment of their life goals. The economic and social costs to society are equally self-evident. As a preventive measure in mental retardation, family planning may well be the single, potentially most significant, and clearly least expensive approach available.

Zero population growth is, of course, rapidly becoming a reality in our society, but it is unrealistic to expect it to apply to all groups. Assuming the continued birth of children who are potential casualties of their environment, can their retardation be prevented?

The Heber (1972) study suggests that it can. The subject population in his program consisted of 50 newborns whose mothers had IQs under 70 and who were randomly assigned to experimental and control groups. From the first 4 weeks of life, infants were given a precisely structured program, including every aspect of sensory and language stimulation, and emphasizing achievement motivation, problem-solving skills, and interpersonal relations. Children participated on a full-day basis throughout the year. They are now of school-age and enrolled in the regular public school systems.

Intervention also included rigorous efforts to modify the family environment. Mothers received training in homemaking and child care and rehabilitation services in the form of occupational training and placement. They were also taught reading and arithmetic as prerequisites for on-the-job training. Even the fathers attended some of the parent meetings. This ensured some carry over from the day care setting to the home.

The most striking differences between the performance of the experimental and control groups is in language skills and measured intelligence. On all dimensions of language and the subcomponents of the Gesell Scales, the former group is far superior. At the age of 66 months, the experimental children have a mean IQ of 125, the controls, 92. This disparity as well as the levels, have remained fairly constant from 3 years of age on. The low average scores for the controls are unexpectedly higher than their siblings and may suggest that the mean scores for both groups may partially reflect the consequence of practice effects. We have still to determine the impact on the experimental group of the recent change from their previous enriched setting to the more stultifying atmosphere of the regular ghetto-located school system. It would appear most unlikely, however, that even under such conditions, could a 50 point loss in IQ occur. Such a loss would put them on the edge of the mental retardation classification.

This project has differed from other intervention efforts which have failed to sustain gains in children in the (a) age of enrollment; (b) intensity and duration of the stimulus conditions; (c) higher vulnerability of the subject population to mental retardation than the poor in general; and (d) range of rehabilitative services provided the families. Which of these variations in the intervention process are indispensable or most critical are points for continuing research. Indeed, until we refine our knowledge about critical developmental periods, effective educational environments, and the role of the family, large scale intervention programs may prove economically and socially unfeasible.

SOME BARRIERS TO PREVENTION

By way of summary, let us now return to the last of my questions posed earlier. Why have we failed to approximate our goals in prevention? The answers vary with the causes of mental retardation and are just as diverse.

In the absence of any concerted, focused effort at prevention, the natural forces at work in our society will produce a relative stand-off. Incidence and prevalence of mental retardation will remain basically unchanged. Suppose, on the other hand, we wish to do something about it?

Consider first the biologically determined conditions. For many of the biochemical abnormalities—mostly inborn—the enzymatic deficiency is known. This knowledge is only a beginning, however. Before the information can be therapeutically applied, still more advanced technologies are needed. The enzyme must be isolated and purified, the metabolic pathways mapped out, and methods for infusion developed. The process is painstaking and time consuming, but the ultimate success of these research efforts will have meaningful application well beyond the specific conditions they hope to remediate or prevent. The cost of such research is a fraction of the cost for life-long support of the severely handicapped.

Genetic disorders, especially Down's syndrome, which occurs with significant frequency and is highly associated with maternal age or aging, can now be largely prevented. But there are barriers. Obstetricians are not yet ready to accept amniocentesis as a routine procedure for their older clients, and despite the Supreme Court decision on abortion, there are still strongly conflicting views on the moral, social, and religious values involved. The issue is perhaps less debatable where a defective fetus is concerned and few women faced with this outlook would choose to carry their pregnancy to term. Here much of the technology is at hand. However, the nation has not yet committed itself to this preventive goal. And it will not generate the necessary community support until women at risk are better informed, physicians incorporate emerging knowledge about genetic disease in their daily practice, and evolving attitudes toward preventing the birth of the defective fetus become more widely accepted.

Prematurity, low birth weight, and malnutrition are also preventable. Prenatal care can help with complications of pregnancy, but more significant inroads can be made through programs of nutrition for mothers and young children and through sex education and birth control information to our young people. The food stamp program has probably alleviated undernutrition to a meaningful degree, but knowing what foods are essential and having access to them is necessary to avoid malnutrition. Our failure to apply these preventive measures stems from economic and attitudinal factors. I am certain they need no elaboration for this audience.

The most strategic approach to the prevention of mild retardation in the socially disadvantaged family, has already been described. These multiproblem families are difficult to reach and often regard social agencies with suspicion and distrust. Some may misinterpret efforts by family planning counselors or social workers to get them voluntarily to control family size. Societal efforts to improve the quality of life in these families have been markedly ineffective. By reducing family size and through better spacing of births, children would receive more parental guidance, mothers would be more able to enter the labor market, economic burdens would be lessened, and all family members would get a greater share of its material and psychological resources. Not all parents would be responsive to such guidance, but many would. Still more would cooperate, given incentives and services and other evidence that society does indeed care.

Early intervention with the children of such families is the next most promising preventive measure. The barriers here are largely economic and of necessity relate to national spending priorities. We need not dwell on these issues or the values which dictate the differential use of our resources. Intervention that starts in early infancy and includes intensive programs to improve child-rearing practices and parental earning power are very costly. Perhaps with more research, we can find ways short of this "saturation" technique of achieving the same goals. Even if we cannot, the investment is still most worthwhile. The cost of social dependency, underachievement, and underproductivity, when coupled with the social ailments that characterize many of these families, is astronomical. We can hardly afford *not* to invest in preventive programs.

Undoubtedly, we have much still to learn

about mental retardation, but in certain aspects of the problem at least, we have only to apply what we already know. We can indeed significantly reduce the incidence and prevalence of mental retardation.

Shall we?

REFERENCES

Antonov, A. N. Children born during the siege of Leningrad in 1942. *Journal of Pediatrics*, 1947, 30, 250.

Birch, H., Richardson, S. A., Baird, D., Horobin, G., & Illsley, R. *Mental subnormality: A clinical and epidemiologic study in the community.* Baltimore: Williams & Wilkins, 1970.

Byers, R. K. Lead poisoning: Review of the literature and report on 45 cases. *Pediatrics*, 1959, 23, 585.

Caputo, D. V., & Mandell, W. Consequences of low birth weight. *Developmental Psychology*, 1970, 3, 363-383.

Douglas, J. W. B. Mental ability and school achievement of premature children at eight years of age. *British Medical Journal*, 1956, 1, 1210-1214.

Drillien, C. M. *The growth and development of the prematurely born infant.* Baltimore: Williams & Wilkins, 1964.

Frazier, T. M., Davis, G. H., Goldstein, H., & Goldberg, I. D. Cigarette smoking and prematurity: A prospective study. *American Journal of Obstetrics and Gynecology*, 1961, 81, 988.

Goodman, S. I. Some advances in the prevention of mental retardation. In I. Schulman (Ed.), *Advances in pediatrics.* Vol. 2. Chicago: Year Book Medical Publishers, 1972.

Hardy, W. G., & Pauls, M. D. Atypical children with communication disorders. *Children*, 1959, 6, 13-16.

Heber, R., Garber, H., Harrington, S., & Hoffman, C. Rehabilitation of families of risk for mental retardation. *Progress Report*, Social Rehabilitation Service, Department of Health, Education and Welfare, 1972.

Hoorweg, J., & Stanfeld, P. The influence of malnutrition on psychologic and neurologic development: Preliminary communication. In *Nutrition, the nervous system and behavior.* Conference proceedings, Panamerican Health Organization, 1972.

Lubs, H. A., & Ruddle, F. H. Chromosomal abnormalities in the human population: Estimates of rates based on New Haven newborn study. *Science*, 1970, 169, 495.

Mercer, J. R. *The eligibles and the labeled.* Berkeley: University of California Press, in press.

Nesbitt, R. E. L., Jr. Perinatal casualties. *Children*, 1959, 6, 123-128.

Nihira, K., Foster, R., Shellhaas, M., & Leland, H. *Adaptive Behavior Scales: Manual.* Washington, D.C.: American Association on Mental Deficiency, 1969.

Richardson, S. A., Birch, H., Grabie, E., & Yoder, K. The behavior of children in school who were severely malnourished in the first two years of life. *Journal of Health and Social Behavior*, 1972, 13, 276-284.

Sigler, A. T., Lilienfeld, A. M., Cohen, B. H., & Westlake, J. E. Radiation exposure in parents of children with mongolism. *Bulletin of Johns Hopkins Hospital*, 1965, 117, 374.

Simpson, W. J. A preliminary report of cigarette smoking and the incidence of prematurity. *American Journal of Obstetrics and Gynecology*, 1957, 73, 807.

Stein, Z., & Susser, M. A. Changes over time in the incidence and prevalence of mental retardation. In J. Hellmuth (Ed.), *Exceptional infant.* New York: Bruner/Mazel, 1971.

Stein, Z., Susser, M. A., Saenger, G., & Marolla, F. Nutrition and mental performance. *Science*, 1972, 178, 708-713.

Takeuchi, T., & Matsumoto, H. Minameta disease of human fetuses. In Nishimura et al. (Eds.), *Methods for teratological studies in experimental animals and man: Proceedings of the second international workshop in teratology, Kyoto, 1968.* Tokyo: Igaku Shoin, 1969.

Tarjan, G., Wright, S. W., Eyman, R. K., and Keeran, C. V. Natural history of mental retardation: Some aspects of epidemiology. *American Journal of Mental Deficiency*, 1973, 77, 369-379.

Thomas, H. V., Milmore, B. K., Heidbreder, G. A., & Kagan, B. A. Blood levels of persons living near expressways. *Archives of Environmental Health*, 1967, 15, 695.

Yerushalmy, J. Mother's cigarette smoking and survival of infant. *American Journal of Obstetrics and Gynecology*, 1964, 88, 505.

CHAPTER 14

A model for deinstitutionalization

R. C. SCHEERENBERGER

Central Wisconsin Colony and Training School

ABSTRACT: *One of the most critical concepts affecting the lives and services for the retarded today involves deinstitutionalization. This paper explores some of the problems associated with this process and considers five aspects deemed important to a successful effort.*

On February 5, 1963, President John F. Kennedy concluded his message to the Congress of the United States with the following challenge:

We as a Nation have long neglected the mentally ill and the mentally retarded. This neglect must end, if our Nation is to live up to its own standards of compassion and dignity and achieve the maximum use of its manpower.

This tradition of neglect must be replaced by forceful and far-reaching programs carried out at all levels of government, by private individuals and by State and local agencies in every part of the Union.

We must act—to bestow the full benefits of our society on those who suffer from mental disabilities; to prevent the occurrence of mental illness and mental retardation wherever and whenever possible; to provide for early diagnosis and continuous and comprehensive care, in the community, of those suffering from these disorders; to stimulate improvements in the level of care given the mentally disabled in our State and private institutions, and to reorient

Reprinted from Mental Retardation **12**:3-7, 1974, with permission.
Author: **R. C. Scheerenberger,** Ph.D., Superintendent, Central Wisconsin Colony and Training School, Madison, and President of the National Association of Superintendents of Public Residential Facilities for the Mentally Retarded.

those programs to a community-centered approach; to reduce, over a number of years, and by hundreds of thousands, the persons confined to these institutions; to retain in and return to the community the mentally ill and mentally retarded, and there to restore and revitalize their lives through better health programs and strengthened educational and rehabilitation services; and to reinforce the will and capacity of our communities to meet these problems, in order that the communities, in turn, can reinforce the will and capacity of individuals and individual families.

We must promote—to the best of our ability and by all possible and appropriate means—the mental and physical health of all our citizens. (Kennedy, 1963, pp. 13-14).

Eleven years have elapsed since this statement was issued and various systems, programs, and techniques have been tried. Some have been successful, some have failed. Today, many community and residential services cannot meet acceptable levels or standards of programming. In 1960, there were 160,000 retarded persons in public residential facilities for the mentally retarded and 53,000 in private residential facilities and mental hospitals (President's Panel on Mental Retardation, 1962). By 1969, the number of retarded persons had increased to 190,000 in public residential facilities and 65,000 in private facilities and mental hospitals (Office of Mental Retardation Coordination, 1972). While there has been a major effort over the past several years to reduce residential populations, many persons have been transferred to inappropriate, under-programmed community facilities.

DEINSTITUTIONALIZATION

All states are attempting to meet the needs of retarded citizens and, at the same time, resolve some of the critical problems confronting most residential facilities through the dual processes of deinstitutionalization and institutional reform. The primary emphasis of this discussion will be upon deinstitutionalization.

Deinstitutionalization encompasses three interrelated processes: (a) prevention of admission by finding and developing alternative community methods of care and training, (b) return to the community of all residents who have been prepared through programs of habilitation and training to function adequately in appropriate local settings, and (c) establishment and maintenance of a responsive residential environment which protects human and civil rights and which contributes to the expeditious return of the individual to normal community living, whenever possible. In contrast institutional reform involves a modification or improvement in attitudes, philosophies, policies, effective utilization of available resources, and increased financing to provide adequate programs to motivate and assist individuals to reach their maximum level of functioning in the least restrictive environment possible (National Association of Superintendents of Public Residential Facilities for the Mentally retarded, 1974, pp. 4-5).

THE COMMUNITY

In order to establish a model from which to proceed, this discussion will emphasize (a) the community, (b) the residential facility, and (c) the mechanics through which each can assume its proper roles and functions. The term "community" can be considered from two points of view: (a) the socio-political community, and (b) the individual's community. Socio-political definitions of a community usually refer to a group of persons with some common background residing within a relatively restricted geographical area:

A community is "a social group of any size whose members reside in a specific locality, share government, and have a common cultural and historical heritage" (Stein and Urdang, 1967, p. 298).

A community is "a general population having a common interest or interdependency in the delivery of services" (NARC Residential Services and Facilities Committee, 1973, p. 72).

The individual's community is concerned with the experiences and mobility that he has within the socio-political community and his interactions with the people, services, and facilities contained within. Normally, the individual's community is smaller than the socio-political community as defined.

The residential facility's community also can be considered within the dual context of a socio-political area and its individual interactions. As shown in Fig. 1, the residential facility exists within a socio-political community and may be part of the individual's community if he uses the services available. Although a residential facility may be located within or near a socio-political community, its services may extend to a number of such communities or, in some cases, throughout the state. Finally, communities also exist within the framework of a larger societal structure (county, state, and nation), all of which may influence to some degree each community and its inhabitants.

By definition (and practice) a residential facility must be considered an integral part of any community. The degree to which it is a successful member of that community depends upon the degree of its involvement and interaction.

The community that is available to the retarded should offer the "least restrictive environment"; however, placements in foster homes, group homes, or nursing homes frequently are more restrictive than residential

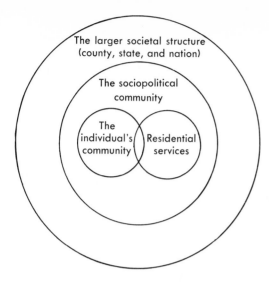

The larger societal structure
(county, state, and nation)

The sociopolitical
community

The
individual's
community

Residential
services

Fig. 1. The interrelationships of communities.

living in a public facility. For example, Murphy, Rennee, and Luchins (1972) studied foster home programs in Canada and concluded:

1. There was very little interaction between residents and family. In fact, one of the authors observed that in most homes there was not merely "a lack of interaction, but a lack of *any* activity whatever" (p. 5).
2. Regimentation and uniformity were common, e.g., certain days were set aside for shaving and others for bathing.
3. In many cases, there was no interaction between residents and other persons or facilities within the community.

Luchins summarized his observations by stating:

. . . it is my opinion that those who think foster home placement enables a patient to escape the disadvantages of an institutional life are mistaken. Foster homes can be as institutionalized as hospitals are, while lacking the compensatory advantages that some hospitals might possess (p. 14).

Time magazine (1973, p. 74) described deinstitutionalization experiences in California:

. . . chronically ill patients have been returned to communities poorly equipped to provide adequate treatment. With no one to care for them, former patients have ended up on welfare rolls, in boarding houses, cheap hotels, and even jail.

and in New York:

. . . since New York state started emptying its mental hospitals of thousands of inmates six years ago, many of them have been jammed into tiny rooms, basements, and garages, and fed a semi-starvation diet of rice and chicken necks. . . . they are taken from the steps of mental institutions by operators who jam them into what can only be described as a private jail and confiscate their monthly welfare checks.

While it cannot be ascertained whether *Time* was referring to the mentally retarded as well as to the mentally ill, the circumstances associated with many of the placements of the retarded over the past several years have been similar.

These comments are not made to condemn the idea of community placement for retarded persons. Nor are they intended, in any way, to justify inadequate practices or services in residential facilities. These statements do, however, clearly demonstrate that any program, regardless of the facility or location in which it is being implemented, must be assessed only in terms of individual needs. According to the National Association of Superintendents of Public Residential Facilities for the Mentally Retarded (1974, pp. 2-3):

While the Association advocates without reservation the rights of the retarded to live in the least restrictive environment and to enjoy fully the benefits of a free and open society whenever possible, it does express concern over the manner in which this goal is being realized. First, the quality of community programs and services being offered to the mentally retarded and other developmentally disabled persons in many parts of the country is inadequate. All too often, "community back wards" and "closeting" are being substituted for institutional "warehousing". Neither community nor residential back wards or "closeting" are justified: the rights of the retarded must be respected wherever they reside. In essence, the Association calls attention to the need not only for continued upgrading of residential facilities . . . but also for a greater interest in quality control for developing community programs.

ROLES AND FUNCTIONS

The respective roles and functions of the community and one of its agencies, the resi-

Table 1. Basic community and residential services

Community services	Residential services

Services which must be available:

1. Adequate home-like environment:
   a. Natural home
   b. Foster home
   c. Group home
   d. Nursing home
   e. Independent living facility
2. Health services
3. Education and training
4. Employment (open or sheltered)
5. Mobility

1. Specialized diagnosis and evaluation
2. Specialized short-term training and treatment program
3. Specialized extended care
4. Specialized back-up and technical consultancy services

Services which should be available:

1. Recreational
2. Religious
3. All other services available to any citizen, e.g., commercial, welfare, family counseling, and protective

dential facility, are outlined in Table 1. No attempt has been made to record all services which should be available. Extensive listings can be found in a number of publications, e.g., President's Panel on Mental Retardation (1962) and the NARC Residential Services and Facilities Committee (1974).

Community services listed have been divided into two categories: those which *must* be available and those which *should* be available. Services which *must* be available include an adequate living environment, health services, training and education if appropriate, some form of employment for older retarded persons, and mobility. The latter is important. The individual not only should be in a position to move freely within the community, but should be trained and encouraged to do so whenever possible, consistent with his needs and desires. Some operators of group and nursing homes are

hesitant to permit residents to leave the premises in fear of potential liability suits or negative public reaction in the event of an accident.

Services which should be available, include any service offered to the general citizenry. The distinction between what must be and what should be available is important. Occasionally, one will encounter residential staff who believe firmly that a retarded person should not be returned to the community until all desired services are developed. Under such circumstances, few retarded persons would ever leave the residential setting. In essence, one has to weigh the advantages of increased opportunities for independence, freedom, and privacy against those residential programmatic offerings which might be lost by an individual when placed in the community.

If the community is capable of providing primary services and programs required by retarded persons, what will be the future role of a residential facility? It can be summarized in one word—specialization.[1] It is anticipated that most residential facilities will function as regional centers, offering specialized short-term, intensive treatment programs; specialized extended care and developmental training for severely and profoundly retarded, multiply handicapped persons; and specialized back-up and consultancy services. One of the primary functions of the residential facility in the future will be to prevent institutionalization.

SUCCESSFUL DEINSTITUTIONALIZATION— FIVE INTEGRANTS

The development of adequate community programs for the retarded, the return of many retarded persons to non-residential settings, and the realization of appropriate roles and functions by both the community and residential facility require five integrants. These are shown in Fig. 2.

---

[1] The position statements of the National Association of Superintendents of Public Residential Facilities for the Mentally Retarded (1974) include a more comprehensive discussion of the future role of residential facilities.

Fig. 2. Integrants to effective programming.

1. There must exist on a local or regional level a visible agency or body with *statutory* authority to plan, implement, and coordinate programs for the retarded. These agencies must be *legally* accountable for services offered to the retarded in general and each individual in particular. (Wisconsin recently passed legislation to create community boards on a county level with the full authority, responsibility, and accountability to provide the 16 services associated with the Federal developmental disabilities act—P.L. 91-517: evaluation, diagnosis, treatment, day programs, training, education, sheltered employment, recreation, personal care, domiciliary care, special living arrangements, counselling, information and referral, follow-up, protective and other sociological services, and transportation. As of January 1, 1974, all state funds, excluding those for public schools and public residential facilities, were channeled through those boards and their professional staffs. There is nothing new about the concept of local boards. Many states have tried similar arrangements, usually with minimal success. The difference is that in Wisconsin the boards have statutory sanction and control over funding. Since their establishment there has been considerable local activity in providing a variety of services to the retarded and other developmentally disabled persons.)

2. An independent standard-setting and monitoring agency must be created. This can be accomplished in several ways: by establishing within the state an independent standard-setting group; by assigning such a task to a state agency; or by requiring accreditation through the Accreditation Council for Facilities for the Mentally Retarded. The essential ingredient is that the setting of standards and their evaluation reflect only the needs of the retarded. Inadequate programs should be given an opportunity to improve; however, if the required improvements are not evidenced according to a set schedule, funding should be terminated. While local boards would not set standards, they would retain responsibility and accountability to see that such standards were met.

3. Local boards and agencies must have access to quality back-up services, including technical consultancy. Many communities will require the expertise of persons who have had extensive experience in dealing with the mentally retarded. Hopefully, residential staff, university personnel, and representatives from established community agencies will pool their talents in a collaborative effort to provide the retarded with the finest programming possible.

4. All community programs, including residential, must receive substantial financial support. Neither the community nor its residential facility can provide for the retarded unless it has access to an adequate resource of funding for programming, training, and research. *Quality services are costly, regardless of where they are offered!*

5. There must exist a tough-minded, strong-willed advocacy program. Three systems have been proposed: (1) legal, (2) agency, and (3) citizen. A system of legal advocacy emphasizes the rights of retarded persons and relies primarily on legally trained advocates. The agency advocacy approach, in contrast, vests broad protectorship in a state department or agency. Protectors, who usually are behaviorally trained professionals, have responsibility to "provide guidance, service, and encouragement in the development of maximum self-reliance to a mentally retarded or other developmentally disabled person, independent of any determination of incompetency" (Ohio. . . . 1972, p. 7). Citizen advocacy according to Wolfensberger (1972, p. 12), is defined as "a ma-

ture, competent citizen volunteer representing, as if they were his own, the interest of
another citizen who is impaired in his instrumental competency, or who has major
expressive needs which are unmet and which
are likely to remain unmet without special
intervention."

Of these three systems, all of which have
distinct value, the legal approach is most critical at this time. The retarded should share
the same advantages and responsibilities as
any other citizen in our society; in other
words, their rights must be recognized. The
question of individual rights is a legal matter
which can best be represented by professionals of that discipline. As stated by Gilhool
(1973, p. 53):

> The language has changed. It is no longer the
> language of favor or benefit. It is no longer the fact
> that what comes to the retarded child and his fam-
> ily comes out of the good will and the graciousness
> of others. It is now the language of rights. What
> comes, comes as a right. It is really not the lan-
> guage of love and kindness but of justice.

When the rights of the retarded have been
clearly enunciated and understood by all,
then, they can be represented more effectively by parents and other advocates with
various experiential backgrounds. Until that
time, the legal advocacy system should receive priority.

REFORM

Deinstitutionalization is both desirable
and feasible. A successful program of

deinstitutionalization, however, will require
institutional reform, community reform, and
juridical reform, and legislative reform. Each
residential facility must reassess its philosophy and services to insure that every resident
is receiving a total developmental program,
individually designed, intended to facilitate
community return. Further, residential services, including technical consultancy, must
be extended to the community at large to
assist in developing local programs and avert-
ing the need for extended residential placement, whenever possible. The community,
in turn, must express a greater willingness to
include the retarded in the mainstream of
everyday life and make a concerted effort to
provide adequate services. The juridical system must recognize and protect the rights of
the retarded and respond to existing in-
equities with alacrity. Legislators, at both
state and national levels, also must recognize
and protect the rights of retarded and
provide those laws and resources necessary
to enable them to live as full and rich a life as
possible within the total society.

SUMMARY

Deinstitutionalization is a desirable aim for
all but a few retarded persons, and it can be
attained within a relatively short period of
time. The needs and rights of the retarded
must be recognized and honored in both the
community and residential setting. Although
there has been considerable reform among
many agencies and professions serving the

retarded over the past several years, much remains to be accomplished. We have yet to "bestow the full benefits of our society on those who suffer from mental disabilities."

REFERENCES

Crackup in mental care. *Times,* December 17, 1973.

Gilhool, T. A commentary on the Pennsylvania Right to Education Suit. In *The rights of the mentally handicapped.* Washington, D.C.: National Coordinators of State Programs for the Mentally Retarded, 1973.

Kennedy, J. *Message from the president of the United States.* Washington, D.C.: House of Representatives (88th Congress), Document No. 58, 1963.

Murphy, H., Rennee, B., & Luchins, D. *Foster homes: The new back wards?* Monograph Supplement #71, *Canada's Mental Health,* 1972.

NARC Residential Services and Facilities Committee. *The right to choose.* Arlington, Texas: National Association of Retarded Children, 1973.

National Association of Superintendents of Public Residential Facilities for the Mentally Retarded. *Contemporary issues in residential programming.* Washington, D.C.: President's Committee on Mental Retardation, 1974.

Office of Mental Retardation Coordination. *Mental retardation source book.* Washington, D.C.: Government Printing Office, 1972.

Ohio 109th General Assembly. *Ammended House Bill No. 290,* 1972.

President's Panel on Mental Retardation. *A proposed program for national action to combat mental retardation.* Washington, D.C.: Government Printing Office, 1972.

Stein, J., & Urdang, L. (Eds.) *Random house dictionary of the English language.* New York: Random House, 1967.

Wolfensberger, W. *Citizen advocacy.* Washington, D.C.: President's Committee on Mental Retardation, 1972.

CHAPTER 15

Human rights and behavior modification

PHILIP ROOS

National Association for Retarded Citizens

ABSTRACT: *Behavior modification is beginning to come under attack as violating ethical and legal principles. The nature of these criticisms is discussed and reasons are presented to explain behavior modification's susceptibility to attack. The author concludes that many other approaches to education and therapy raise similar ethical questions. Specific suggestions are presented to minimize criticisms while preserving the viability of behavior modification.*

We are plummeting into a future of accelerating change, a future which is generating excitement, uncertainty and anxiety (Toffler, 1970). The field of mental retardation is not immune to the transience, novelty and diversity which Toffler has identified as the major ingredients of the future (Roos, 1972a). Yet our technology is still in its early infancy. Recent developments in behavior modification (Watson, 1970; Roos, 1972b; Ullman & Krasner, 1965) herald the beginning stages of scientific control of human behavior. We may soon develop a technology which will allow us to shape individual futures and, perhaps, which will give us some control over the destiny of our race.

ETHICAL ISSUES

Behavior modification is being confronted with critical ethical and moral issues; specific programs have already come under serious attack. The litigation against the Partlow (Al-

abama) State School (Wyatt vs. Stickney, 1971) resulted in standards mandated by the Court which included specific reference to behavior modification procedures. One of the state institutions in Florida subsequently came under serious attack by the news media for alleged cruel and dehumanizing practices resulting from a program described by its administrator as behavior modification. These events are not likely to remain isolated instances but could be the precursors of increasing criticism and scrutiny of behavior modification—a trend related to the mounting legal action on behalf of the human rights of retarded persons (Abeson, 1972; Roos, 1972a; Friedman, 1973).

At least three distinct issues must be faced by behavior modifiers. Each has important legal and ethical implications.

Use of aversive conditioning

Aversive stimuli has been used in behavior modification programs for avoidance conditioning, escape conditioning, punishment and classical conditioning (e.g., Tate & Baroff, 1966; Watson, 1970). The most commonly used forms of aversive conditions in-

Reprinted from Mental Retardation 12(3):3-6, 1974, with permission.
Author: **Philip Roos**, Ph.D. (University of Texas), Executive Director of the National Association for Retarded Citizens.

clude painful stimuli (such as electric shock), cost contingency (loss of earned tokens) and time-out (as being confined to a relatively isolated chair for a short, prescribed period of time). The use of aversive conditioning raises three types of important questions:

Are the procedures successful and, if so, are they significantly more successful than other procedures? The answer to this question is obtainable from empirical evaluation; it is essentially a research question.

Are the means used intolerable? Do the aversive procedures constitute dehumanizing or abusive practices? To answer these questions value judgments are required rather than empirical data. Ethics rather than science is the basis on which conclusions will have to be reached. Criticism and legal condemnation have primarily focused on this aspect of aversive conditioning—specific procedures, such as use of cattle prods, have been considered to be intolerable.

Do the ends warrant the means? Are procedures which would usually be considered intolerable acceptable if they are successful in eliminating even more intolerable conditions? It can be argued, for example, that elimination of severe self-abusive behavior warrants the use of painful stimuli, since the damage to the subject is relatively milder and of much shorter duration. Again, these questions are ethical rather than empirical in nature and value judgments must be made in reaching decisions. The making of value judgments is inescapable in such cases, since deciding not to use aversive conditioning is itself a decision based on value considerations which can have major consequences for the subject. For example, without recourse to aversive conditioning, prevention of self-injury or possible death may require indefinite use of restraint which can effectively totally curtail the individual's development and freedom of action.

"Control" of behavior

By definition, behavior modification aims to alter behavior along predetermined, specified lines. The establishment of such simple skills as toothbrushing or toileting is likely to remain relatively non-controversial. On the other hand, modification of complex behavioral repertoires effecting change in what might be described as "attitudes" or "personality" may be viewed with alarm by those who advocate the concept of individual "freedom" and interpret motivation as a product of "autonomous man" (Skinner, 1972). The behavior modifier is open to the criticism that he is curtailing the "freedom of choice of other human beings" by manipulating their "personality." The ethical question can therefore be raised as to what degree and under what conditions is the shaping of human behavior to be socially sanctioned?

Selection of goals for behavior modification

Assuming that the shaping of behavior is desirable under some conditions, the question can be raised regarding the selection of goals or "target behaviors." On what basis should goals be selected, and by whom? There would probably be general agreement that goals should be selected by the client rather than by the modifier, but this principle may prove to be inapplicable in the case of clients who are seriously psychotic, severely or profoundly retarded, criminal, addicted, "perverted" sexually or young children. Situations in which the client is unable to set goals or in which he selects goals which clearly conflict with cultural standards or the client's own welfare raise the issue of determining the conditions under which the behavior modifier's goals should supersede those of his clients.

OTHER APPROACHES

Behavior modification differs from other therapeutic and educational approaches with regard to these ethical issues only in degree. The issues are fundamentally identical. Indeed the basic purpose of such other approaches—including various forms of psychological and somatic "treatment"—is almost always to alter or modify behavior.

Use of aversive condition

Much human learning is the result of aversive conditioning occurring in the "natural" course of events. Fire burns, falling hurts, provoked dogs bite, and when treated with obvious hostility people retaliate in kind. The folkways in many of our subcultures advocate an approach to education and socialization based on letting a child "take his lumps," that is, letting painful consequences modify his behavior.

Many of our social systems and institutions likewise incorporate the use of aversive consequences. Parents typically rely on punishment (physical and/or psychological), time-out (e.g., locking the child in his room or prohibiting him from playing with peers), and cost-contingency (e.g., explicit or implicit withdrawal of love or withholding the child's allowance) as effective means of shaping their child's behavior. The enforcement of laws is based almost exclusively on a complex set of aversive consequences, including cost-contingency (fines), time-out (imprisonment), and punishment (social condemnation, capital punishment).

Many of our specialized "therapeutic" techniques also rely on aversive consequences, although their aversive characteristics are usually implicit rather than explicit. For example, the use of Antabuse in the treatment of alcoholism is predicated on aversive conditioning—drinking alcohol while undergoing this form of "treatment" precipitates a highly aversive physical reaction. The relationship between specific behavior and aversive consequences is not always so apparent, but it is real nonetheless. Insitutionalization follows certain forms of culturally condemned behavior, electroconvulsive shock follows depressive behavior, and lobotomy follows "uncontrollable psychotic episodes." Even the manipulation of the "therapeutic milieu" or the "psychotherapeutic relationship" often involves aversive consequences predicated on behaviors which have been selected for deceleration.

"Control" of behavior

Usually attempts to modify behavior are thinly disguised by use of such terminology as "influencing attitudes" or "changing personality." Our society is replete with examples of systematic efforts to "control" human behavior. Examples included child-rearing and education, military programs, law enforcement, propaganda, religious proselytizing, advertising campaigns and political campaigns.

Counseling and psychotherapy are, in the majority of cases, specifically designed to "modify personality," "change attitudes," "reorganize goals and objectives"—in short, modify client behavior.

Selection of goals

Regardless of the specific techniques used, all efforts to alter human behavior in a specific direction are based on explicit or implicit goals. Hence parents usually want their children to adopt the parental standards; advertising campaigns are designed to foster the purchase of specific products; political campaigns aim to elect specific politicians, and religious missionaries seek to convert persons to a specific religion.

Likewise psychotherapeutic efforts are typically based on (often implicit) value judgments. The following oversimplified list is illustrative of the types of judgments likely to underlie therapuetic activities:

"Secondary process" thinking is preferable to "primary process" thinking (Arieti, 1955).

Heterosexuality ("genital primacy") is preferable to homo- or autosexuality (Freud, 1957).

Interpersonal intimacy is preferably to isolation (Sullivan, 1953).

Insight is preferable to low self-awareness (Rogers, 1951).

Rationality is preferable to irrationality (Ellis, 1973).

Economic productiveness is preferable to economic dependency (basis for most vocational rehabilitation).

Ideologies in the field of mental retardation also embody specific objectives predicated on value judgments. Hence the "developmental model" (Roos, McCann & Patterson, 1970) assumes that the retarded should be optimally developed; "normalization" (Wolfensberger, 1972) assumes the retarded should be as much like the non-retarded as possible; "hedonism" (Roos, 1969) assumes the retarded should be as happy as possible; and certain approaches to prevention (such as amniocentesis) assume it is better to have no child than a retarded child.

The issues raised by behavior modification are no different, than, from the issues raised by other strategies which aim to alter human behavior. Yet behavior modification has been targeted for criticism more frequently and more vehemently than many of these other approaches. Behavior modification is apparently more vulnerable to attack.

VULNERABILITY

In this age of consumerism and increasing insistence on the protection of individual legal rights (Roos, 1972a), it is likely that behavior modifiers will find their technology restricted by increasingly rigid external controls. It may seem ironic that psychosurgery, insulin, coma and electroconvulsive shock therapy flourished for years with minimum public criticism while behavior modification has come under attack relatively early in its application to human beings. Behavior modification's vulnerability may be in part the result of changes in socio-cultural conditions, but it is also a function of the fact that the technique differs in several significant dimensions from most other attempts to change people.

1. The very success of behavior modification opens it to criticisms of "controlling" human beings. Objectives are often achieved more quickly and with greater frequency than with other techniques. The relationship between means and ends is usually explicitly stated, so that the success of the procedures is readily ascertained. Obviously, techniques which do not succeed in achieving predictable outcomes are not likely to be criticized as "controlling;" they do not, in fact, succeed in "controlling" anything tangible.

2. The high degree of specificity in defining objectives emphasizes the "controlling" aspects of behavior modification. Approaches which strive to accomplish such vague or ill-defined objectives as "fostering self-actualization," "fulfilling human potentials" or "serving society" are much less vulnerable to this criticism. These diffuse objectives do not threaten such constructs as "free will" and "autonomous man."

3. By defining their procedures in highly specific and objective terms, behavior modifiers are vulnerable to criticisms of being "mechanistic" and "dehumanizing." In contrast, approaches using esoteric and ambiguous procedures (often couched in humanistic and idiosyncratic verbiage) foster the impression of "art rather than science."

4. Emphasis on clearly stipulated, immediate consequences likewise fosters the impression of a manipulative and controlling approach. Other techniques tend to favor subtle and delayed consequences, particularly when they are aversive. "Manipulation of the transference," use of "direct interpretation," and transferring clients from one ward to another within an institution are examples of the types of consequences, frequently used by psychotherapists, which are less likely to arouse criticisms of attempting to "shape behavior."

5. Finally, the emphasis placed on frankly manipulating the physical and interpersonal environment of the subject renders the behavior modifier more vulnerable to attack as a controlling agent than his colleagues who operate in the relative isolation of the "therapeutic hour." Involvement of families in implementing consistent regimens of reinforcement and attempts at human engineering of physical environments are particularly prone to excite criticisms of behavior modification.

MINIMIZING CRITICISMS

Recognizing that behavior modification is vulnerable to criticisms predicated on deeply rooted cultural values dealing with the essence of man and the nature of freedom, behavior modifiers can adopt strategies designed to minimize these criticisms and to harmonize their practices with these prevailing cultural values. The following principles are suggested as helpful in achieving this goal:

1. Goals and objectives should be carefully selected to reflect the values of the client. In those cases where the client is unable to participate in goal selection (as in very young children, some profoundly retarded individuals, or some seriously psychotic persons), the client's advocate should be involved in selecting goals. The behavior modifier needs to guard against letting his personal values supersede those of his client or inadvertently assuming that his cleint's goals are identical with his own.

2. Use of aversive consequences should be avoided or minimized. Use of painful stimuli, in particular, has been the major focus of criticism of behavior modification. The following guidelines should prove helpful:

a. Techniques relying on aversive conditioning should be used only when alternative procedures have proven to be ineffective and/or when use of aversive techniques is advantageous over alternatives. Positive reinforcement should routinely be attempted as the initial appoach and only when, after a fair trial, it proves to be ineffective should aversive techniques be considered.

b. When aversive consequences are used, they need to be clearly defined and differentiated from procedures which are likely to meet with social condemnation. For example, "time-out" should be differentiated from "seclusion;" the former is usually acceptable as a valid conditioning procedure while the latter is often interpreted as a dehumanizing practice devised for staff convenience.

c. Care must be exercised that the ends warrant the means. The potential value of successfully modifying behavior (e.g., suppressing self-mutilation) must be carefully weighed against the probable consequences of aversive procedures. Particular care must be exercised that value to the client rather than value to his advocate or to the staff entrusted with his care remains the basis for deciding whether to use aversive conditioning.

d. The client or his advocate should be fully informed of the specific aversive conditions which are to be used, and he should agree to their use before their initiation. Rachman and Teasdale (1969, p. 174) have made a similar point: "Aversive therapy should only be offered if other treatment methods are inapplicable or unsuccessful and if the patient gives his permission after a consideration of all the information which his therapist can honestly supply."

3. Behavior modification should be systematically monitored on a continuing basis. The specific aversive conditions being used should be reviewed to ensure that they do not violate general cultural standards. Whenever possible the procedures should be supported by the research literature. Likewise the objectives selected for behavior modification need to be monitored, with particular attention to the long range implications of the procedures, generalization and extinction phenomena, the occurrence of "spontaneous recovery" (Hovland, 1951), and the appearance of "symptom substitution" (Neuringer, 1970). The possible effect of conditioning procedures on the behavior modifier deserves special attention. Procedures which lead to rapid and dramatic changes in clients are likely to be highly reinforcing to the behavior modifier and hence he is more likely to repeat such procedures. Care must be exercised, therefore, to ensure that the selection of procedures is not a function of their reinforcing effect on the behavior modifier. Another important aspect of monitoring is to keep the administrator who is responsible for the program completely informed of all activities. At least one institution superintendent has recently been severely criticized for supporting a program described as behavior modification of which he was only superficially aware.

4. Behavior modifiers should systematically involve key individuals and groups to ensure maximum conformity with contemporary cultural values. As previously noted, the client or his advocate should participate in the selection of specific objectives and techniques. In addition, the overall program should be periodically reieved and evaluated

by a human rights committee (including consumers or their representatives) to assure protection of individual human and legal rights. Periodic review of the overall program by a professional advisory committee, including professional peers, is desirable to assure the validity of the specific program goals and the appropriateness of specific techniques used.

5. Results should be continually subjected to scientific evaluation. In view of the considerable enthusiasm often generated by behavior modification, it is particularly important to guard against dogmatism, fanaticism, "cultism," or reliance on authority for justification of programs. Objective evaluation of results will foster the scientific objectivity so essential to the continued viability of behavior modification.

6. Since the science of shaping behavior is in its infancy and changing rapidly, it is essential that the behavior modifier keeps current of research findings and new technology. He must remain highly flexible, abandoning cherished tenets whenever evidence favors alternative approaches.

7. Means must be carefully differentiated from ends. Behavior modification refers to means or methodology which have the potential for achieving desirable or undesirable results. As Skinner (1972, p. 150) has stated: "Such a technology is ethically neutral. It can be used by villain or saint. There is nothing in a methodology which determines the values governing its use."

CONCLUSION

The growing concern with "abusive practices" refers primarily to aversive conditioning. This concern addresses itself to only the most obvious and perhaps the simplest of issues. Still in the very earliest stages of the science of behavior—a period of gross, primitive technology—professionals are enamored of their own tools, as they catch glimpses of their potential impact on the human condition.

As increasing control is gained over our destiny, behavioral scientists are being confronted with ethical and moral issues which have taunted man since the beginning of history. All ethical and moral responsibilities for the effects of our technology could be avoided by rationalizing that scientists are only tools of society—technicians charged with implementing cultural decisions. Though probably attractive to many, this would be a naive and irresponsible refuge from reality.

The time has come for behavioral scientists to monitor their own activities, to recognize their legal and ethical implications, and to participate in resolving the ethical and moral dilemmas which are confronting the race of man.

REFERENCES

Abeson, A. *A continuing summary of pending and completed litigation regarding the education of handicapped children.* Arlington, Virginia: Council for Exceptional Children, 1972.

Arieti, S. *Interpretation of schizophrenia.* New York: Robert Brunner, 1955.

Ellis, A. The no cop-out therapy. *Psychology Today,* 1973, 7 (2), 56-62.

Freud, S. *Collected papers.* London: The Hogarth Press, 1957.

Friedman, P. *Mental retardation and the law: A report on status of current court cases.* Washington, D.C.: Office of Mental Retardation Coordination. U.S. Department of Health, Education, Welfare, 1973.

Hovland, C. I. Human learning and retention. In S. S. Stevens (Ed.), *Handbook of experimental psychology,* New York: John Wiley & Sons, Inc., 1961.

Neuringer, C. Behavioral modification as the clinical psychologist views it. In C. Neuringer and J. L. Michael (Eds.), *Behavior modification in clinical psychology.* New York: Appleton-Century-Crofts, Meredith Corporation, 1970.

Rachman, S. & Teasdale, J. *Aversion therapy and behavior disorders: An analysis.* Coral Gables, Florida: University of Miami Press, 1969.

Rogers, C. R. *Client-centered therapy.* Boston: Houghton Mifflin Company, 1951.

Roos, P. *Current issues in residential care.* Arlington, Texas: National Association for Retarded Children, 1969.

Roos, P. Mentally retarded citizens: Challenge for the 1970's. *Syracuse Law Review,* 1972a, 23 (4), 1059-1074.

Roos, P. Reconciling behavior modification procedures with the normalization principle. In W. Wolfensberger (Ed.), *Normalization.* Toronto: National Institute on Mental Retardation, 1972b.

Roos, P., McCann, B., & Patterson, E. G. *A development model of mental retardation.* Paper presented at the 1970 Annual Convention of the National Association for Retarded Children. Arlington, Texas: National Association for Retarded Children, 1970.

Skinner, B. F. *Beyond freedom and dignity.* New York: Alfred A. Knopf, 1972.

Sullivan, H. S. *The interpersonal theory of psychiatry.* New York: W. W. Norton & Company, Inc., 1953.

Tate, B. G. & Baroff, G. S. Aversive conditioning of self-injurious behavior in a psychotic boy. *Behavior Research and Therapy,* 1966, 4, 281-287.

Toffler, A. *Future shock.* New York: Random House, Inc., 1970.

Ullman, L. & Krasner, L. (Eds). *Case studies in behav-ior modification.* New York: Holt, Rinehart, & Winston, 1965.

Watson, Jr., L. S. Behavior modification of residents and personnel in institutions for the mentally retarded. In A. A. Baumeister & E. Butterfield (Eds.). *Residential facilities for the mentally retarded.* Chicago: Aldine, 1970.

Wolfensberger, W. *Normalization.* Toronto: National Institute on Mental Retardation, 1972.

Wyatt *vs.* Stickney, 325 F. Supp. 781 (M.D. 5 Ala.) and 334 F. Supp. 1341 (M.D. Ala. 1971).

SECTION THREE

Discussion questions

1. What are some of the "barriers to prevention" that are discussed by Begab and how do they relate to the ethical issues presented by Roos?
2. What are some of the broader societal influences that have an impact on deinstitutionalization as discussed by Scheerenberger?
3. What social factors do you see operating in your world that are influencing clinical progress? Think in terms of both positive and negative influences.

SOCIETY AND LEGAL ISSUES

The right to be human, based upon the principles of equality, is applicable to all individuals. However, this democratic principle is too often violated in relation to the mentally retarded citizen. There is today a significant movement, initiated by parents and professionals, to establish the legal rights of the retarded. It is certainly ironical that these concerned individuals are advocating the "establishment" of basic human rights, when in reality the rights of the retarded under the constitution should be no different than those of the nonretarded citizens. Consequently, the issue confronting society is not the establishment of basic human rights, but the enforcement of the rights guaranteed every individual.

The present section is intended to confront the reader with several social and legal issues facing the public in regard to the role of the retarded individual in society. The first two articles in this series discuss several pertinent factors related to the denial of educational and social rights for the retarded. Elizabeth Ogg stresses the lack of service continuity in community and educational programs. The underlying basis for this problem is reflected in the vague and imprecise standards regarding the legal

rights of the retarded within our social system. The general public takes for granted certain fundamental rights but does not view these rights as basic to all citizens. Ed Skarnulis suggests that mentally retarded individuals have been denied their human rights, not only by the public, but by professionals in the field including social workers and educators. These authors discuss and analyze several issues related to the enforcement of human rights, including the right to due process, the right to treatment in institutions, the right to choice regarding marriage and sterilization, and the right to education. The roles and responsibilities of parents, friends, and professionals are delineated as they relate to the concept of normalization.

Robert Perske expands the present discussion of legal issues to include the retarded citizen's right to individuality and growth. This involves the concept of "risk-taking" in the person's everyday life experiences and, therefore, implies the possibility of failure. The right to fail has traditionally not been perceived as necessary or appropriate for the emotional or intellectual growth of the retarded individual, yet this right must be considered an integral part of the normalization concept. Perske's article is a distinctively unique view of exemplary community programs for the retarded that stress "normal risk-taking experiences." The discussion centers upon the Scandinavian perspective of normalized community living, employment, and interpersonal relationships. Implications for the American system of services are generated.

The misconception that all mental retardation is genetic in origin has, perhaps, had the most debilitating effect on potentially constructive community and educational programs for the retarded. These theories of heredity have resulted in preventative marriage, sterilization, and segregation laws that dehumanize retarded individuals and create irrational public fears of this population.

The next article in this series, by Robert A. Burt, examines the stereotyped sexual imagery of retarded persons through several dimensions. Burt analyzes such controversial issues as compulsory sterilization, child-rearing practices, guardianship, and abortion. The impact of these issues on the retarded individual as a competent and potentially productive member of society has been devastating. This becomes particularly alarming when viewed with current incidence data on the high percentage of individuals who come under the classification of environmentally retarded.

The final article in this section, by Robert L. Marsh, Charles M. Friel, and Victor Eissler, reviews the procedural inadequacies of our criminal justice system as it affects the legal rights of the retarded individual. Marsh, Friel, and Eissler discuss incidence data reflecting the overrepresentation of mentally retarded individuals in the penal system. Legal processing of the retarded is examined as it relates to court trials and incarceration practices. The authors cite the lack of effective training and rehabilitation programs for this population, and recommendations are made regarding the appropriate means for handling the retarded individual in a manner suitable to his or her needs. There is a need, for example, to be able to determine an individual's competency to stand trial and still maintain the principle of due process. This article effectively reflects the problems associated with the lack of mental competence and the intricacies and inconsistencies associated with our judicial system.

CHAPTER 16

Securing the legal rights of retarded persons

ELIZABETH OGG

Indiana, 1968: Theon Jackson, 27, is accused of robbing two women of a total of nine dollars—a charge he vehemently denies. A deaf mute able to communicate only by sign language, and with a mental age of four years, Jackson is held incompetent to stand trial. He is then committed to a state mental hospital "until he should become competent."

There is no cure for mental retardation, so "until he should become competent" is likely to mean life imprisonment. Yet Jackson has not been convicted of a crime. Indeed, the standards under which he was forcibly hospitalized are much looser than those governing civil commitment in Indiana. What became of his right to bail, his right to due process and a speedy trial, his right to equal protection of the laws under the Fourteenth Amendment? No one, it seems, was giving these rights a thought.

Nearly 10 percent of the patients in our public mental hospitals are, like Theon Jackson, retarded, not mentally ill, and the hospitals can do little to help them. More than 200,000 adults and children live in state institutions for the retarded, many of which are hardly more than warehouses. About 21,000 retarded people, many of whom may be innocent, are in jail, where they get no help and are often abused.

Of the estimated 6 million mentally retarded Americans, almost 2½ million are under 20 years of age. Although tax-supported investment in special education had doubled in the past decade, more than half of our school-age retarded children still are not served either by the public schools or by state-funded special schools. How can we square this with our historical commitment to educational opportunity for all?

Rights and privileges which are not written into law but which most of us take for granted—like the right to enter into a contract, or to join a union and work when jobs are available—are often denied to retarded persons.

But how can we accord such rights to people who lack mature judgment; who cannot act responsibly? To answer that question, we must first understand what mental retardation is, and how widely it varies.

WHAT IS MENTAL RETARDATION?

The American Association on Mental Deficiency defines mental retardation as "subaverage intellectual functioning which originates during the developmental period and is associated with impairment in adaptive behavior." It is not the same as mental illness or emotional disturbance, although a retarded person may, like anyone else, become emotionally disturbed.

A person with normal mental faculties may

Reprinted from Public Affairs Pamphlet, No. 492, 1973, with permission.
Elizabeth Ogg *is a well-known freelance writer. She is the author of many Public Affairs Pamphlets, including* Sensitivity Training and Encounter Groups, The Rehabilitation Counselor, *and* Homosexuality in Our Society.

become mentally disturbed at any age. Worry, frustration, shock, dozens of pressures may precipitate mental illness. If the condition is diagnosed early, the patient often can be treated successfully. Retarded persons, however, suffer incomplete mental development, which limits their ability to learn.

Low intelligence and limited ability to adapt to new situations are relative, however. Actually, 89 percent of all retarded persons in the U.S. are only "mildy," so. In IQ tests—which at best are only rough measures of certain kinds of intelligence—they score approximately 55 to 69. If allowed to learn at their own pace, with teachers who understand their limitations, they can be taught social and vocational skills, and can earn their living in simple jobs. They may marry; and they may have normal children. This group, the majority, is called educable mentally retarded.

About 6 percent are "moderately" retarded, with an approximate IQ range of 40 to 54. While they cannot go much beyond second grade in academic subjects, they can be trained in manual skills. They can hold jobs too, but they need living arrangements that give them some supervision. They are classified as trainable mentally retarded.

Only 5 percent are either "severely" retarded, with IQs from about 25 to 39, or "profundly" retarded, with IQs below 25. They require constant care.

Clearly, there is no logical basis for denying legal rights to the vast majority of retarded persons. They are much more like than unlike normal people. They can develop their potentials through appropriate education, work and support themselves, vote, and live in the community, like most people, if they are allowed to.

Whether or not retarded persons can enjoy their legal rights now depends largely on geography and on the decisions of local officials. Important victories have been won for them recently in some states; but in most states their rights still are not recognized, much less guaranteed.

THE OBSTACLE COURSE

To see what this means, let us follow the obstacle course encountered by a typical mildly retarded boy and his parents. Joey Norton lives in a small Pennsylvania town, where his father owns a hardware store. Had Mr. Norton taken out a family insurance policy while his wife was pregnant with Joey, the unborn child would automatically have been included for standard health coverage. But when he finally did so, Joey, then three and already diagnosed as retarded by his pediatrician, was barred from coverage. (Since the insurance industry has no actuarial studies of retarded children as health risks, this type of exclusion seems to be prejudicial.)

An educational vacuum

The Nortons were dismayed to learn that the local schools provided no special education for retarded children. There were too few such children, they were told, to justify the expense of special classes. Nor were there facilities to guide parents. So, hoping for the best, the Nortons entered Joey in the first grade at six like a normal child. The results were disastrous. When Joey couldn't count or follow the teacher's instructions, the other children made fun of him. Humiliated and enraged, he began to hit back. "This child is disruptive and can't learn in a group," concluded the school authorities. They offered instead two hours of home instruction a week—a poor response to Joey's educational and social needs.

A year later, the Nortons enrolled their son in a private special day school in a neighboring city, and Mrs. Norton drove him there daily. It was expensive in both time and money, but worth it, they felt. Joey had lost a valuable two years, but soon he began to make progress. He was able to stay in this program until he was twelve.

Progress in Pennsylvania

Then came another two-year gap in Joey's education, spent mainly watching TV or helping out in his father's store. By the time he was fourteen, however, the parents of retarded children in his state had joined forces. In 1971, the Pennsylvania Association for Retarded Children (PARC), on behalf of fourteen school-age retarded children, and representing all others similarly situated in Pennsylvania, brought suit against the state for its failure to provide them with a free public education. In a court decree, reached by consent agreement, the State Department of Education acknowledged its responsiblity to offer educational programs for *all* mentally retarded children in the state, including those in institutions. The agreement affirmed that none should be rejected, that all are educable in some sense, if only in self-care. It added that:

> . . . the earlier . . . education and training begins, the more thoroughly and the more efficiently the mentally retarded person will benefit from it; and, whether begun early or not . . . a mentally retarded person can benefit at any point in his life and development from the program of education and training.

While a number of educational alternatives were to be offered, placement in a regular public school was to be the preferred choice, placement in a special public school class the second, homebound instruction the third, and placement in a residential institution only a last resort. This is in line with the so-called "normalization principle"—allowing retarded persons to live as nearly normal a life as possible.

No child was to be denied admission to a public school program, or to be shifted from one program to another, without advance notice to his parents and the opportunity for a formal "due process" hearing. This included the right to be represented by legal counsel and to present evidence, such as independent medical, psychological, and educational evaluations of the child.

Finally, the State Department of Education agreed to reach out to find all retarded persons between the ages of 6 and 21 in the state, and offer them access to free public education and training appropriate to their capacities as soon as possible.

Training for job

So, in January 1972, Joey Norton was able to enroll in a vocational high school, where a pilot program for slow learners was getting under way with help from the state's Bureau of Vocational Rehabilitation. A counselor assessed each student's potentials and interests and then, in cooperation with the teachers and the school administration, planned his or her training program. (Since the students were not learning to substitute new skills for old ones lost because of their handicap, but were starting from scratch, the programs represented "habilitation" rather than rehabilitation.)

Joey had a choice of working part-time in the school cafeteria or helping the janitor with cleaning and minor repairs. First he tried out in the cafeteria, but the nosy noonday crowds flustered him. After he switched to helping the janitor, a patient man who gave him a lot of encouragement, he was more successful.

In class, Joey was learning the ways of the workaday world. Lessons centered on filling out job application blanks, rehearsing job interviews, proper job conduct and dress, handling money. Whatever problems cropped up with his janitoring job were also discussed in class.

The following fall the counselor found Joey a part-time paid job, which he could combine with his school work. Three mornings a week he worked as an assistant cleaner in a church. He was elated with his success in handling this job, and with the money he earned.

What of Joey's future? He is 15, and he has ambitions. Like most young people his age, he wants to be independent and live a life of his own, away from his parents. His father encourages him to think along these lines, but his mother worries that he won't be able to cope on his own—that he will meet with social rejection or get into trouble with the law. He would like to own a car. Since Joey is only "mildly" retarded, he certainly could learn to drive and pass the licensing test. But where could he buy auto insurance? When is is 18, he will be eligible to vote. If the Nortons lived in a big city, this wouldn't present any problem, but in his home town an election official, knowing Joey's background, may arbitrarily bar him from the polls In the city, too, Joey probably would be able to get a marriage license without much difficulty. But again, in his home town, a clerk might turn down his application, although there is no law authorizing him to do so.

OUT OF A BENIGHTED PAST

The roots of such rejecting attitudes lie in the past. The hard life of the American colonists left few emotional and material resources to spare for the handicapped. Mentally retarded persons whose families couldn't care for them were boarded out at public expense—often like dogs in unheated kennels—or were thrust into jails. Later, lunatic asylumns and almshouses became the dumping grounds for these unfortunates.

In the mid-nineteenth century, the success of pioneering French efforts to train the mentally retarded spurred similar undertakings in America. In 1848, the Massachusetts legislature authorized an experimental school in Boston to train ten "pauper idiots" for three years. After the trial period, the school was incorporated as the Massachusetts School for Idiotic and Feeble-Minded Youth (later the Fernald School). In 1851, New York launched a similar school in Albany. Within little more than a decade, there were special schools in Pennsylvania, Ohio, Connecticut, Kentucky, and Illinois as well. They were the earliest acknowledgement of state responsibility for educating retarded children.

The pioneer educators were enthusiastic about the possibilities of training the mentally retarded, and they did show that many could be trained. But in their zeal they failed to see that some—the most severely retarded and those with antisocial impulses—would have to remain in institutions indefinitely. They didn't yet know how to differentiate the various degrees of retardation, and how to adapt their training methods to each kind. The public didn't differentiate either, but took the most helplessly feeble-minded as its stereotype for all mentally retarded persons. Sour jokes about the folly of trying to "teach idiots" were all too common.

Eugenics in the dark

By the turn of the century, a reaction of disillusionment, even alarm, about the feeble-minded had set in. Studies (later discredited) of families like the Jukes and the Kallikaks, which showed a high incidence of mental retardation, crime, and delinquency, gave rise to a popular belief that all mental retardation was hereditary and potentially criminal. There was no recognition of how social and economic deprivations can retard mental development and foster antisocial behavior.

The thrust of the movement to "do something" for the mentally retarded thus gave way to concern with protecting society from the "threat" they posed. They must be isolated from society in remote asylums. And to prevent them from passing on their deficiencies to succeeding generations, they must be sterilized.

By the early 1920s, twenty states had responded to these fears with statutes providing for compulsory sterilization of retarded persons residing in state institutions. Ironically, these residents, segregated as they were by sex, had little or no opportunity to propagate themselves, as retarded persons abroad in the community presumably had. Yet the laws, with a total lack of logic, did not mention at all those living outside institutions.

The case of Buck v. Bell

From the outset, the laws were challenged, on the ground that they mandated cruel and unusual punishment, or ignored the procedural rights of the retarded. One case reached the Supreme Court in 1927. It concerned a mentally retarded 18-year-old woman named Carrie Buck, whose mother and illegitimate daughter were also labelled retarded. The superintendent of the state institution to which Miss Buck was committed obtained court approval of his petition to have her sterilized. Through her court-appointed guardian, Miss Buck appealed.

The Supreme Court decision, set forth by Justice Holmes, sustained the state's authority to compel eugenic sterilization for the promotion of the general welfare. The Justice likened this to compulsory vaccination, hardly a precise analogy. His famous comment, "Three generations of imbeciles are enough," reflected the misconceptions of the time. (In fact, the "third generation" in this case may not have been retarded at all. Miss Buck's daughter, labelled mentally defective *at the age of one month*, completed the 2nd grade before she died of measles in 1932, and her teachers found her to be "quite bright.")

The Holmes opinion did at least specify certain procedural rights for a person faced with a sterilization order. They included notice of a hearing, the right to attend a hearing and present evidence, access to a permanent record of the hearing, and the right to appeal. In practice, however, these guarantees have meant little. Without legal aid, a retarded person—who would probably be judged incompetent to stand trial—can make no constructuve use of the right to notice and to present evidence. Yet only seven states appoint counsel to represent retarded persons who are the subject of a sterilization order.

Compulsory sterilization

Over 70,000 operations have been performed under the compulsory sterilization statutes, more than half of them on retarded persons. Today, the number appears to be stabilized at around 400 a year, despite the fact that 25 states still have laws providing for such operations on noncriminal grounds.

The main reason for this decline is that research has uncovered some 200 cases of retardation, only a fraction of them genetic. Retardation may also be due to blood incompatibility, infection, poison, injury, metabolic disorder, growths in the brain, environmental factors, and a large group of still unknown conditions that may be present before, during, or after birth. These conditions

have nothing to do with parental brainpower. Scientists have therefore concluded that even sterilizing all defectives—if that were possible—would not significantly reduce the number of mentally retarded persons.

Legal experts also attacked the Holmes opinion for its flimsy logic and as a violation of the equal protection clause of the Bill of Rights. The revulsion people felt against the Nazi sterilizations of Jews and Poles under the infamous Nuremberg laws of 1935 probably helped to discredit in the public mind the once-popular eugenics theories.

Yet compulsory sterilization continues and so does the debate about it. Some courts sanction it on social rather than eugenic grounds, holding that retarded persons would be unfit parents. It's true that even high-level retarded persons often need help in meeting the complex demands of parenthood, and out-of-wedlock pregnancies do occur—especially among young girls released from state schools for the mentally retarded, whose naiveté tends to make them susceptible to sexual exploitation.

The state schools themselves contribute to problems related to sexual behavior. As a rule, male and female residents do not associate in any way, not even for meals or recreation, and receive no sex education. The only outlets for their sexual impulses are masturbation and homosexual relationships. (Of course, retarded persons outside of institutions may face similar problems.) The more severely a person is retarded, however, the less his interest in sex.

In some schools, the rigid sex segregation is easing. In 1970, two residents of one such school applied for a marriage license. Confronted with the question, "Have you ever been in a state institution for the mentally retarded?", they realized that a Yes answer would probably kill their plans. So they answered No, got the license, and were married. After their return to the institution, their secret came out. The superintendent then took them to court to have the marriage annulled, but the judge sustained it. Another retarded couple decided to answer that question Yes, and were refused a marriage license. But with the help of an American Civil Liberties Union lawyer, they went to court and won the judge's permission to marry.

The judges in these cases saw no reason to deny retarded couples the right to marry. As for the more problematic question of childbearing, most professionals feel that, although intrauterine devices and contraceptive pills are less reliable methods of preventing pregnancy, they are preferable to sterilization, unless the latter is voluntary. "Compulsory sterilization," says one lawyer, "is playing God."

While the furor over "hereditary" feeblemindedness was subsiding, vocational rehabilitation of disabled people were gaining ground. The knowledge and skills developed by federal and state rehabilitation services set up after World War I, and by private organizations, began to be applied to mentally retarded persons. In 1943, Congress made this handicapped group eligible for services under the federal-state program. From then on, efforts to habilitate the retarded became much more realistic, setting modest but achievable goals. While some of these efforts fells short on genuine training, others demonstrated that retarded persons could master a wide range of marketable skills.

PARENTS TAKE A HAND

For the parents of retarded children, however, habilitation was too little and too late. They began banding together, at first in informal groups to share experiences and ideas, then in organizations that created new services for their children—diagnostic clinics, nursery schools and day care centers, social and recreation programs. Soon these organizations were demanding more public services for the retarded and better performance from those already in existence, while they lobbied for changes in state laws affecting their children. In 1951, they joined together to form the National Association for Retarded Children, now the National Association for Retarded Citizens (NARC), which assembled a professional staff to guide them,

and raised funds for research and training in mental retardation.

The question of guardianship

One question of deep concern to parents is who will care for their retarded child after they are dead. State laws dealing with legal guardianship of incompetents are a patchwork of different approaches. Many lump mental retardates with the mentally ill, epileptics, alcoholics, and the senile, and make no allowance for varying degrees of incompetence.

A legal guardian may be a private individual (or group) or a public official. His role is to guard the person or the property of an incompetent, or both. A guardian of a mentally retarded person is expected to see that his ward has adequate living arrangements, clothing, medical care, and so on, and to step in in emergencies. A guardian or property, sometimes called a conservator, is appointed to manage the property and finances of his ward in the latter's best interests. Both types of guardian are accountable to the court.

Parents are apt to think first of a relative as guardian of their retarded child, an aunt or uncle who will give loving care as well as management. But an aunt or uncle isn't likely to live as long as the child. Because any individual guardian poses this risk, a bank or trust company is often proposed as property guardian. But most banks cannot profitably handle estates worth less than $50,000, nor is bank administration of smaller estates worth the cost to the ward. The same applies to an individual trust fund.

Trust funds

To deal with this dilemma, parent groups in some states created trusts for the retarded. In the one set up by the Massachusetts Association for Retarded Citizens (MARC), for example, a parent pays an annual membership fee (currently $20). When the parent member dies, a social worker employed by the trust helps the family—including the surviving parent, if any, or the legal guardian—to plan for the retarded persons' needs and, where necessary, makes referrals to appropriate agencies. Trust representatives visit periodically to make sure the plans work out. As a rule, no direct financial aid is given. However, a bequest of $10,000 or more to the MARC Friendship Trust is invested and used for the named retarded person during his lifetime.

Other trusts have fallen into disuse either because they couldn't insure that income from a gift or bequest would be used solely for a particular beneficiary, or because they couldn't finance both money management and guardianship of the person.

The New York State Association for Retarded Children (NYSARC) has set up a trust with only one function—to manage sums left for the benefit of individual retarded persons during their lifetimes. Three separate funds under the direction of one professional investment firm offer a variety of options to the donors.

Standby and limited guardians

Under the New York State Guardianship Statute, revised in 1969, parents can have a standby guardian (possibly an aunt or uncle) and alternates (possibly a brother, sister, or cousin) appointed to take over the guardianship of the child after both parents are gone. The choice of older standbys and younger alternates promises continuity of guardianship. The statute also recognizes that a self-supporting retardate doesn't need total supervision of his finances. It provides for a limited guardian to manage any large sums he receives, while leaving him free to spend his own earnings, and to contract up to $300 or one month's earnings, whichever is greater.

A retarded person with no brothers or sisters or cousins to be named as successor guardians may at some time in his life be left alone. The New York statute therefore permits a nonprofit corporation such as NYSARC to take on the role of guardian with full legal responsibility.

In 1972, the Ohio State Division of Mental Retardation developed a system of protective services. The agency may be appointed by the probate court as guardian or trustee of mentally retarded or other developmentally disabled persons.

After making a broad study of guardianship for the mentally retarded, the President's Panel on Mental Retardation, appointed by President Kennedy in 1962, recommended that a protective service, organized in one state agency, should initiate all guardianship proceedings and supervise all private guardians. The courts, the Panel said, should consider each retarded person individually and determine his guardianship needs, whether full or limited, on the basis of a complete clinical evaluation. And, since many retarded persons can, with help and through experience, learn to manage their own affairs, the Panel also recommended that the courts periodically review each case to see if grounds exist for terminating the guardianship.

Citizen advocates

Whatever the legal guardianship provisions, certain crying needs of the retarded are overlooked. A relatively new idea for meeting them is a citizen advocate for each retarded person.

A citizen advocate is a mature volunteer who makes a long-term commitment to represent a retarded person's interests as if they were his own. The need may be for occasional guidance in the use of transportation or leisure time, preparation of tax returns, buying a car, or getting a loan. If the retarded person lives a barren life with an unloving family or in an institution, the citizen advocate may be a warm-hearted friend who frequently telephones, exchanges visits, sends letters and gifts. For the retarded citizen who must deal with agencies of one kind or another, the advocate sees that he "gets his rights."

Most agency staff members can't fill such a role. Some may even see a vigorous advocate as a "pain in the neck"! Yet to make the idea work, an agency, an advocacy office, must be set up. Its job is to define the advocacy role, recruit and orient volunteers, establish guidelines for their conduct, bring advocates and retarded persons together, and review their relationships from time to time.

The first citizen advocacy services were launched in Nebraska early in 1970. One—started by the Capitol Association for Retarded Children in Lincoln—has concentrated on supplying advocates for retarded persons coming back into the community from institutional life. The other, a statewide service, buses young advocates to state institutions for the retarded on weekends, and encourages one-to-one and two-to-two relationships between them and residents of the same or lower age.

Although citizen advocacy, parent groups can gain wide support. In Lincoln, for example, many advocates joined the local Association for Retarded Children. It seems likely that, in the future, coalitions of citizens, parents, and professionals in legal, medical, rehabilitation, and social services will work with the mentally retarded persons themselves, to help them win their full legal rights.

Taking matters to court

Although they made some small headway in matters of guardianship, parent groups were disappointed in the uneven results of their efforts to upgrade public services for the retarded.

The civil rights movement of the 1960s added fuel to the fires of protest. Parents and their professional allies—physicians, psychologists, teachers—saw in the lack of opportunity for the retarded another kind of gross discrimination. "These, too, shall be equal," became their battle cry. Their first tactic was to promote legislative recognition of the right of retarded persons to public services and to the public financing of such services. Although most states responded that they lacked the necessary funds, personnel, or other resources, some innovative programs were begun. The differences within and between various state agencies, however, produced islands of excellence while leaving many areas and age groups unserved.

Where their pleas proved futile, the parents resorted to the courts. In the 1970s, they began to sue state authorities on behalf of not only their own children but whole groups of children in the same plight. Such "class action suits" became a powerful new weapon in the strugggle for reform.

THE RIGHTS OF THE INSTITUTIONALIZED

One basic right that several class action suits have asked the courts to confirm is the right to treatment when institutionalized. While treatment can't cure the retarded of their basic handicap, it can and should keep them in good physical health and help them develop the potentials they have. Otherwise they don't stand still—they deteriorate.

The right to treatment

A landmark Alabama case, started in 1971 on behalf of state mental hospital patients, was later expanded to include the mentally retarded residents of the Partlow State School and Hospital. The judge allowed the American Psychological Association, the National Association for Mental Health, the National Association for Retarded Children, the American Orthopsychiatric Association, the American Civil Liberties Union, the American Association on Mental Deficiency, and the federal government to serve as *amici curiae*, friends of the court. After touring the Partlow buildings, experts from these organizations testified to the appalling conditions there. The court found that:

. . . the evidence . . . has vividly and undisputedly portrayed Partlow State School and Hospital as a warehousing institution which, because of its atmosphere of psychological and physical deprivation, is wholly incapable of furnishing habilitation to the mentally retarded and is conducive only to the deterioration and the debilitation of the residents. . . .

An interim emergency order issued by the court required the state to make the Partlow buildings fire-safe at once, and to control the distribution of drugs to residents. Even if it meant bypassing the usual civil-service procedures, 300 new aides were to be hired immediately. This goal was met.

In April 1972, the court issued its final order and opinion, detailing 49 standards for operating Partlow. These included minimum physical, staffing, and nutritional requirements; a prohibition against institutional peonage; a provision for individualized evaluations and habilitation programs for residents, with observance of each one's right to the least restrictive setting necessary for his habilitation; and appropriate transitional care for residents released from Partlow. Habilitation was defined as "the process by which the staff of the institution assists the resident to acquire and maintain those life skills which enable him to cope more effectively with the demands of his own person and of his environment, and to raise the level of his physical, mental, and social efficiency." It was to include, but not be limited to, programs of formal education and training for those able to profit from them.

The judge also appointed a seven-member human rights committee for Partlow which included one resident. The committee was to "review all research proposals and all habilitation programs, to insure . . . the dignity and human rights of patients. . . ."

Although the state of Alabama appealed this case, some improvements were made at Partlow even before the appeal was heard in December 1972. Publicity arising out of the court action helped to induce the state legislature to increase appropriations to the Mental Health Board, and the daily per-resident expenditures at Partlow in 1972 were more than twice the 1967 level. In November 1974 the Appellate Court upheld the decision.

Similar class action suits were filed in New York, Massachusetts, and Georgia in 1972. Two groups of parents brought suit against the Willowbrook State School for Mentally Retarded Children, accusing New York state officials of denying their children adequate treatment, and of violating their rights under the 1st, 8th, and 14th Amendments. Among the allegations in the complaint, which was backed by NYSARC, were gross overcrowding; inadequate diets; overuse of tranquilizers; medical experiments on residents without their consent or that of relatives; solitary confinement under incredibly brutal conditions (five persons were confined for more than a year and three for more than five years); no schooling for 80 percent of the school-age residents; residents forced to perform involuntary labor; and substandard sanitary conditions. An order providing extensive relief was handed down in April 1975. It is based on the theory of "protection from harm," holding that lack of treatment causes deterioration.

Plaintiffs in the Massachusetts suit—parents of Belchertown State School residents, joined by MARC—demanded treatment defined in even broader terms that in the Alabama case. Accepting this definition, the court ordered the defendants to formulate "comprehensive treatment for all residents [of Belchertown] which will provide for adequate and proper medical, dental, educational, nutrition, physical therapy, occupational therapy, psychological, social, recreational, speech therapy, and vocational therapy services." Final resolution of this suit is still pending.

In the Georgia case, brought on behalf of the mentally ill as well as the mentally retarded in state institutions, the lower court dismissed the suit. It held that, while there might be a moral or social obligation to render adequate treatment to patients involuntarily confined in a state institution, this right was not to be found in the U.S. Constitution. On appeal by the plaintiffs, the case was heard in conjunction with the Alabama right-to-treatment suit. The decision was reversed.

Freedom from involuntary servitude

Both the Alabama and New York cases exposed the practice of forcing residents to perform services for the upkeep of the institution—labor which otherwise would be done by workers hired under contract. This practice is sometimes defended as habilitation, but no real training is involved. A class action in Tennessee, filed in February 1972 on behalf of four residents of Clover Bottom

Hospital and School and similarly situated state residents, concentrated on this issue.

The plaintiffs complained that they were compelled to perform services during the entire term of their residence at Clover Bottom, and that such involuntary servitude was still the practice there. Labor of this kind was covered by the U.S. Fair Labor Standards Act, they argued, yet their wages, 6½ cents an hour, were far below the minimum wage set by the Act. Moreover, the failure of the school administration to withold social security taxes from their wages was in violation of both U.S. and Tennessee law.

In March 1973, the American Association on Mental Deficiency and the National Association for Mental Health filed suit seeking to compel the U.S. Department of Labor to enforce the Fair Labor Standards Act for work done by residents of every institution for the mentally retarded in the country. The suit was decided in their favor and the Labor Department issued enforcement regulations.

Protection from abuse

Certainly institutional peonage is a form of abuse. But some institutions for the retarded are guilty of more flagrant cruelty.

In November 1970, a class action complaint was filed in Illinois on behalf of two mentally retarded youths, Robert Wheeler and Dennis Duffee, who had been committed to Elgin State Hospital. It alleged that the defendants—the director of the state Department of Mental Health and the hospital authorities—had violated the plaintiffs' constitutional rights by binding Wheeler and Duffee to their beds in spread-eagle fashion for 77½ consecutive hours, and by forcing them to wash walls for over 10 consecutive hours on more than one occasion, to punish and humiliate them.

The mere initiation of a court action in this case was enough to produce reform. In August 1971, the court granted the defendants' motion to dismiss the complaint, on the ground that they had already corrected the alleged abuses. They had indeed done so, by enforcing new, strict rules on the use of restraints at Elgin. The plaintiffs appealed only the dismissal of that portion of their complaint which sought monetary compensation for their suffering. In January 1973, the appeals court reversed the lower court's decision and returned the case for reexamination of the request for damages.

The right to due process

Nowhere is the right to due process and equal protection of the laws more crucial to a mentally retarded person than in commitment proceedings, whether civil or criminal. In civil commitment hearings, there is often no one to speak for the retarded person. His parents are not always on his side; some simply want to get rid of the problem. At issue are two questions: whether the person should be institutionalized at all and, if so, in what kind of institution.

A class action suit in Illinois centered on these questions. The plaintiffs were all under 18 years of age. One was mentally retarded and all were in the custody of the Illinois Department of Children and Family Services—an agency legally bound to provide proper placement, custody, and treatment for its wards. Yet, according to the complaint, it institutionalized the plaintiffs, not only without due process of law, but also contrary to the repeated recommendations of psychiatrists and psychologists in the Department of Mental Health. These experts hold that the young people concerned are not so seriously handicapped as to need hospitalization—all they require is special care such as might be given in a foster home. The suit was withdrawn when an Illinois court in another case gave institutionalized children who were wards of the state the right to leave institutions and affirmed the state's responsibility to secure placement for them.

The situation of a retarded person accused of a crime is grim indeed. The whole process of arrest, interrogation, and trial is much more terrifying to him than to a normal person. If the police, the lawyers, the judge, and the jury don't know he is retarded, they tend to interpret his flustered, frightened behavior as an indication of guilt. In his anxiety to please, he may make incriminating statements, though he may be innocent. If he is found guilty, a judge who has not been advised of the defendant's retardation will sentence him to prison, where he will get, not treatment, but abuse. At best, if allowance *is* made for his mental level, he will be committed to a state institution for the mentally ill or the mentally retarded for an indefinite term.

Although the mentally retarded make up only 3 percent of our population as a whole, they comprise at least 10 percent of our prison population, ranging from 2 percent in some Midwestern jails to 27 percent in some Southern jails. Some probably are innocent of any wrongdoing. Many, perhaps came into conflict with the law because, being highly suggestible, they were prodded into committing a crime by smarter persons. One lawyer tells of a retarded teenager who was called out of his home by members of a neighborhood gang who knew him. They led him to the place where other gang members had pinned down the leader of a gang they were feuding with. Handing their retarded friend a gun, they urged him to shoot the rival leader in the back. Only too willing to oblige, the retarded boy did so. Of course he was easily caught, and easily persuaded to admit what he had done. Now he is accused of murder—a charge he does not understand.

The Miranda ruling, which requires arresting police officers to remind a suspect of his right to say nothing without the advice of counsel, is meaningless to a retarded person. Even providing him with an attorney is no great help, unless the lawyer understands his client's difficulties in grasping meanings and in expressing himself.

The usual tests of criminal responsibility are of little use to a retarded offender. Temporary insanity—the so-called McNaghten rule or right-wrong test—doesn't apply to him. Nor does the "irresistible impulse" test exonerating an offender who, although aware that his act was wrong, was unable to control his behavior (as in "crimes of passion" or under the influence of drugs). The American Law Institute advocates another type of defense, more applicable to a retarded offender—that he could not appreciate the nature or consequences of his act.

But what of the retarded accused person who, like Theon Jackson, is judged incompetent to stand trial and is then committed to an institution?

Through his lawyers' appeals, Theon Jackson's case eventually reached the Supreme Court. At the hearing before the Court, the American Association on Mental Deficiency and the Council for Exceptional Children, acting as a single *amicus curiae*, presented a brief. They pointed out that, under Indiana state law, before civil commitment of a person judged to be mentally ill, the court must show that this person needs either treatment or custodial care in a mental hospital *to guard against harm to himself or others.* Before civil commitment of a "feeble-minded" person, it must determine that he is unable *to properly care for himself.*

In Mr. Jackson's case, the only hint of danger to others was the unproven charge of robbery, which he denied. Far from being unable to care for himself, he was working at the time of his indictment. Despite his handicap, he had a kitchen-helper job in a local restaurant. Previously, he had worked in building construction. Moreover, had he been civilly committed as either mentally ill or retarded, he would have been eligible for release at any time that the institutional staff decided that he no longer required care for his own or others' safety, or that he could properly care for himself. The brief concluded:

It would better serve petitioner's interests, assuming that the state had a sufficiently compelling case for conviction, to be convicted and sentenced to a term which he could then satisfy rather than to be committed to a limbo status of quasi-criminal, quasi-insane—bad and mad—from which he might never hope to emerge.

In June 1972, three and one-half years after Mr. Jackson's indictment, the Supreme Court handed down its opinion. It read in part:

. . . a person charged by a State with a criminal offense who is committed solely on account of his incapacity to proceed to trial cannot be held more than the reasonable period of time necessary to determine whether there is a substantial probability that he will attain that capacity in the foreseeable future. If it is determined that this is not the case, then the State must either institute the customary civil commitment proceeding that would be required to commit indefinitely any other citizen, or release the defendant.

Shortly afterward, Theon Jackson was released.

A RIGHTFUL PLACE IN THE COMMUNITY

Class actions have also achieved sizable gains for retarded persons living in the community. The rights affirmed by these suits promise to keep more and more mentally retarded persons out of institutions and permit them to lead relatively normal lives. In addition to those rights mentioned—education, employment, voting, housing—a normal life means the right to enjoy the same privileges as any other citizen. These include obtaining licenses, insurance, recreation, for example, on a nondiscriminatory basis.

The right to education

Education is crucial to living a normal life. As we have seen, the Pennsylvania right-to-education case led to a consent agreement, with the State Department of Education undertaking to provide free education for all retarded young people in the state. More far-reaching in its implications was a 1972 class action suit against the District of Columbia Board of Education, which affirmed the constitutional right of every child to individually appropriate public education, regardless of mental, physical, or emotional handicap.

In ruling in March 1973, however, that unequal educational systems based on property taxes are not invidiously discriminatory, a 5-4 majority of the Supreme Court ruled that education is *not* a fundamental constitutional right, and tossed back to the states and municipalities the problem of how it should be financed.

Since the D.C. court's decision was not appealed, however, its decrees presumably stand. It ordered the school board to offer educational facilities within 30 days to all identified plaintiffs; to set up procedures to guarantee that no pupil would be assigned to a special education program or be suspended from school for more than two days without a formal hearing; to prepare a comprehensive written plan for special education facilities; and to identify the plaintiffs [the children] in need of such facilities within 45 days. The judge warned that he would appoint an educational expert as a special "master" if his order was not carried out.

The court's ruling demolished the familiar excuse of lack of funds that educational authorities offered for not serving the retarded. It stated:

If sufficient funds are not available to finance all of the services and programs that are needed and desirable in the system, then the available funds must be expended equitably in such a manner that no child is entirely excluded from a publicly supported education consistent with his needs and ability to benefit therefrom.

Recognizing the normalization principle, the court stressed that among alternative programs, placement in a regular public school class with appropriate supplementary services was preferable to placement in a special school class.

Civil rights for retarded persons

Artificial barriers to employment and voting, such as discrimination against minority groups, are forbidden by federal civil rights laws. Illinois, Michigan, New Jersey, and Rhode Island now have statutes extending this prohibition against discrimination to the mentally retarded. In Illinois, for example, a General Civil Rights and Right to Work law contains a provision for the "prevention of discrimination among persons by reason of . . . physical or mental handicap." It covers discrimination in voting as well as employment.

In a period of general unemployment, it might seem unwise to push for retarded persons' right to work. Yet, it has been found that they gladly fill tedious, repetitive jobs that normal workers don't want, and generally stick with them, so there is little turnover. Many unskilled and semiskilled jobs are available in the service areas of hotels, hospitals, and laundries; butchers and bakers need helpers; there is a chronic labor shortage in plant nurseries and grounds maintenance services; domestics are in short supply. Educable retarded persons (89 percent of all retarded persons), with appropriate training, can fill all these jobs. And in sheltered workshops, many others who are trainable can do useful, paid work on industry subcontracts, such as assembling ball-point pens or toys, and enjoy a sense of achievement.

The right to the least restrictive alternative

As we have seen, judges in Pennsylvania and the District of Columbia have affirmed the right of retarded children to the least restrictive (most normal) alternative in education. A struggle is now underway to apply the same rule to placement.

Retarded persons for whom the least re-

U.N. DECLARATION ON THE RIGHTS OF MENTALLY RETARDED PERSONS

. . . *Proclaims* this Declaration . . . and calls for national and international action to ensure that it will be used as a common basis and frame of reference for the protection of these rights:

1. The mentally retarded person has, to the maximum degree of feasibility, the same rights as other human beings.
2. The mentally retarded person has a right to proper medical care and physical therapy, and to such education, training, rehabilitation, and guidance as will enable him to develop his ability and maximum potential.
3. The mentally retarded person has a right to economic security and to a decent standard of living. He has a right to perform productive work or to engage in any other meaningful occupation to the fullest possible extent of his capabilities.
4. Whenever possible, the mentally retarded person should live with his own family or with foster parents and participate in different forms of community life. The family with which he lives should receive assistance. If care in an institution becomes necessary, it should be provided in surroundings and other circumstances as close as possible to those of normal life.
5. The mentally retarded person has a right to a qualified guardian when this is required to protect his personal well-being and interests.
6. The mentally retarded person has a right to protection from exploitation, abuse, and degrading treatment. If prosecuted for any offense, he shall have a right to due process of law with full recognition being given to his degree of mental responsibility.
7. Whenever mentally retarded persons are unable, because of the severity of their handicap, to exercise all their rights in a meaningful way, or it should become necessary to restrict or deny some or all of these rights, the procedure used for that restriction or denial of rights must contain proper legal safeguards against every form of abuse. This procedure must be based on an evaluation of the social capability of the mentally retarded person by qualified experts and must be subject to periodic review and to the right of appeal to higher authorities.

—20 December 1971

strictive alternative consistent with their needs and capabilities would be to live in a group home, with a "house parent" as supervisor, still meet with community opposition. In a residential area in a Connecticut town, for example, when eight airline stewardesses rented a house together, no one complained that the zoning ordinance was being flouted. But when the women moved out and the house was sought as a group home for retarded workers, the zoning ordinance was invoked to bar them. Similar protests often greet the plan to establish a sheltered workshop in a given neighborhood.

Some of these obstacles to deinsitutionalizing retarded persons can be removed through community education. It is essential to convince people that the retarded are no threat, if they've had social and vocational training. Regardless of IQ, they can live in a group home similar to the halfway houses for patients discharged from mental hospitals. In one such experiment, arrangements were made for the residents' pay checks to be paid into a bank, which then apportioned the money for various purposes. For example, cash handed to a depositor in a red envelepe was for rent, cash in a blue envelope for board, and so on. Once people learn about the effectiveness of such schemes, and understand their human value—as well as the tax savings that result when mentally retarded residents remain in the community rather than in institutions—they may be less reluctant to have retarded persons as neighbors.

Even so, in many places, zoning ordinances that outlaw occupancy by unrelated persons remain a roadblock to the retarded person's return to the community. If persuasion doesn't move a city planning commission, a court action may be necessary. One such suit is now in process against the San Francisco Planning Commission.

THE BALANCE SHEET

Our mentally retarded citizens have come a long way in the last two decades. Thanks to the leadership of the National Association for Retarded Children and its affiliates, and the President's Committee on Mental Retardation, more people today understand that mental retardation is not a disgrace but a misfortune that can happen in any family— President Kennedy had a retarded sister, General de Gaulle a retarded daughter. There is wider public awareness, too, of the potential of many retarded persons for full citizenship.

Perhaps the gain that means most for the future is the growing acceptance of the normalization principle in the field of law— international, national, and state. This principle is strongly affirmed in the Declaration on the Rights of Mentally Retarded Persons, adopted by the United Nations General Assembly in December 1971. It is honored in two bills now before Congressional committees—the Javits bill in the Senate and the Vanik bill in the House. And as we have seen, the courts and legislatures of several states have acted to normalize the lives of retarded persons as much as possible in education, in institutions, in voting, and in work opportunities.

But judges' orders and legislative enactments are not enough. Before the lives of the retarded can indeed be normalized, and developed to their greatest possible potential, we must see that the orders and statutes are fully implemented.

"We have committed the nation's third century," said President Nixon in 1970, "to the quality of life." As long as we continue to deny retarded persons their full legal and civil rights, can that commitment become a reality?

CHAPTER 17

Noncitizen: plight of the mentally retarded

ED SKARNULIS
Eastern Nebraska Community Office of Retardation

Revelation of the deplorable conditions that exist in this country's residential programs for the mentally retarded has, after years of public indifference to the problem, triggered a lively reaction. Public uproar over the situation at Willowbrook—one of the residential institutions for the mentally retarded in New York State—and a national fund-raising telecast are examples of this awakening concern. Despite this, many people tend to deny the reality of the injustices, perhaps because they either have a relative who is mentally retarded or a relative who works in that field.

When scandalous conditions are revealed, one hears such statements as: "That's probably an isolated example; at least our son is being cared for properly." Or "It's nice to know *our* state has a good institution." Or "How can these people do such things?" Even with such wholesale denial, litigation is currently being carried on in at least ten states charging that the rights of mentally retarded persons are being denied. The evidence presented and its repeated documentation of atrocities is incontrovertible.

Recent court litigation at the state level has proposed the right to treatment, the right to

Reprinted with permission of the National Association of Social Workers, from Social Work, vol. 19, No. 1 (January 1974), pp. 56-62.
Ed Skarnulis, MSW, is Director of Family Resource Services, Eastern Nebraska Community Office of Retardation, Omaha, Nebraska.

the least restrictive alternative in the provision of services, and the right to education for mentally retarded citizens. Court action concerning civil rights and consumer rights is bound to bring social service for the mentally retarded to the attention of the community.

Adams describes the traditional position of social work on mental retardation in these words:

> Stereotyped thinking about mental retardation is disappearing gradually, but a residual lingers in the reluctance in some quarters of the social work profession to invest resources in the care of the retarded—or, where there is willingness, in the recognized lack of expertise in how to provide this care.

In general the mainstream of social work in America has not demonstrated a concern for retardation and its social implications commensurate with that given to other problem areas or with the needs of this client group. Therefore, responsibility for social service to this category of handicap has been borne by a small number of social workers operating in the specialized retardation facilities—mainly the state institutions and more recently the community evaluation clinics. Although a tradition of conscientious and imaginative service has been maintained, the isolation of their professional settings has prevented those workers from making a significant impact upon the main body of social work.[1]

RIGHTS OF THE RETARDED

Historically, the mentally retarded have been perceived as creatures to be pitied, feared, abhorred, or treated as inconsequential. At the opposite end of a confused spectrum, they have been perceived as holy innocents, objects of pity, burdens of charity, or eternal children.[2] Such stereotypes strip the mentally retarded of their dignity as human beings. Worse, the constitutional rights accorded to all United States citizens are selectively denied to mentally retarded citizens.

From personal observation, the author would estimate that at least 60 percent of all retarded children in the country are not getting a public education. Within existing residential programs it is rare to find children attending school, and for the few fortunate ones, two hours a day seems to be the generally accepted standard.

The principle of normalization has been defined by Nirje as "making available to the mentally retarded patterns and conditions of everyday life which are as close as possible to the norms and patterns of the mainstream of society." Although this principle is beginning to affect channels of communication, in many residential programs there is still censorship of mail.[3] Such programs rarely provide books, magazines, or newspapers. Furthermore, for those children or adults who are unable to read, there is virtually no provision for someone to read to them, nor are there "talking books" for the retarded who are blind.

All children, and frequently adults, must obtain permission from parents or guardians before they are exposed to basic sex information. In most residential programs males and females are strictly segregated. An inviolate taboo against sexual intercourse prevents the dissemination of information about sexual relations and denies distribution of contraceptive devices to all but the most promiscuous. In other words, the system rewards those who cleverly escape the rules. If pregnancy does occur, a retarded woman does not have the right to an abortion that a nonretarded woman would have. She can obtain an abortion only if her parents allow it. Not to allow a woman to have an abortion is to use childbirth as a form of punishment.[4]

According to Douglass, the executive director of the President's Committee on Mental Retardation, de facto sterilization is still a reality.

Although there has been a significant decline in sterilization in retarded persons during the last 30 years, several hundred such operations still take place each year. Even when these are supposedly done on a voluntary basis, one must be skeptical whether true consent has been given. What about cases where a woman is told she can be released from an institution if she will "consent" to be sterilized? The American Neurological Association warned against this more than 35 years ago, and as recently as 1968, this very issue came up to the U.S. Supreme Court from Nebraska, but was not ruled upon. It was interesting to note that what prompted the order to sterilize the Nebraska woman as a condition of her release was the fact that her existing children were provided for largely by public aid. Apparently, the old chestnut of perpetuating poor stock has given way to fear of simply perpetuating the poor.[5]

Within existing residential programs, there is a widely circulated myth that mentally retarded citizens are receiving expert vocational training, medical services, educational services, and psychiatric care. It has assumed that these citizens are provided with adequate food, shelter, and clothing. Professionals in the field claim that the mentally retarded are "special" people who need the extraordinary complex array of services that the residential programs ostensibly provide. But is this true? Evidence is pouring in from all over the world that mentally retarded persons respond better to "normalized" environments—that in the vast majority of cases, by being placed in "special" environments, they are actually deprived of growth-producing experiences. Current litigation has raised a second question: Even if there is a need for "special" services, are they truly being provided? Blatt comments on the conditions that exist in these institutions as follows:

Why have I seen a state school superintendent who did not call for a post mortem, an inquiry, or even a staff conference to determine the possibility of negligence or other unusual circum-

stances surrounding the death of a severely retarded child who choked when an attendant fed
her a whole, hard-boiled egg?

Why have I seen a severely retarded ambulatory resident; stabbed in the testicles by an unknown assailant while he slept, and who almost
died because the night attendant bandaged him as
best she could, with no one doing anything else for
the wound until ten hours later?

Why have I seen children at the state school go
to bed each night wearing dungarees instead of
pajamas, on mattresses without sheets, without
pillows, and not one child "owning" even a single
article of clothing? Why have I seen children lying
on filthy beds, uncovered, flies crawling all over
them?[6]

RIGHTS OF PARENTS

In sanctioning a total denial of rights to the
mentally retarded, society was presented
with the quandary of assigning those ex-
tracted rights. The perception of the mentally
retarded as "eternal children" facilitated del-
egating to their parents not only the authority and responsibility that they already exercised over their nonretarded children, but a
godlike absolute power.

The doctor's traditional concern for his patient
seems to have been displaced by his concern for
the parents, the patient's family or even the community. In other words, once the initial diagnosis
is made and the retardate is neatly classified, the
role of the physician, as it pertains to treatment,
becomes focused on the parents. If one believes
what is being written it would almost seem it is the
parents rather than the retardate who is deemed
to be in greatest need of treatment.[7]

All children are subject to the dictates of
their parents. Rubin, an attorney for the National Council on Crime and Delinquency,
observes:

Parents have the right to beat their children.
The law—including presumably protective
juvenile court laws—gives other custodians of
children parental rights including beating the
children. A commission has recently prepared a
proposed new federal criminal code. One section
provides that the person responsible for the care
and supervision of a minor under 18, or a teacher
or other person responsible for the care and
supervision of such a minor, may use force upon
the minor "for the purpose of safeguarding or

promoting his welfare, including prevention and
punishment of his misconduct, and the maintenance of proper discipline." It is marvelous how
what is honestly called punishment of a child in
one breath is also said to be "promoting his welfare" in another.[8]

If a child is retarded, society's sanction of
parental power extends even further. In
1971, the parents of a Down's syndrome
child chose to forego a simple surgical procedure designed to keep the child alive. The
attending physician and staff were instructed
to withhold nourishment; it took fifteen days
before the baby became so dehydrated that
he died. Another couple has said that if they
could find a place where their mentally retarded child could be taken and put to sleep
forever, they would do so. These same parents have steadfastly refused to provide training programs that would strengthen the
child's body, to purchase medication to make
it easier for the child to breathe, or even
name the baby.[9]

Another case exemplifying the extent of
parental power, even when the offspring has
reached adulthood, is that of June, who is
mildly retarded, has no health problems, and
is one of the outstanding employees of the
dietary department at the institution where
she is a resident. Her behavior is above re-
proach and she frequently assists in the care
of other residents. Her eligibility for placement in the community seems irrefutable.
However, June is the offspring of a brother
and a sister living in one of the metropolitan
areas of the state. The family is wealthy and
politically prominent. Shortly after she was
born, June was placed in the institution; her
parents went on to build their separate lives
and became established in the power structure of the state. Attempts by the institution's social service department to place June
in the community have been rebuffed by the
superintendent and on at least one occasion
by the governor.

A further example of abridged rights is illustrated by the case of a young man named
Al. The court committed Al to a state institution at the age of three, and he has lived
there for twenty-three years. His parents

have never visited him and are living outside the state. Although his acceptance into a vocational and residential program in the county is assured, the director of social services at the institution insists that permission for placement must be obtained from the parents. The parents refuse. Thus, even though Al has passed his majority, is court comitted (and therefore technically a ward of the state), and even though the parents have not seen him in twenty-three years, their wishes have to be followed.

The laws operate on the premise that institutionalization is for the benefit of the child. Indeed, many urge that the parents' application for commitment be made as easy as possible. Yet it would seem that a great many people are institutionalized less for their own benefit than for the comfort of others.[10]

RIGHTS OF PROFESSIONALS

As agents of society, social workers have supported the parents of the mentally retarded child in making their decision to institutionalize him. Professional involvement began as an acquiescence to parental requests for help, but developed into open support and encouragement for residential placement. Concurrently, institutional involvement degenerated often from a temporary provision of educational services to placement for life.

Social workers became agents who could translate society's prejudices into the professional jargon required for admission to a residential facility. They assuaged parents' guilt, placated the conscience of society at large, and lent an air of respectability to specious admission procedures. Menolascino made a study of ninety-five randomly selected individuals at an institution for the mentally retarded and identified eight reasons for admission:

1. Realistic family parameters, e.g., mother suffered postpartum cerebral hemorrhage with resultant diplegic status; seven other children currently at home; three other preschoolers in the home; marginal income (12 patients).
2. Needs of siblings; predicted on the parents'

impressions of possible social-developmental hindrance to the other siblings in the family (9 patients).
3. Major emotional illness in one or both parents presenting crisis situation, e.g., mother could come home from state hospital if her mongoloid daugher was first institutionalized (14 patients).
4. Recurrent major medical problems in child (3 patients).
5. Overt psychiatric disturbance; most common behavioral complaints were adjustment reactions, signs of a brain syndrome—especially judgment deficits that involved lack of caution with streets, livestock, etc. Marked behavioral reactions, impulsivity, hyperactivity, "driven behavior," unprovoked aggressiveness, etc. (33 patients).
6. Iatrogenic factors; commonly rather dogmatic pronouncements by family physicians, e.g., "Happier there" or "Best for him" (11 patients).
7. Need for special education services not available in the local community (9 patients).
8. No reasons given (4 patients).[11]

All of these rather commonly accepted reasons deserve scruitiny in terms of *type* and *degree* of treatment. If a child were of normal intelligence (and the word "child" is appropriate here since 95.8 percent of the total sample were under the age of 12 at the time of admission), how would these referrals have been handled?

Realistic family parameters

Why was this child singled out for removal from the home? What Solomon-like wisdom dictated which child should be removed from a family? More important, what gives anyone the right to make such a decision? If the purpose of such action is to effect a more healthy family group, how much real impact will the removal of one child have? The expulsion of a child is reminiscent of a witch doctor driving out the "evil spirts" while ignoring the malaria.

Needs of siblings

Under what circumstances would a child of normal intelligence be removed from the family, and what salubrious effect might this have on his siblings? If the mother is devoting too much attention to one child at the expense of the others, would not the appropriate treatment be to provide casework services or timesaving appliances to reduce the disparity? If either the mother or the siblings are exhibiting pathological behavior patterns, must one automatically assume that this was caused by the presence of a mentally retarded individual?

Major emotional illness in parents

Social workers and other professionals often use this as a two-part rationale. The decision to remove the child from his home can be explained by saying that the situation is deleterious to the child's well-being—a valid concern. A more dubious explanation is that a cause-and-effect relationship exists, which presupposes that the parents were "driven" to their present state by the presence of a retarded child. At a recent conference a nurse informed the audience that a profoundly retarded child, only five years old, had already "caused" two divorces and was about to "cause" a third!

Recurrent medical problems in children

Under normal circumstances, Americans mobilize every available resource to help children with medical problems. Emotion-laden newspaper features plead the case, kindly patrons make enormous donations, entire communities organize to help pay the costs. However, in the case of the mentally handicapped, one witnesses a return-on-investment syndrome. Because there is no assurance that the patient's physical health will increase his ability to provide a return on the investment, the medical situation appears less urgent.

We often begin with the noblest of intentions and refer to "specialized" institutions for these "special" children. The fallacy in such reasoning is glaring when one examines current institutional programs. Because these institutions are isolated, they rarely attract competent medical practitioners and the facilities seldom compare in quality to others in our communities. Most important, the attitudes of the staff often militate against the provision of even marginal medical services. Recently the medical director of a large institution for the mentally retarded criticized certain expenditures on the grounds that these children were "human vegetables" who could scarcely appreciate such "lavish" surroundings.

Overt psychiatric disturbance

Menolascino observed that all the children he studied could have been treated more appropriately in an outpatient setting.

Children who perhaps could have responded quite well to outpatient psychiatric care, preferably within a highly structured interpersonal environment (e.g., the family and/or a special education setting) were seemingly admitted to an institutional setting as an alternative treatment of choice—even though most institutional settings for the retarded are devoid or thinly staffed as to ongoing psychiatric services, and poorly staffed as to a close interpersonal contact which these particular patients so desperately need. Thus, institutionalization frequently produces a continuation of, rather than treatment for, such behavioral problems. It also commonly precludes the child's entry into the special education program available in the institutional setting. Accordingly, it will come as no surprise that the majority of the children that we noted in this group had continued to display the behavioral difficulties which have been noted at the time of their admission.[12]

Iatrogenic factors

This category could just as well have been subsumed under "No valid reason."

Need for special education services

A ruling of the Pennsylvania courts confirming the right of children to a free public education may some day make this reason for referral a thing of the past. At present, however, there are gaps in community resources. Only if the residential facility does, in fact, provide special educational services, can this be a realistic basis for referral.

No reasons given

Not only are the reasons for commitment often inappropriate, but there is no requirement to review the situation when the child reaches his majority. In normal circumstances, when a youngster has been committed to a state training school, he is released at age 21 (or whatever the age of legal majority may be in that state). No so for the mentally retarded. At the time of admission a nonjudicial procedure takes place, which usually includes representatives of the parents, the staff of the residential facility, and sometimes the county welfare department or other political subdivision that has referred the case. But the principal party most affected by the proceedings—the child—is not formally represented.

The profession of social work needs to review current methods of providing service to mentally retarded citizens and their families. In referring and admitting case and in giving clinical advice to parents, there must be caution equal to that exercised with other client groups. The community social worker who refers the case and goes to elaborate lengths to justify it, the institutional social worker who allows admission, and the social worker who participates in institutional atrocities share the responsibility for the deprivation of rights of the retarded, for the inordinate power given the parents, and for the failure to create alternative programs in the community.

EMOTIONAL NEGLECT

The mentally retarded have been stripped of their rights. Parents have been accorded supervisory rights and professionals, rather than sharing this responsibility, have found themselves in the rather comfortable position of advising helpless parents but not being held accountable for that advice. Some parents are permitted to choose between life or death for their retarded child. In most instances, however, the choice is not that dramatic; children are permitted to be sent to institutions or stay at home in a back room and suffer a slow death. Mulford defines emotional neglect as

. . . the deprivation suffered by children when their parents do not provide opportunities for the normal experiences producing feelings of being loved, wanted, secure and worthy,

which result in the ability to form healthy object relationships. . . . (Emotional deprivation stunts normal development as deprivation of Vitamin D stunts bone development, producing rickets; as psychic traumata injure the personality makeup and handicap its function, as rheumatic fever injures the heart and handicaps cardiac functions.)

Deprivation of needs is most marked in the realm of human love. It is within the atmosphere of warm, tender, protective love that the infant experiences his first pleasure of human relationship. . . . Spitz has shown that deprivation of this love, if complete, may lead to severe infant withdrawal with only fearful reactions to persons, and final wasting away into marasmic death.[13]

Virtually thousands of mentally retarded children residing in large and impersonal institutions have been emotionally neglected.

An increasing number of court cases may be filed on behalf of such children on the grounds that they have been inappropriately placed. Legal action may also be taken against professionals who ignore existing knowledge of child development and who routinely continue to make unsuitable referrals or engage in program planning based on a stereotyped understanding of mental retardation.

In short, juvenile law and by analogy the law of incompetents does not assume an identity of interest between child and parent where institutionalization is in the offing. The parent may be motivated to ask for such institutionalization for a variety of reasons other than the best interests of the child himself, i.e., the interests of other children in the family, mental and physical frustration, economic stress, hostility toward the child stemming from the added pressure of caring for him, and perceived stigma of mental retardation. The retarded child's best interest may well lie in living with his family and in the community, but theirs may not lie in keeping him. In such a sea of human turmoil, the law cannot presume that the parent's voluntary act is also the child's voluntary act when he seeks to institutionalize his child; the parents' consent may not be substituted for the child's.[14]

The right of a parent to rear his child in the manner he thinks best is not an absolute right. Protective services are sometimes needed and the parents' rights may be partially or totally abrogated.[15] In the past, child protective services agencies have focused on cases involving *physical* abuse or *physical* neglect. However, with the expansion of knowledge in the area of child development, social workers must legitimate court action on the grounds of *emotional* neglect. Continued referrals to dehumanizing programs and failure to act against those programs will implicate the social work profession as one more group that rides the backs of those it purports to serve.

NOTES AND REFERENCES

1. Margaret Adams, *Mental Retardation and Its Social Dimensions*, Studies of the Child Welfare League of America (New York: Columbia University Press, 1971), pp. 52-54.
2. *See* Wolf Wolfensberger, "The Origin and Nature of Our Institutional Models," *Changing Patterns in Residential Services for the Mentally Retarded* (Washington, D.C.: U.S. Department of Health, Education & Welfare, 1972), pp. 59-160.
3. Bengt Nirje, "The Normalization Principle and Its Human Management Implications," in ibid., pp. 179-195.
4. Sol Rubin, "Children As Victims of Institutionalization," *Child Welfare*, 51 (January 1972), p. 9.
5. Joseph H. Douglass, "The Rights of Retarded Persons." Excerpts from a speech given at Glassboro State College, Glassboro, New Jersey, March 1972.
6. Burton Blatt, "Man Through a Turned Lens." Excerpts from a speech given at Syracuse University, Syracuse, New York, 1972.
7. Paul H. Pearson, "The Forgotten Patient: Medical Management of the Multiple Handicapped Retarded," *Public Health Reports*, 80 (October 1965).
8. Rubin, op. cit., pp. 9-10.
9. Paul Wilkes, "When Do We Have the Right to Die?" *Life Magazine* (January 14, 1972), p. 52.
10. "Plaintiff's Brief in Opposition to Defendant's Motion for Dismissal," U.S. District Court for the District of Nebraska, CU-72-L-299, p. 35.
11. Frank Menolascino, "Down's Syndrome: Clinical and Psychiatric Findings in an Institutionalized Sample." Unpublished study, 1972.
12. Ibid., pp. 12-13.
13. Robert M. Mulford, *Emotional Neglect of Children* (Denver, Colo.: The American Humane Association, Children's Division, 1958).
14. "Plaintiff's Brief in Opposition to Defendant's Motion for Dismissal," p. 34.
15. "Due Process of Child Protective Proceedings" (Denver, Colo.: The American Humane Association, Children's Division, 1971).

18

The dignity of risk and the mentally retarded

ROBERT PERSKE

*Director of Chaplaincy Services, Kansas Neurological Institute
and Staff Affiliate, The Menninger Foundation, Topeka, Kansas*

RISK AND THE RETARDED

In the December, 1969, issue of McCall's, S. I. Hayakawa, one of the nation's leading authorities on semantics, made the statement that there are hidden meanings in the word "mental retardation." When this word is used, the thought "how tragic" automatically flashes into the minds of many hearers. This is a paradox to Hayakawa since one of the happiest members of his family is a teenage mentally retarded son named Mark.

There are other hidden meanings in the term "mental retardation." For many who work with the retarded, this term triggers such action words as "protect," "comfort," "keep safe," "take care," and "watch." Acting on these impulses, at the right time, can be benevolent, helpful, and developmental. But if they are acted upon too intensely, or if they are used exclusively without allowing for each retarded person's individuality and growth potential, he becomes overprotected and emotionally smothered. In fact, such overprotection endangers the retarded person's human dignity and tends to keep them from experiencing the normal taking of risks in life which is necessary for normal human growth and development.

Wolfensberger (1969), in his historical

Reprinted from Perske, R.: The dignity of risk and the mentally retarded, Mental Retardation, February 1972, with permission of the American Association of Mental Deficiency.

study of American attitudes toward the mentally retarded, has shown that there was a period of history in which we saw the mentally retarded as "objects of pity." But this period did not last long; soon, pity degenerated into loathing as the retarded began to be perceived as a "menace to society."

Wolfensberger's history forces us to ask a rather piercing question: Why has it seldom occurred to us that a mentally retarded man or woman can be seen as a courageous person? There are those who are; but what has kept us from seeing them all as such?

In 1966, a ten-year-old, severely retarded boy, named Billy, wandered away from the midwest institution where he lived and became lost in the woods that skirted the institution grounds. The temperature was below freezing. All off-duty personnel were called back to the institution to form emergency parties to search for the boy. Two moderately retarded teenage boys, Ray and Elmer, asked a staff member if they could search for Billy, too. The staff member "moved through channels," and, after some time, received approval for the boys to join in the search, and they found the lost boy! At a later-program, the superintendent gave Ray and Elmer special recognition and letters of commendation. By this time, many of the staff were haunted by the fact that there were 35 adolescent boys and 40 girls in the institution who functioned every bit as well as

Elmer and Ray. Since this particular wooded area is not terribly large, they might have been mobilized more efficiently and quickly than the staff.

All this helps one to see the many ways in which the mentally retarded can be denied their fair and prudent share of risk-taking. Many who have worked in the field of retardation for any length of time can be aware of the clever ways in which all of us have built the virtually total avoidance of risk into the lives of the mentally retarded by limiting their spheres of behavior and interactions in the community, jobs, recreation, relationships with the opposite sex, etc. Even buildings constructed for the benefit of the retarded are filled with things designed to help the residents avoid risk. Fortunately, there is a growing awareness and many beginning efforts in America to allow the retarded to assume a fair and prudent share of the risk, commensurate with their functioning.

SOME NEW ATTITUDES TOWARD RISK AND THE MENTALLY RETARDED IN SCANDINAVIA

With the backing of a Rosemary Dybwad International Award from the National Association for Retarded Citizens, it was my opportunity to travel to Scandinavia and study the ways in which Swedish and Danish people have given human dignity to their mentally retarded citizens. During this study, one of the most exciting things I observed was the many new, and different ways these people are attempting to put reasonable risk back in the life of the retarded persons in their midst. Though these attempts are still rather new and somewhat isolated, sound principles underlying what is being done seem to be developing.

The beauty of it all is that new attitudes toward risk seem to be one of the quite unforeseen by-products of Denmark's and Sweden's crash programs for the mentally retarded. It is my hunch that neither the Danes nor the Swedes completely planned or predicted this new and fresh attitude when Denmark passed the "Act of 1959" (Bank-

Mikkelsen, 1969), and Sweden enacted the "Normalization Law" in 1968, (Nirje, 1969).

In this paper, I will present first-hand observations of incidents where workers in these two countries allowed their retarded to experience a reasonable amount of risk. Since we in America, are beginning to struggle with this problem as well, it is hoped that these incidents will illuminate and clarify the directions and attitudes we may choose to take in the future.

PROGRAMMING RISK-TAKING EXPERIENCES IN SCANDINAVIA

Some Scandinavian workers with the retarded are developing innovative ideas to literally "push the retarded out of the nest" as a means of finding new growth. Such experiences in a number of areas of living are illustrated below.

Normal risk in community experiences

Bengt Nirje, the Secretary General (Executive Director) of the Swedish Association for Retarded Children, has developed as a side interest the formation of youth clubs in Stockholm, where both college students and mentally retarded youths serve as coworkers. In four years, the first Flamslattsklub has grown into 24 clubs. Kept to approximately 20 members each, these clubs plan a wide range of recreational and educational activities. To be a member in full standing a retarded person must first learn to find his own way from his home to the clubroom in the center of downtown Stockholm.

Nirje has attempted to build into each club something he calls "hidden social training." Members are required to do for themselves what they have never done before. For example, a group may travel for a special program to a section of Stockholm where they have never been before. When the program is over, they are expected to find their way home alone, even though this involves the struggle of asking questions of strangers, getting one's own direction, finding the right bus or subway, etc. At another time, a day's outing at a particular amusement area may be planned and then the leaders may be "called away," leaving the retarded persons to entertain themselves.

There are a variety of experiments where mentally retarded persons are allowed to live in apartments in the city. The degree of supervision while living alone in these apartments ranges from intensive to none. In a boarding school outside Vingaker, this period of self-reliance may amount to a weekend after which the mentally retarded return to the school to evaluate their experiences. In Flen (also in Sweden), institutionalized persons move into a rented hotel for a period of training and supervision. Later, they move into apartments and live alone.

The different plans for programming experiences of being left alone in a city or of being placed in a strange apartment varies with the region and the agency, but I was amazed at the great number of such programmed risks that have been developed.

Normal risk in industry

Workshop personnel anywhere can be very imaginative in designing jigs and fixtures or in modifying industrial equipment, either to simplify an operation, or to make it safe. In either case, such ingenuity may be the critical element in opening up many tasks to severely impaired persons. However, in our good intentions, one may go too far, and once more lose sight of individual differences in the capabilities of the retarded. To reshape a task that might be performed by an ordinary industrial worker solely because a retarded worker is to perform it is dehumanizing if the retarded worker is capable of performing the same task on the same equipment as safely and/or as well as the industrial worker.

The general movement from basket weaving, ceramics, potholder making, and other occupations of a handcraft variety, to productive manufacture of useful and marketable items has served to expose many retarded Scandinavian persons to the normal risks found in any industry. For example, in the Orebro district in Sweden, I saw a nineteen-year-old mongoloid man sitting at a large punch press with all its mechanical shafting and mechanisms standing ten to twelve feet high. He pushed a button and a mass of metal came hurtling down on the press plate with a thud. There would not be much left of his hand if it got in the way. This type of operation was also observed in Gothenburg, Uppsala, and in a Danish Workshop in Farum.

Throughout these two countries, one can see retarded persons operating heavy-duty punch presses, drills, and saws while they do simple repetitive operations on a Volvo automobile finder, on brass fittings, or on Danish Modern furniture, to name only a few. It was noticed that the risks these persons took were normal for industry in these countries.

In Orebro, the Frykstagarden workshop contains a work force of 15 deaf, mentally retarded adolescents and young men who turn out routine machined items on heavy duty lathes. Their foreman, Karl Bargguist, felt the need to tell me: "That's not easy, you know. A regular worker can hear when the machinery is going to break and fly in his face. These people can't hear. So, I teach them to watch things with an alert eye."

There was danger here! In fact, there was enough danger to put great fear in the heart of any worker with the mentally retarded who tended to be over-protective. But, the remarkable thing about these workshops was that their foreman expected their workers to be safe. For the most part, these persons lived up to the expectations of the leaders. It could be conjectured that there would have been tragic consequences if the foremen expected the retarded workers to get hurt.

Normal risk in heterosexual relationships

In healthy human beings attempts to build close, creative human relationships, there is always a risk and a chance for failure and pain. We have yet to completely evaluate what we do to the human dignity of a mentally retarded person when such relationships are denied. Now, we are beginning to wonder about our "safe" segregation of men and women—sometimes for life.

Bo works in an assembly line for TV terminal strips at the Frykstagarden workshop in Orebro. Approximately 26 years of age, he suffers from spastic paralysis, but has an ingenious way of putting metal pieces into plastic parts using a vice (others can do the same operation much more readily with a hammer). Marie, age 21, works elsewhere in the line; she is spastic also. Bo and Marie look forward to being together in the lunch room. Sara Wendahl, the social worker, pointed them out to me, saying, "they're in love." Slowly these two persons, with professional help, were working out plans for the day when they could live together and make a closer relationship. Because of the spasticity of both of these persons, sex could hardly be a very large issue, but there seemed to be so many other creative possibilities between them. It was obvious that everyone respected these two and their attempts to find one another.

Older men and women with many years of institutionalization behind them are given the chance to attempt a life together when the chance for failure is not terribly great, though in any close human relationship there must be some risk. Many human beings choose to live out their lives keeping distance between themselves and others, a fact also true of many of the mentally retarded. But there are some who would not choose isolation. Throughout Denmark and Sweden, there seems to be a movement away from dormitories of men and dormitories for women, with a "never-never land" in between. Instead, the tender, patient, sensitive building of closer human relationships under supervision was observed in many areas of both countries. The healthy, carefully evolved decisions of these retarded persons were honored and regarded by the helpful professionals as being within the limits of normal human risk.

Normal risk in building design

For years, in both Scandinavia and the United States, when architects were contracted to build a facility for the mentally retarded, they automatically drew up plans for a "heavy-duty" and a "super-safe" facility. In both countries, the building codes have reinforced this attitude. But now there seems to be a struggle to change.

If a small "family" of mentally retarded persons are to be housed in a two-story home, some local governments will demand an outside fire escape, special exists, expensive fire detection systems, and special electrical wiring and plumbing, to name only a few restrictions. If a professional attempts to move his own family of the same size into the same two-story home, these "special" standards do not apply. In both America and Scandinavia, we are becoming aware of the fact that the most human facilities for the mentally retarded are those that have not been built for the mentally retarded. Instead, they are properties built for other purposes and later they are rented to agencies for the mentally retarded.

Sweden and Denmark are now struggling to break this tradition, and have already made much progress in this direction. New institutions for the mentally retarded are being constructed more and more the way homes for normal, happy human beings are constructed. They are being designed with plenty of glass, many doors to the outside, and lots of brigtly colored fixtures and furniture. Beautiful hanging lamps can be seen everywhere, and nobody seems to swing from them—because it is expected that no one will. This new architecture is saying some powerfully hopeful things to and about human beings who happen to be mentally retarded.

Sweden has a penchant for spiral staircases. They are rather beautiful but dangerous. One can stand at the top of one of these staircases and look down at the inner pole and see nothing but a spiral of space curling around and around. Walk down on the wrong side of one of these staircases, and you can be maimed or killed! Yet, such staircases can now be seen time and again where the mentally retarded live.

We are now beginning to learn that there is such a thing as the "language of a building" (Wolfensberger, 1969). We do "say something" to the mentally retarded person who lives in the building that we build for them. We can say: "We will protect you and comfort you—and watch you like a hawk!" Or we can say: "You are a human being and so you have the right to live as other humans live, even to the point where we will not take all dangers of human life from you."

THE NEW SCANDINAVIAN ATTITUDE TOWARD RISK AND THE MENTALLY RETARDED: IS IT APPLICABLE TO THE AMERICAN SCENE?

What is it that we in America who work with the mentally retarded can learn from Sweden and Denmark's attitude of allowing the mentally retarded to experience normal risk? Before an answer is attempted, it might be well to recall how much they have learned from us. In an endless range of situations, they can quote American experts—even to the point where a Swedish man was able to inform me that Henry Ford called his first automobile the Model "T", because it was the first "tempo" manufactured car. These people seem to be the skilled implementers and appliers of a wide range of knowledge from other lands. They seem to do it in the same way that they gather raw materials from all over the world and then design and manufacture some of the most excellent products on the face of the earth. Most of these ideas about risk-taking were not new with the Scandinavians. We have theorized about such things for years and years, but in many cases, they implemented what we often only felt or talked about.

It would be spurious to try to make Swedes and Danes out of Americans. We gave up such "missionary" action years ago. But it would be expedient to watch the hopeful struggle in which the Scandinavians are involved, focus on their attitudes, and see which would be compatible with healthy American life and which would not. God knows, we cannot continue the type of overprotection we usually give the mentally retarded in our country.

The world in which we live is not always safe, secure and predictable. It does not always say "please" or "excuse me". Everyday we wake up and live in the hours of that day, there is a possibility of being thrown up against a situation where we may have to risk everything, even our lives. This is the way the real world is. We must work to develop every human resource within us in order to prepare for these days. To deny any retarded person their fair share of risk experiences is to further cripple them for healthy living.

A book has recently been published in German that could haunt us all (Teufel, 1960). It graphically describes the human responses of children and adults in a 700-place institution at Stettin, Germany when, in 1940, two gray buses with windows painted gray drove up to the institution for the first of many trips. The driver presented a list of residents who were to be "transferred," and then drove them off after saying to a worker: "Soon there will be seventy-five less idiots in the world." During an extended period of time, 322 of the 700 were driven off to be gassed and cremated. But, the most interesting thing in this account is that it makes one aware of the fully human reactions of these people in the face of this risk.

The ambulatory persons became deeply concerned for the non-ambulatory, knowing they had little chance to fend for themselves. Many used their best wits to scout and plan special hiding places to which they fled every time they saw the buses coming up the road. One boy instinctively ran to his hiding place when the critical time came. He then returned after the buses were gone saying, "They didn't catch me, I'm smarter than they." Karl fought with the driver and ran away shouting, "I'll hang myself before I'll die like that." Richard, who was paralyzed, knew he did not have a chance; with calm and purpose he gave his pocket money and watch to his closest friend. He discussed the situation with his housefather, and they prayed together as he made himself ready to die like a man with dignity. "Cool" Emily calmly got into line on the day her name was called and walked to the bus. But, as she came near the door of the bus, she calmly walked right on by and nobody even noticed. Later, when the bus was gone, she returned to the institution and busied herself with her assigned task of scrubbing steps. All this points up how mentally retarded persons may, can, will and should respond to risk with full human dignity and courage.

It is my firm belief that we now need to insure this dimension of human dignity for the mentally retarded and prepare them for facing real risk in a real world. Where many of us worked overtime in past years to find clever ways of building the avoidance of risk into the lives of the mentally retarded, now we should work equally hard to help find the proper amount of normal risk for every retarded person. We have learned; there can be such a thing as human dignity in risk. And there can be a dehumanizing indignity in safety!

REFERENCES

Bank-Mikkelsen, N. E. A metropolitan area in Denmark: Copenhagen. In R. Kugel & W. Wolfensberger (Eds.), *Changing patterns in residential services for the mentally retarded.* Washington: President's Committee on Mental Retardation, 1969, 227-254.

Nirje, B. The normalization principle and its human management implications. In R. Kugel & W. Wolfensberger (Eds.), *Changing patterns in residential services for the mentally retarded.* Washington: President's Committee on Mental Retardation, 1969, 179-195.

Teufel, W. *Das schloss der barmherzigkeit.* Stuttgart: Quell-Verlag, 1960.

Wolfensberger, W. The origin and nature of our institutional models. In R. Kugel & W. Wolfensberger (Eds.), *Changing patterns in residential services for the mentally retarded.* Washington: President's Committee on Mental Retardation, 1969, 59-171.

19

Legal restrictions on sexual and familial relations of mental retardates—old laws, new guises

ROBERT A. BURT

Professor of Law, The University of Michigan

Several kinds of state laws currently limit the freedom of those labeled "mentally retarded" to engage in sexual relations, to marry, and to rear children. In a significant number of states, persons found "mentally retarded" can be compulsorily sterilized, can be denied marriage licenses, or can lose custody of their children. In recent decades these laws apparently have been rarely invoked. This may be because the most likely targets for these laws are those "mental retardates" whom we have placed and forgotten in long-term custodial institutions. Greater efforts are now under way to avoid institutionalization of the retarded. This new emphasis demands that we scrutinize the existing state laws which threaten to curtail the freedoms that community placement for the retarded is intended to assure.

In 1966, twenty-three states had statutes providing for compulsory sterilization of mental retardates. In eight of these, the statutes permitted sterilization whether or not the person found retarded had been institutionalized on that ground. For the rest, sterilization laws applied only to institutionalized mental retardates.[1] As a general matter, however, these laws are rarely applied today. It may be that little necessity for their application is seen, on the ground that life-long confinement in a single-sex unit of a residential institution is an even more effective means of constricting heterosexual relations than sterilization.

In practice, the prime targets for compulsory sterilization appear to be those retardates who are being released from institutions. Some state laws have in fact explicitly required sterilization as a condition for release.[2] Even where there is no state law authorizing compulsory sterilization, it apparently is often imposed as a condition for institutional release, usually with the pretense that sterilization is "voluntarily accepted."[1] (Similarly, state laws removing custody of children from the "mentally deficient"[3] or prohibiting the retarded from marrying—variously identified in state marriage licensing laws as "mental deficients," "idiots," "imbeciles," "feebleminded" and the like[3]—are most likely to be applied to those with prior histories of institutionalization.) There are no reliable statistics available on the frequency of application of any of these laws. The most recent report I have found regarding compulsory sterilization for mental deficiency in this country indicates a decline from 1,643 cases in 1943 to 643 in 1963.[1]

I believe the laws that single out "mental retardates"—or any stigmatized group,

Reprinted from de la Cruz, F., and LaVeck, G. D., editors: Human sexuality and the mentally retarded, New York, 1973, Brunner/Mazel, Inc., with permission.

clearly identified as such—for special restrictions in sexual or family life violate the United States Constitution. The simple existence of laws that aim at vulnerable, stigmatized groups as such presents intolerable dangers of abuse and over-use.

The mentally retarded are not the only stigmatized group against whom special sexual and familial restrictions are directed. The retarded share this distinction with those whom we label "mentally ill" and "criminal." Virtually all state laws authorizing compulsory sterilization of mental retardates apply equally to the "mentally ill"[3] and about half of those laws also apply to "hereditary criminals."[3]

The stereotypes that are projected onto these deviant groups are remarkably similar in attributing dangerous sexual appetites. The Nebraska Supreme Court, in its 1968 opinion upholding the constitutionality of the state's compulsory sterilization law for institutionalized mental defectives, stated: "It is an established fact that mental deficiency accelerates sexual impulses and any tendencies toward crime to a harmful degree."[2] This statement has of course no empirical support. As an expression of popular prejudice, however, the statement could apply equally to those considered "mentally ill" or "criminals."

The prevalence of sexual imagery and fears regarding blacks in this country is a related phenomenon. The laws which forbade intermarriage among blacks and whites—rationalized by a potpourri of genetic and social arguments[4]—have a close kinship with the restrictive laws applied to the mentally retarded. Indeed, one important attribute of slave status in this country (but not, interestingly enough, in the Latin American countries where slavery also flourished) was that slaves were forbidden to marry, and that familial ties between parent and child were disregarded as a matter of course.[5] Mental retardates share with these other stigmatized groups the popular perception of "less-than-humanness" and they, like these other groups, become the target and repository of a cluster of fears that are felt to assault our "humanness" in general. Among these fears, unabated sexual appetite ranks high.

This special vulnerability of mental retardates as an irrationally feared and stigmatized group has important legal implications. It means that, as a group, they warrant particular protection, most notably against the operation of legislation aimed at their sexual and child-rearing behavior. Mental retardates are "a discrete and insular minority . . . [against whom prejudice] tends seriously to curtail the operation of those political processes ordinarily to be relied upon to protect minorities, and . . . [on whose behalf] a correspondingly more searching judicial inquiry [may be called for]."[6] For blacks—another such "discrete and insular minority"—the Supreme Court has increasingly done battle. In this pursuit, the Court has ruled unconstitutional the state laws prohibiting marriage between blacks and other races in a case appropriately denominated *Loving v. Virginia*.[7] This result was dictated by a prior series of Supreme Court holdings (beginning with the famed 1954 school segregation case) which invalidated any form of state action that singled out blacks as a group for special derogatory treatment.[8] Whether or not a similarly broad principle should be followed by the courts to protect mental retardates, their rights to sexual freedom should be judicially protected. The special status of family and sexual conduct in this society has been acknowledged in various Supreme Court cases as fundamental rights "to marry, establish a home and bring up children,"[9] the right of "privacy surrounding the marriage relationship,"[10] "the right to satisfy [one's] intellectual and emotional needs in the privacy of [one's] own home."[11] The Supreme Court has recently stated,

> If the right of privacy means anything, it is the right of the individual, married or single, to be free from unwarranted governmental intrusion into matters so fundamentally affecting a person as the decision whether to bear or beget a child.[12]

These familial and sexual freedoms, which the Court properly sees as the core of the right to privacy, are drastically and wrongfully infringed by such laws as sterilization and marriage prohibitions directed specifically against the mentally retarded.

Some state legislation imposes disabilities only on a specially designated class among mental retardates. The Utah Code, for example, provides for compulsory sterilization, among the retarded, only for those who are "probably incurable and unlikely to be able to perform properly the functions of parenthood."[13] This apparently more limited application does not, in my judgment, save the statute from the vice inherent in all of the restrictive legislation that singles out the mentally retarded as such. However uncertain our capacities to distinguish among good and bad parents generally, this society, and its officialdom, clearly is in the thralls of a strongly irrational attitude regarding the sexuality of the mentally retarded. Our officials share the incapacity of most people in this society to look at the retarded without inappropriate fear or pity, to look at them with sufficient clarity to permit sensible differentiation among them. Because the mentally retarded as a group are so readily victimized, because they are a vulnerable "discrete and insular minority," compulsory interventions in their child-bearing activities which might be tolerable for the general population are constitutionally intolerable if limited to the retardate group alone.

Justice Holmes' famous—indeed, notorious—opinion for the Supreme Court in 1927 upheld a state compulsory sterilization law with the aphorism "three generations of imbeciles are enough."[14] But Holmes' Court wrongly failed to appreciate their special role in protecting vulnerable minorities. A 1942 Supreme Court case, invalidating a state's compulsory sterilization law for habitual criminals on grounds that it made irrational distinctions between those criminals who should and those who should not be sterilized, reveals a different, and more enlightened, Court attitude.[15] The Court has not yet administered a *coup de grace* to these laws, though it appeared ready to do so when it took jurisdiction over the 1968 Nebraska Supreme Court's decision, noted earlier.[2] The Nebraska Legislature, perhaps reading between the lines of the Court's writ, repealed its compulsory sterilization law before the Court had an opportunity to rule on its constitutionality. When the Court is finally given the opportunity to rule on such laws, I have little doubt that it will overturn them.

But this Court action, when it comes, will remove only the easiest problem. Even if my argument here is accepted, and the courts strike down all sterilization, marriage prohibitory and child removal laws specifically limited to the mentally retarded, that will eliminate only the most obvious of legal impediments afflicting mental retardates. Most notably, such court action will not invalidate child abuse and neglect laws which generally authorize compulsory removal of children from their parents. Although these laws apply to the population at large, I believe that they will fall with particular harshness on parents who, by their residence in sheltered homes for the "mentally retarded" (often supported by public funds and thus highly visible to other public agencies), appear to flaunt their diagnostic label and thereby remain peculiarly vulnerable to community restrictions on sexual and child-rearing activities.

Child abuse and neglect laws of virtually every state are sufficiently broad-gauged to authorize compulsory removal of a child from a parent who is regarded as incapable of child-rearing merely because of mental deficiency. The Minnesota child neglect statute, for example, authorizes the state to take custody of any child "whose . . . condition, environment or associations are such as to be injurious or dangerous to himself."[16] Inevitably the fears and prejudices that stigmatize mental retardates will intrude on the judgment of court and social agency personnel who will apply these statutes.

But though these open-ended statutory invitations to state intervention bring this risk of abuse, these statutes cannot be overturned on this ground alone. Numerous procedural guarantees—such as right to counsel and opportunity to rebut all adverse evidence—should be provided to all parents, including the mentally retarded, who are subjects of child abuse or neglect proceedings. But the statutory standards for state intervention cannot be so narrowly defined as to eliminate the possibility of misuse without inappropriately withholding the possibility of state intervention to help children in serious jeopardy from inadequate parenting.[17] The opportunity for victimizing the mentally retarded in the application of child abuse and neglect laws must, regrettably, remain a reality.

This special vulnerability creates an obligation on the part of those planning new modes of introducing retardates into community life to defend their clientele—preferably, in my view, by appending special plans for intensive child-rearing services to any plans for sheltered community living in which normal heterosexual contacts are envisioned. Unless those who specially care for the mentally retarded can convincingly attest to the rest of the community that the children of retardates are being well-bred, it seems that these children will be lost, lost in many ways. The need for these special child-rearing programs seems to me even more urgent than the need for similar programs for those parents in the "normal" population who share the child-rearing disabilities of a portion of the mentally retarded population. The label of retardation threatens loss to all who bear it; it is to protect them, as much as to protect those among the retarded population who all "right-thinking people" would agree are incapable parents, that special protective programs are needed.

A second problem must also be faced. Statutes that authorize voluntary sterilization, abortions, or relinquishment of children present quite troublesome issues regarding mental retardates. The argument for compulsory sterilization of mental retardates founders in part on the uncertainty of genetic predictions. But new advances in intrauterine diagnosis—which permit wholly accurate detection of Down's syndrome and other kinds of developmental anomalies—change the context of the argument.

It seems unthinkable that the state would ever compel therapeutic abortions for the general population, even if development defects were detected *in utero*. But therapeutic abortions for mothers who so choose are increasingly accepted in state laws. Should maternal choice also govern if the mother herself is "retarded?" In what ways can the "retarded mother" be adequately helped to exercise choice? Should someone exercise choice for her? No matter how euphemistically we describe this last alternative, it is compulsory abortion limited to those whom we label "mentally retarded."

Legal authority to make such choices on behalf of mental retardates appears available in the guardianship laws in all states, which authorize the appointment of custodians for, among others, "mentally deficient" persons who are not institutionalized but are nonetheless regarded as incompetent to handle some portion or all of their affairs.[3] The potential for abuse of these guardianship laws is clear.

A case recently decided by the Kentucky Supreme Court should serve as a warning. In *Strunk v. Strunk*,[18] the court authorized the appointment of a 27-year-old institutionalized retardate's mother as his guardian in order to permit her to consent on his behalf to remove one of his kidneys to donate to his otherwise doomed, intellectually normal older brother. The court did not seem troubled by the mother's at best necessarily ambivalent role in making this decision for her retarded son.

But no matter who is given such power of choice over child-rearing for a retardate, similar conflicts—whether conscious or unconscious—are bound to be provoked. Can, for example, an administrator of a sheltered home for retardates address the question whether one of his charges should abort her genetically flawed child, or surrender her normal child, without being influenced by the impact of his decision on community approval of his enterprise generally and the implications of that approval for the welfare of all his charges?

I believe that a retardate who might require a guardian to make, or assist in, this choice is entitled at least to someone who is sufficiently trained and sufficiently detached to view the matter from the retardate's perspective, with other conflicting perspectives banished to as great a degree as possible. The laws and the judicial personnel involved in authorizing appointment of guardians for mental retardates are not sufficiently sensitive to these kinds of conflicts of interest that work against the deserved freedoms of mental retardates. If we intend to offer greater freedoms to those retardates whom we now institutionalize, we must assure that this problem is adequately addressed.

I have no easy answer to these questions. There is serious danger that generally applicable child neglect laws, for example, will be discriminatorily applied against the retarded. But I am unwilling to conclude that this danger is so great that we must leave the decision with the mother—no matter what her capacities—regarding, for example, whether to surrender her child for adoption. Reliance on parental choice in all child-rearing matters must be our primary goal. But I believe there will be cases in which such reliance would be misplaced, and detrimental to the child's interests.

We cannot blithely trust legal institutions to make wise and sensitive discriminations in applying authority to override parental choice. But in my judgment we cannot wholly deprive the state of this authority to protect against its abuse. We must instead maintain constant vigilance to protect the interests of those among us, including the mentally retarded, who are always vulnerable to excessive deprivations by those purporting to act for their benefit.

It is likely that courts can be persuaded to apply the Constitution in order to invalidate the injustices that previous generations of law-makers have imposed on the mentally retarded in their sexual and family lives. It is equally likely that, unless careful thought and planning is undertaken in conjunction with efforts to bring the retarded into community life, the same injustices will be imposed on the mentally retarded under new legal guises.

REFERENCES

1. Ferster, E.: Eliminating the Unfit—Is Sterilization the Answer? 27 *Ohio State Law Journal* 591 (1966).
2. See *In re Cavitt*, 157, N.W. 2d 171 (Nebraska Supreme Court, 1968), *certiorari granted*, 393 U.S. 1078 (1969), *certiorari dismissed*, 369 U.S. 996 (1970).
3. Lindman & McIntyre: *The Mentally Disabled and the Law* (American Bar Foundation, 1961).
4. See *Perez* v. *Lippold*, 198 P. 2d 17 (California Supreme Court, 1948).
5. Tannenbaum: *Slave and Citizen* (1946).
6. *United States* v. *Carolene Products Co.*, 304 U.S. 144, 153 n 4 (1938).
7. 388 U.S 1 (1967).
8. *Brown* v. *Board of Education*, 347 U.S. 483 (1954).
9. *Meyer* v. *Nebraska*, 262 U.S. 390, 399 (1923).
10. *Griswold* v. *Connecticut*, 381 U.S. 479, 486 (1965).
11. *Stanley* v. *Georgia*, 394 U.S. 557, 565 (1969).
12. *Eisenstadt* v. *Baird*, 92 Sup. Ct. 1029, 1038 (1972).
13. Utah Code Ann. §64-10-7 (1968).
14. *Buck* v. *Bell*, 274 U.S. 200, 207 (1927).
15. *Skinner* v. *Oklahoma*, 316 U.S 535 (1942).
16. Minn. Stat. Ann. §260.015 (Supp. 1965). See also Paulsen, The Legal Framework for Child Protection, 66 *Columbia Law Review* 679, 693-94 (1964).
17. See Burt, Forcing Protection on Children and Their Parents, 69 *Michigan Law Review* 1259 (1971).
18. 445 S.W. 2d 145 (Kentucky Supreme Court, 1969).

CHAPTER **20**

The adult MR in the criminal justice system

ROBERT L. MARSH
Boise State University

CHARLES M. FRIEL
Sam Houston State University

VICTOR EISSLER
Sam Houston State University

ABSTRACT: *Adult mental retardates are increasingly being processed through the criminal justice system. The Anglo-American concept of mental incompetence provides little protection to insure the special handling and treatment a retarded person requires. The retarded person, because of the lack of mental competence in addition to the intricacies of the criminal justice system, is often incarcerated. This incarceration does little to improve the retarded person. Recommendations are made to improve the detection of mentally retarded persons and handle them in a manner more suitable to their special needs.*

DESCRIPTION OF THE INCARCERATED

Today there are in excess of 230,000 adult males and females incarcerated in state prisons throughout the nation. A review of those studies which have attempted to characterize the background of these individuals indicates that the majority are undereducated,

Reprinted from Mental Retardation 13:21-25, 1975, with permission.
Authors: **Robert L. Marsh**, Ph.D., Assistant Professor, Department of Criminal Justice Administration, Boise State University; **Charles Friel**, Ph.D., Professor and Director of Research, Institute of Contemporary Corrections and the Behavioral Sciences, Sam Houston State University; **Victor Eissler**, Alcoa Foundation Fellow, Institute of Contemporary Corrections and the Behavioral Sciences, Sam Houston State University.

underskilled, and come from culturally and financially impoverished backgrounds.

As part of President Johnson's Commission on Law Enforcement and the Administration of Justice, the National Survey of Corrections conducted a number of studies to assay the background characteristics of the nation's inmate population. Their studies indicated that while the median education achievement level for the general population was 10.6 years, that of the nation's inmates was only 8.6 years. Similarly, they found that the incidence of inmates with no vocational skills was five times as high as the national average. Studies were also conducted to determine the earning capacity of inmates prior to their incarceration. The results indicated that 90% of the nation's inmates were earning less than

$5000 a year as compared with only 56% of the general population who fell within the same income level.

The recognition that the nation's inmate population tends to be substandard with respect to a number of background characteristics including intelligence is not a recent discovery. Goddard and other early researchers responsible for the development of intelligence testing technology conducted many studies on the intellectual capacity of juvenile delinquents and adult offenders. The results of their early work indicated that a preponderance of the offenders studied represented the lower end of the intelligence continuum. These facts encouraged the development of a theory which alleged that mental retardation itself predisposed a person to the commission of criminal acts. Goddard and Hill (1944) concluded that if mentally retarded individuals were not properly supervised, they would inevitably become criminals. This conclusion was based upon their studies of delinquency from which they generalized that 25% of all delinquents are mentally defective. In one study, Goddard obtained data from 16 institutions for delinquent males and females in which he found that the incidence of mental retardation ranged from 28% to 89%. Similarly, the Gluecks completed a survey of 500 women paroled from a women's reformatory in Massachusetts in 1934 and found the sample to contain 11 imbeciles, 150 feebleminded individuals, and 76 borderline mental defectives.

Zeleny conducted a review of the literature regarding mental retardation studies from 1910 to 1930. He noted that there was a general lack of agreement among investigators regarding the relationship between feeblemindedness and criminal conduct because of the variability in standards used for testing. He attempted to standardize the testing criteria and the degree of mental retardation into total population and found the studies basically in agreement. He concluded: "For men criminals we may expect to find 3.2 percent and for women criminals we may expect to find 5.9 percent feebleminded."

Through the years the studies conducted in this area have repeatedly found the incidence of borderline mental defectives and mental retardates among correctional populations to be significantly high. One impact of these studies has been the development of a negative stereotype regarding the treatment potential and rehabilitation of the mentally defective offender. If it is assumed that retardation itself precipitates anti-social behavior, and that the person's retardation status is irreversible, it is only natural for a philosophy to develop which views the retarded offender as a poor risk for rehabilitation. However, the assumption that mental retardation itself precipitates criminal behavior should be explored in greater detail. This assumption is based on the fact that a large number of the individuals in correctional institutions are intellectually sub-normal. To generalize these findings to the criminal population at large is to assume that the incarcerated population is a representative sample of the criminal population.

During 1970, for example, there were approximately 6.5 million arrests in the United States for all types of offenses. Yet, during the same year, state correctional institutions received approximately 75,000 convicted felons. Recognizing that some arrests involved the apprehension of the same individual more than once, it would appear that no more than 1% of arrested individuals are ever committed to state correctional institutions. The remainder are either dismissed from the criminal justice process, fined, incarcerated in county jails, or granted probated sentences and returned to the community. If intelligence is a factor in determining the sentencing of criminal cases, then the disproportionate number of individuals with low IQs in state correctional facilities would represent an administrative artifact of the administration of criminal justice and not evidence for the theory that mental retardation precipitates criminal behavior. There are several lines of evidence to suggest that a disproportionate number of individuals with low IQs are sentenced to prison. The National Survey on Corrections has reported that approximately 3 out of every 5 individuals convicted of criminal acts are placed on probation as opposed to being incarcerated. In almost all jurisdictions, a prerequisite for probation requires that the individual either have or acquire a steady job. Since it is reasonable to assume that the mentally retarded have less marketable job skills, a higher percentage would have difficulty in meeting this requirement for probation. As a result, probably a significant number are sentenced to prison in lieu of being granted probation.

Brown and Courtless (1967) found that the mentally retarded compose a small minority of those incarcerated in American correctional systems. "The significance of the problem [however] far outweighs the small number of people involved. . . ." Based on 1963 National Prisoner Statistics figures, approximately 20,000 of the 189,202 prisoners in the entire system were considered retarded. This figure represents 9.5 percent of the 90,477 inmate comparative sample of all prison facilities in the United States. This figure of nearly 10% takes on added significance when compared to the statistically projected 3% mental retardation figure for the entire country. These numbers include only those persons with IQ test results of less than 70, and when the data of those scoring less than 85 IQ (the upper limit for qualification for special education in many states) is added, the percentage jumps to 40, or approximately 76,000 inmates. This "relative small minority" is no longer easily ignored.

The authors have estimated the incidence of mental retardation of male inmates entering the correctional system to be 10%; this estimate is based on scores from a number of different psychological tests. Retarded inmates tended to be older, and eight out of ten were either black or Mexican-American.

Treatment and ultimate rehabilitation of the offender is emphasized by various philosophical schools of thought as well as state statutes. The American Correctional Association (1966) states: "Penologists in the United States today are generally agreed that the prison serves most effectively for the protec-

tion of society against crime when its major emphasis is on rehabilitation."

Rehabilitation has been defined at different times as meditation, harsh punishment, hard labor, psychiatric care, and various mixtures in-between. Regardless of the particular treatment modality of a certain institution, a distinction must be made between the methods employed for the "average" and the retarded inmate.

The problem of the mentally retarded in a correctional institution does not rest with the correctional administrator; administrators generally have no control over the type of inmate that is received. Often, even in cases of severe mental retardation, the administrator cannot send someone to a residential facility for the retarded because of statutory limitations.

THE CONCEPT OF MENTAL INCOMPETENCE

An important concept of Anglo-Saxon legal tradition is that an accused may not be tried on a criminal charge if at the time of the trial his mental condition is such that he cannot appreciate the nature of the proceedings and participate intelligently in his defense. A determination that the accused is mentally incompetent to stand trial does not cancel the trial altogether, but merely postpones it until the accused becomes competent to stand trial. The general practice in such cases is to commit a mentally incompetent offender to a mental institution until he becomes competent, at which time the trial will resume.

For the mentally retarded individual accused of a crime the laws of incompetency pose special problems—the laws are designed more for the mentally ill or the insane than the mentally retarded. The laws of incompetency do not recognize mental retardation per se as a kind of mental condition that renders an accused incompetent to stand trial. Little, if any, research has studied the effect of mental retardation on a person's ability to understand the criminal proceedings or participate effectively in his defense. The idea of postponing a trial until the mentally incompetent offender regains competency may be appropriate for a psychotic defendant but is inappropriate for the mental retardate whose chances of becoming mentally competent are neglible. Therefore, since there is little hope that a mentally retarded person found mentally incompetent to stand trial will ever become competent regardless of the amount and/or quality of treatment, a commitment in a mental institution amounts to a life sentence without parole.

How do the present laws affect the handling of a retarded offender? Since medieval times, Anglo-American criminal law has made provision to exempt mentally disabled persons from criminal responsibility on the grounds of "insanity." Commonly known as the defense of insanity, this exemption is perhaps one of the most widely discussed, yet least agreed upon topics in criminal law. Most of the arguments have centered around who should be included in the class of mentally disabled persons eligible for the defense of insanity and the consequent legal rules (or operational definition) of this class. Scant attention, however, has been paid to the mentally retarded. Few have addressed the question of whether mental retardation should or should not relieve the defendant of culpability. In fact, it is not certain whether existing legal rules recognize mental retardation as a basis of excusing criminal liability. The problem becomes one of determining how an insanity defense affects the mentally retarded, and how, if advisable, it should be modified to take into account the mentally retarded.

"Insanity" as used in reference to the defense of insanity is a legal term with no corresponding medical or psychiatric description. As used in legal context, it roughly means "the degree or quality of mental disorder which relieves a person of culpability for his actions."

The defense of insanity is unlike the concept of mental incompetency to stand trial. Though both halt the criminal proceedings against the defendant, a finding of incompetency to stand trial suspends the proceedings until the defendant becomes competent,

while a finding of "not guilty by reason of insanity" ends the proceedings forever. Though both usually result in the commitment of the defendant, a defendant incompetent at the time of the trial must still stand trial after he is released from commitment, while a defendant acquitted on the basis of insanity at the time of the crime will often go free after release. Finally, though both are concerned with the mental disability of a defendant, the function of incompetency laws is to prevent, for reasons of fairness and humanity, the trial of a person incapable of understanding the criminal proceedings. The insanity defense relieves a person of criminal responsibility.

Yet, for the mentally retarded, the insanity defense, despite its different operation and function, presents many of the same basic problems as the laws of incompetency. First, there is the question of whether mental retardation is or should be the kind of mental condition that excuses a person of culpability. If so, then what degree of mental retardation is, or should be necessary to excuse the accused? Also, how can the legal rules for the defense of insanity be formulated to accommodate mental retardation? Second, if a mentally retarded person is excused from culpability, under what circumstances is it permissible for the state to commit him to a mental institution, and under what circumstances should the state commit him? Must the mental retardate be dangerous to himself or society before he is committed? Can rehabilitation justify commitment? Does the fact that he successfully pleaded the defense of insanity authorize the state to commit him to a mental institution? Finally, for how long can the state confine a mentally retarded defendant acquitted by the defense of insanity?

LEGAL PROCESSING OF THE MENTALLY RETARDED

The way in which the statutes are written influence the handling of the mentally retarded offender. There are a number of other considerations concerning the actual operation of the criminal justice system that frequently are overlooked but are critical in determining how the mental retardate will be handled.

Over 90% of all criminal cases are disposed of by the defendant pleading guilty. Stated in another manner, less than 10% of all cases (both felony and misdemanant) result in a jury trial. Pollack and Smith (1972) state: "Instead of each accused standing trial before an impartial judge and jury, with skilled legal counsel who examine the case from different points of view, . . . most defendants arrive in the court room only to stand before the judge and plead guilty."

The process by which defendants "plead out" their case is termed "plea bargaining." The advent of plea bargaining is principally the result of the need to handle the increasing number of criminal defendants. As the number of criminal defendants has continued to rise, the amount of money appropriated for jails, prosecutors, courts, and judges has not risen at an equal rate. As a result, the court system is generally overburdened.

If the accused cannot make bail, he may wait in jail in some states for over a year for trial. This creates an additional shortage of space in local jails. If the defendant makes bail, he may commit new crimes before the trial date. If the trial is delayed for an inordinate long period, witnesses may move, disappear, die, or forget crucial details. These events increase the pressure to dispose of the backlog of cases as soon as possible.

The attorney, in an attempt to get the best possible decision for his client, may offer to change a plea of "not guilty" for a serious charge to a "guilty plea" for a lesser charge. Pollack and Smith (1972) point out that:

> While superficially this may seem a convenient and efficient way to handle accused persons, it is obvious that it is a short-circuiting of the entire judicial process, because the determination of guilt has been made, not by judge or jury in open court, but by two lawyers in private conferences.

This process of plea bargaining is further legitimized by the judge who customarily asks the defendant if any special promises were made to him in return for his guilty plea. The defendant denies that any promises were made to him.

The process of the negotiated plea frequently obviates the utility of the pre-sentence investigation. If the person has agreed to a negotiated plea in return for a lesser sentence, the judge may fail to utilize the pre-sentence report in determining the sentence. Thus, the pre-sentence report becomes little more than an expensive formality.

The mentally retarded offender, caught within this quiet complex system of justice, suffers because of his limited mental capacity. Quite often his attorney, not being able to obtain acquittal by reason of insanity because this defense is quite time-consuming, tries to plea bargain in order to obtain a lesser sentence.

If the mentally retarded offender is poor, in addition to his mental handicap, he has an even smaller chance for special consideration by the court. Court appointed attorneys often do not have the time to expend as much effort on an indigent as a regular client. Because of this, many cases are "pled out" as quickly as possible. Again the mentally retarded offender is not handled according to his own special needs.

If the mentally retarded defendant goes to trial and the case is not "plea bargained" then he still is at a decided disadvantage. All jurisdictions appear to allow the defendant, the prosecution, or the court, on its own initiative, to raise the issue of the defendant's competency to stand trial. In *Pate* vs. *Robinson* the Supreme Court made it clear that all parties have a duty to raise the issue of incompetency whenever there is any evidence of incompetency. Since the trial of an incompetent violates his due process right to a fair trial, and since it is difficult if not impossible to make accurate retrospective determinations of incompetency, the Court held that whenever there is a *"bona fide doubt"* about the defendant's competency to stand trial, the court must conduct a competency hearing before proceeding to trial. Thus, not only may the defendant, his counsel, the prosecution, or the court raise the issue of incompetency, but a failure to raise the issue and determine the defendant's mental condition where there is some evidence of incompetency may violate due process and render his trial and conviction unconstitutional.

Avoiding legal errors in trials and convictions of the mentally retarded presents a difficult problem for the courts and prosecutors alike. At present, it seems that many mentally retarded persons are tried, convicted, and sentenced without having their competency to stand trial determined. For example, in their 1966 survey of mentally retarded federal prisoners, Brown and Courtless found that for 92% of the mentally retarded prisoners in the study the issue of competency to stand trial was not raised. In 88% of the cases of these retardates no appeal was made, the post-conviction relief was not requested in 84% of the cases. Several reasons may account for the widespread failure to inquire into the competency of mentally retarded offenders. Most, if not all, jurisdictions have no systematic procedure for testing the intelligence of an accused before or during the trial, which leaves the detection of a defendant's mental retardation to chance. Unless the defendant behaves in a bizarre manner, or a medical record revealing his retardation is brought to the attention of the court, or unless the judge, prosecutor, or defense counsel suspect mental retardation, it would seem unlikely that a mentally retarded defendant will have his competency questioned. The swift, routine manner in which many accused persons are processed through courts—with a guilty plea only requiring a few minutes in many courts—reduces even more the probability that a defendant's mental retardation will be noticed and his competency questioned.

What may be the most significant reason for the failure of all concerned to raise the issue of competency is the common misunderstanding of what competency to stand trial means. The issue of competency and the issue of criminal responsibility are often confused. As a result, if a defendant appears to know right from wrong (the usual test of criminal responsibility), no one will bother to inquire into his capacity to stand trial. Although the tests vary from state to state, basically competency requires that the person must have the ability to understand the nature of the criminal proceedings and be able to participate intelligently in his defense. A mentally retarded person may have some ability to distinguish right from wrong, but such ability is no guarantee that he possesses the mental capacity to stand trial. Through training, conditioning, or the like, a mentally retarded individual may acquire a sense of what kind of conduct is socially acceptable and, therefore, wrong, yet he may lack the intelligence to participate effectively at his trial. However, as long as the courts, defense lawyers and prosecutors think of competency to stand trial in terms of criminal responsibility, even if they recognize mental deficiency in the defendant, there will always be the danger that mentally retarded persons will be tried and convicted without having their competency to stand trial questioned, let alone judicially determined.

THE MENTALLY RETARDED IN PRISON

Since prisons are not designed to treat the mentally retarded, it is no surprise that little programming exists that attends to this group's special needs. Furthermore, the low funding priority of most correctional systems insures that programs must be geared to the average rather than the retarded inmate. It is doubtful that the retardate could be helped in prison even with the establishment of special programs since mental retardation is usually considered to be irreversible.*

---

*EDITOR'S NOTE: This statement is the position of the authors of this article and is therefore presented in the context of this article. Opinions concerning this statement vary considerably, and this statement may be a fruitful focus of debate for the reader.

RECOMMENDATIONS

As in other areas of criminal law, there is a wide variability from state to state in the application of the law to the mentally retarded. Before any program or differential handling of the mentally retarded can be initiated, it is necessary to determine the incidence of mental retardation in inmate populations, both juvenile and adult. If as indicated by the limited number of studies on the subject the incidence of mental retardation is exceptionally high in inmate populations, then specific changes should be made.

There is significant ambiguity in the law regarding the prosecution of the mentally retarded offender. Two areas of law that seem particularly ambiguous are tests of competency to stand trial and tests of criminal responsibility.

Legal competency refers to the defendant's knowledge and awareness of the proceedings in which he is involved and his capacity to participate in his own defense. For the mentally retarded person accused of a crime, the laws of incompetency pose special problems, mainly because they are designed for the mentally ill or the insane instead of the mentally retarded. Very little empirical information is available of the effect of mental retardation on a person's ability to understand the criminal proceedings or to participate effectively in his defense. The common practice of committing an incompetent individual to an institution until he regains competency presents a peculiar difficulty to the mentally retarded individual because, unlike mental illness, the condition of retardation is considered irreversible. Commitment in such instances constitutes institutionalization comparable to a life sentence without due process of law.

The second area of legal ambiguity involved in the prosecution of mentally retarded offenders relates to tests of criminal responsibility. In fact, it is not certain if the existing legal rules for the insanity defense recognize mental retardation as a basis for denying culpability. To alleviate this existing ambiguity, the legal definition of insanity and the use of insanity as a defense should be expanded to allow mentally retarded defendants to avoid penal dispositions where such dispositions are inappropriate.

Research should further be undertaken to determine existing alternatives for adult courts in the handling of the mentally retarded. These alternatives should be studied in conjunction with the total needs of the state or area, the current operating capacity of the institutions, and the present percentage utilization of the operating capacity. This study would undertake to evaluate existing services and delivery services based on the needs of the mentally retarded in the area.

If as indicated by the limited number of studies completed, a significant shortage of services for the mentally retarded exists, liaison should be established with state and local planners to develop funding resources for the mentally retarded.

REFERENCES

Allen, R. C. The retarded offender, unrecognized in court and untreated in prison. *Federal Probation*, 1968, 32(3), 23.

American Correctional Association. *Manual of correctional standards* 3rd ed. Washington, D.C.: The American Correctional Association, 1966.

Brown, B. S. & Courtless, T. F. *The mentally retarded offender*. Washington, D.C.: U.S. Government Printing Office, 1967.

Brown, B. S. & Courtless, T. F. The mentally retarded in penal and correctional institutions. *American Journals of Psychiatry*, March, 1968, 124(9), 1164.

Clark, R. *Crime in America*. New York: Simon and Schuster, 1970.

Federal Bureau of Investigation, U.S. Department of Justice. *The Uniform crime report: 1970*. Washington, D.C.: U.S. Government Printing Office, 1970.

Fink, A. E. *Causes of crime*. New York: A. S. Barnes and Company, 1962.

Glueck, S. & Glueck, E. T. *Five hundred delinquent women*. New York: Alfred A. Knopf, 1943.

Goddard, H. H. *Feeble mindedness, its causes and consequences*. New York: Macmillan, 1914.

Pate vs. Robinson, 383 U.S. 375 (1966).

Pollack, H. & Smith, A. *Crime and justice in mass society*. Waltham, Massachusetts: Xerox Publishing Co., 1970.

President's Commission on Law Enforcement and the Administration of Justice. *Task force report: Corrections*. Washington, D.C.: U.S. Government Printing Office, 1967.

President's Commission on Law Enforcement and the Administration of Justice. *The Challenge of crime in a free society.* Washington, D.C.: U.S. Government Printing Office, 1967.

U.S. Department of Health, Education and Welfare. *Correctional Administration and the Mentally Incompetent Offender (CAMIO).* Washington, D.C.: Research Grant No. ROI-MR-07006, 1973.

U.S. Department of Justice and the Federal Bureau of Prisons. (Reprinted by the Law Enforcement Assistance Administration). *National prisoner Statistics,* 1970.

Zeleny, L. D. Feeble-mindedness and criminal conduct. *American Journal of Sociology,* 1933, 38(4), 564-576.

SECTION FOUR

Discussion questions

1. Skarnulis discusses public and professional responsibility in the enforcement of human rights for the retarded. In what ways have professionals denied the retarded their legal and human rights? What are some of the specific responsibilities of parents and friends in securing legal and human rights for the retarded individual?

2. Discuss several assumptions that are associated with the concept of "risk." How have Scandinavian countries assimilated risk-taking experiences for the retarded into everyday functional living? Why do you think risk might be a difficult concept for parents and professionals to understand and accept?

3. Why does Burt refer to current legislation on sexual and familial relations for the retarded as old laws under new guises?

4. The adult mentally retarded are increasingly being processed through the criminal justice system and incarcerated in prisons. Discuss several factors that can be attributed to the high incidence of crime associated with the retarded individual. Has incarceration improved the social capabilities of the retarded adult? What are some possible recommendations to alleviate this situation?

PART II

EDUCATIONAL AND VOCATIONAL ISSUES

DELIVERY PATTERNS AND INSTRUCTIONAL CONSIDERATIONS

Social and educational delivery patterns for the mentally retarded have generated a major area of controversy within the field. Social issues have centered around the necessity, appropriateness, and administrative feasibility of institutional vs community-based programs. However, the dispute over institutional or community-based program emphasis translates into a much more primary concern: segregated vs integrated programs for the retarded individual. This controversy is currently paralleled in the educational system as well. The debate has actually focused upon two basic educational issues: (1) mainstreaming vs self-contained special classes and (2) mandatory education for the moderate and severely handicapped individual and the role of the public school. These two issues have received an abundance of attention in the literature. Strong advocates with supportive efficacy data have continually emerged to support one side or another. It is therefore very important that the various delivery patterns be examined from several perspectives. The articles in this sec-

tion will present some of the more recent alternative positions and literature reviews of educational delivery systems for this population. Current trends in the field will be examined and critiqued by several contributing authors.

Many special educators would suggest that the field is in a state of change or transition. Special educators in the past have promoted the need for totally self-contained instructional programs for the mild, moderate, and severely handicapped. This was to compensate for the regular educator's lack of training and insight regarding exceptional children in their classroom. Consequently, primary responsibility for the child was shifted to the special educator. More recent theories of the roles and responsibilities of special education have brought about a reorientation of earlier positions. Special education is viewed as a support service to regular education personnel with the primary responsibility for the child remaining in the regular class program.

The first article in this section attempts to identify the issues and trends that have brought about the current state of transition regarding special education's responsibilities within the educational realm. The overrepresentation of minorities in special classes as a result of culturally-biased testing is discussed and analyzed. In addition, the efficacy of special classes is examined in relationship to the current movement of returning the exceptional child to regular class programs. Donald L. MacMillan discusses the advantages and disadvantages of the mainstreaming trend and relates this to a functional noncategorical approach to instructional programming. Several other relevant issues are also reviewed, including deficit labeling, appropriate service to all children, early intervention, and accountability in the classroom. MacMillan calls for several investigative studies to further clarify the status and operational feasibility of these recent trends within the field.

The next two articles in this series present distinctly differing viewpoints regarding appropriate delivery patterns for the retarded individual. David A. Sabatino analyzes the justifications for special classes and draws some negative conclusions utilizing nonsupportive efficacy data. The article criticizes the special class as the major delivery pattern for the mild or moderately retarded child. The author questions whether special classes serve the purpose of administrative convenience or educational relevance. Two alternative delivery systems are then examined: the resource room and the itinerant teacher. The resource room is defined in theory as a support service within the framework of regular education programs. The resource and itinerant teachers are described as diagnosticians, programmers, and consultants. Efficacy studies are presented in support of the resource or support service theory.

This criticism of special class placement as a major delivery pattern for the retarded is not shared by Oliver P. Kolstoe. This article examines basic allegations against traditional educational programming and special classes for the retarded. These allegations involve the disappearance of mild retardation during the adult years, harms of labeling, lowering the child's self-concept, fruitlessness of special classes, self-fulfilling prophecy, and the expanded provisions of regular education curricula. Kolstoe refutes these allegations in several different arenas. These include alternative data in support of special class programs, lack of follow-up information from previous investigations, and methodologic weaknesses within efficacy studies criticizing special class placement. In conclusion, the author suggests that the criticisms leveled against special classes are more related to administrative function than to instructional theory.

The final article in this section deals with the practicality of serving the more severely handicapped through public education. Recent court decisions have called for mandatory education of all handicapped children, thus creating some difficult administrative and curricular problems for the public schools. Ed Sontag, Philip J. Burke, and Robert York indicate that there is a lack of comprehensive programs currently available to the severely handicapped. The article discusses problems of administrative feasibility, the need for appropriately trained personnel, the role of the multidisciplinary team in the public schools, and transportation considerations. The authors propose several practical alternatives that public education must attend to in order to be prepared to meet the needs of this population.

CHAPTER 21

Issues and trends in special education[1]

DONALD L. MacMILLAN
University of California at Riverside

ABSTRACT: *This paper represents an attempt to identify and describe the issues and trends which have led special education to be in a state of transition. The writer's intent is to describe the trends for those professionals concerned with handicapped children, but who are not special educators and therefore do not have time to read extensively special education literature. Since handicapped children are of concern to a variety of professionals in related disciplines, it is important that they be aware of the trends in special education, and that special educators be aware of trends in these allied fields.*

For the past 5 years, the field of special education has been engaged in a serious re-evaluation of its mission, the assumptions underlying certain practices, and its effectiveness in delivering services to handicapped children. Stemming from this re-evaluation have been several trends—some of which evolved from this self-evaluation,

[1]This paper is based on an invited address delivered to the First National Convention of the Federación Venezolana de Asociaciones de Padres y Amigos de Niños Excepcionales in Caracas, Venezuela, October 29, 1972. This investigation was supported in part by the National Institute of Child Health and Human Development Grant No. HD-05540 and General Research Support Grant No. FR-05632 from the General Research Support Branch, Division of Research Facilities and Resources, National Institutes of Health. Reprinted from Mental Retardation 11(2):3-8, 1973, with permission.
Author: **Donald L. MacMillan**, Ed.D. (U.C.L.A.), is Associate Professor of Education at the University of California, Riverside, and Research Specialist for Pacific-Neuropsychiatric Institute Research Program. He has published over 40 articles and has authored one book, *Behavior Modification for Educators* (March, 1973) and recently completed work on an edited book with Dr. Reginald L. Jones, *Special Education in Transition.*

and several other directions one can identify which arose out of pressure from minority groups and the courts. Regardless of the source of the impetus, special education, probably more than any other discipline involved in the delivery of services to handicapped children, has engaged in self-examination and has modified some longstanding practices.

MILD RETARDATION AND MINORITY CHILDREN

Clearly the hottest issue in special education today in the United States concerns the over-representation of minority children in special classes for the mildly retarded. In 1968, Dr. Lloyd Dunn published an article in which he questioned the efficacy of special classes for minority children classified as educable mentally retarded. In so doing, he criticized the classification procedure, the practice of labeling of children as "retarded," the isolation and segregation of children so classified from other children in the school, and the ineffectiveness of teaching procedures used in the special classes. The Dunn (1968) article has been widely read and directly or indirectly resulted in serious challenges to the use of intelligence tests, labeling children with deficit labels (such as mentally retarded), and providing separate and "different" educational experiences for mildly retarded children.

At the same time, increasingly more militant minority groups decried the abundance of minority children being classified as mentally retarded. Pressure was brought to bear by these groups on state and local educational agencies. Court cases were being brought on behalf of minority children for damages stemming from their being classified as mentally retarded and being barred from regular educational experiences. Hence, the courts have played a major role in determining a trend toward the "decertification" of great numbers of children heretofore classified as mentally retarded. In the state of California, for example, over 19,000 educable mentally retarded (EMR) children were decertified between 1969 and 1972 and returned to regular classes.

Probably the most widely known court case brought on behalf of a minority child who had been classified as mentally retarded is *Diana vs the State of California* (1970). In this case in which the court was found to be in favor of the child, six mandates were issued to the state. Four of the mandates related to the use of intelligence tests with minority children. The mandates issued by the court were:

1. The child must be tested in her native language.
2. The child should be retested with a nonverbal test of intelligence.
3. The state was directed to develop ethnic norms for intelligence tests.
4. The districts must make plans for revising testing programs.
5. Districts had to present an explanation for ethnic disproportions in special classes.
6. The districts were directed to provide transitional programs which would aid decertified EMR children to move back into the regular educational program.

It is interesting to note that only the last provision was truly educational in nature. In most of the litigation pertaining to the issue of the disproportionate representation of minority children in special classes (Ross, DeYoung, & Cohen, 1971), the primary issue deals with the use of verbal intelligence tests with which to identify such children as mentally retarded.

Issues in the area of assessment will be discussed further in another section of this paper, but here the intent is to focus on the trend toward the movement of many children who were EMR back into regular classes. First, these children failed repeatedly in regular classes before being placed in special classes. Hence, what evidence is there to indicate that these same children are now going to be able to succeed in the regular class? The learning problems they possessed initially cannot be legislated away by legislatures or mandated away by judges. Yet, the result of this action is that the decertified children no longer qualify for any additional assistance for their learning problems since they do not fit into any categories for which funding is provided. (Temporary funding is provided in California for transitional programs.) It remains to be seen whether this action is beneficial or detrimental to the children it affects.

NONCATEGORICAL APPROACH FOR DELIVERY OF SERVICES

A recurring problem in special education when a state provides funding for exceptional children by categories (e.g., blind, deaf, retarded) has been that some children with learning problems do not fit any of the existing categories, and thereby cannot be given the needed assistance. In essence, such children "fall between the keys," and require that another category be created lest these handicapped children go unaided. Creation of new categories has led to a proliferation of categories, and still some children in need of help fail to qualify for any of these numerous categories.

At a 1971 conference held at the University of Missouri on the Categorical/

Noncategorical Issue (Meyen, 1971), the clear recommendation coming from almost all involved was toward a noncategorical approach for the delivery of services to children with learning problems. It was recognized that with certain groups of children (e.g., blind, deaf, severely retarded), the prospects for successful integration into regular classes was unlikely. However, in the case of mildly handicapped children (e.g., learning disabilities, educable mentally retarded), sentiment clearly supported their return to regular classes.

While many agree in principle with the trend toward a noncategorical approach, certain problems arise. First, it has been recognized that the categories such as blind, deaf, and retarded are categories with which legislators and the general public understand and sympathize. Hence, in raising money for programs, there is support among legislators for the disability groups into which handicapped children have been grouped traditionally. Legislators vote rather generously for such groups, but if educators go to legislators and request money for children with "learning problems" without differentiation, the feeling (Meyen, 1971) is that legislators will not be as supportive.

Another problem concerns the basis for grouping children educationally if the old categories are discarded. Clearly, the children must be grouped on some educational basis (achievement level, nature of learning problem), but the feasibility of grouping on such bases remains to be demonstrated. Attempts of grouping children across certain of the old disability groupings (Hewett, 1971) have shown some promise. However, to do the same thing on a district or state basis raises many additional problems not encountered in a one classroom project. Since little evaluation has been attempted on new programs, the problems must be hypothesized, and efficacy cannot yet be "assumed."

Yet another problem arises when one moves from policy to implementation. While most agree that in principle mildly handicapped children should be educated in regular classrooms, it is questionable as to whether

in practice such a move can be carried out. Are regular class teachers going to be receptive toward these children? Do regular class teachers have the skills needed to reach the learning needs of these children? With the larger class sizes in regular classes, can the child receive the needed individual attention? These questions only begin to scratch the surface, but they show some of the problems likely to be encountered. It should be emphasized that while problems of implementation do occur they do not invalidate the principle; yet, policy makers must also be sensitive to the realities of implementation.

AVOIDANCE OF DEFICIT LABELS

The labeling issue is in actuality a subissue of the noncategorical issue, but one which has received considerable attention in its own right (Jones, 1972). Concern arises, particularly in the case of the mildly handicapped children who are able-bodied and are unidentifiable before they come to school, do not stand out as different in social situations outside the school, and who, upon completion of school careers may blend into society and meet the demands of society. These children have been referred to as the "six hour retardates" who are said to be retarded only for the time they must spend in school. The question raised is whether the practice of labeling these children as "retarded" is justifiable, and whether such a label detrimentally affects the child's feelings of self and the behavior of others (peers, teachers) toward that child so labeled.

Several authors (Dunn, 1968; Mercer, 1972; Jones, 1972) have challenged the labeling of children with deficit labels. Each presents some evidence in support of their position; however, the complexity of the labeling process has yet to be explored, much less understood. For example, Jones (1972) has presented data which do indicate that children do not like being called "mentally retarded." Otherwise, no data have been presented which support the detrimental effects hypothesized for labeling. Dunn (1968) extrapolated from the work of Goffman (1963) in mental hospitals, and Rosenthal and Jacobsen (1968) with a highly selected non-retarded group; however, such extrapolations seem hazardous if not illegitimate. . . . The only evidence with which this author is familiar extends the Goffman (1963) notions of "strippings" and "mortifications" of the self to retarded subjects; it is the work of Edgerton and Sabagh (1962). In the Edgerton and Sabagh study, mildly retarded residents in a state institution were actually found to experience "aggrandizements" of the self in being able to compare themselves to less able patients; and in some instances they were better able to cope with institutionalization in that they attributed their placement (and labeling) to discrimination and inaccurate diagnosis. Furthermore, in the institution they were not constantly confronted with evidence of their inability since the institution was geared to their intellectual level.

In preparing a review of the literature on labeling of mental retardates it was found that about the only clear dimension which emerges is the complexity of the issue. Whether a child's being labeled has a detrimental effect probably depends on a host of variables, including: (a) whether the child accepts or rejects the label as accurate; (b) the extent to which the child experienced informal labeling prior to formal labeling (i.e., being called "dummy" or "stupid") by peers, parents, or teachers; (c) the age of the child at the time of labeling; (d) the presence or absence of physical stigmata in association with the presence of mental retardation; (e) ethnic status; and (f) compounding effects of additional deficit labels (e.g., "culturally deprived").

High quality research is needed on the labeling issue to move the controversy from a plane of rhetoric to one of empiricism. Data are needed on which to base decisions, and those data are lacking at the present time.

RESPONSIBILITY OF STATES TO PROVIDE EDUCATIONAL PROGRAMS FOR THE SEVERELY RETARDED

In the education of the severely retarded, court cases are also promising to have a profound effect on programs. In the majority of states, entrance into classes for the trainable mentally retarded have required that the child be toilet trained and be able to communicate his needs. In addition to programs for the TMR, some states such as California, have provided Child Care Centers for children not able to meet the criteria specified here. Other states have not provided for these children through their Departments of Education. For example, if pressed for an explanation of why there was no provision for children functioning at a level below TMR, state officials responded that they were provided for by the Department of Mental Health or Social Welfare; these children could be placed in a state institution for the mentally retarded and were therefore not the responsibility of the Department of Education.

While this was accepted by parents for years, class action court cases may force states to provide for children functioning at very low levels under the auspices of the State Department of Education. For example, in Pennsylvania, a recent court case was brought on behalf of a severely retarded child against the state, charging that the state must provide for the education of *all* children, regardless of the severity of their retardation. The state counsel decided that the evidence presented by plaintiff was so compelling that the state could not win. The case was settled on a "gentleman's agreement" before a judgment was made, and as a result, no precedent was set. However, it is anticipated that similar cases will be brought in other states, forcing some decision on this issue.

In another case in California, suit was brought on behalf of an autistic child against the state in an attempt to prohibit the state residential school for the multihandicapped deaf from dropping the child from school. The contention was that if she is dropped from school there is no other school in the state which can serve her, and thus the state is neglecting its responsibility to provide for her education. It was the contention of the state that her presence in the program detracted from the quality of education able to be provided for the other children in the program, and that given her characteristics, it is more reasonable for a Department of Mental Hygiene facility to care for her than for a group of teachers relatively untrained in the care of severely disturbed children. Again, this case *(Lori vs the State of California)* raises the same issue as that in the Pennsylvania case: which agency in the state is responsible for the education of severely handicapped children?

The California case was tried and the court found against the plaintiff (i.e., the child). The judge wrote two conclusions which are at odds with the trend mentioned previously:

1. Training of a child of diminished mental capacity in such basic human needs as eating, toileting, and simple acts of self-preservation is not education within the purview of the Education Code.
2. A person teaching a child of school age with diminished mental capacity to eat, use toilet facilities, wash, dress and avoid dangers in her immediate surroundings, and in addition caring for such child on a custodial or care basis, is not educating such a child within the meaning of the Education Code.

If a trend can be identified, it would seem to be that educational agencies are going to be ordered to provide for children heretofore cared for by mental health agencies. This will mean drawing up guidelines for such things as: (a) What should these children be taught? (b) What should be the maximum enrollment in these classes? (c) What should be the qualifications for certification of teachers serving these children? If the direction continues to be the one in which we are moving, these questions will need answering in the near future.

EARLY IDENTIFICATION AND INTERVENTION

In the United States during the past decade, considerable amounts of money have been spent on Headstart and similar preschool programs for children coming from areas in which there is a high incidence of learning problems and mental retardation.

Starting with an intervention program conducted by Kirk (1958), the field of special education seems to have adopted the point of view that many of the mild cases of retardation can be ameliorated if identified early enough. Kirk (1958) reported that those children who were given a preschool educational experience at the age of four had somewhat more successful early elementary careers; also fewer cases of mental retardation were identified as compared to a group of children from the same area for which no such program was provided. In keeping, Bloom's (1964) analysis of the stability of intelligence led to the conclusion that intelligence stabilizes very early (age four was found to be a critical point), and if one wishes to influence its development, one must intervene very early in the child's life.

The outgrowth of these works has been the position that with "high risk" children, educators must identify those who are high risk very early and intervene with programs to ameliorate their learning inefficiencies. Recent reviews (Caldwell, 1970; Spicker, 1971) summarize the rationale for such intervention and provide summative data on programs which have been tried. The results to date have not been promising with mildly handicapped children from low socioeconomic status backgrounds (see Jensen, 1969). However, no agreement has been reached on what the nature of the early program should be. For example, should it be intensive drill in academic tool subjects, or should it be very low-keyed and provide the child with opportunities and experiences, such as trips to the zoo or the beach, typically provided for middle class children? These programmatic considerations are in need of review and evaluation. Or does the implicit intent to make second class middle class children out of lower class children doom these programs to failure in spite of programmatic inputs?

The principle of early intervention, however, can and has been extended to more severely handicapped children. In the area of deaf, for example, children have been started on communication training very early in life, and the results are quite positive. In the area of the severely retarded, less attention has been given to this approach, but these children also would seem likely candidates for training in toileting and the learning of other self-help skills as early as possible, to enable later training to move into areas more directly related to academic tool subjects, social skills, and vocational skills. In light of the evidence from operant conditioning research with mentally retarded subjects, it seems reasonable to hypothesize that ways may be developed for teaching these children skills previously thought beyond their capabilities. If so, then what are the earliest ages at which severely retarded children can be taught toileting, recognition of simple signs. etc.?

ACCOUNTABILITY AND SPECIAL EDUCATION

Public education has been free to determine what should be taught to children for years. In the process, education has been somewhat of a sacred cow of which everyone was supportive. Seemingly no one questioned the decisions made by educators.

Recent developments have led the public to ask that the schools be held accountable. The schools, like industry or business, are asked to show how tax money is spent. More importantly, schools must be able to show that they are accomplishing what they claim they are accomplishing. Many states have passed legislation which requires evaluation. In California, functioning is tied to the ability to demonstrate that a given district has achieved goals it set out to achieve; teachers must set behavioral objectives for stated time periods and gather objective data to demonstrate that objectives were met.

In special education, teachers have been held less accountable than have teachers in general education. If the children in a TMR class failed to learn anything over a year's time, where did the responsibility lie? If the teacher were confronted, she could relate the failure to characteristics of the children ("After all they are mentally retarded"), implying that the disability resides within the child, and the failure to learn can be explained in terms of the mental incapacities of the child. With the advent of accountability, the teacher will be held responsible, regardless of intellectual level. Failures on the part of education now become teaching failures rather than child failures.

Accountability is upon us whether we like it or not. The ramifications of this program are beginning to be realized, and some of these ramifications are seen as undesirable by some. For example, can the teacher set trivial objectives in order that they be easily obtained? Should the teacher who fails to achieve the objective be given less money, fewer materials, or more money and more materials in order that the objective be achieved in the next year? Some of these issues are dealt with in articles by Barro (1970), Cook (1972), and Drew et al. (1972).

ASSESSMENT OF ASSESSMENT PROCEDURES

In the process of questioning the efficacy of the special class, one of the major issues is the misidentification of children as mentally retarded. The school psychologist bears the brunt of this criticism as it is his responsibility to identify and classify those who are retarded. The major issue raised in court cases pertains to the validity of instruments such as the Stanford-Binet and Wechsler Intelligence Scale for Children when used with children from culturally different backgrounds. Barnes (in press) and Mercer (1972) are most critical of the use of these instruments, since they hold that identification as mentally retarded depends heavily upon performance on these tests. Barnes (in press) contends that test content is invalid for children coming from low socio-economic status and/or minority backgrounds. Mercer (1972) contends that the norms are relatively uninfluenced by minority groups, as they constitute such a small percentage of the population on which the tests are normed. This aspect of intelligence testing is receiving a great deal of attention; yet the issue is far from resolved.

Another criticism leveled at intelligence tests is that they are only useful to classify children (retarded, average, gifted), but are not useful in diagnosing areas of strength or weakness in a given child. The argument goes that what is needed for educational programming is information which pinpoints strengths and weaknesses—information which is not forthcoming from intelligence tests. Out of such concern grew a movement to develop such tests as the Illinois Test of Psycholinguistic Abilities (ITPA) and the Frostig tests of visual perception to assess underlying basic abilities judged necessary to succeed in school. Mann notes that:

> From the basic abilities standpoint, we assume in dealing with a learning disabled child that (1) he has certain organismic "learning" disabilities that are interfering with or limiting his potential for learning and that (2) if we provide him with appropriate training, either remediating his disabilities by working in so-called deficit areas or helping him compensate for his disabilities by teaching to his strong ability areas, we will help him overcome his learning problems (1971, p. 323).

Mann (1971) goes on to contend that one must recognize, however, that one is not assessing an entity (perceptual disability, psycholinguistic ability), but rather sampling behaviors of the child.

While the Mann (1971) criticism of abilities testing and training is leveled at the conceptualization of basic abilities, another movement, behavior modification, has continually criticized the kind of evidence collected by psychometrists. The behaviorists have contended that behaviors emitted by children reflect what that child's environment has reinforced in the past; i.e. that a child behaves in a certain fashion because it pays off—he gets the rewards he wants by behaving in a given manner. Furthermore, the behaviorists have argued that the psychometric approach puts the onus upon the child—the child is mentally retarded, the child is learning disabled—the problem resides within the child rather than in the contingencies and reinforcements in the environment.

Instead of collecting data like IQ, achievement, and personality scores, the behaviorists have opted for precise descriptions of the behavior and what happens immediately following the behavior in question. For a child who is constantly out of his seat, the behaviorists see no value in diagnosing him as minimally brain damaged or emotionally disturbed because it is the child's getting out of his seat that is of concern. Hence, the behaviorist would count how often the child gets out of his seat and for what duration. Then he would attempt to determine what is the "pay off" for his getting out of his seat. By manipulating the consequences of the behavior, the behaviorists attempt to alter target behavior.

The behaviorists have exerted considerable influence on the role of the school psychologist. Whereas in the past, the psychologists spent considerable time testing children and interviewing, these individuals are spending increasingly more time in the classroom observing, recording, and designing intervention programs based on operant conditioning principles.

Another trend within the assessment area concerns the interpretations placed on test results. A distinction which is being made by some (Bortner & Birch, 1970; Cole & Bruner, 1971) between performance and capacity is an important one to make. When a child gets an answer correct, one has little problem interpreting what that means. However, when a child does not get the answer correct it may be due to limited capacity, but it may also be due to any one of a number of other variables such as motivation, anxiety, failing to understand what is being asked, feeling ill on the day of testing. The evidence reviewed in the two articles mentioned in this paragraph clearly indicates that it is hazardous to assume that test performance necessarily reflects the best a child can do.

USE OF PARAPROFESSIONALS

One set of circumstances has forced special education to look to ways of getting additional personnel to serve children in special education settings. There has been a gap between special educational needs and the number of professionals available to provide for these needs. Three major populations have been used to fill this gap: (a) nonprofessional adults, (b) older children performing cross-age tutoring, and (c) parents.

The most attention is being given to the use of nonprofessional adults working in concert with a fully certified teacher. With the additional adult in the classroom, the adult/pupil ratio is reduced, thus enabling each child to receive a greater amount of individual attention. These paraprofessionals have been used in a variety of ways. Some teachers have used the teacher's aide only to perform clerical duties, supervise non-academic activities, and perform housekeeping duties. However, other teachers have seen fit to use the teacher's aide in the instructional arena. Mitchell (1970) characterizes the effective paraprofessionals as "individuals who by personality, life experience, or common knowledge have a good deal to offer others (p. 42)."

In other ventures, there have been attempts to teach parents to use certain behavior controlling techniques, principally, how to use behavior modification techniques. In having the parent employ behavior modification at home while it is concurrently a technique being used in school, the child is handled with consistency. Otherwise, the child may learn that he has to behave in a given way in school but not at home.

Cross-age tutoring has been used for centuries. Recently it has been demonstrated that older retardates and gifted children can be effective teachers with younger retarded children. In attempts to specify why cross-age tutoring works with children who fail to respond to teachers, one reason often presented is that the older child is perceived by the recipient of tutoring as less authoritarian. Another explanation posited with older children as recipients is that the peer group becomes increasingly more powerful as a reinforcing agent, and the older tutor is perceived as a peer. Little attention has been given to determining whether cross-age tutoring exploits the child tutor, or whether it may be detrimental to some children for whom tutorial service is offered by peers.

The evidence on the use of paraprofession-als is indeed promising since the gap between needed personnel and the number being prepared annually gets increasingly wider. What seems needed now is for further investigation to uncover the personality attributes correlated with success, and the ways in which these paraprofessionals can be employed with maximal benefit to the children they are serving.

CONCLUSIONS

An attempt has been made to describe generally the trends and issues in special education in the United States. The next decade should reveal which of these trends crystallized into standard procedure and which failed to pan out. The one healthy aspect of the number of trends apparent in special education today is that there is constant re-evaluation of practice and a questioning attitude among at least some professionals in the field. More obvious is the need for special educators to address themselves to questions which are empirical in nature, with a research approach. Despite the fact that most of the questions leading to the trends discussed were empirical in nature, many professionals in the field have tended to search for answers through logic and philosophy. It is hoped that the next decade in special education will be one in which penetrating research questions are asked and research methodologies refined to the point where valid evidence is collected in attempts to answer these questions.

REFERENCES

Barnes, E. J. Cultural retardation or shortcomings of assessment techniques. In Jones, R. L. & MacMillan, D. L. (Eds.), *Special education in transition*. Boston: Allyn & Bacon, in press.

Barro, S. M. An approach to developing accountability measures for the public school. *Phi Delta Kappan*, 1970, L11, 196-205.

Bloom, B. S. *Stability and change in human characteristics*. New York: Wiley, 1964.

Bortner, M. & Birch, H. G. Cognitive capacity and cognitive competence. *American Journal of Mental Deficiency*, 1970, **74**(6), 735-744.

Caldwell, B. M. The rationale for early intervention. *Exceptional Children*, 1970, **36**, 717-726.

Cole, M. & Bruner, J. S. Cultural differences and inferences about psychological processes. *American Psychologist*, 1971, **26**, 867-876.

Cook, J. J. Accountability in special education. *Focus on Exceptional Children*, 1972, **3**, 1-14.

Drew, C. J., Freston, C. W., & Logan, D. R. Criteria and reference in evaluation. *Focus on Exceptional Children*, 1972, **4**, 1-40.

Dunn, L. M. Special education for the mildly retarded —Is much of it justifiable? *Exceptional Children*, 1968, **35**, 5-22.

Edgerton, R. B. & Sabagh, G. From mortification to aggrandizement: Changing self-conceptions in the careers of the mentally retarded. *Psychiatry*, 1962, **25**, 263-272.

Goffman, E. *Stigma*. Englewood Cliffs, N.J.: Prentice Hall, 1963.

Hewett, F. The Madison Plan as an alternative to special class placement. *Education and Training of the Mentally Retarded*, 1971, **6**, 29-42.

Jensen, A. R. How much can we boost IQ and scholastic achievement. *Harvard Educational Review*, 1969, **39**, 1-123.

Jones, R. L. Labels and stigma in special education. *Exceptional Children*, 1972, **38**, 533-564.

Kirk, S. A. *Early education of the mentally retarded*. Urbana, Illinois: University of Illinois Press, 1958.

Mann, L. Psychometric phrenology and the new faculty psychology: The case against ability assessment and training. *Journal of Special Education*, 1971, **5**, 3-14.

Mercer, J. R. The meaning of mental retardation. In R. Koch & J. Dobson (Eds.), *The mentally retarded child and his family*. New York: Brunner/Magel, 1972.

Meyen, E. L. *Proceedings of the Missouri Conference on the Categorical/Noncategorical issue in special education*. Columbia: University of Missouri-Columbia, 1971.

Mitchell, M. M. Nonprofessional personnel become professional teachers. Paper presented at the 48th Annual International Convention of the Council for Exceptional Children, Chicago, Illinois, April 19-25, 1970.

Rosenthal, R. & Jacobsen, L. *Pygmalion in the classroom*. New York: Holt, Rinehart & Winston, 1968.

Ross, S. L., DeYoung, H., & and Cohen, J. S. Confrontation: Special education placement and the law. *Exceptional Children*, 1971, **38**, 5-12.

Spicker, H. H. Intellectual development through early childhood education. *Exceptional Children*, 1971, **37**, 629-640.

CHAPTER 22

Resource rooms: the renaissance in special education

DAVID A. SABATINO, Ph.D.
Northern Illinois University

What is special education? Is it a special curriculum, or a special teaching environment, or some combination wherein a teacher has fewer pupils and can individualize instruction? The justification for special education has been that many children are seemingly unable to profit from regular instruction and need adapted curricula and teaching assistance on a more individualized level. Most schools, especially at the time they place a child into some type of special education class, justify special placement to themselves and parents on the basis of smaller class size and specialized instruction. This justification may be mere rationalization.

It is now fairly well agreed that special classes generally do not provide increased academic achievement for the educable mentally retarded (EMR) children placed into them. An example is Sparks and Blackman's (1965) study, which determined that the academic achievement of mentally retarded (MR) children placed in special classes was significantly poorer than that of those remaining in regular classrooms. A further review of the research literature (Bennett, 1963; Cassidy & Stanton, 1959; Elenbogen, 1957; Johnson, 1962; Pertsch, 1936; Thurstone,

Reprinted from The Journal of Special Education 6:335-347, 1972, with permission.

1960) indeed allows the general conclusion that retarded children do not function as well academically in special classes as do their confrères in regular-class settings. It has been found that the EMR in special classes have manifested better social-personal adjustment (e.g., Cassidy & Stanton, 1959). Though some of this research is suspect because of poor design and subject-selection problems, there is little doubt that societal and parental stress for social skills has led many special educators who are concerned with curriculum for the retarded to emphasize social content.

However, on the debit side of the social-behavioral issue, there have been suggestions that special classes for the ERM have certain undesirable side effects. Zito and Bardon (1969) showed that retarded children in special classes are impaired (a) in their goal-setting behaviors, and (b) in their expectancies for achievement growth when compared with retarded children in regular classes.

In any case, special classes for the MR have not fulfilled the promise that was once perceived. They are being developed at a significant increase in school per-capita expenditures, while serving only limited numbers of children. The more recent development of special classes for children with other learning disorders (emotional disturbance, brain damaged, and learning disabilities)[1] has been based on a limited appreciation of special-class effectiveness. Even if conclusive data showed that self-contained classes for children with learning disorders were more effective than any other single curriculum delivery system, additional instructional procedures would still be necessary simply because it is doubtful that school systems can provide enough space or funding to place the large number of children with learning disorders into special classes. While it is true that special classes frequently have limited enrollments, it should not be assumed that a reduction in the number of pupils in a class ipso facto improves instruction. In fact, these are two reasons why individualization of instruction in special education classes may presently be impossible. First, the number enrolled in a class is too great. One teacher can individualize work for one or even two children; she stands less of a chance with three children. In rare cases, she may even be able to provide fairly individualized work for four handicapped children. But no teacher, even one equipped with the best methods and materials, can individualize work for 5, 10, or 15 children. This is so because of the second reason: the instructional homogeneity of categorically defined handicapped children is a faulty assumption; to find five children needing precisely the same teaching approach at the same time would requite a huge population-sampling procedure.

Class size is an unknown variable that has received little attention. There is some evidence that it is generally more difficult to plan a group curriculum as class size exceeds 20 to 25 children. But it may be just as difficult to plan for five children as for five groups. The point is that there can be no appropriate use of, or formulation for, specialized curricula unless the *instruction* can be individualized. It may be possible to teach each child individually in a small, manageable group if all the children in that group are working from essentially the same teaching method or material. However, the adaptation or adoption of any curriculum, teaching method, or material is impossible, in the author's opinion, when the teaching environment is directed at more than four children.

What *should be special* about special education is a continuum of teaching environments that permits special educators from all the different areas—school psychology, speech and hearing, remedial reading, and the different teaching areas—to focus on handicapped children. The first priority should be to determine the needed specific instructional objectives for handicapped children. We in special education realize by now that medically borrowed labels—which we have converted to convenient administrative categories—lend little to the type of instruction we provide children. There is no instructional homogeneity in most classes of EMRs, emotionally disturbed, and brain-damaged children. There are few instructional similarities in classes for the visual or hearing impaired, and it is ludicrous to create a special class for these or any other categorical type of handicapped children and view it as an all-encompassing learning center.

Special classes may be more aptly described as instructional nightmares in which a single teacher is expected to perform an impossible task. Her academic preparation included perhaps the history of some aspects of special education, a superficial acquaintance with the needs and characteristics of handicapped children, and a limited preparation in applying a few curricula to an artificial disability. This training is not only irrelevant but has also failed to help teachers prepare for their real job: to render meaningful educational prognosis while establishing realistic instructional objectives, and to develop the methods and materials to implement and validate these objectives. Most university training programs perpetuate the state of the art by preparing teachers for special classes when such classes are instructional impossibilities for the teacher as well as for at

---

[1] Learning disorders and learning disability are being differentiated according to federal guidelines and definitions.

least 50% of the handicapped children they are supposedly designed to serve.

The failure of special education classes for the EMR to show significant academic efficiency has prompted the special educator to reevaluate their educational value. The special educator was previously too eager to justify newly found positions and accepted far too many casualties for almost any reason. (One problem is that most special educators have no say in the selection of children they will teach.) Regular-class teachers were not only relieved at the possibility of reducing their teaching loads but generally were delighted at the absolute shift of responsibility for children with educational miseries to the special educator. Special placement depended on IQ scores and neurological or psychiatric examinations. Dependence on such examination procedures was supposed to insure that a categorical label was appropriately applied. The fact that handicapped children cannot be homogeneously grouped on the basis of these instructionally irrelevant criteria seemed unimportant to the administrator and sent the noneducational diagnostician laughing all the way to the bank. As a result, most special education classes resembled a box of assorted candies because of the diversity of the children and their educational disabilities. The responsibility for instructional planning within the special class was almost exclusively the teacher's. Her dream of individualized instruction for each child was far too frequently a nightmare of hyperactivity, emotional reactions, chronic "failurisms," and parental guilt and denial; all of this was due most of all to the impossibility—not the challenge—of establishing instructional goals, developing curricula, and preparing material to teach 5, 10, and even 20 children in any one day. Special educators are now ready, I believe, to turn a corner and recognize the realities of teaching. At least two efforts provided the major impetus for new directions in planning the future of special education: Dunn's (1968) now classic article on the efficiency of special classes and his statement that 20% of the better special-class teachers should be retrained as diagnostic-prescriptive teachers; and Moss's (1971) original position paper on the regional resource centers.

Recent litigation has shown that many children placed in special classes have cultural-linguistic or other sociocultural problems and are not handicapped in the sense implied by the traditional categories. The problem is that when a turning point is reached, something must be turned *to* and an alternative position or set of positions must be achieved. One definition of a professional person might be knowledge about his discipline and ability to render sound, responsive, and responsible decisions to those he serves. The profession (if it is one) of special education seems to wait for others to make its decisions for it. It was born through the will of parental pressure, not educational planning, and it could succumb to the combined social forces of parental, minority, or court action unless it can support a sound position that reflects the federal and state dollars it spends and the magnitude of the social responsibility thrust upon it. We, as special educators, should realize that if we fail to make decisions, others such as the courts will make these decisions for both the children we serve and for us. What we need to offer is diversity of educational systems, i.e., a set of alternative programs for children, providing efficient instructional delivery vehicles and multiple academic-planning and teaching environments. Our strategy of using medically related labels of handicapping conditions and hardening these categories has limited the development of programs based upon instructional deficits of children. The fact is that we do not suffer from too many administratively convenient categories; rather, we suffer from too few educationally relevant ones. Until the time that ample diversity in special education instructional delivery systems and teaching environments is achieved, the more precise acts of specifying curriculum for a particular child's learning and behavioral strengths or weaknesses cannot be initiated or validated.

THE RESOURCE ROOM

Resource rooms in their many forms may be a first step in developing a continuum of special instructional environments. What are resource rooms? Reger and Koppman (1971) made the most concise statement in the literature regarding resource rooms. They wrote:

Resource room programs for children with problems are not new, but there seems to be a large degree of variation among programs, and there is not universal understanding of this kind of approach [p. 460].

The literature has described resource-room programs for emotionally disturbed teenagers (Connor & Muldoon, 1967) which represented a combination of public school and community agencies and included special classes and tutoring services for aggressive, withdrawn, or disoriented adolescents. Clark (1969) described a learning center which bridged the gap between the broad-based unit curriculum of the pre-1960 era and the precision of diagnostic-prescriptive teaching. She illustrated how a learning center could make the diagnostic-prescriptive process immediately available to teachers—a system of blending master teachers and school psychologists as a team. The technology and special materials were provided by the learning center. She emphasized that "the classroom teacher must have more of an 'even chance' at managing the problems of working with children—and this system 'equalized the odds' [p. 17]."

Hillerich (1969) recommended the resource room as a "creative learning center" whose sole objectives are to increase language facility and improve the child's self-concept. He saw the disadvantaged child as requiring not only rich language experiences but also a teacher "who recognized his [the child's] worth, and has time to let him know it [p. 262]."

Comparing the achievements of children served by the resource rooms with those in special classes, Weiner (1969) concluded that the former serves more handicapped children more effectively. He emphasized the desirability of a widely varied approach, as opposed to using any specific technique of instruction.

A prime example of resource rooms used to implement a varied approach to remediation is the Learning Resource Center for Exceptional Children in Sacramento City, California (Vallett, 1970). The evaluation and programming for each child are the result of consultation between teachers, coordinators, and psychologists, rather than the product of one diagnostic assessment or assessor. This multifaceted resource-room program includes parent and pupil counseling, parent education, in-service teacher training, and educational therapy.

The personnel that staff a resource room may range from one coordinating teacher to a team of specialists. The *coordinating teacher* has been described as a "trouble shooter, problem-solver, consultant, demonstration teacher, and research scientist (Cienion, 1968)." One general criticism of resource rooms has been that their teachers try to be all things to all children—too much of an undertaking, some feel. Cienion listed specific functions of a learning-resource teacher:

1. The learning-resource teacher teaches six or seven sessions daily, except Friday (a half-day).
2. She acts as resource person for all classroom teachers from 8:30 to 9:00 a.m. and 3:30 to 4:00 p.m.
3. She meets weekly with the special-subject teachers, either as a consultant for lesson planning or in an advisory capacity.
4. She prepares stand-by resource lessons for classroom use when a child cannot function within the framework of the regular lesson.
5. She observes in the classroom in an advisory capacity by invitation.
6. She confers with the classroom teacher about the progress of the children attending the resource room.
7. She is responsible for a written evaluation of the children's progress in both the classroom and the resource room.

8. She confers jointly with parents and classroom teachers and initiates separate parent conferences, when indicated.
9. She initiates the integration of children into the parent class on a full-time basis, when indicated, and serves as supportive resource teacher until transition is complete.
10. She prepares in-service training materials as the need arises.
11. She serves on the Special Learning Disabilities Committee.
12. She is part of the screening team for special learning disabilities and is responsible for the final evaluation report of each referral.

The resource-room teachers of the National Regional Resource Center for Pennsylvania have five major functions identified under two Plans. Plan A incorporates direct service to individuals and small groups of children in resource rooms. Plan B is more consultative and includes (*a*) assisting teachers (both regular and special) to establish instructional objectives for the handicapped children, (*b*) obtaining suitable teaching methods and materials to augment those objectives while validating their use, and (*c*) demonstrating special education curriculum frequently by teaching in regular or special classes with groups or total classes for short blocks of time.

THE ITINERANT TEACHER

The resource room is frequently a specific physical setting in a fairly large elementary building. In such a setting, the special educator can better individualize instruction by providing essential materials and building fairly elaborate teaching stations. However, not all elementary buildings can support a resource room. One alternative is the itinerant resource teacher, who functions in the same way as a resource-room teacher but serves several schools.

The philosophy of educators of the visually impaired has long been to keep partially sighted children in the regular educational mainstream, supplemented by large print, parapatology, and so forth. In their article on educational plans for partially sighted children, Stephans and Birch (1969) recommended the use of itinerant as well as resource-room teachers.

Education of the visually handicapped, an area of special education that has attempted to serve a few geographically scattered handicapped children in regular education, has in the past stressed the use of itinerant teachers working between buildings while serving a base population. The size of the population served by any itinerant teacher may vary widely, depending upon the social-cultural environments the children represent. A suburban school may have difficulty identifying 20% of its children for such programs, even when using a broad definition of handicapped such as "educational misery." On the other hand, 50% to 60% of the children in a selected rural or inner-city population may be found to have significant handicapping conditions or learning problems associated with perceptual and receptive-expressive language deficits. According to Sabatino and Hayden (1970), in a Maryland county with wide variation between its suburban and rural schools, it was noted through annual psychoeducational screening procedures that the incidence of learning-disabled children was directly related to the size of their communities. Less than 20% of suburban elementary populations had any perceptual or language deficit, whereas as high as 50% of the rural population showed considerable developmental lag on these behaviors.

An itinerant special education teacher's schedule must reflect the amount of disability she or other school personnel can identify, not an arbitrary teacher-pupil ratio such as 500 to 1.

The itinerant teacher is one more alternative or, more precisely, derivative of the resource room. Obviously, the itinerant teacher's travel time can subtract from her teaching time. She also needs a strong back to carry materials but has less elaborate space needs. Sabatino and Hayden (1970) observed some general personality differences between effective resource-room, itinerant, and self-contained class teachers. The resource-room teacher can tolerate ambiguity more than the special educator who prefers the self-contained class. The itinerant teacher has less need for a teaching home and children she can call her own. Both the itinerant and resource-room teachers need a strong feeling for service but have less need for social relationship with other teachers, favoring a more salesman-like attitude for working with multiple personalities.

A functional difference between resource-room and itinerant teachers is that the latter may serve more children by shortening the daily time a child receives a supportive program. In other cases, the number of days each week that a child receives a supportive program may be altered. The issue is that of massed versus spaced practice. Studies to date have generally supported massed practice and, in fact, a 6-week massed (blocked) schedule may be as effective as a twice-a-week schedule continued over a year. Several speech therapists have attempted to determine if articulation errors can be corrected more efficiently by scheduling children every day for perhaps one-half hour periods (block therapy), as opposed to the more spaced twice-weekly visits.

Van Hattum (1959) reported on 5 years of a program that used both a twice-a-week method of scheduling and an intensive system of 2-week sessions. The intensive system was found to be more effective as judged by the number of children dismissed from therapy.

Ervin (1965) showed that the block-therapy method produced more improvement in functional disorders of articulation in second and third graders than did a cycle-therapy program. However, Ervin cautioned against making generalizations to other areas without further investigations. Weaver and Wollersheim (1963) gave similar credit to the block system when it was used in comparison with an intermittent program. It was found that both teachers and principals preferred the block program because of ease of scheduling, improved motivation, increased speech benefits, and better rapport between clinicians and faculty. Teachers who preferred the intermittent system also cited increased disruption of class time as a major disadvantage of the block system. Grassi (1971) concluded that spaced practice (seeing children over longer periods of time) was more effective with 11- and 15-year-old brain-damaged children. The difference between the results from the Grassi and Ervin studies may have been due to the different ages of the subjects, or the type of problem, or the type of intervention. Children 10 years of age and younger may not have the language-retention skills to transfer training over distributed practice. The Grassi study suffered from design fatigue and is in need of replication that varies the age and type of handicapped children.

AN EVALUATION OF RESOURCE ROOMS, SPECIAL CLASSES AND ITINERANT SERVICES

Sabatino (1970), in evaluating and comparing a resource-room and itinerant program, found that the 27 children who visited a resource room for 1 hour per day during the academic year did as well as 11 children in a self-contained class. Forty-eight children seen in an itinerant program did not equal the reading-comprehension gains of children in self-contained classes, but they showed similar growth in word recognition and perceptual and language skills, which facilitated positive academic growth.

The resource-room plan provided the teacher with the opportunity to combine a behavior-modification and a remedial approach. It was found that the 1 period permitted 40 minutes of instruction, with about 20 minutes accounted for by going to and fro and the all-important conversations with home room teachers. The 1-hour period seemed to encourage teacher support while maximizing language interplay necessary for reentry into the regular-class learning process.

Under the itinerant plan, there was the least academic gain in the reading achievement areas. This fact does not negate its value. The itinerant required more ongoing consultation and a closer liaison with the regular classroom teachers. It may be that regular-classroom teachers who refer children for extra help and are anxious to see them aided (even if it means extra demands on themselves) might find real advantages in this instructional period, actual teaching time amounted to about 20 minutes. Twenty minutes is approximately the attention span of most children for a given activity, and it was also about the time necessary to present one activity per training session. The gain of a year or more in academic growth for children with a history of limited academic growth suggests that the itinerant plan was a viable instruction alternative to special classes. The problem was that neither the behavioral data from the psychoeducational assessment nor the diagnostic prescriptive teaching procedures was sufficiently refined to provide reliable prognostic statements about children's learning. In other words, it appears that some children profited as well from a one-half hour, twice-a-week prescriptive program as others did from a self-contained special class. Thus, more than 11 of the 48 children in the itinerant program gained as much as did 11 children in the self-contained class.

THE SPECIAL EDUCATION TEACHER-CONSULTANT

The resource room may serve multiple functions. In many cases, the concept of resource rooms may be broadened to include functions other than direct services to children. One may envision the resource room as a small special education laboratory of teaching methods and materials, in addition to the teaching stations described earlier. These materials can be used to support instructional objectives for "handicapped children" and children with "educational miseries" in regular or special classes. A special educator teacher-consultant would be the person to deliver these methods and materials once she has worked through a diagnostic-prescriptive procedure to insure that they (the materials or methods) are efficient and the instructional objective(s) is reasonable.

The special education teacher-consultant

or strategist (or whatever title) is a special educator who works largely in educational diagnosis, rendering instructional objectives and special education curricula to be used primarily by other teachers. She may develop special education curriculum units for special groups, adaptive procedures for a specific handicapped child, or an entire instructional process which emphasizes perceptual or language development for an entire class. She may team-teach or provide instructional support by teaching within one of the above structures in both the regular and special class. In the author's experience, she provides two additional roles. The first is obvious: she supports the work of handicapped or learning-disabled children in the regular or special class. The second role is not so obvious: she provides a front line of defense in establishing priorities for referrals to other school personnel or community agencies.

Special- or regular-class teachers are frequently not sure when to refer a child for speech, reading, medical, or psychological services. Interaction between the resource teachers and referring teachers can help to determine whether a behavior or academic deficit is severe enough to warrant referral. This same "two heads are better than one" premise also works in the resource room, where the resource teacher and special education teacher-consultant can interact regarding the problems of the day or a particular child.

An important new concept is the *relief teacher*. Relief teachers staff resource rooms, relieving the regular or special class teacher so that the latter may visit the resource room periodically while children from her room are working there. This makes possible increased interactions between resource room teachers and referring teachers. Without such formal communication systems, the resource room teacher and referring teacher may have to rely on a hit-or-miss relationship which stands just as good a chance of missing as of hitting. In addition, the referring teacher doesn't have the opportunity to learn special teaching techniques that she may use with other children and which would support the work of the resource-room teacher. The magic of a three-headed team—resource room teacher, special educator teacher-consultant, and relief teacher—is that each supports the work of the other in emphasizing the necessity of instructional objectives and the use of special instructional techniques in the special class and, particularly, in the regular class. It is the author's contention that 90% of special-class teachers do not have instructional objectives specific enough to be meaningful, and that those who do have specific instructional objectives frequently lack the teaching materials to implement them.

TRADITIONAL ASSESSMENT-TEACHING RELATIONSHIPS

One of the most controversial problems in education is too little versus too much assessment. Traditionally, teachers teach children, and other professionals from other disciplines, such as school psychologists, assess children. The extent of communication between the two may be a hurried conference in the hall between classes. There has been a feeling that each should stick to his task (teaching or assessment) and that a cooperative team approach of both to both tasks—especially teaching—would be wasteful. Diagnostic teaching has suffered greatly because teachers feel that the diagnosis is "complete" when they receive the "diagnosed" child and that they must begin immediately to teach him.

When should the diagnostic process terminate? The answer is deceptively easy: when it has been achieved. On this point, however, the medical and educational models part company—and radically so. Medicine, or medical pathology, achieves a diagnosis of pathogenesis by isolating the specific disease entity. It is easy to test this working model by watching how differently a physician approaches chronic illness and acute illness. Frequently, acute illness can be managed medically with one diagnosis and/or treatment. Chronic illness involves long-term care and continued diagnosis. Handicapping conditions or educational dis-

ability are forms of chronic illness, in that the isolation of a specified disease entity will not by itself specify behavioral or instructional management. The handicapped child's education is dependent upon a continuously changing instructional pattern, based upon his needs and functions. There is no one diagnostic statement that can cover any more than one educational planning period. In short, then, the term diagnostic-prescriptive implies that diagnosis should have an immediate relationship to teaching if it is to have any instructional value. The problem is that educational diagnosis is dynamic, continuous. The one-shot approach to psychoeducational child study sadly lacks the capability to validly sample behaviors leading directly to the instructional management of handicapped children.

A medical, clinical, psychological, or any other isolated, insular assessment scheme is valueless to instructional planning. That is not to say that if a medical condition exists, it should be ignored. The need for medical management must always be acknowledged. But the literature supports the fact that specific disease entities are not directly related to how a human functions in his learning skills. Likewise, the psychologist's appraisal of a child's general ability and language or perceptual functions is valuable; it is even more valuable when the perceptual-discrimination and retention functions in both the auditory and visual modalities are examined. This kind of appraisal permits initial teaching hypotheses. It is impossible to relate an isolated IQ score or a medical diagnosis to a teaching hypothesis.

There is a need for continuous behavioral- and educational-assessment procedures for learning disabilities which include rationales for instruction. This is the initial teaching hypothesis, and it is based on careful behavioral, sociological, academic, and medical observations and assessment. There must be continuous monitoring or evaluation for a reasonable period of time—no longer than 2 weeks for one-half hour a day per each instructional objective. Such monitoring permits validation of each instructional procedure against appropriate goals, instructional objectives, or aims. The system is far from perfect, but it offers direction. Without an instructional objective, teaching is like heading off on a trip without any idea of the route to follow.

Education has been so busy protecting its arts, and especially the black art of a one-shot diagnosis with magical instruments, that it has failed to collect baseline data on any given set of human performances in relationship to academic achievement for handicapped children (or regular children, for that matter). It is not fair to blame the medical or psychological diagnostician for this failure. The medical evaluations for a candidate for some type of special class were more the work of special education administrators than of practicing physicians. Similarly, education has mandated psychological appraisal as the major procedure in identifying handicapped children for special classes; as a result, practically all handicapped children placed into special education classes have been recommended by the school psychologist. The psychologist became gatekeeper between regular and special education.

In his role as "gatekeeper," the school psychologist has communicated very little with teachers either in the world of regular or special education. Regular-class teachers have been conditioned to comply with the procedure of referring children for special-class placement and not for behavioral or learning management. It is little wonder that they are confused when a resource teacher requests a referred child remain in the regular class. It may even shock them when the resource teacher begins to explore a diagnostic scheme with the regular class teacher for an obviously handicapped child.

Too many school psychologists have conveyed the impression that special education classes are the cure-all for hundreds of different educational ills. But the cure-all is really a catch-all, and we are segregating children into medical categories instead of enough into educationally relevant ones. School psychologists literally sold their professional skills to educational administrative dictums,

thereby reducing their function to that of testers in the eyes of most teachers.

The etiology of our diagnostic-assessment hangups is easily determined: It is the special class seen as the one-shot cure for the one-shot diagnosis. *Too bad, it didn't work.* The difficulty is to group the needed disciplines, primarily school psychologists and special educators, for one purpose—to provide the information necessary for establishing the type(s) of teaching environment needed and the type(s) of instructional goals desirable.

THE FUTURE

The year is 1971, and in Pennsylvania we have just witnessed a judicial decision[2] that necessitates the notification of parents for a due process hearing before special education class placement of their child can be made. Thus, a legal precedent has been established that special instruction is still desirable, but parents, lawyers, physicians, psychologists, and a multiplicity of other professions have a say in its design. I believe that a moratorium should be placed on special education class placement by the next academic year.

Our major task should be to remove the legal, administrative, and medical labels and structures which force us to depend upon categorical programming. In their place, we need a continuum of program alternatives which will encompass the educational problems, and therefore the instructional goals, which lead to educational and behavioral management. The term "management" implies the interdependence of academic learning and social, cultural, behavioral, and medical information. It implies that before academic or vocational skills can be taught, a child may need behavioral training of a perceptual or language skill. It implies a total instructional accountability and a culminating effort from all the disciplines, while keeping a central purpose—education. The fanciful-sounding *zero reject model* means to many that every child has a place to go within

---

[2] Pennsylvania Association for Retarded Children, Nancy Beth Bowman et al., plaintiffs, v. Commonwealth of Pennsylvania, David H. Kurtzman et al., defendants. Civil Action No. 71-42, October 7, 1971.

the system of education. I should like to think that it also implies that we have a sound, preplanned option for every child, long before he approaches rejection by the system. To accomplish this end, special education should have begun the 1972 academic year thinking prognostically and in terms of resource-room approaches. Every child should have the opportunity to visit a prognostic learning center 1 hour each day, for at least a 6-week initial assessment period. Meaningful instructional goals should then be established for him and a set of meaningful interventions and educational materials developed and validated.

Should the 1-hour assessment class fail to provide answers to resilient learning problems, some children could be provided a full day's prognostic class structure for longer periods of time. In essence, many special classes of today could become a program-planning activity where master special educators work with their consultants to determine and develop programs for children. The continuum of services and programs should include these prognostic learning centers, resource rooms, and itinerant special educators, as well as the language, perceptual, psychological, medical, and speech/hearing personnel needed in curriculum support roles. Each school district should have at least one elementary and one secondary resource room, staffed by special educators, backup staff members from other disciplines, the special educator-consultant, and relief teachers.

If just one such prognostic learning center could be placed into each elementary population of 1,000 children and an era of program planning begun, creative alternative teaching structures could develop by 1973. If they don't develop by 1973, I believe societal pressure will eliminate most initiative from special educators; in fact, this process has already begun. Many special education directors in Pennsylvania are spending nearly one-half of their time in due process hearings—not in creative planning. If the trend continues, and if we lose the little initiative for self-direction that remains, we will

be left with no other recourse but to take direction from those nonspecial educators who will gladly provide it.

REFERENCES

Bennett, A. A. *A comparative study of the progress of sub-normal pupils in the garden and in special classes.* New York: Columbia University, 1963.

Cassidy, V., & Stanton, J. *An investigation of factors involved in the educational placements of mentally retarded children: A study of difference between children in special and regular classes in Ohio.* Columbus, O.: Ohio State University 1959.

Cienion, M. Some aspects of a learning-resource room. In J. I. Arena (Ed.), *Successful programming many points of view.* Pittsburgh: Association for Children with Learning Disabilities, 1968.

Clark, P. The magic of the learning center. *California Teachers Association Journal,* 1969, **65**, 16-20.

Connor, E. M., & Muldoon, J. F. Resource program for emotionally disturbed teenagers. *Exceptional Children,* 1967, **34**, 261-265.

Dunn, L. M. Special Education for the mildly retarded—Is much of it justifiable? *Exceptional Children,* 1968, **35**, 5-22.

Elenbogen, M. A. A comparative study of some aspects of academic and social adjustment of two groups of mentally retarded children in special and regular grades. Unpublished doctoral dissertation, Northwestern University, 1957.

Ervin, J. E. A study of the effectiveness of block scheduling versus cycle scheduling for articulation therapy for grades two and three in the public schools. *Journal of Speech and Hearing Association of Virginia,* 1965, **6**, 17-18.

Grassi, J. R. Effects of massed and spaced practice of learning in brain-damaged, behavior-disordered and normal children. *Journal of Learning Disabilities,* 1971, **4**, 237-241.

Hillerich, R. L., The creative learning center. *Elementary School Journal,* 1969, **69**, 259-264.

Johnson, G. O. Special education for mentally handicapped—a paradox. *Exceptional Children,* 1962, **19**, 62-69.

Moss, J. W. Resource centers for teachers of handicapped children. *Journal of Special Education,* 1971, **5**, 67-71.

Pertsch, C. *A comparative study of the progress of sub-normal pubpils in the grades and in special classes.* New York: Columbia University, 1936.

Reger, R., & Koppman, M. The child oriented resource room. *Exceptional Children,* 1971, **37**, 460-462.

Sabatino, D. A. An evaluation of resource rooms for children with learning disabilities. *Journal of Learning Disabilities,* 1971, **4**, 84-93.

Sabatino, D. A., & Hayden, D. L. The information processing behaviors related to learning disability and educable mental retardation. *Exceptional Children,* 1970, **37**, 21-30.

Sparks, H. L., & Blackman, L. S. What is special about education revisited: The mentally retarded. *Exceptional Children*, 1965, **5**, 242-249.

Stephens, T. M., & Birch, J. W. Merits of special class, resource, and itinerant plans for teaching partially seeing children. *Exceptional Children*, 1969, **35**, 481-486.

Thurstone, T. *An evaluation of education of mentally retarded handicapped children in special classes and in regular grades.* Chapel Hill, N.C.: University of North Carolina, 1960.

Vallett, R. E. The learning resource center for exceptional children. *Exceptional Children*, 1970, **36**, 527-530.

Van Hattum, R. J. Evaluating elementary school speech therapy. *Exceptional Children*, 1959, **25**, 411-415.

Weaver, J. B., & Wollersheim, J. P. *A pilot study comparing the block system and the intermittent system of scheduling speech correction cases in the public schools.* Champaign, Ill.: Champaign Community Unit 4 Schools, 1963.

Weiner, L. H. An investigation of the effectiveness of resource rooms for children with specific learning disabilities. *Journal of Learning Disabilities*, 1969, **2**, 49-55.

Zito, R. J., & Bardon, J. I. Achievement motivation among Negro adolescents in regular and special education programs. *American Journal of Mental Deficiency*, 1969, **74**, 20-26.

CHAPTER 23

Programs for the mildly retarded: a reply to the critics

OLIVER P. KOLSTOE
University of Northern Colorado

Recently, there have appeared in the literature numerous writings from diverse sources which suggest that provisions for children who show mild mental retardation do more harm than good. Indeed, the entire March 1972 issue of *Exceptional Children* addressed that subject. The implication from the writings is that methods of identifying the retarded and programs for educating them actually impede their development. If this is true, it would be most difficult for those of us who work in educational programs for the educable retarded to justify our positions. In view of the widespread criticisms leveled at our efforts, it would seem important to examine some of the data used to support the charges.

The six basic allegations to be considered are:

1. That mental retardation is noticeable during the school years but that the condition disappears in adult years.
2. That labeling harms the children.
3. That special class placement is bad for the child's self concept.
4. That segregated programs are fruitless.
5. That teachers contribute to the self fulfilling prophesy of low achievement.

Reprinted from Exceptional Children **35**:51-55, 1972, with permission.
Oliver P. Kolstoe is Professor of Special Education, University of Northern Colorado, Greeley.

6. That general education is capable of dealing adequately with individual differences in the regular classrooms.

DISAPPEARANCE OF MILD RETARDATION (ALLEGATION 1)

The notion that mild mental retardation is noticeable during the school age years but disappears in adulthood seems to have been given credence from several surveys, notably the Onondago, New York, survey of 1955 (Kirk & Weiner, 1959) and Weiner's survey of Hawaii in 1958. Although the surveys are not comparable in technique, in common they report the lowest rates of incidence of mental retardation below the age of 5 years and above the age of 15 years. The 1929 study in England by Lewis as reported by Farber (1968) likewise indicated that between ages 5 and 9 years, there were 15.5 mentally retarded children per thousand children; between 10 and 14, 25.6 per thousand; between 15 and 19, 10.8 per thousand; between 20 and 29, 8.0 per thousand; between 30 and 39, 6.0 per thousand; between 50 and 59, 4.0 per thousand; and over 60, 2.0 per thousand.

A conclusion drawn from these figures is that the retarded appear to be inadequate because the demand of the school are academic and somewhat unrealistic, but when faced with the most realistic demands of acceptable vocational performance and self management, these same children now grown up are no longer retarded because they can cope with those societal demands. In other words they are inadequate in learning but adequate in adaptive behavior.

The validity of this conclusion depends primarily on evidence from followup studies of the adult retarded. Nearly all of the followup studies are confounded by failure to account for the effects of social class on adult living patterns and the degree of retardation studied. Fortunately, one study that does control both severity and social class is the 1948 study by Kennedy and her 1960 followup (Kennedy, 1965).

Kennedy compared the family background, marital adjustment, economic adjustment, antisocial behavior, and social participation of 256 retarded children (IQ's 50 to 75) and 129 nonretarded children (IQ's above 75) matched on age, sex, ethnic background, religion, and father's occupation. In every area of comparison, the retarded were inferior in some important characteristic (for example, employer satisfaction). The crucial point, however, is that in 1960 the retarded were just as inferior to the nonretarded as they had been in 1948. For example, median weekly earnings in 1960 were $88.50 for the retarded versus $102.50 for the nonretarded. Thus, when the retarded are compared with peers who differ only in IQ, it appears they are no more adequate as adults than they were as students in school.

HARM OF LABELING (ALLEGATION 2)

The disproportionate number of black and chicano youngsters found in special classes for the retarded (about 3 times as many blacks and 2 times as many chicanos as would normally be expected) have led to charges that special classes have become dumping grounds for problem children from minority groups. This apparently is achieved by using an IQ test which is highly culturally biased. Any IQ which is significantly below average (generally using a cutoff of 70 to 85) is interpreted to signal the presence of the condition of mental retardation and therefore qualify the youngster for special class membership. Once in the class all the other ills discussed in this paper are presumed to follow, but the major injustice is labeling a child retarded on the basis of an unfair test.

The charge that labeling negatively affects the performance of youngsters has been investigated by Jones (1972). In two separate but related studies, he found no evidence to support the charge. Neither the groups with negative labels nor those with positive labels performed any differently than any other group. The task was a simple digit symbol one so that any change in motivation would have been reflected in output.

On the other hand, it has been pointed out by Gallagher (1972) that labeling has made it possible for society to identify a major social problem and to marshal vast resources of money, facilities, and talent to attack the problem. Had there been no labeling, literally millions of youngsters would have never had any special attention given their learning needs. Gallagher questioned the negative effects attributed to labeling in the following words:

If we can accept the results of the Coleman report (Coleman, Campbell, Hobson, McPartland, Mood, Weinfeld, & York, 1966), we could expect that inner city, lower income children would receive an inferior education in an overcrowded classroom by an overworked teacher surrounded by classmates not oriented to learning or education. That is not a recipe for success in our technological society.

Since children labeled as retarded stand at the bottom end of even their minority peers in measured ability, their chances of a favorable educational or vocational outcome would be even less than for the average of their subgroups. So we cannot have much faith in the decision not to label as turning out well merely because the children who have been labeled achieved limited academic success [p. 528].

From the results presented, it seems that labeling does not have a negative effect on the performance of the children, and labeling does have the positive effect of allowing society to work for the solution of a problem. So far the case for labeling is more convincing than the case against.

LOWER SELF CONCEPTS (ALLEGATION 3)

Two studies are generally pointed to in support of the idea that special class placement is bad for the child's self concept. In 1962 Meyerowitz used the *Illinois Index of Self Derogation* (HSD) with two groups of 6 year old retarded youngsters, half of whom were in special classes and half of whom were in the regular grades. The HSD consists of 22 pairs of statements, one neutral or positive and one derogatory. The child chooses which statement is most like him and the index then is the number of derogatory statements he chooses. In the Meyerowitz study, the mean number of derogatory statements was 3.0 for the retarded in regular classes and 3.4 for the retarded in special classes. In 1967 Carroll replicated the study, but this time with two groups of youngsters who were slightly over 8 years old. One group was in a totally segregated program, the other in a partially integrated one. The HSD was given in the fall and repeated again 8 months later in the spring. The mean scores for the segregated group fall and spring were 6.50 and 7.60, while the mean scores of the partially integrated were 7.53 and 6.11. The increase of 1.1 versus the decrease of 1.42 is a statistically significant difference which has been interpreted to mean that youngsters in segregated special classes develop a poorer self concept than youngsters in partially integrated special classes.

The believability of this research pivots on the reliability of the HSD In this conncection Meyerowitz indicated that the test-retest reliability of the HSD is 80 percent, that is, 4 out of 5 choices do not change from test to test but 1 does. In the 22 item test, 4.4 items or 2.2 plus and 2.2 minus could be expected to occur by chance alone. Assuming a mean score of 6.50 on a first test, by chance, retest scores could run from 4.3 to 8.7 with no presumption of reflecting a real change in self concept. In neither the Meyerowitz nor the Carroll study is there any evidence that spe-

cial class placement had a negative effect on the self concept of the youngsters. It may have had some negative effect, but the data does not prove it.

The other side of the coin, however, is what happens to retarded youngsters who remain in regular classes. Here the classic studies of Johnson and Kirk in 1950 are our most reliable source of information. Using a sociometric technique these investigators found in 25 classrooms with 689 children:

1. Three times more stars among non-retarded than retarded children.
2. 69 percent isolates among retarded versus 39 percent nonretarded children.
3. Over 10 times more rejectees among retarded than among nonretarded children.

Johnson and Kirk pointed out that the retarded child in a regular class is as socially isolated as he would be if he were not physically present. Jordan (1966) further emphasized the point indicating that special class placement does not precipitate a cleavage between the retarded child and his peers since the cleavage already exists whether the retarded child is in school or not. From an acceptance point of view it does not appear that we do the retarded child any favors by permitting him to stay in the regular classes.

FRUITLESSNESS OF SPECIAL PROGRAMS (ALLEGATION 4)

The question of the efficacy of special classes has been a continuing one, but it was given major visibility by Johnson in 1962 who pointed to the paradox that special classes were accomplishing their educational objectives at the same or a slower rate than regular classes. Dunn in 1968 likewise questioned the effectiveness of special classes and then voiced a plea to stop expanding programs which he felt were undesirable for many of the children in the programs. Dunn presented no original data to prove his allegation of undesirability and relied instead on Johnson's evidence. Johnson, however, cited studies by Pertch done in 1936, Bennett in 1932, Baller in 1936, Kennedy in 1948, and

Charles in 1953. None of these studies followed the fundamental principle of random assignment, and therefore none had an appropriate group of youngsters who could be compared with the special class children.

One study which did have equivalent groups was the 1965 study of Goldstein, Moss, and Jordan. These investigators screened all entering first grade children in schools in three communities in central Illinois. All children who had individual IQ test scores below 85 were randomly assigned to regular or special classes. After 4 years it was found that:

1. Both groups had raised their average IQ's from 75 to 82.
2. Neither group was superior in academic achievement.
3. Neither group was superior on a test of social knowledge.

Johnson's allegation that the special classes were no better than the regular classes in fostering academic achievement was therefore confirmed. However, Dunn's allegation that the classes were undesirable was not. The special classes were no better, but they were likewise no worse; the achievement of the groups was equal.

However, the major function of programs for the retarded is not simply to teach reading, writing, and arithmetic; it is to teach skills of employability and self management. On this measure, all of the studies point to superior results from work oriented programs. As an example, the 1958 study of Porter and Milazzo found 77 percent of retarded students from the special class employed versus 17 percent of others.

The 1971 study of Chaffin, Spellman, Regan, and Davison seems to be even more believable. Youngsters from work-study and non-work-study special classes were carefully equated to assure that they were similar and then compared for employment success after they left school. The non-work-study group had 68 percent employed, but the work-study group had 94 percent employed, a 50 percent improvement. In 1971 when the groups were restudied, the percentages shifted from 68 to 75 percent for the non-work-study and 94 to 83 percent for the work-study (still a significant superiority).

If this were an isolated instance, there might be room for skepticism but similar results are reported from Michigan, Missouri, and California. In the area of preparation for employment, there exists no evidence to suggest that regular class placement is superior to special class. Indeed, all the evidence suggests that regular class placement is inferior.

SELF FULFILLING PROPHESY (ALLEGATION 5)

The believability of the charge that teachers contribute to the self fulfilling prophesy of low academic achievement depends on the validity of the research of Rosenthal and Jacobson, authors of *Pygmalion in the Classroom*. They contended that the achievement of children was influenced by the expectation of teachers. The review of the research which supports the prophesy was written by Thorndike in 1968. That reviewer pointed out that the alleged effect of the prophesy appeared in only 19 children in grades 1 and 2, not in all the children nor in all the grades, and that one of the classes had a reported average IQ of 31. His comment was, "They just barely appear to make the grade as imbeciles!" After reviewing the rest of the data presented on all of the children studied he asked: "What kind of a test, or what kind of testing is it that gives a mean IQ of 58 for the total entering first grade of a rather run-of-the-mill school [p. 710]?"

Thorndike discussed similarly suspicious results and then closed his review by saying:

In conclusion, then, the indications are that the basic data upon which this structure has been raised are so untrustworthy that any conclusions based upon them must be suspect. The conclusion may be correct, but if so it must be considered a fortunate coincidence [p. 711].

Thus, there does not appear to be data to support the self fulfilling prophesy charge.

EXPANDED PROVISIONS OF GENERAL EDUCATION (ALLEGATION 6)

Supposedly, general education is better able to adequately provide for a wide range of individual differences than it has been. Although attention to individual differences in learning style is becoming more common in our schools, the implementation of the findings from this attention is far short of universality. Indeed, programs such as computer based instruction are so rare they are still being reported in the literature.

Melcher (1972) indicated that in the 33 teacher education institutions in Wisconsin not one requires even one course on exceptional children for teachers in regular education. Additionally, he reported a study of 92 administrators by Bullock in 1970 which found that 65 percent of the administrators had no courses, 33 percent had one, and only 12 percent had two or more. If this condition is widespread, it does not appear that many colleges or universities are doing much to prepare teachers and administrators to accept and work with the handicapped.

Even the much heralded programs which espouse the use of operant conditioning as a teaching technique do not reach many pupils and do not deal with learning performance much beyond perceptual learning or sensitivity training. Furthermore, a sensitivity program designed to teach tolerance resulted in a decrease in the positive attitude of counselors after an inservice program which informed the counselors about the characteristics and needs of the retarded (Jones, 1972). Perhaps the programs in regular education are better able to cope with individual differences than they once were, but they are still a substantial distance from being widespread.

One other development casts some doubt on the readiness of general educators to serve the handicapped. Blatt (1972) reported that in Massachusetts, when vouchers were given to parents to allow them to purchase special services, some schools actually discontinued the services they had, thus forcing the parents to patronize private agencies.

A FURTHER CONSIDERATION

There is a further consideration which needs discussion and that is the nature of the special class programs. First, although the classes vary widely in their approaches, even the most traditional academically oriented classes are tuned to individual differences and do not present impossible tasks to the children. For example, reading is not expected of children until their mental ages are sufficiently high to assure a good probability of success—usually a mental age of about 6 given a chronological age of 8 or 9. Thus the classes expect achievement which is consistent with the ability levels of the children. Second, the teachers use concrete materials for instruction. This allows the children to participate actively in learning rather than be passive recipients, because the lessons typically do not require them to deal with abstractions which they are ill equipped to understand. Third, the large majority of programs now lead to work training experiences with eventual job counseling and placement—something not provided in most regular programs.

There are a number of other characteristics of good special class programs, such as an emphasis on developmental physical training and a recreational skill component, but these are not found in all programs. Nevertheless, they are almost never found in regular class or tutorial types of programs. In a nutshell, special classes generally gear the programs to fit the abilities and needs of the children more than general education programs.

POSSIBLE SOLUTIONS

It appears the present criticisms aimed at special classes are not so much criticisms of the classes as they are criticisms of some of the administrative aspects of the program: (a) the use of IQ test scores to identify the retarded, (b) a failure to reevaluate the effectiveness of the program on a regular basis, and (c) the absence of a work preparatory sequence of experience which bridges the gap between school and community living.

If this is the case, then the solution to

these problems would seem to be quite possible. First, the use of the IQ to define mental retardation needs clarifying. Recently it was suggested that mental retardation is demonstrated when an individual is unable to develop appropriately complex methods of thinking as a function of maturation and environmental interaction (Kolstoe, 1970). The mentally retarded are unable to achieve the skill of formal thought as described by Piaget. Thus the thought processes of the child reveal his mental capability. The IQ, however, is a quantitative measure so it may or may not reflect these thought processes and therefore cannot be accepted as an indication of the condition of mental retardation.

A low IQ is, however, an alerting symptom which heralds a learning problem. Therefore, a young child who has a low IQ for whatever reason should have immediate special attention given to his academic needs. These could take a variety of forms, but they would have the common goal of improving his learning efficiency. However, if significant improvement in learning efficiency is not demonstrated within a period of a few months, then the child's learning problems should be tentatively considered to be chronic and a long term development program should be offered the child. In every case, early intervention of a remedial nature should be available to every child who has a low IQ.

Second, reevaluation should take place on a regularly scheduled basis. Exit from the program should be as systematic as entry into the program.

Finally, every program should lead to training in skills needed for work and independent living. Provisions should be made for continuing education well into adult life.

Fortunately, this prescription is already standard procedure in many programs. What seems to be more difficult is to dispel the distortions and half truths which plague our profession. Simply because some programs have not been completely satisfactory is no reason to eliminate all programs. The record of special classes which provide work-study components has been successful employment for 8 out of 10 clients.

On the other hand, if it can be demonstrated empirically that other kinds of services are more appropriate for some children, then there would be every reason to provide a variety of special programs, but they should be in addition to, not in lieu of, special classes.

REFERENCES

Blatt, B. Public policy and the education of children with special needs. *Exceptional Children*, 1972, **38**, 537-545.

Carroll, A. W. The effects of segregated and partially integrated school programs on self concept and academic achievement of educable mental retardates. *Exceptional Children*, 1967, **34**, 93-99.

Chaffin, J. D., Spellman, C. R., Regan, C. E., & Davison, R. Two followup studies of former educable mentally retarded students from the Kansas work-study project. *Exceptional Children*, 1971, **37**, 733-738.

Dunn, L. M. Special education for the mildly retarded—Is much of it justified? *Exceptional Children*, 1968, **35**, 5-22.

Farber, B. *Mental retardation: Its social context and social consequences*. Boston: Houghton Mifflin, 1968.

Gallagher, J. J. The special education contract for mildly handicapped children. *Exceptional Children*, 1972, **38**, 527-535.

Goldstein, H., Moss, J., & Jordan, L. A study of the effects of special class placement on educable mentally retarded children. US Cooperative Research Project No. 619, University of Illinois, 1965.

Johnson, G. O. A study of social position of mentally handicapped children in regular grades. *American Journal of Mental Deficiency*, 1950, **55**, 60-89.

Johnson, G. O. Special education for the mentally handicapped—A paradox. *Exceptional Children*, 1962, **29**, 62-69.

Johnson, G. O., & Kirk, S. A. Are mentally handicapped children segregated in the regular grades? *Exceptional Children*, 1950, **17**, 65-68.

Jones, R. L. Labels and stigma in special education. *Exceptional Children*, 1972, **38**, 553-564.

Jordan, T. E. *The mentally retarded.* (2nd ed.) Columbus, Ohio: Charles E. Merrill, 1966.

Kennedy, R. J. R. A Connecticut community revisited: A study of the social adjustment of a group of mentally deficient adults in 1948 and 1960. In T. E. Jordan (Ed.), *Perspectives in mental retardation.* Carbondale, Ill.: Southern Illinois University Press, 1965.

Kirk, S. A., & Weiner, B. B. The Onondago census— Fact or artifact. *Exceptional Children*, 1959, **25**, 226-228, 230-231.

Kolstoe, O. P. A new definition of mental retardation. Paper presented at the USC Ninth Annual Distinguished Lecture Series in Special Education and Rehabilitation, Summer 1970.

Melcher, J. W. Some questions from a school administrator. *Exceptional Children*, 1972, **38**, 547-551.

Meyerowitz, J. H. Self derogation in young retardates and special class placement. *Child Development*, 1962, **33**, 443-451.

Porter, R. B., & Milazzo, T. C. A comparison of mentally retarded adults who attended a special class with those who attended regular school classes. *Exceptional Children*, 1958, **24**, 410-412, 420.

Thorndike, R. L. Review of *Pygmalion in the Classroom* by Robert Rosenthal & Lenore Jacobson. *Review of Education Research*, 1968, **5**, 708-711.

Weiner, B. B. Hawaii's public school program for mentally retarded children. Unpublished doctoral dissertation, University of Illinois, 1958.

CHAPTER 24

Considerations for serving the severely handicapped in the public schools

ED SONTAG
U.S. Office of Education

PHILIP J. BURKE
U.S. Office of Education

ROBERT YORK
University of Wisconsin at Madison

ABSTRACT: *Due to recent court decisions the exclusion privilege, previously allowing school systems to deny public education to severely handicapped children, is becoming a legal option no longer. This article examines the administrative concerns and problems regarding the education of severely handicapped children and attempts to offer some general solutions and plans of implementation.*

The suit brought by the Pennsylvania Association of Retarded Children (1971) in Federal court and its resulting decision clearly stated that free public school education should be provided for mentally retarded persons. However, another suit and its resulting decision of even greater significance to the special education community is the *Mills v. Board of Education of the District of Columbia* (1972) case. This decision expanded the implications of the Pennsylvania right to an education situation in that all handicapped children, not just those labeled as mentally retarded, have a right to a public education. In addition, the Mills case is considered "a final and irrevocable determination of plantiffs' constitutional rights [Friedman, 1972]" while the Pennsylvania

decision is based on a consent agreement and does not possess as strong a precedential valve as the *Mills v. Board of Education of the District of Columbia* decision.

In his summary statement, U.S. District Court Judge Joseph C. Waddy, on August 1, 1972, stated:

That no child eligible for a publicly-supported education in the District of Columbia public schools shall be excluded from a regular public school assignment by a Rule, Policy or Practice of the Board of Education of the District of Columbia or its agents unless such child is provided (a) adequate alternative educational services suited to the child's needs, which may include special education or tuition grants, and (b) a constitutionally adequate prior hearing and periodic review of the child's status, progress, and the adequacy of any educational alternative [Abeson, 1973 p. 3].

The judgment also stated that the defendants and those working with them be en-

Reprinted from Education and Training of the Mentally Retarded 13:20-26, 1975, with permission.

joined from taking any actions which would exclude plaintiffs and members of their class from a regular public school assignment and/or not provide the students with alternatives at public expense and a constitutionally adequate hearing. Furthermore, the District of Columbia shall provide each child of school age ". . . a free and suitable publicly-supported education regardless of the degree of the child's mental, physical or emotional disability or impairment . . . [Abeson, 1973 p. 3]." Thus, insufficient resources may not be used as a basis for excluding these children from their right to an education. It is this decision which demolishes the traditional "if we had the money, we'd be glad to help these kids" argument.

In the above case, the defendants offered the response that they could not:

. . . afford plaintiffs the relief sought unless the Congress appropriated the needed funds, or funds were diverted from other educational services for which they had been appropriated. The court responded: The defendants required by the Constitution of the United States, the District of Columbia Code, and their own regulations to provide a publicly-supported education for these 'exceptional' children [Abeson, 1973 p. 2].

The precedent established by these cases and the impetus supplied by other litigation concerned with the denial of civil rights for handicapped children has placed new demands on the special education community. It is then the purpose of this article to examine the administrative concerns regarding the education of the severely handicapped child previously excluded from public education.

THE PROBLEM

For years, many school systems in the United States have had programs for orthopedically handicapped, trainable level retarded, deaf blind and/or emotionally disturbed students. However, it is the rare school system that has provided comprehensive programs for severely involved retarded, severely emotionally disturbed, and immobile mutiply handicapped students. Now that the exclusion privilege is becoming no

longer a legal option, school administrators will have to provide educational services for *all* children in their districts. This includes students who are not toilet trained; aggress toward others; do not attend to even the most pronounced social stimuli; self multilate; ruminate; self stimulate; do not walk, speak, hear, or see; manifest durable and intense temper tantrums; are not under even the most rudimentary forms of verbal control; do not imitate; manifest minimally controlled seizures; and/or have extremely brittle medical existences.

Obviously, when large enough numbers of the above mentioned children enroll in the schools over a brief period of time, the special education community will be confronted with problems and challenges. These problems and challenges will be at least in degree, if not in kind, something which the schools have never confronted on such a large scale.

When viewed generally, severely handicapped students do not present as many problems for administrators as they have had presented to them in the past by other students. However, in our view, the problems presented by the severely handicapped are usually more pervasive, more intense, and more expensive to solve. That is, most administrators experience difficulties in relation to medical services, transportation, parent-school interactions, scheduling, student-teacher ratios, affiliations with nonschool agencies. In comparison, these problems are not of the same degree as those faced by administrators of public school programs for severely handicapped students.

ADMINISTRATIVE CONSIDERATIONS

The following is a brief presentation of some traditional considerations as they relate to school programs for severely handicapped students.

Cluster and dispersal approaches

One of the initial considerations facing any administrator of programs for severely handicapped students is the location of classes for these students. For organizational purposes, service delivery models range from a self contained school approach, to classes of severely handicapped students dispersed throughout a school district.

If the administrators choose to adopt the cluster approach then it appears that many of the same advantages and disadvantages of placement in a residential institution are relevant. For example, if the severely handicapped students were clustered, the following advantages are possible:

1. If the program were a separate entity, it would have high community visibility and teachers, parents, the general public, and administrators could relate to the salient needs of the specified group.
2. If grouping were done on the basis of functioning level then neighborhood boundaries would be irrelevant.
3. Inservice training would be easier because the staff could discuss their own successes and failures with each other as well as with external consultants.
4. Teacher morale and cooperation would be better because teachers could share common challenges and problems and not feel that they were "the only people in the world" with such intense problems.
5. The provision of ancillary services (nurses, physical therapists, psychologist, social workers, speech and language therapists, etc.) would be more efficient because professionals would spend less time traveling from school to school and more time with the teachers and students.
6. The delivery of medical services would be particularly suited to the clustered approach because (a) severely handicapped students generally have more medical problems than less handicapped students, (b) the standard school ratio of nurses to pupils would be reduced for these students, and (c) a higher nurse-student ratio would be tolerated if a nurse was assigned full time to a particular school.
7. It would be easier for local school officials to design and implement a relevant and efficient curriculum because students could move fluidly from program to program.

8. Involvement with teacher training and research agencies could be more fruitful because potential teachers would be more easily supervised and exposed to students with varying age and functioning levels. In addition, researchers could be more easily induced to attempt to solve the day to day instructional and management problems presented by the students.

While there have been and will continue to be many advantages to a clustered approach, the history of the care and treatment of severely handicapped persons undoubtedly casts a great deal of suspicion upon clustering. For example, many parents will consider clustering as another form of institutionalization. The students will be, by administrative fiat, categorically excluded from "normalization factors" as they relate to education. The educational community at large will not be given the opportunity to desensitize to individual differences. The students in a special school will be deprived of interacting with, observing, and imitating students of different behavioral repertoires. Depending upon the location of the school, certain students will be required to spend an inordinate amount of time in transit, etc.

However, by choosing to disperse these special clustered classes throughout a school district, other advantages can be seen:

1. The programs for severely handicapped students would be represented in nearly every school, making contact with regular educational programs, personnel, and students the norm. Integration of the severely handicapped into the community and acceptance of these students may be enhanced by this widespread mutual contact of regular education and special education students.
2. Despite grouping by functional level which must be utilized in the school system, most children would be placed in schools near their homes. School placement in close proximity to a student's home may yield the advantages of convenience, fewer transportation problems, superior community accceptance and adjustment, etc.

3. The unique problems presented by severely handicapped students (medical, transportation, behavior management) are also dispersed across a greater range of settings and personnel. This may encourage diversified attempts to remediate these difficulties, eventually yielding the most effective and practical solution.

An important consideration in a decision to disperse classes for severely handicapped students is the physical structure of the schools to be utilized. Since most schools are designed for ambulant students who experience few sensory-motor impairments, the typical facilities may require modification. Obvious examples of potentially troublesome structural facilities are stairs, crash bar doors, combination lockers, toilet facilities, and even limited flow faucets, or spring loaded toilet paper dispensers.

Unfortunately, despite the above considerations, the sudden influx of large numbers of new students into the already overburdened school systems will mitigate against deliberations concerning the most educationally sound service delivery model. What seems to be happening and what will continue to happen over the next few years, is that students will be placed where there is space, whether that space is in a rented store, a leased private school or church basement, a regular school, a special school, or a school maintained by the public school system in a residential center.

Personnel

In our view, there is a direct relationship between the level of the students' disability and the competencies of the teachers, i.e., the more pronounced the level of disability, the more specific and precise are the competencies required of the teachers. Most nonhandicapped and mildly handicapped students acquire information and skills from many diverse and nebulous sources: parents, teachers, siblings, peers, TV, toys, etc. These children can develop in spite of a poor teacher or an unconcerned parent. However, severely handicapped students have not been able to acquire the general basic skills and information in any way, from anyone, or anything. Therefore, unless drastic environmental manipulations are engineered, severely handicapped students will not be able to acquire the needed general basic skills and information. Procedures that are typically used by parents, TV producers, siblings, and most classroom teachers to impart skills and information to nonhandicapped and mildly handicapped students are of little utility with severely handicapped students.

The issue then becomes "What competencies are needed by the teachers of severely handicapped students?" In our view, the teachers' competencies are directly related to the instructional problems and acquisition deficits presented by the students. Thus, if the students are not toilet trained, but are physically capable of becoming so, the teacher must have within her instructional repertoire an applicable technology which will result in such students becoming toilet trained. If students are nonimitative, nonverbal, and/or do not attend or respond to social stimuli, then the teacher must be able to teach the students to speak, imitate, and/or to relate to social stimuli.

Concomitantly, the teachers must be able to do away with self mutilating behavior, stereopathics, temper tantrums, and various escape and avoidance behaviors. In addition, the teachers must be able to teach the students to play with and acquire information from materials, self feed, self dress, ambulate, write, read, compute, etc. Finally, it is the teacher who will be the major source of practical information for the parents of the students in her charge. Thus, the teacher must be able to function as an effective parent-trainer.

At this point in time, it is a rare teacher who has been able to acquire all the skills needed to teach severely handicapped students merely from the experiences obtained in his or her college level special education training program. Assuming that the previous statement is accurate, then it seems logical that there are very few teachers in the field who have the competencies to teach severely handicapped students and that there are very few, if any, teacher training programs producing teachers with these needed competencies. Thus, most of the new classes arranged for these students will be staffed by untrained teachers.

Unfortunately, this situation will exist until special education training programs around the country develop programs that actually train teachers to teach the severely handicapped. This too, will require a major reorientation of special education training programs and the development and infusion of needed technological information either from research in special education or from allied disciplined areas (experimental psychology, applied behavior analysis, etc.).

Severely handicapped students often present instructional and management problems and this necessitates lowering the pupil-teacher ratios even lower than those considered conventional in special education. At first glance, it might seem tenable to suggest ratios of 7, 6 or 5 to 1. However, a class can be disturbed if only one student ruminates or aggresses towards others, or self mutilates and is required to sit in a chair, even if the remaining students are passive and cooperative. This dilemma is particularly debilitating if the teacher is not allowed to use physical restraints or contingent aversion stimulation (punishment). Until teachers are trained to alleviate severe management problems, one option which the teacher might consider is to use other persons (parents, volunteers, university and high school students, teacher-aides, work-study students) when attempting to respond to an individual student's problems.

In addition to the lowering of student-teacher ratios demanded by severely handicapped students, these students also require programming throughout the school day. This is especially relevant to the traditional slack times in the regular teacher's day. Recess, lunch, or free time before or after school are times when the students cannot be left to themselves or lumped into the high student-teacher ratio situations usually encountered. Initially, these periods must be considered instructional time and the students should be taught how to play, eat, and occupy their free time. The additional staff and programing necessitated by this total day approach is considerable and requires careful administrative consideration for success.

The inservice needs for teachers of severely handicapped students are different from those found in regular education, thus the people who have the most to offer these teachers are usually not school personnel. Psychologists, experienced in applying behavior modification procedures and institutional personnel experienced with severely handicapped students, often provide a more valuable contribution to these teachers.

Just as the special education community will be presented with unique problems, due to the influx of severely handicapped students, so will those professionals attempting to provide ancillary or supportive services. Consider the dilemma of the art, physical education, and music teachers. They will be confronted with groups of students who eat paint and guitar strings, do not follow verbal directions, do not imitate, who self stimulate, and self mutilate. Consider the school social worker or guidance counselor who is concerned with helping parents and students "adjust to their problems." Parents' "problems" in turn, center around children who do not self feed, throw temper tantrums at the slightest provocation, aggress toward peers and siblings, bang their heads on walls, chew their fingers and hands, and fake seizures. Consider the school psychologist whose evaluation instruments are usually designed for a less handicapped population and who is asked by the teacher for help with a child who screams or sleeps all day long, who eats inedibles, or who sits on the floor looking at his right hand for hours on end.

The point is, that teachers cannot expect to receive direct assistance from traditional ancillary personnel. This is why it was previously emphasized that the teachers must be trained to function as behavioral management specialists, speech therapists, parent trainers, etc., until the ancillary service community itself trains individuals to function with the severely handicapped.

Medical problems encountered while working with severely handicapped individuals are more numerous and oftentimes more extreme than those encountered with the typical school population. Seizures, congenital defects, sensory-motor deficits, etc., are common among the severely handicapped. It is these situations which necessitate extraordinary services from teachers and medical personnel within the school system. The ability to administer medicine (as prescribed by physicians) becomes an essential part of the teacher's role, as does her ability to handle seizures, physical positioning, and daily exercise regimens. This in itself, suggests the need for a liason between medical and school personnel never before realized.

Motility

The area of transportation for severely handicapped students represents another problem which requires special consideration by administrators. Most students either walk, bicycle, or ride buses to schools. However, severely handicapped students due to present physical or intellectual functioning, may be unable to transport themselves via walking or bicycling. Also, many parents have not taught their severely handicapped children to traverse streets safely and/or are fearful of the child getting lost or abused, exploited or teased by other persons, or becoming incapacitated in the streets due to manifestations of various physical anomalies (seizures, crutches), or inclement weather conditions.

One alternative is that the parents take the student to school or arrange for an older more adept person to supervise the transportation. While this option may alleviate some of the problems, what can be done if the parents work and cannot be present, or if other willing and able persons cannot be found, or if the severely handicapped student does not attend the same school as the potential transporters?

As schools come under mandate to provide educational programs, it is likely that they will be held responsible for getting the students to school. Aside from increased expenditure, at least in terms of vehicles and drivers, transportation by bus presents other problems. The severely handicapped students may display hyperactivity, physical aggression, stereotyped behavior, self mutilation, severe seizures, or other behaviors which cannot be ignored or dealt with in the typical manner by untrained bus drivers. What does a driver do if a student has a seizure, starts self mutilating, throws feces, aggresses towards other students, screams all the way to and from school?

Indeed, it is the rare driver who has, without training, the expertise to manage these problems. One obvious solution would be to provide the driver with an aide. Another is that school systems will have to reconsider the use of various physical restraints in order to protect the students from themselves and others. While these may be temporarily expensive measures, they are insufficient. That is, in our view, most severely handicapped children can either be taught to traverse to school or to behave on a school bus.

Furthermore, travel skills should be a part of the school personnel technological repertoire when parents lack such skills. What remains then, is the special bus and seating arrangement for physically handicapped children, help in boarding and disembarking from these buses, and the elimination problems for children not yet toilet trained.

TODAY AND TOMORROW

School districts confronted with implementing either mandatory court decisions or legislative actions are in different situations from those districts which have the time to think and plan for the day when the problem will directly confront them. Nevertheless, it appears to us that there are at least two levels within which the entire educational community must operate.

The first level may be called structural. Within the structural level, we must secure facilities in which to house the students during the school day, appropriate the money to operate a program, hire personnel, locate all those children who are not now being served in school, furnish the classrooms with equipment and materials, orientate parents, arrive at reasonable student-teacher and student-nurse ratios, make attempts at inservice training, and strive for some semblance of success.

The second level we must operate in may be called functional. Once the students have a room, a budget, a teacher, equipment, and a reduction in the immediate pressure, we then have to go about the more difficult task of upgrading the level of instruction. This must be done in order to effect substantial changes in the life styles of the students. Success at the functional level will be more costly, will take more time, and will require more resources than success at the first. In our view, success at the functional level will require the following:

1. The development of relevant and efficient preservice and inservice teacher training programs.
2. The development of highly specialized doctoral level, teacher training, research, and instructional design personnel.
3. The development and dissemination of a more efficient instructional technology, instructional content (scope and sequence), and instructional materials.
4. The development of parent training programs which will enable the parents to prepare their severely handicapped children for school and work intensively with teachers toward optimal student development.

5. The development of relevant vocational skill training programs.
6. The development of life encompassing service plans so that after 15 or 18 years in a public school program the students can avoid spending the remainder of their lives in dehumanizing residential institutions.

Finally, it seems that the educational community is receiving the brunt of parental, legal, and legislative pressures. While in many ways this pressure is justified, educators must communicate to the community that the school experience cannot and should not be responsible for or ever become involved in the total life styles of the students it attempts to serve. Other persons and community agencies must develop with and adapt to the problem.

REFERENCES

Abeson, A. (Ed.) *A continuing summary of pending and completed litigation regarding the education of handicapped children.* Arlington, Va.: The Council for Exceptional Children's State-Federal Information Clearinghouse for Exceptional Children, 1973. Pp. 1-5.

Friedman, P. *Mental retardation and the law: A report on status of current court cases.* Washington, D.C.: Office of Mental Retardation Coordination, Department of Health, Education, and Welfare. 1972.

Mills v. Board of Education, Civil Action No. 1939-71 (District of Columbia), August, 1972.

Pennsylvania Association for Retarded Children v. Commonwealth of Pennsylvania, Civil Action No. 71-42 (3 Judge Court, E.D. Pennsylvania), January, 1971.

Discussion questions

1. What is a resource room? How does this placement alternative differ from the concept of "special class"?
2. Do you see the resource room eliminating the need for the self-contained special class? What are the positions of Sabatino and Kolstoe? What is your position? Cite supporting evidence for both sides of this issue.
3. The "effects of labeling" has always been a controversial issue in the field of mental retardation. Discuss the allegation that "labeling harms children." Do you agree with the positions of MacMillan and Kolstoe? Why? What are some alternatives to labeling?
4. Due to recent court decisions public education can no longer deny services to the severely handicapped child. Do you agree with the concept of mandatory education for all children? What about the problems of practicality? Discuss some of the recommendations made by Sontag, Burke, and York. Are they functional for programs that you have encountered?

IMPLICATIONS FOR TEACHER PREPARATION

The developments and trends in educational delivery patterns discussed in the previous section have significant implications for preparing teachers. This has been a mutual impact that has combined the interactive influence and leadership of professionals in the field, state departments of education, and institutions of higher education. The details and change agent forces have varied greatly from situation to situation. There is no plan that is guaranteed to generate program change and improvement in all settings. Even to describe all of the approaches that have succeeded and failed would require many more pages than can be allocated in this volume. It is important, however, to present an overview of how innovative delivery patterns relate to certain dimensions of teacher preparation. That is the purpose of the present section.

One trend that has received considerable attention in recent years has been the principle of normalization. The principle of normalization was initially formulated by Nirje (1969) as ". . . making available to the mentally retarded patterns and conditions of everyday life which are as close as possible to the norms and patterns of the

mainstream of society" (p. 181). This principle has been restated in a variety of forms, and its basic conceptual tenants are familiar to special educators in general as well as those specifically concerned with mental retardation. The principle of normalization is seductively appealing. It would be difficult to find individuals who would not agree with it either ideologically or emotionally. In many cases, however, the vast ramifications with regard to societal implementation have not been thoughtfully considered. The deceptive simplicity of the concept, as well as the emotional loading, have often led to naive interpretation and lack of serious attention to what the resulting implications are. These statements should not be interpreted as being in opposition to the principle of normalization. They are, instead, made as a plea for careful and comprehensive consideration of the action and arrangements necessary if the principle is to be honestly and realistically embraced. The first article in this section, by Charles Kokaska, explores one aspect of this arena, implication for teachers.

The second article in this section continues an examination of issues and trends in special education and draws further implications for teacher preparation. In this paper John Ostanski emphasizes the careful and thoughtful consideration of changes in preparation programs before they are implemented extensively. This caution is balanced with the urging to move ahead on what he terms a "trial and success basis." Combined with recommendations for changes in teacher preparation is the basic challenge to move ahead with caution and deliberate speed but to avoid the pitfalls that are always present in change, that of falling prey to ill-conceived or poorly thought out fads. This is an extremely important message for professionals working with mentally retarded individuals.

The third article in this section provides a logical sequel to Ostanski's paper by presenting a challenging description of change in teacher preparation. This article, by Florence Christoplos and Peter Valletutti, illustrates some of the many issues and trends influencing change that were alluded to by Ostanski. It also exemplifies the complex and multifaceted considerations involved in responsive teacher preparation. Although Christoplos and Valletutti present their model in the general framework of special education, the nature of their discussion demands attention by those who consider themselves exclusively in the "area" of mental retardation.

The final article in this section addresses an area that has received increasing attention in recent years, the area of severely and profoundly handicapped. For the most part, teacher preparation during the last two decades has attended to the mildly handicapped. Only recently, as mainstreaming and normalization principles have been actively debated, have special educators in teacher preparation begun to address the needs of the severely handicapped. The previous posture was more informal happenstance than a conscious exclusion of this segment of the population. It was, however, quite real and also aimed at response to the needs of those individuals who constituted the largest percentage of the retarded population. The article by Susan and William Stainback and Steven Maurer represents a crucial statement for teacher educators and students who are moving into the severely and profoundly handicapped arena.

REFERENCE

Nirje, B.: The normalization principle and its human management implications. In Kugel, R., and Wolfensberger, W., editors: Changing patterns in residential services for the mentally retarded, Washington, 1969, President's Committee on Mental Retardation, pp. 179-195.

CHAPTER 25

Normalization: implications for teachers of the retarded

CHARLES KOKASKA

California State University at Long Beach

ABSTRACT: *The author identified three major implications for teachers' functions which can be drawn from the principle of normalization. They involve the utilization of risk components within instruction, recognition of the transience of the teacher-learner situation, and modification of attitudes toward the retarded's participation in society.*

Within recent years the term "normalization" has been added to the nomenclature in the field of mental retardation. The term and its principle components were initiated in the Scandinavian countries and introduced to American practitioners in a monograph sponsored by the President's Committee on Mental Retardation (Kugel & Wolfensberger, 1969). Although primarily presented in relationship to the care and management of institutional populations, normalization has been expanded by authors to demonstrate the practical applications in the continuum of services for the mentally retarded (Bruininks & Rynders, 1971; Perske, 1972; Wolfensberger, 1972). The principle of normalization places particular emphasis upon the congruence between the process and goals of service for the retarded. The intent of this discussion is to identify the implications of this means-ends relationship for the educational setting.

Reprinted from Mental Retardation 12:49-51, 1974, with permission.
Author: Charles Kokaska, Ed.D. (Boston University), Associate Professor, California State University, Long Beach, California 90840.

THE ELEMENT OF RISK

In his observations of the Scandinavians' approach to normalization, Perske (1972) described planned activities which included degrees of risk in one's functioning. He provided accounts of retarded individuals being allowed to live in apartments in Stockholm, operate heavy-duty punch press machines on assembly lines, or being placed in social situations which required self-initiated decisions.

Perske contended that denying an individual exposure to normal risks commensurate with his functioning tended to have a negative effect on his sense of human dignity and delayed the development of a sense of responsibility. In addition, the removal of all risk diminished the individual in the eyes of others who imagined him to be without ability and, consequently, without social status. The "positive self-concept" will not thrive under conditions which by their very nature and structure convey the covert message that one is regarded as being incapable of fulfilling a respected role.

Introducing the element of risk into the teaching process may be easier in the situations Perske described as compared to those encountered by public school personnel. First, his descriptions included adult experiences in community settings which are not as easily duplicated in public schools or at the elementary levels. Secondly, several examples of risk fall within the category of potential physical danger. School codes define the teacher's responsibility for the physical safety of the student; this would tend to discourage forms of experimentation that involved those kinds of risk. However, if one moves from the specific examples provided by Perske to the concept involved in the experiences, the chances of generalization to related classroom instruction are increased.

Risk is one element in the process of problem solving. The characteristics and amount depend upon the teacher's estimation of the individual's capacity to deal with the problem as well as the consequences of the encounter. Teachers have always estimated "risk" as defined by such social factors as self-esteem, popularity with peers and, even, teacher approval. The student who attempted to read to the class or solve arithmetic problems at the blackboard encountered risk and, hopefully, the teacher was aware of its configuration and consequences.

The essential element is that teachers continually involve students in problem solving which includes what may be termed "risk components." The risk components are integral to the process and provide a degree of status to the results. This process includes decisions and is initiated by "How can . . . ?" questions. For example, "How can you place three body parts on the floor (as in movement exploration)?" "How can you count to 100 (as in mathematics)?" "How can you make a fire (as in science)?"

Basic knowledge is required for each question, but the possibility for numerous answers allows students to be "correct" while engaging in search and analysis procedures. Students must be provided with the practice of reaching decisions long before society expects them to make choices commensurate with their chronological status as an adolescent or adult.

Teachers often deal with "What if . . . ?" queries in the realm of fantasy, which can be changed to "reality encounters" by transforming the questions into situational decisions. For example, the teacher may misplace the key to the classroom so that students must determine a way to enter or leave, or arrange for the school bus to be a "trifle late."

The idea is to place strategic hurdles in the educational environment which foster independence of action and provide practice in solving problems that establish one's status as a competent human being. This requires that the teacher view her classroom activities from a frame of reference which includes the continual question "Does that activity provide experience with responsibility and prepare the student to cope?"

HOME BASE

Normalization requires a closer coordination between the instructional activities of the classroom and home. Teachers and parents must be mutually informed about expectations and experiences of the two settings which are related to the overall attempt at integration in society. This is especially crucial if the professionals' interpretation of "mainstreaming" and its corresponding requirements varies from that of the parents'. Differences of opinions and practices have been reported in such areas as vocational expectation, recreation, and sex education. In all cases, the variance of opinions can interfere with the combined effort toward normalization.

Teachers must be particularly aware of one fact: Although the school is a major service system for normalization and teachers are major agents, the parents constitute the base to the entire process. It is the parents that span the elements of time and space and must, at this stage of the development and coordination of our varied service systems, be considered the crucial agent of continuity. It is the parents who must continually encounter decisions about testing, special classes, vocational training, insurance plans, etc. In a period of history which has been described as increasing in transience (Toffler, 1970), teachers "come and go." No doubt, some individuals are permanent in their teaching positions and locations thus constituting a reliable support for students and parents. But, the classic permanence of *Mr. Chips* can not be projected as a characteristic of the majority of professionals within the field. Balow (1971) estimated that production of special class teachers per year is slightly ahead of the attrition (18,000 compared to 16,000). However, these figures do not include "job switching" within the field due to geographic movement or advancement.

It is the author's contention that teachers must recognize that they are in various stages of transience and utilize this realization to further prepare both students and parents to encounter situations within the normalization process. Teachers would be advised to:

1. Provide instruction to the family which would foster normalization. This would include knowledge of community agencies and their services, projected decision situations, and alternatives and techniques to develop appropriate social behaviors which can be practiced in the home.

2. Anticipate and coordinate a "goodness of fit" as the student functions within and between various social settings and systems. The "goodness of fit" would require that the teacher be in contact with colleagues to facilitate adjustment and success when a student, for example, transfers from special to regular class, school to employment, or home to independent living.

MODIFICATION OF ATTITUDES

The projection of the retarded in such roles as parent, voter, or employee is an important ingredient to the teacher's efforts. Certain individuals will not function at the required level of competence to successfully fulfill defined personal or occupational roles. However, the question is not whether individuals defined as retarded will attain desig-

nated levels of behavior at some future date, but whether teachers can visualize these future functions within present time frames and develop methods which would prepare students for intended participation. The student may attain such roles without assistance. The omission of teachers' participation does not preclude role attainment; but the achievement may be in spite of the teachers' efforts and, in effect, is the most severe condemnation of the profession.

Change in the projected role of the retarded requires corresponding alterations in the functions of those professionals who will provide the appropriate training and support services. Progression toward increased efforts to "mainstream" exceptional learners in the academic and social domains will redefine both the competencies and educational settings for teachers. These modifications and implications for teacher training, diagnostic/prescriptive capabilities and systems for merging special and regular students have received increased attention in the total area of education for exceptional individuals (Reynolds & Davis, 1972; Deno, 1973). Regardless of whether the teacher of the retarded will function in a segregated special class or in some variation of a specialist role, he will be required to appraise his attitudes and activities in relationship to the long-term goals of normalization. It is this author's opinion that the principal requires the instruction to be an "active agent" in coordinating the classroom, home, and community efforts to provide enabling experiences.

The teacher must also concern himself with the congruence between his colleagues' perception of the retarded's ability and projected role in society. Gottwald's (1967) study on public awareness of mental retardation reported a survey of attitudes toward the retarded based on a national probability sample of 1515 individuals. The opinions were relative to the retarded's participation in various activities/function/roles. The following percentages of negative responses were recorded on questions of whether the retarded should:

Go downtown alone	58.0%
Drink liquor	83.8%
Drive a car	77.5%
Marry	53.9%
Have a family	66.1%

Approximately 40% of those responding negatively did not present a reason that could be evaluated by the investigator.

One possible reflection upon the survey results may be that the respondents reported their attitudes toward "what should be regardless of the retarded's actual participation in society." Secondly, the respondents may have been unable to project a particular mental image of a retarded individual (for example, the various retarded children that have appeared in public service advertisements) into the required adult roles as presented in the survey.

One would imagine the other professionals in the school would not record the same amounts of negative responses. However, any one of them could encounter similar difficulties in relating a current status of mental retardation to a projected role and its implied competencies. The "active agent" should anticipate these potential contradic-tions. They must be countered by consistent demonstrations of the individual's ability to achieve and, most certainly, his right to achieve.

REFERENCES

Balow, B. Teachers for the handicapped. *Compact*, 1971, **5**, 43-46.

Bruininks, R. & Rynders, J. Alternatives to special class placement for educable mentally retarded children. *Focus on Exceptional Children*, 1971, **3**, 1-12.

Deno, E. (Ed.) *Instructional alternatives for exceptional children.* Arlington, Virginia: Council for Exceptional Children, 1973.

Gottwald, H. *Public awareness about mental retardation.* Grant No. OEG 3-6-062448-1889. Washington, D.C.: Office of Education, 1967.

Kugel, R. B. & Wolfensberger, W. (Eds.) *Changing patterns in residential services for the mentally retarded.* Washington, D.C.: President's Committee on Mental Retardation, 1969.

Perske, R. The dignity of risk and the mentally retarded. *Mental Retardation*, 1972, **10** (1), 24-27.

Reynolds, M. & Davis, M. *Exceptional children in regular classrooms.* Mineapolis, Minn.: Department of Audio-Visual Extension, University of Minnesota, 1972.

Toffler, A. *Future shock.* New York: Random House, 1970.

Wolfensberger, W. *The principle of normalization in human services.* Toronto, Canada: National Institute on Mental Retardation, 1972.

CHAPTER 26

New dimensions and considerations in the training of special education teachers

JOHN OSTANSKI
University of New Orleans

INTRODUCTION

If we look around us and if we review the literature, there appears to be a definite trend toward significant change in Special Education today. Also, there is no indication that this is "change for change's sake," but rather a much needed, long overdue re-evaluation of our system. Whether this change will result in returning many of the "mildly retarded" to the regular classroom or whether we are headed for a completely "noncategorical" arrangement remains to be seen. But one consideration seems abundantly clear, namely, new approaches will be needed in the training of Special Education teachers.

The implications of these approaches may manifest themselves in new names. The special education teacher may come to be known as some sort of "resource teacher," or perhaps as a "behavioral manager," or even a "teacher-therapist." But regardless of the title, the idea of competency must be explored fully; and this exploration must include a careful definition of the concept of competency. In short, we should know what we are talking about, we should attempt to research our ideas as well as possible, and we should provide for an on-going evaluation. This is

imperative if we dare to move out to make major changes. Education, as a whole, is notorious for attempting to make sweeping changes without full mature thought, without adequate researching, and without any idea of the consequences. As was pointed out by Rusalem and Rusalem (1971) the status quo of special education can be defined on the following grounds:

(1) Research concerning the shortcomings is equivocal.
(2) The reformers have diverse ideas concerning a new structure.
(3) Much of the current special education is worth retaining.
(4) Changes would require more money and personnel when the present system is already funded.
(5) Communities are reasonably well satisfied with the present programs.

If this be true, then it would appear that we have the makings of a dilemma. On one hand, we are saying that change is needed and that change is coming; in fact, it is already underway in various parts of the country. On the other hand, we are saying that perhaps we have not done our homework well enough. Do we know the full implications of the changes; are we aware of what is worth retaining and what "must" go; and worst of all, are we in danger of simply giving

Reprinted from Education and Training of the Mentally Retarded 10:117-119, 1975, with permission.

the communities more of the same only under new and different names?

The point of today's presentation is twofold. First, let us emphasize the importance of "thinking through" these changes before implementing them on any large scale. In line with this point, let us be very careful not to lose what we have already learned in Special Education. Secondly, let us realize that we need not wait and continue to reinforce the mistakes we may have made over the years in Special Education, but rather let us move now on a "trial and success" basis. Let us move out of the special classroom and down the hall and into the mainstream of education.

If there is a corollary to these two points, it is that we must be competent to make the changes.

TRENDS

In looking to the literature it is apparent that, in varied forms, the concept of competency based education is gaining great acceptance (Cates, Flynn, & Berlin, 1972). In line with the principle that schools are accountable for their products is the idea that colleges of education must supply teachers who can demonstrate an actual ability to teach. This would assume, of course, contact with children in their schools and training aimed at these chidren. In the case of Special Education, experience with exceptional children becomes vital.

Smith (1969) described a view of the process of training special education teachers in which contact with exceptional children is the important aspect and in which the underlying tenets of teacher training are constantly empirically verified through evaluation of their usefulness. Smith described one view of special education as positing a defect in the child and blaming the child for not learning. Another view, he says, is that it is the child's environment which is at fault and that those who manage the child's environment, the teachers, must share blame for failure in learning.

Smith claims that exceptional children need to be exposed to behavioral managers who are competent and who can explain and justify what they do. They need, he says, to have teachers who place emphasis on resolving attitudinal disorders. Also, they need effective individualized curricula.

College level special education training, Smith says, must prepare teachers who can use research and understand it. A college level program in special education should further require a minimum demonstrated level of competence in such areas as diagnosis, prescription, behavior modification, and so on. This requires evaluation, he says, by a systematic observation of student teachers working with special classes. The proposal Smith describes attempts to set up a curriculum along these general lines. Finally, he states that

> If merit is seen in emphasizing the need for special education personnel to identify and then demonstrate skill in certain areas, the certification criteria would most certainly have to change. We might then be able to do away with the familiar course names and credits as criteria for certification and require the candidate to demonstrate skill in those performance areas which are viewed as necessary [p. 35].

This paper does not propose changes in certification or degree requirements for any particular state or college, though in some instances this might not be a completely unmeritorious idea. Instead, changes in the manner of organization and execution of certain special education courses and programs are suggested. These suggestions for change are not without some general precedent in some parts of the country and would not interfere greatly with present general university requirements of degree programs. They would require fundamental change in the introductory and methods courses in mental retardation, emotional disturbance, and learning disabilities.

Rochford and Brennan (1972) describe a competency based program of inservice graduate credit in special education, specifically learning disability and behavior problem classes, as well as resource room teachers. A cooperative effort of a school district and a local college in this case used behavioral objectives and work in and on actual classes of exceptional children. The authors state that in view of the problems of defining clear, observable behavioral objectives for an entire program, it may be better to not delay implementation for want of objectives but to begin a program, and then expand it.

Bonham (1970) described a program consisting of readings, films, discussion and observation of exceptional children and their placement. Methods courses consisted of weekly meetings with an instructor, individual readings, and supervised work in classrooms for special children.

It is the position of this paper that these are moves in the right direction. Bringing the student teacher and the exceptional child together in an organized, in-depth manner is seen as the goal of the program herein described. This would go beyond the usual practicum experience so that the goal of relating research and theory to real children can be met. Further, more work with children gives more opportunity to demonstrate competence in education, more opportunity to relate to the problems of children with multiple handicaps, and more opportunity to develop a view of special education based on geniune needs of real children as these needs relate to theory in texts and in the literature.

IMPLICATIONS AND RECOMMENDATIONS

Based on what has just been said, it seems that we can put forth the following as possible new dimensions and considerations in the training of special education teachers:

(1) Cease training "special class" teachers, but rather train teachers more broadly so that they might serve as resource persons, consultants to all teachers, innovators in education, et cetera.

(2) Make certain that the student teachers have much more contact with exceptional children.

(3) Implement fundamental changes in course work, especially methods courses, which would aim at competency.

(4) Prepare teachers to be meaningful consumers of research in so far that continuous new knowledge can be brought to bear in working with children.

(5) Somehow, attempt to "build into" the training program an "understanding and communication system" with school administrators. This last point is of particular importance if we do attempt to channel many of the mentally retarded into the mainstream of education.

Obviously, significant changes in curricula and training programs come slowly and often are far-reaching, having effects on certification requirements, et cetera. This takes time and should come only after proper evaluation and research. Moreover, there is no reason why an existing, somewhat traditional special education program in a school system cannot make certain "administrative adjustments" which would provide for innovation, resourcefulness, and a broadening of the education horizon for handicapped children.

REFERENCES

Bonham, J. L. Training teachers of exceptional children: A participant observer approach. *School and Community*, April 1970, **56**, 42-43.

Cates, P., Flynn, A. & Berlin, B. Panel: Competency based education. Second Annual International Symposium on Learning Disabilities, Miami Beach, Fla., 1972.

Rochford, T. & Brennan, R. A performance criteria approach to teacher preparation. *Exceptional Children*, 1972, *38*, 635-639.

Rusalem, H. & Rusalem, H. Implementing innovative special education ideas. *Exceptional Children*, 1971, 37, 384-386.

Smith, R. M. Preparing competent special education teachers. *Education Canada*, December 1969, **9**, 31-36.

CHAPTER 27

A noncategorical and field-competency model for teacher preparation in special education

FLORENCE CHRISTOPLOS, Ph.D.
Bowie State College

PETER VALLETUTTI, Ed.D.
Coppin State College, Baltimore, Maryland

Teacher-preparation programs in special education reflect a confusing array of conflicting goals, conflicting philosophies, and conflicting procedures. There is little agreement on the issues of whether to stress (a) cognitive or affective goals; (b) a psychological and learning-theory basis for classroom decisions or an educational-cookbook basis for selecting teaching methods and curricula; (c) practicum experiences over course work, and in what balance; and, finally, (d) how to define the elements of good teaching and how to delineate the permissible ways in which teachers can demonstrate them. Recently another teacher-preparation issue has been raised: Shall teachers continue to be prepared for a particular area of exceptionality, or shall common clusters of teacher competencies across areas of exceptionality be the basis of teacher preparation? The Bureau for the Education of the Handicapped of The Office of Education, has sponsored several national and regional conferences on this issue of "categorical" or "non-categorical" approaches.

A confounding factor in teacher preparation is the rapid change in public school

provisions for exceptional children, making uncertain the nature of the situations into which "prepared" teachers will step. The effect of teacher preparation is largely happenstance and unmeasurable unless teachers are given the support and opportunity in their classrooms to use the knowledge and skills in which they have been prepared. In addition, not only must the achievement of the children that teachers work with be measured, but the children's achievement must also be measured in those behavioral areas *taught them by the teachers.* It is senseless to measure what children learn without at the same time measuring what the teacher has been teaching them.

In order to resolve or reach intelligent decisions about the problems of teacher education in special education, it is necessary to have clear philosophical guidelines arrived at by interinstitutional consensus (colleges, public school systems, and state agencies serving a particular geographic population of exceptional children). Cohesive and consistent action in education is dependent on functional guidelines for selection of priorities in goals, competencies, and procedures. A major cause for the absence of long-range effects of intervention procedures is inconsistency in *what* and *how* material is

Reprinted from The Journal of Special Education **6:** 115-120, 1972, with permission.

being and will be taught. Successfully taught short-range goals will be lost if these goals are not used in ensuing programs. To achieve such consistency in curricula requires clarity of priorities.

The program model to be discussed in this paper is based on the overriding assumption that to develop cooperative behaviors based on respect for the dignity and worth of all individuals is a priority educational responsibility (if not *the* responsibility) in special education. To discharge it logically requires heterogeneous experiences to a large degree at all levels of education. Segregation by exceptionality is incompatible with cooperation, and hence with respect, for human variations in interests, behaviors, and beliefs.

A noncategorical approach in public schools and in teacher-preparation programs in special education is based on grouping by common goals rather than by common symptoms. Such grouping provides greater heterogeneous opportunities for mutual cooperation. If another type of grouping is found to be a more effective means of achieving academic goals, the question of priorities arises. The unequivocal bias of the present writers is that goals of cooperation and respect (even if they are not as objectively measurable as academic ones) must not be sacrificed for other goals that are more measurable, and certainly not *because* other goals are more measurable.

In addition to a broad-based program model such as noncategorization by exceptionality, classroom activities may be identified that constitute short-range, measurable objectives that hold a self-evident criterion relationship to the long-range goals of cooperative endeavors involving mutual respect among individuals. Two examples are interstudent tutoring and use of questioning techniques that stress evaluative responses rather than convergent ones. These two procedures for teaching academic materials are consonant with the proposed philosophical guidelines. Successful interstudent tutoring is a self-evident way for students of

different abilities to interact with each other cooperatively and respectfully.

Successful use of nonjudgmental evaluative questioning is, again, an operational way to have children consider alternative beliefs and behaviors and respect differences in beliefs more than, or at least as much as, convergent correct answers. Thus long-range goals can guide the selection of priorities in skills, methods, and organization of classes in special education. A guiding philosophy is more useful for educational decision making than atomized research findings about effectiveness of single (usually academic) programs for exceptional children.

Teaching strategies, consonant with program goals and philosophy, are most effectively developed and evaluate in field practice. To describe appropriate strategies accurately, or to respond well to questions about strategies, are very different skills from successfully using strategies with students. In addition, to teach college students to use certain strategies in the field requires a very different college-preparatory program than if verbal or written responses *about* strategies are the college objectives. Thus field experience and a field-evaluation model is required for effective implementation of any program that professes to prepare teachers to teach in the schools.

In addition to the *(a)* noncategorical, competency-based education of exceptional children and the *(b)* noncategorical, field-competency evaluation of students in teacher-preparation programs, a third concept must be added if the model is to be consistent throughout a teacher-preparation program: The assignment of special education college faculty to teaching and supervisory responsibilities must be on the basis of faculty competency.

A widely supported principle of effective teaching is to provide models of the desired behavior for those who are to learn it (Bandura, 1969; Christoplos, 1971; Miller & Dollard 1941). A major reason for a noncategorical program organization and a field-competency evaluation at the teacher-preparation level is that it provides a model for the teachers of how to teach exceptional children in the public schools, i.e., to group exceptional children by goals rather than by symptoms, and to evaluate exceptional children in terms of behaviorally stated competencies. It is only logical to further reinforce this model by the noncategorical and competency approach to college faculty assignment.

A variety of difficulties arises in trying to dislodge thinking from the traditional categorical approach to grouping. Since this paper is concerned with initiating changes at the college level, the first objective is to identify the desired competencies of college students upon which to base the selection of curricula for the teacher-preparation program. Two competencies have already been identified: tutoring and evaluative-questioning techniques. Other competencies must also be measurably defined and opportunities provided for the field practice and field evaluation of the competencies. Priorities in these competencies must be identified as opposed to merely listing the competencies. Priorities, of course, are based on the continually reemphasized philosophy of cooperation and respect for differences.

The second objective is to organize the teacher-preparation program and curricula so that students from the specialized areas (e.g., mental retardation, emotional disturbance, learning disability) attend classes together as much as possible. Such heterogeneity will broaden their viewpoints and lead to the development of a generalized special educator rather than a specialized special educator. The goal of heterogeneity of children (noncategorization) in public school classes, both regular and special, can be best achieved if the concept is modeled on the heterogeneity of student interests in college classes. Approaches to mutual problems from a variety of specialized interests should benefit attitudes and, in the long run, professional behavior. Techniques of interstudent tutoring and evaluative questioning may also be effectively *modeled* by the college faculty

under heterogeneous college class circumstances.

The third objective is to emphasize field or simulated experiences above the minimal requirements of hours spent in a traditional number of lecture courses. College credit should be shifted from a time basis to a competency-evidenced basis. If emphasis is placed on practicum and demonstration (not instead of, but at least equal to, lecture and discussion), flexibility will be required to schedule the student's time as well as that of the college faculty. The type of experiences and the number of hours in practicum or observation must be individually determined from an evaluation of the student's entering competencies. Guidelines for the extent of required experiences should be clarified and formalized by the faculty during the early stages of program implementation, so that the unique characteristics of the student body in a particular college are exploited.

A fourth objective is to identify college staff competencies and use these as the basis for assignment of responsibilities. More effective use of staff should evolve from faculty self-analysis in regard to their competencies and strengths. On this basis the faculty may then be assigned to teach sections of courses rather than total courses. College-course procedures, program organization, and content thus become a model to which students can adapt their own eventual teaching procedures. In the area of assignment of faculty advisors to students, however, the traditional category division may continue for some time until there is greater familiarity and experience with the noncategorical approach.

The final objective is to use more effectively those competencies of the part-time college staff that may be lacking in the full-time staff. In hiring part-time staff, competencies in needed areas should be the criteria rather than degrees or other traditional and probably irrelevant criteria. For such student goals as effective inter- and intraprofessional relations, students should have the opportunity to observe practitioners with superior effectiveness in such relations and to question and discuss what they observe.

Obviously these goals are far-reaching, pervasive, and unusual enough to require gradual, careful, and closely scrutinized implementation. Several difficulties in achieving the goals will be clear at the start, and no doubt more difficulties will emerge. The resolution of most problems will take time, and there will be continuing problems to face afresh. For a start, however, the following six problems are perhaps the most urgent:

First, the critical competencies needed by students must be identified. This requirement raises the issue of the values and ideals of the faculty, college, and school system. If the college staff effectively determines the final competencies of their students in all priority areas of professional behavior, and if the college students, in turn, have an equally effective and pervasive influence on their students, the importance of ethical issues in choosing competencies and behaviors cannot be overestimated. Increased effectiveness in controlling behaviors leads to wider implications for the ethical responsibility of the decision makers. The implications of what competencies are chosen to be taught may become awesome enough to prevent consideration of necessary immediate decisions. The long-range possibilities must be borne in mind, nevertheless, as decisions are made about choosing desirable short-range competencies and effective ways of assuring their continued demonstration.

A second task emerging from the identification of critical competencies is to develop tests, devices, and procedures for periodically measuring the competencies. The evaluation, for the most part, should deal with field competencies exhibited during internships or after full teaching responsibility is assumed. The major purpose of the latter type of evaluation would be to improve college programs; it should no longer affect the teacher's certification or degree status. Once professional certification has been granted, the professional rights of a teacher to select procedures and curriculum must be respected by the college (regardless of the

less-than-professional status granted to teachers by public school supervisors, principals, and administrators).

If the instruments and measurements are to reflect what a particular faculty is teaching, they will have to be refined and revised on a continuous basis. Ongoing appraisal and modification of the program will necessitate a new evaluation of the content validity and predictive validity of measuring devices. Evaluation must be a permanent component of any program. Evaluation devices should be chosen for their appropriateness to specific programs; it will be some time before there will be sufficient program stability to allow for the inclusion of construct validity in evaluative devices. Evaluation approaches must be empirically rather than theoretically oriented for some time.

A third problem is to design program materials and sequences to effect the desired changes. This aspect of the program especially, should depend predominantly on the individual initative of each faculty member. Extensive use of community resources, audiovisual materials, and materials centers will enrich the program and facilitate goal achievement.

The fourth problem is administrative: What is a feasible rate for implementation of the various aspects of a competency-based, noncategorical program? If each faculty member teaches specific competencies to all or a majority of the enrolled students, eventually an increased student/teacher ratio may result in increased efficiency. At the start the more traditional classroom ratio may be necessary. However, teaching loads may need to be significantly reduced if the staff is to be involved in the measurement of the students' field competencies. The possibility of using outside evaluators should be considered. The question of internal versus external evaluation is an important consideration but beyond the scope of this paper.

The fifth problem, also concerning feasibility, is how to meet state or county certification requirements during the interim period of change and when the final program is established. As long as local certification is oriented to course and degree rather than to competency and experience, colleges will have to maneuver in this regard. Professional pressure must promote total program certification. To this end, state education personnel should be asked to participate in program development and meetings on a continuing basis.

Related to the problem of certification is the task of persuading school systems to hire teachers who are "generally" rather than categorically prepared in special education. In order for these teachers to use competencies and curricula in which they have been trained, much of the training will have to be accomplished in the schools. It thus becomes critical to involve public school personnel as well as state department of education personnel. Only in this way can there be effective teacher placement and evaluation.

The sixth and final problem is one of the most difficult: to identify college faculty competencies. A college program is built largely around the unique competencies of faculty members as well as around student needs. Most college faculty would agree that *who* teaches a course very often determines *what* is taught in the course. Rather than try to minimize teacher effect, it may be well to use it—an "if you can't lick' em, join 'em" approach. Each faculty member must therefore define his or her own competencies to provide demonstrations, lectures, and learning experiences of various types for students. Needless to say, faculty competencies will affect the identification and selection of student competencies the faculty will seek to develop (the first objective discussed). Obviously a program must be flexible enough to change as faculty and faculty competencies change. Not only the needs of the students, but the competencies of the faculty will affect content, format, evaluation, and achievement. Administrators and faculty must be prepared for continuous evaluation and modification of goals and programs.

These objectives are proposed as guidelines for developing a noncategorical field-competency-based program in teacher education in special education. The program is based on the conviction that cooperation and respect for human variations are priority educational responsibilities in special education. Such an approach has not yet been proven effective or feasible. Nevertheless, to implement the approach on a piecemeal basis without this unifying philosophy is to assure failure or to eviscerate the essential change. Piecemeal changes are simply concessions to those who press for change per se; they rarely lead to meaningful change. If the noncategorical, field-competency approach is to be given a chance, it must be treated as more than a fad. Gradual implementation may be necessary but should not stall at, or be confused with, a stage of only partial implementation. A philosophical approach must imbue the entire plan, and the program must progress to its stated goals.

REFERENCES

Bandura, A. *Principles of behavior modification.* New York: Holt, Rinehart & Winston, 1969.

Christoplos, F. Influence of a model of commitment in mild retardation. *Mental Retardation,* 1971, **9,** 26-28.

Miller, N. E., & Dollard, J. *Social learning and imitation.* New Haven, Conn.: Yale University Press, 1941.

CHAPTER 28

Training teachers for the severely and profoundly handicapped: a new frontier

SUSAN STAINBACK
WILLIAM STAINBACK
STEVEN MAURER
University of Northern Iowa

ABSTRACT: *Due to recent litigation and legislation, there will be an influx of severely and profoundly handicapped individuals into community based public education programs. As a result, teachers who possess the knowledge and skill to foster the growth of these individuals will be needed. The onus of responsibility is on the universities to prepare competent teachers. This article examines the basic components that will have to be integrated into the existing structures of teacher training programs to adequately prepare teachers of the severely and profoundly handicapped.*

The severely and profoundly handicapped consist of a group of individuals who until recently could generally be found on the back wards of large state institutions. They were frequently found in cribs responding very little to the limited stimuli present. Sontag, Burke and York (1973) describe these children as those who self multilate, regurgitate, ruminate, aggress towards others, display stereopathics (rocking, handwaving), manifest durable and intense temper tantrums, have serious seizures, and/or have ex-

tremely brittle medical existences. Included are those who do not suck, swallow or chew, imitate, ambulate, speak, see, toilet themselves, respond to simple verbal commands and/or those who do possess multiple handicaps. They have been labeled untrainable, profoundly retarded, seriously disturbed, multiply handicapped, crib cases and custodial.

It was not until behaviorists (Bensburg, Colwell & Cassel, 1965; Fuller, 1949; Rice & McDaniel, 1966) began conducting research with this population that the learning potential of the severely and profoundly handicapped was recognized. While the necessary initial research was being conducted, parents of these individuals began lobbying through such strong parent groups as the National Association for Retarded Citizens (NARC).

Reprinted from Exceptional Children **42:**203-210, 1976, with permission.
Susan Stainback is Assistant Professor, **William Stainback** is Associate Professor, and **Steven Maurer** is Graduate Assistant, Special Education Division, University of Northern Iowa, Cedar Falls, Iowa. The preparation of this paper was supported in part by HEW Special Project Grant No. 451AH50558.

They worked to gain for their children educational and training opportunities to enable them to develop their full potential. This parental pressure resulted in several major court decisions (e.g. Pennsylvania Association for Retarded Children v. The Commonwealth of Pennsylvania, 1972) that have expanded public educational services to include the severely and profoundly handicapped.

Along with this emphasis on the right to education for these individuals, the "deinstitutionalization philosophy" has evolved which postulates that equal education for this group should come under the jurisdiction of public education. It is noted that education is the job of public educational agencies, not of social services in an institutional setting. As a result of this philosophy, court decisions, and parental pressures, laws have been passed in many states (Education Commission of the States, 1972) that place the responsibility on the public schools for the education and training of the severely and profoundly handicapped.

Other events have signaled a growing commitment to the education of this group.
1. In March/April, 1975, the NARC held a national training meeting on the education of the severely and profoundly retarded,
2. A new American Association for the Education of the Severely and Profoundly Handicapped has been formed (Haring, 1975a)
3. The Bureau of Education for the Handicapped has cited as one of its top priorities the education of the severely and profoundly handicapped (Martin, 1975).

THE NEED FOR TRAINED TEACHERS

As the focus changes from custodial care to education and training for the severely and profoundly handicapped, highly trained teachers will be needed in public education.

Here the onus of responsibility rests on teacher training institutions to design and implement teacher education programs specifically aimed at preparing persons to further develop multiply

handicapped, severely retarded children. (Smith & Arkans, 1974, p. 501).

The number of trained teachers needed will be substantial, especially if one accepts a teacher/student ratio of no more than 1:5. This ratio is tenable when the learning, behavioral, and physical characteristics of the severely and profoundly handicapped are considered.

When estimating the number of teachers needed, the necessity of early intervention should be considered also. Even the more profoundly handicapped preschooler has the potential for learning, among other things, visual and auditory awareness, motor control of the head and trunk, and a rudimentary understanding of vocabulary. It should also be noted that early intervention can prevent the development of abnormal body structure from prolonged periods of bed rest (Luckey & Addison, 1974). In many cases early correct body positioning can prevent physical deformities frequently found in older handicapped individuals (Robinault, 1973).

On the other end of the life continuum, continued education and training during adulthood is imperative to maintain and expand the skills of work productivity and daily existence. It has been recently demonstrated that the markedly handicapped can learn to participate in work activities (Gold, 1973) previously thought beyond their capabilities.

In essence, a teacher/student ratio of 1:5 and the necessity of life long intervention will require that institutions of higher education train teachers competent to aid the growth of severely and profoundly handicapped individuals. In addition, it should be noted that (a) recent medical advances are keeping many children with serious handicaps alive who would otherwise not have lived, and (b) today there is virtually a void of trained teachers of the severely and profoundly handicapped.

TRAINING REQUIREMENTS

Universities have focused their teacher training in special education toward the mildly and, in some cases, the moderately handicapped. The potential special education teacher has received more diagnostic techniques and remediation approaches than the regular classroom teacher. With few exceptions, the basic techniques and materials presented teachers of the mildly handicapped and teachers of so called "normal" students have been the same with changes mainly of emphasis.

The functioning level of the severely and profoundly handicapped will require a wide deviation from what has been the mainstay in university teacher training. The following is a discussion of the training needs of prospective teachers of the severely and profoundly handicapped to provide an impetus for critical evaluation of the content of some elements necessary in teacher training. Discussed here are: (a) diagnostic evaluation, (b) curriculum, (c) methodology, (d) interdisciplinary team work, (e) field experience, (f) parent training, and (g) prosthetic aids.

Diagnostic evaluation

The standard diagnostic and evaluation tools presently employed with the mildly handicapped such as readiness and achievement tests will generally be of little use to teachers of the severely and profoundly handicapped. Even the social maturity tests at the preschool level are frequently too high and/or have too large a gap between skills to accurately assess the functioning level of many severely or profoundly handicapped individuals for training purposes.

Due to the infantile functioning level of some of these individuals and the small achievement increments made over time, it is imperative that teachers of the severely and profoundly handicapped have a thorough working knowledge of human growth and development patterns from birth through beginning preschool as well as the basic readiness and early academic learning process. A high degree of insight into child development during the infancy stage such as visual tracking, responding to stimuli, lifting head, reaching for objects, grasping objects and turning over is needed since it is within this range of functioning that teachers will find many of the severely and profoundly handicapped.

These diagnostic evaluation needs require going beyond the present educational literature. Teachers must become aware of the psychological and medical information concerning infancy and early childhood development. Developmental instruments such as the Gesell Developmental Schedules (1947), the Cattell Infant Intelligence Scale (1940), the Bayley Infant Scales of Development (1969), the Denver Developmental Screening Test (1970), and the Piagetian based Albert Einstein Scale of Sensory-Motor Intelligence (Corman & Escalona, 1969) will need to be closely examined. Most teachers are not aware of, for example, the developmental sequence for evaluating and/or teaching such skills as ambulation.

It is obvious that educational diagnosis and evaluation as we know it for the mildly handicapped and normal student will need modification for teachers of the severely and profoundly handicapped. It should be noted that a few special educators and psychologists (Balthazar, 1971; Sailor & Mix, 1975) have already begun developing diagnostic and evaluation instruments for the severely and profoundly handicapped.

Curriculum

As in all educational situations, the goal of the curriculum for the severely and profoundly handicapped is to move each individual to higher levels in the developmental sequence. The major differences relate to the range of the developmental functioning levels of concern. In the education of mildly handicapped and normal students, the major focus is on readiness for and achievement in reading, writing, arithmetic and social skills. With the severely and profoundly handicapped the curricular emphasis is on response to environmental stimulation, head and trunk balance, sucking, swallowing and chewing, grasping, movement of body parts, vocalizations, and at higher levels, imitation, language acquisition, self feeding, ambulation, dressing skills, toilet training, social/recreational behaviors and functional academic skills. Vocational skills, as with any individual, are important. When individuals reach this level, the bagging of golf tees, stapling packages, or more complex tasks such as the assembly of 14 piece bicycle brakes (Gold, 1973) are a few of the possible additions to the curriculum.

The curricular needs are widely divergent from the mildly handicapped or normal child. Despite the newness of this area, ideas and materials for curricular development are becoming available (Ball, 1971; Meyers, Sinco & Stalma, 1973.)

Methodology

Presently educators and psychologists are finding that the behavior modification methodology is very effective with the moderately and severely handicapped (Haring & Phillips, 1972) with many implications for teaching the most profoundly handicapped.

When classroom teachers have used behavior modification, the stress has been on the manipulation of stimuli that occur after the response to increase or decrease the intensity, duration, or frequency of responses.

With the severely and profoundly handicapped, teachers must continue to apply reinforcement principles. They will need only to become more sophisticated. The concepts of reinforcement sampling, discrimination training, generalization, stimulus control, shaping, backward chaining, contingent aversive stimulation, prompting, fading, modeling, etc. will have to not only be understood, but also incorporated into daily teaching sessions. In addition, the manipulation of antecedent stimuli will be essential. With the severely and profoundly handicapped, responses will not only have to be shaped but elicited. The teacher who waits for the emission of a particular response in order to apply reinforcement principles will waste much precious learning time. Also, knowledge of the most efficient methods for modifying behavior is imperative in controlling severe management problems. Finger chewing, headbanging, aggressing toward others, and feces throwing can quickly and totally disrupt classroom learning.

The precise measurement of behavior will take on new importance. Progress with the severely and profoundly handicapped may not always be easily recognizable. The morale of the teacher as well as plans for the next teaching session will depend upon correct identification of progress.

Perhaps the most important skill that teachers must have is the ability to task analyze behavior. It has been found that breaking down tasks into small sequential steps enhances the speed and quality of response acquisition in the severely and profoundly handicapped (Brown, 1973).

Interdisciplinary teamwork

The importance of interdisciplinary teamwork becomes evident when the daily life of the severely and profoundly handicapped is examined. Many severely and profoundly handicapped individuals live an extremely brittle medical existence. They frequently are under the supervision of medical staff; sometimes gaining nourishment through tubes, urinating through catheters and/or living with reduced spasmodic seizures by continuous medication. (These children will challenge the literal meaning of "zero reject." Here we are referring to community-based education in hospital wards or schools as well as special classes, special schools, and residential centers.)

Due to multiple handicaps, the activities of these individuals must be carefully considered by physicians as well as by physical and/or occupational therapists in terms of strenuousness, bone and muscular involvement, and body positioning. Misunderstanding or overlooking an individual's needs may cause irreparable damage. In addition, these individuals may suffer from partial or total blindness, deafness, and/or paralysis which further complicates the communication process to which ophthalmologists, audiologists, and speech clinicians can contribute their expertise. No one person can be expected to possess all the expertise required to facilitate the development of a profoundly retarded child who is also blind, deaf, and/or cerebral palsied.

Some supportive and ancillary personnel may be unfamiliar with the characteristics of the severely and profoundly handicapped. The school counselor, assistant principal or itinerant art teacher, for example, may never before have worked with children who eat their crayons, self mutilate, stare at their left hand for hours, and/or indiscriminately wail throughout the day (Sontag, et al., 1973).

Receiving medications is a frequent occurrence with the severely and profoundly handicapped. A child who is alert and responsive one day may be docile and unresponsive the next. In their teacher training sequence, teachers will need to be made aware of the reasons certain drugs are administered and their side effects.

These and other aspects will have a bearing on how the teacher works with such individuals. The teacher will be required to design an educational program, but not be the sole contributor. The element of interdisciplinary teamwork is mandatory.

Because of this need for teamwork, it is important that teachers be trained to communicate efficiently and effectively with other disciplines. Courses in speech acquisition and psychology will be needed. Exposure to clinical syndromes and the medical aspects of physically handicapping conditions will also enhance the teacher's ability to communicate.

Finally, it is imperative that teachers be thoroughly aware of their own and other team members' roles. They must know their particular areas of competency as well as the competencies possessed by other professionals and be able to conduct their duties in terms of them.

Extensive field experience

Teachers of the severely and profoundly handicapped will be faced with a population previously considered untrainable. Gains may be slight and tediously slow in coming. This combined with the precise skill application required to effect gains emphasizes the need for immediate feedback and support while actually working with children.

Field experiences will permit prospective teachers to determine if they have the abilities and attitudes required. The enhanced

precision required in the teaching process will be too difficult for some; the development of appropriate attitudes will be impossible for others. For example, an attitude that permits *normal* risk taking is essential. As for any child, the severely and profoundly handicapped must be allowed to experience pleasure from self discovery even at the risk of minor bumps and bruises. Field experience can assist prospective teachers to develop attitudes that will avoid overprotection.

A teacher training program which includes curriculum, methodology, and field experience may help us avoid some of the pitfalls experienced in the earlier training of teachers for the mildly and moderately handicapped (e.g. knowledge of definitions and characteristics, but no teaching skills). Hopefully, we can reduce the frequency of the first teaching day syndrome: "I know the definitions and characteristics, but what do I do?"

Parent training

With the severely and profoundly handicapped the training of parents and/or parent surrogates by the teacher is an important factor. Without the necessary information and support, home care will be beyond the abilities and tolerance level of many parents.

Since the teacher is most closely involved in the overall daily planning and training he/she will be called upon to provide information and support to the parents or parent surrogates. With strong lines of communication between the school and home, a consistent and comprehensive 24 hour program can be devised and implemented.

In order for teachers to assume the role of parent trainers, they must become knowledgeable in several areas. This constitutes another component not previously emphasized in many teacher training programs. A few of the specific competencies needed by teachers to be effective in parent or parent surrogate training include:

1. Explaining student abilities and progress to help parents overcome the problems of under or over protection and inappropriate expectations (either too high or too low);

2. Training parents to deal with explosive, stereotype, self stimulative behaviors as well as appropriate motor responding and verbalization behaviors. This, of course, will make home living a more realistic alternative for the handicapped child, siblings and parents;
3. Being a source of information concerning community resources that can provide health care, social interaction, recreation, etc. This will also include knowledge concerning foster and group home alternatives for parents who are unable to cope with their handicapped child within the existing family structure;
4. Providing parents with knowledge of sources of special clothing and equipment that can aid in easing home care problems and encourage greater independence and self care;
5. Training parents in lifting, carrying, and positioning the nonambulatory;
6. Training parents in techniques for fostering sensory awareness, motor development, communication, eating, toileting, bathing and dressing, etc.
7. Explaining the importance of having the nonambulatory child up and correctly positioned for part of each day in a chair, even if strapped in, rather than flat on his back in a crib or bed. (In addition to enhancing motor development, the child can see and respond to stimuli in his environment other than the ceiling.)

Use of prosthetic aids

In order to successfully deal with the severely and profoundly handicapped population, teachers must be well versed in the use of modification tools such as prosthetic aids. A prosthetic aid is a device used to modify an individual or environment so a previously handicapping condition can be bypassed or eliminated in a given set of situations. Smith and Neisworth (1975) list five broad categories of prosthetic devices. These are locomotion, life support, personal grooming and hygiene, communication, and household aids. It can be observed from these categories that the use of prosthetic aids can permeate almost every phase of life from breathing to brushing teeth to recreation.

Due to the high incidence of multiple handicapping conditions in the severe and profound population, many of them use one if not several prosthetic devices in their daily lives. Teachers of these children will find themselves in classrooms with such items as creepers, walkers, standing tables, cut out trays, splints, motorized beds, wheelchairs, built up and/or modified spoons, knives, and forks. In addition, special prosthetic devices will be used in getting some of these individuals to and from school (e.g. adjustable base lifter). Teachers, when helping children load or unload from the transportation vehicle, will need to be familiar with these devices in order to avoid possible accidents. Potential teachers of the severely and profoundly handicapped should be provided the opportunity to acquire a strong working knowledge of prosthetic aids. They should know how to use and maintain the devices so maximum efficiency and effectiveness can be achieved in the classroom setting.

New devices are being designed to help modify the results of the handicaps of blindness, deafness, paralysis, and voice, muscular, and bone aberrations. As research, development, and use of these devices continues, the need for teachers to become familiar with them will increase.

SOURCE OF EXPERTISE

We have discussed why and in what areas teachers of the severely and profoundly handicapped should be trained. Now the question is where will the universities get the expertise to train prospective teachers of the severely and profoundly handicapped?

Educators are rapidly gaining the legal right to provide education and training for the severely and profoundly handicapped. With or without this expertise, public schools will establish classes for the most profoundly handicapped. Colleges and universities will begin training teachers. We will accomplish the task of providing education and training for the severely and profoundly handicapped. However, if we are to do the most efficient and effective job, we must recognize our current lack of knowledge of training procedures and begin to correct it.

The recent work of Blatt and Garfunkel (1973), Bricker (1972), Brown (1973), Gold (1973), Haring (1975), Hayden (1975), Lent (1975), Sailor and Mix (1975), Tawney (1974), and others should serve as prime sources of reference for the identification of materials, techniques, and procedures found effective for training the severely and profoundly handicapped. In addition, the excellent work of prominent institution personnel (Azrin & Foxx, 1971; Bensburg, et al., 1965; Gardner, Brust & Watson, 1971; Luckey, Watson & Musick, 1968; Watson, 1967) should be closely examined.

The focus on available expertise does not minimize the need for further research and study to update and expand what is currently known. It is only to insure that these relatively early efforts are not ignored.

Although we are for the most part inexperienced in dealing with the severely and profoundly handicapped, public education does provide real advantages for this population. Through public education the severely and profoundly handicapped will receive, by the nature of the organizational arrangement, a considerable increase in environmental stimulation by such aspects as living in a community setting, being transported to and from school, and exposure to many normal activities throughout the day. For example, the simple act of being transported back and forth to school provides a wide array of experiences (e.g. active and/or passive interaction with people). It is this involvement in ordinary daily living (normalization), not our current expertise, that largely justifies community based public school education for the severely and profoundly handicapped.

CONCLUSIONS

Laws and court decisions have been and are being enacted that will mandate a right to education for the severely and profoundly handicapped.

The right to education, if it is implemented, will bring into our special education orbit those children and adolescents who were not previously considered to have the necessary academic potential or even to be capable of acquiring the basic life skills for community living or who are not of the traditionally prescribed age for education. Many special educators never before saw them . . . They were invisible. (Goldberg & Lippman, 1974, p. 331.)

Few teachers are trained to teach these children and few professors of special education are prepared to instruct teachers in educating the severely and profoundly handicapped. This is not to say we cannot do the job. We can and should. However, careful planning will have to occur, if we are to meet this new challenge.

Although laws are being passed to insure public school education for the severely and profoundly handicapped, little money is being appropriated for personnel training. This, of course, enhances the risk of repeating the same mistake made when we first began trying to meet the needs of the less markedly handicapped in regard to the use of ill prepared and unprepared teachers. Because of the pressure to provide special services to the mildly and moderately handicapped, many teachers were not prepared for their jobs. Unfortunately, some handicapped children have suffered, as well as the overall reputation of special education. Although some states are just beginning to overcome the critical lack of trained and certified personnel for the mildly and in some instances the moderately handicapped, we will be faced with new demands for trained personnel for the severely and profoundly handicapped.

Unless adequate support is forthcoming for personnel training, classrooms for the severely and profoundly handicapped are likely to be staffed by untrained teachers. If this happens, these children may fail to progress in an educational environment. This could happen if untrained teachers establish babysitting centers or a watered down curriculum. The severely and profoundly handicapped do not need this kind of educational programing. They need well planned and designed programs developed by rigorously trained special education teachers.

REFERENCES

Azrin, N. H., & Foxx, R. M. A rapid method of toilet training the institutionalized retarded. *Journal of Applied Behavior Analysis*, 1971, *4*(2), 89-99.

Ball, T. (Ed.). *A guide for the instruction and training of the profoundly retarded and severely multihandicapped child.* Santa Cruz CA: Santa Cruz County Board of Education, 1971.

Balthazar, E. E. *Balthazar scales of adaptive behavior for the profoundly and severely mentally retarded.* Champaign IL: Research Press, 1971.

Bayley, N. *Bayley infant scales of development.* New York: Psychological Corporation, 1969.

Bensburg, G. J., Colwell, C. N., & Cassel, R. H. Teaching the profoundly retarded self-help activities by behavior shaping techniques. *American Journal of Mental Deficiency*, 1965, *69*(5), 674-679.

Blatt, B., & Garfunkel, F. Teaching the mentally retarded. In R. M. Travers (Ed.), *Secondary handbook on research on teaching.* Chicago: Rand McNally, 1973.

Bricker, D. Imitation sign training as a facilitator of word-object association with low-functioning children. *American Journal of Mental Deficiency*, 1972, *76*, 509-516.

Brown, L. Instructional programs for trainable level retarded students. In: L. Mann and D. A. Sabatino (Eds.), *The first review of special education*, 2. Philadelphia: Ise Press, 1973.

Cattell, P. *The measurement of intelligence of infants and young children.* New York: Psychological Corporation, 1940.

Corman, H. H. & Escalona, S. K. Stages of sensorimotor development: A replication study. *Merrill-Palmer Quarterly of Behavior and Development*, 1969, *15*, 351-361.

Education commission of the states. *Handicapped Children's Education Program Newsletter*, 1972, *1*, 3.

Frankenburg, W. K., Dobbs, J. B. & Fandal, A. *The revised Denver developmental screening test manual.* Denver: University of Colorado Press, 1970.

Fuller, P. R. Operant conditioning of a vegetative human organism. *American Journal of Psychology*, 1949, *62*, 578-590.

Gardner, J. M., Brust, D. J., & Watson, L. S. A scale to measure skill in applying behavior modification techniques to the mentally retarded. *American Journal of Mental Deficiency*, 1971, *75*, 617-622.

Gesell, A. *Infant development: The embryology of early human behavior.* New York: Harper & Row, 1952.

Gesell, A., & Amatruda, C. S. *Developmental diagnosis.* New York: Harper, 1947.

Gold, M. W. Research on the vocational habilitation of the retarded: The present, the future. In N. R. Ellis (Ed.), *International review of research in mental retardation.* New York: Academic Press, 1973.

Goldberg, I., & Lippman, L. Plato had a word for it. *Exceptional Children*, 1974, *40*, 325-334.

Haring, N. G. Personal communication, May 2, 1975.

Haring, N. G. *Curriculum development for the severely and profoundly retarded students.* Presented at the National Training Meeting on the Education of the Severely and Profoundly Mentally Retarded, April, 1975.

Haring, N. G., & Phillips, E. L. *Analysis and modification of classroom behavior.* Englewood Cliffs NJ: Prentice Hall, 1972.

Hayden, A. *Training early intervention specialists.* Presented at the National Training Meeting on the Education of the Severely and Profoundly Mentally Retarded, New Orleans, April, 1975.

Lent, J. R. Developing daily living skills for the mentally retarded. In J. M. Kauffman & J. S. Payne (Eds.) *Mental retardation. Introduction and personal perspectives.* Columbus: Charles E. Merrill, 1975.

Luckey, R. E., & Addison, M. R. The profoundly retarded: A new challenge for public education. *Education and Training of the Mentally Retarded*, 1974, *9*(3), 123-130.

Luckey, R. E., Watson, C. M., & Musick, J. K. Aversive conditioning as a means of inhibiting vomiting and rumination. *American Journal of Mental Deficiency*, 1968, *73*(1), 139-142.

Martin, E. W. *The federal commitment to education of severely and profoundly retarded students.* Presented at the National Training Meeting on the Education of the Severely and Profoundly Mentally Retarded, New Orleans, March, 1975.

Meyers, D. G., Sinco, M. E., & Stalma, E. S. *The right-to-education child: A curriculum for the severely and profoundly mentally retarded.* Springfield IL: Charles C Thomas, 1973.

Pennsylvania Association for Retarded Children v. The Commonwealth of Pennsylvania, 343 F., Supp. 279 (E.D. Pa., 1972).

Rice, H. K., & McDaniel, M. W. Operant behavior in vegetative patients. *Psychological Record*, 1966, *16*, 279-281.

Robinault, I. P. (Ed.). *Functional aids for the multiply handicapped.* New York: Harper & Row, 1973.

Sailor, W. S., & Mix, B. J. *The TARC assessment system* (User's Manual). Lawrence KA: H & H Enterprises, 1975.

Smith, J. O., & Arkans, J. R. Now more than ever: A case for the special class. *Exceptional Children*, 1974, *40*, 497-502.

Smith, R. M., & Neisworth, J. T. *The exceptional child: A functional approach.* New York: McGraw Hill, 1975.

Sontag, E., Burke, P. J. & York, R. Considerations for serving the severely handicapped in the public schools. *Education & Training of the Mentally Retarded*, 1973, *8*, 20-26.

Tawney, J. W. Acceleration of vocal behavior in developmentally retarded children. *Education and Training of the Mentally Retarded.* 1974, *9*, 22-27.

Watson, L. S. Application of operant conditioning techniques to institutionalized severely and profoundly retarded children. *Mental Retardation Abstracts*, 1967, *4*, 1-8.

Discussion questions

1. How do the seemingly simple concepts involved in normalization become complicated as one thinks of implementation? What plans must receive attention in advance of implementation?
2. What do you see as important differences between preparing teachers for the more severely handicapped as compared to teachers of mildly handicapped children?
3. What do you think the term "competency" means? What might be some of the strong points and problems with competency based teacher preparation?

VOCATIONAL CONSIDERATIONS AND MENTAL RETARDATION

Vocational issues have long been recognized as important if full service to mentally retarded individuals is to become a reality rather than rhetoric. The problems, however, in attaining such a goal are varied and complex. In many cases these difficulties echo the attitudinal postures of society as a whole that interfere with programming efforts in mental retardation. In others, the stark realities of economic considerations come into play. The papers in this section discuss these considerations

and present the reader with a broad examination of mental retardation in the world of work.

The first paper in this section reviews a variety of issues related to employment and mental retardation. Penetrating the very core of vocational problems, Harry P. Bluhm discusses such topics as the employability and employment market in terms of retarded individuals, employer attitudes, and factors influencing employment success. The reader is likely to find the influences and complex interaction between these issues somewhat overwhelming at first. It is exactly this complexity that has historically deterred comprehensive vocational planning on a widespread basis. As noted earlier, however, a solution must be sought if a full service goal is to be attained.

The second paper in this section describes a vocational delivery system for mildly retarded individuals. Relating to some of the issues discussed in the first paper, Bluhm presents this delivery system in the context of competitive employment and the preparation of retarded individuals for such functioning. Including both prevocational and vocational phases, Bluhm illustrates vividly the many dimensions requiring consideration in a delivery system. The reader should remain cognizant of the fact that this delivery system focuses primarily on one segment of the retarded population—persons who are mildly handicapped. With this in mind it is easy to see how workers in mental retardation have been somewhat overwhelmed by the magnitude of the task at hand.

The third and final article in this section focuses specifically on vocational evaluation. In this selection Donn Brolin makes a plea for more coordination of school programs with the life of retarded individuals after they leave school. Additionally, he presents a model for vocational evaluation and placement.

The papers in this section present only a brief glimpse into the complex world of vocational considerations for the mentally retarded. A full and complete examination of this area would require many more pages than can be allocated in the present volume. As with many other facets of mental retardation, the problems are longstanding. Broadly based, well-conceptualized solutions remain the future task of professionals in the field and those yet to enter the discipline.

CHAPTER 29

The right to work: employers, employability, and retardation

HARRY P. BLUHM
University of Utah

The rights of retarded individuals are being affirmed in a variety of arenas by the courts and promoted strongly by agencies representing the interests of this population. The rights to education, treatment, and fair compensation have been upheld by the courts (U.S. Department of Health, Education and Welfare, 1973). Professional organizations such as the International League of Societies for the Mentally Handicapped have also declared that the retarded have a right to productive work and to meaningful occupational opportunities. These efforts have resulted in vocational training programs that are sponsored by public and private institutions and agencies to prepare the retarded for gainful and productive employment.

The purpose of the present paper is to discuss a variety of questions related to employment and mental retardation. These questions cover a broad range of topics such as: Are the retarded employable? What is the status of the employment market for retarded individuals? How are retarded individuals placed on jobs? What are the attitudes of employers toward hiring retarded individuals? What factors affect the employability of retarded individuals and their success in employment? What benefits accrue to society, the retarded person, and his or her family through employment?

EMPLOYABILITY OF RETARDED PERSONS

It has been estimated that there are six million mentally retarded persons in the country with more than half in the working ages of 16 to 64 years (Wolfbein, 1967). Not all of these individuals can qualify and hold jobs in the competitive labor market. Retarded persons who are unable to function at this level of employment may, however, be engaged in productive work under sheltered conditions. Wolfbein (1967) suggested that nearly nine out of every ten mentally retarded persons can be gainfully employed if they receive the proper kind of special training, guidance, and counseling and job development.

A significant relationship seems to exist between level of employment and level of IQ. Conley (1973) conducted a detailed analysis of twenty-two follow-up studies of retarded adults with IQ's ranging from 36 to 89. He found that competitive employment for retarded persons with IQ's less than 40 was impractical. Those severely retarded adults who did hold jobs in the labor force primarily had IQ's in the 40 to 50 range. The employment potential of severely retarded persons at the lowest levels (IQ's between 10 and 20) does not exist since many cannot even walk, talk, or perform simple tasks (Bolanovich, 1972).

The data seem to suggest that the majority of working age retarded persons are employable with the level of employment—competitive or sheltered—dependent upon their IQ level.

STATUS OF THE EMPLOYMENT MARKET FOR RETARDED PERSONS

In studying the status of the employment market for retarded persons, consideration will be given to such subtopics as: (1) the type of jobs retarded persons have held in the labor market, (2) efforts by government, business, labor, and other organized groups to prepare and place the retarded in competitive employment (3) the employment rate for the retarded, and (4) suggestions concerning how job opportunities for the retarded might be expanded.

Types of jobs retarded persons typically hold

The retarded individual generally functions in jobs that are simple, repetitive, and routine. These individuals may be found, however, in a variety of occupations—service, clerical, sales, agriculture, and the gamut of unskilled to skilled jobs. Examples of types of jobs they have held include waiters, dishwashers, barbers, cosmeticians, laundry workers, custodial workers, service station attendants, clerks, store sales personnel, bakers, tailors, dressmakers, painters, routemen, mechanics, and upholsterers (Kruger, 1963; Schumacher and Townsell, 1960; Strickland, 1964; and Bolanovich, 1972).

Organized efforts to place retarded individuals

The first organized attempts involving government, business, labor, and service agencies for the retarded to promote the employment of retarded persons occurred during the mid 1960's. In 1963 President Kennedy requested all federal executive departments to consider retarded individuals for employment in positions

. . . where they meet the necessary performance requirements, or in positions where the performance requirements can be modified to take advantage of their abilities without detriment to the service . . . [U.S. Civil Service Commission, 1963, Letter Number 339-4].

The U.S. Civil Service Commission became responsible for the administration of this program. In the period January 1964 through November 30, 1968, 5284 individuals were placed. Of this number, 62% were retained in their positions with 40% receiving job advancements (Oswald, 1968).

During its operation, the W. T. Grant Company was one of the first national companies that established a corporate policy for the hiring, training, and integrating of the retarded. In 1964 the company earned the first employer of the year award from the National Association for Retarded Children (President's Committee, 1968; National Association for Retarded Children, 1966). Since that time many large and small businesses throughout the country have instituted hiring procedures to employ the retarded. Companies receiving national recognition for their efforts have included Howard Johnson Restaurants (Wall Street Journal, 1966), Iona Manufacturing Company (Sleith, 1966), and Sky Chef, Inc.—American Airlines (National Association for Retarded Children, 1967).

Training programs have been a vehicle for preparing the retarded individual for placement in the labor force. Typically, these programs have been funded by the federal government under the auspices of service organizations for the retarded. Two exemplary programs have been the National Association for Retarded Citizen's (NARC) On-the-Job Training project and the Institute of Industrial Launderer's National MDTA-OJT project.

The NARC On-the-Job Training project was initiated in 1966 with the Bureau of Apprenticeship Training, Department of Labor. This program provides on-the-job training by employers who are reimbursed for training costs. Over 400 individuals were trained during the first 3 years of the project with approximately 80% retained in employment after training (Bolanovich, 1972). For the fiscal year 1977 the Department of Labor has allocated nearly a million dollars to help train 4405 mentally retarded persons in forty-seven states and the District of Columbia (American Personnel and Guidance Association, 1976).

The MDTA-OJT project operated from 1965 to 1968 and was jointly sponsored by the Institute of Industrial Launderers, the Vocational Rehabilitation Administration, and the Bureau of Apprenticeship Training of the Department of Labor. This project attempted to fill 1000 job openings in the laundry industry. Although this number was not achieved, individuals received training during the 3-year period. Their performance as appraised by employers was excellent (Browning, 1974).

As indicated above, a variety of efforts have and are currently being made to secure increased employment of the retarded. These efforts in turn raise immediate questions concerning what proportion of working-age retarded individuals are employed in the labor market.

The employment rate for the retarded

Definitive figures regarding the employment rate of retarded persons in the labor force are difficult to obtain. Conley (1973) states that employment rates of the retarded are affected by (1) changes in the level of economic activity—retarded individuals are more affected by adverse conditions than persons who are not retarded, (2) sex—retarded females have more difficulty finding work and are less likely to work than retarded males, (3) race—a higher percentage of black retarded persons are unemployed compared to Caucasian retarded persons, (4) IQ—employment is highest among the mildly retarded, and (5) community attitudes toward accepting the retarded.

The earliest attempt to estimate the number of retarded individuals employed was made in 1966 by Mary Switzer, Commissioner of Social and Habilitative Services. She reported that over one million retarded men and women were out of work and capable of working while two million were employed (National Association for Retarded Children, 1966).

Examining employment data for 1970, Conley (1973) estimated that among non-institutionalized retarded individuals ages 20 to 64 years, 55.6% were employed. A larger percentage of males, 81.2%, were employed, compared to only 30.4% of females. These figures seem to indicate that a goal of full employment for the retarded will be difficult if not impractical to attain. For the economically idle retarded persons, however, it would seem that persistent and continual efforts must be applied to find them jobs.

Suggestions for securing job opportunities for the retarded

Recommendations for increasing the employment potential of retarded persons have been made by Kruger (1963), Gitlow (1968), Conley (1973), and Bolanovich (1972). Kruger (1963) had advocated that those who seek to place the retarded in the labor force should study the labor market for trends and possibilities. He specifically identified the multifacet service occupational groups as good prospects for placing the educable mentally retarded.

Gitlow (1968) volunteered four suggestions for expanding job opportunities of the retarded: (1) realistic job hiring requirements reducing the artificially high levels of education being demanded of lesser-skilled jobs; (2) better on-the-job training programs for unskilled workers; (3) job redesign, removing routine and repetition from high skilled jobs and placing it in newly created positions that could be filled by the unskilled; and (4) active recruitment of unskilled workers to fill existing jobs.

Conley (1973) has stressed the need to utilize regular employment channels in industry and government to obtain jobs for the retarded. The government in particular, he feels, should seek to influence the composition of demand for retarded workers. Training is accented by (1) training retarded individuals for occupations in which the demands for workers exceeds the supply, and (2) training retarded persons for those occupations that best suit their abilities. Another consideration is the need to secure additional jobs through sheltered workshops as a preparation for placement in the labor market.

Bolanovich (1972) has proposed a system that aims to move the unemployed retarded person to full employment. The system provides for (1) the identification, classification, and development of the employability of the mentally retarded to make them "work ready," (2) identification of employment opportunities for the retarded defining the degree of economic and social security provided by these opportunities, and (3) developing and matching of the individual's capacities and needs to employment opportunities. Certain principles have been included in the system to facilitate promoting greater employment of the retarded. Among them are: (1) employment must be preceded by a long-term training process beginning in the schools; (2) vocational training must be a continuous process for each retarded person, from school through final job adjustment; (3) qualified employers must be active participants in preemployment evaluation and training; (4) specific occupational training programs must be organized under the aegis of better qualified employers as permanent community training resources; (5) rehabilitation agencies, state agencies in particular, must provide roles for employers and must supply guidance to them; and (6) training and informational programs must be maintained to ensure better communication between employers and representatives of the retarded.

JOB PLACEMENT FOR RETARDED INDIVIDUALS

It is estimated that 500,000 retarded individuals will enter new employment each year (Bolanovich, 1972). How do these individuals secure their jobs? The majority seem to obtain employment on their own by making direct contact with an employer. Generally the employer does not identify these individuals as retarded (Bolanovich, 1972). The remaining retarded individuals receive assistance in securing jobs through the efforts of vocational, rehabilitative (private and state), and employment counselors as well as dedicated special education teachers.

Prevocational programs in the schools are designed to help retarded youngsters prepare for the world of work. When they come of working age, the vocational counselor typically becomes their representative. The counselor may seek to gain employment for the retarded person by working directly with an employer or by working cooperatively with an employment or rehabilitation counselor.

State vocational rehabilitation agencies have been charged since 1943 with providing services to the mentally retarded. The function of the counselor assigned to work with the retarded person is to provide such services as: diagnosis of the rehabilitation problem, counseling, guidance in the planning and preparation for a job, suitable placement in a job, and follow-up of the performance in that job. It has only been within the past 15 years that a substantial number of retarded individuals have received the services of state agencies. A total of 155,743 mentally retarded clients were rehabilitated by agencies throughout the country between 1945 and 1970 with 93% of that number being rehabilitated during the decade of the 1960's (U.S. Department of Health, Education and Welfare, 1970).

Private rehabilitation agencies such as the Federation for Handicapped in New York City, the Kansas City Rehabilitation Center, the Cleveland Vocational Rehabilitation Agency, the local chapter of the National Association of Retarded Citizens, the Goodwill Industries, and the Jewish Employment and Vocational Service materially help in obtaining employment for the retarded. Counselors who work for these agencies generally work with severely retarded individuals (Bolanovich, 1972). Employment counselors in state agencies also serve as a source of help in securing employment for the retarded. The individuals they serve, however, typically are recipients of help designed for the disadvantaged or those in poverty circumstances.

ATTITUDES OF EMPLOYERS TOWARD HIRING RETARDED INDIVIDUALS

Employers hold the key to employment of retarded persons. How receptive are they toward hiring these individuals? Some factors that seem to be related to receptivity include: educational level of employers, size of businesses, personnel managers' length of time in employment and in personnel work; employers' realistic concept of mental retardation; and the degree of acquaintanceship employers have had with the retarded in employment. These factors are interesting and have a variety of implications for employment of the mentally retarded, some of which follow:

1. Regardless of the type of business, large businesses were more favorably inclined to hire the retarded (Phelps, 1965; Hartlage, 1965; and Posner, 1968).
2. The longer a personnel manager had been in his or her present position and in personnel work, the less likely he or or she will be to hire the retarded (Phelps, 1965).
3. Companies that have previously employed the retarded seem more accepting toward them than companies who have not knowingly hired retarded persons (Bolanovich, 1972).
4. No relationship was found between receptivity and employers' realistic concept of mental retardation. Employer attitudes, it was concluded, are formed irrespective of their knowledge of mental retardation (Cohen, 1963).
5. The relationship between educational level of employers and receptivity seems inconclusive. Cohen (1963) found a significant negative relationship between employers' years of schooling and receptivity. Employers with a lesser amount of education were believed to have a greater degree of empathy with the relatively uneducated retarded persons. Phelps (1965), however, obtained conflicting results. Employers with an eighth-grade education or less seemed to be more prejudiced toward the retarded than those

with training at the college level. This contradiction is heightened by Hartlage's (1965) finding of no significant differences in receptivity as a function of the educational levels of employers. Part of the contradiction seems to center on the characteristics of the employers sampled.

The test of employer receptivity lies in the percentage of businesses that actually hire the retarded. The results of a 1968 survey of a limited number of companies across the country provides some indication. Only 24% of the respondents reported that they had knowingly employed persons identified as mentally retarded (Bolanovich, 1972). It appears from these findings that employer receptivity is conditioned by many factors, some more definitive than others. The small percentage of firms that seem willing to hire the retarded implies that barriers yet exist that must be lowered. It seems as though programs designed to help employers understand the retarded and their work potential must be continually promoted.

FACTORS AFFECTING EMPLOYABILITY OF RETARDED INDIVIDUALS AND THEIR SUCCESS IN EMPLOYMENT

Factors that seem to affect the employability of the retarded may be worker related, employer related, and/or external. Improper vocational training resulting in poor work habits (Conley, 1973; Wolfbein, 1967; Bolanovich, 1972) and the level of intelligence seem to be two major worker-related factors restricting the placement of retarded individuals in the labor market. Retarded persons with an IQ less than 40, as noted previously, rarely, if at all, obtain competitive jobs. Employers who have hired retarded persons with inadequate work preparation have cited, in rank order, the following problems they have encountered: take more time to break in, cannot perform enough different tasks, take too much of supervisor's time, may have accidents, and cannot maintain expected level of quality (Posner, 1968).

Employer receptivity, as mentioned earlier, is critical in assuring placement of the retarded. Other important employer-related factors (Bolanovich, 1972) include (1) logistical problems—trying to match the "work ready" retarded individual to the right job at the right time, (2) excessive paper work, (3) failure to grasp the full obligation undertaken when hiring and training the retarded, and (4) discrimination—hiring nonretarded persons though the retarded may be equally qualified (Conley, 1973; Cohen, 1960).

External factors may be societal in nature, such as a depressed economy and the effect of automation, both of which may restrict the number of unskilled and semiskilled jobs open to retarded individuals. Also included are the roles played by federal and state governments and labor unions in influencing the climate for employment of the retarded; attitudes and perceptions of parents and counselors relative to the work potential of retarded individuals; and the failure by agencies working with the retarded to coordinate their functions (Bolanovich, 1972).

Vocational success

The vocational success or adjustment of the retarded has been extensively studied. The reported findings, however, have often been contradictory. One of the reasons for this is the lack of agreement among investigators and practitioners concerning what vocational success means. Different criteria have been employed such as employer satisfaction, tenure of employment, successful job performance, self-directed responsibility, responsible work orientation, and the quality of work. Agreement is also absent on such issues as whether a single criterion should apply to all retarded persons in all of the different work settings and whether norm-referenced or criterion-referenced data should constitute the yardstick for measuring vocational success (Browning, 1974).

The variables studied regarding vocational success have been varied. Most have been subject related, although the use of situational variables such as community attitudes, type of training given, and placement process have also been advocated (Cowan and Goldman, 1959; Wolfensberger, 1967). Subject variables have been intellectual (IQ, academic achievement scores); personal (habits, attitudes, appearance, strength); social (peer relations, relationship with supervisors); biographical (sex, age, ethnic background, socioeconomic status); and vocational skills (specific, related).

The findings of studies relating intelligence to vocational success have been the most conflicting. Jackson (1968), in summarizing such studies, found results supporting four different conclusions: (1) a positive relationship exists, (2) a negative relationship exists, (3) no relationship exists, and (4) a curvilinear relationship exists between intelligence and work success. Conley (1973) in a thorough analysis of the literature pertaining to vocational success, concluded that when vocational failure does occur, intellectual deficiency is usually not the major cause except in cases of severe retardation. He states that vocational failure occurs as a result of the combination of intellectual deficiency with other employment impediments such as attitudes prejudicial to work or physical disabilities. Employment impediments are more likely to be encountered by persons whose intellectual deficiency is severe. To support this position he cites the following reasons: (1) since most jobs available to the retarded require physical labor, the combination of intellectual deficiency and physical disability materially reduces the chances of succeeding vocationally; (2) employers seem reluctant to hire a person who is both mentally retarded and physically handicapped; and (3) the combination of employment impediments such as being both blind and mentally retarded reduces the individual's capacity to adjust.

Personal-social variables as reported by some investigators seem to be a prime cause of vocational failure (Robinson and Pasewark, 1951; Collman and Newlyn, 1957; Huber & Sofonenko, 1963; Kantner, 1969; Sali and Amir, 1970). Such traits as punctuality and consistent attendance (Voelker, 1957; Cohen, 1960; Peckham, 1951; Kolstoe, 1961; Daniels, 1974), good interpersonal relations with work colleagues and supervisors (Voelker, 1957; Porter and Milazzo, 1958; Tarjan,

1960; Cohen, 1960; Sali and Amir, 1970), and good personal appearance (Daniels, 1974; Voelker, 1957; Kolstoe, 1961) have been found to be related to vocational success.

Situational variables that have been found to have a relationship to vocational success include type of training provided (Deardon, 1951; O'Brien, 1952), lack of supportive services (Conley, 1973), community acceptance of the retarded (Cohen, 1960), and parental attitudes and home conditions (O'Connor, 1954; Warren, 1955; Cohen, 1960; Ferguson and Kerr, 1958; Conley, 1973). The findings of these studies demonstrate that it is not necessarily the inability of the retarded individual to work but primarily personal-social behavior that causes job failure.

BENEFITS ACCRUING TO SOCIETY, RETARDED INDIVIDUALS, AND THEIR FAMILIES THROUGH EMPLOYMENT

The retarded individual has a moral and legal right to be engaged in productive work and to be gainfully employed. Rehabilitative agencies, organizations representing the retarded, the U.S. Civil Service Commission (1963), and committed employers have conscientiously been promoting programs and services to fulfill this goal. When employment is secured and maintained by the retarded individual, benefits accrue to the individual, his or her family, and society.

Employment seems to have a positive effect on retarded persons. They become happier, and feelings of self-esteem and accomplishment are enhanced. Employment signifies the attainment of adult status, resulting in the acceptance of the retarded individual by his or her family and the community. Obtaining disposable earnings has a two-fold benefit. First, the economic outlay of the family is reduced, and second, the retarded individual is able to use the earnings to buy products and services enjoyed by the majority of community residents (Wolfensberger, 1967).

Conley (1973) has studied the cost-benefits of rehabilitating retarded citizens compared with institutionalization. In terms of 1970 dollars, he has estimated it would cost $400,000 to institutionalize a retarded individual for a lifetime. In contrast, a mildly retarded male who entered the work force at age 18 years in 1970 could expect a lifetime earnings of $600,000. The dollars spent, therefore, on vocational rehabilitation stand to benefit society. Each dollar expended on the vocational rehabilitation of an 18-year-old retarded individual should generate, according to Conley, an expected increase in future earnings of $14 in 1972 value terms. This ratio would decline among older retarded individuals, women, and the more severely retarded but in all cases would be equal to or greater than the critical value of "one," and in most cases the ratio would be far above this value.

Historically, the retarded have been dehumanized. Viewed as menaces to society, they have been ridiculed, labeled, used as scapegoats, segregated, and considered ineligible for human rights and privileges (Wolfensberger, 1972). It has only been recently that the retarded were considered to have rights—the right to dignity, to education, to treatment, to legal process and redress, and to work. The retarded have demonstrated that, when given the opportunity, they have the ability to work. They are employable. Jobs exist in the labor market that they can perform. With proper training, placement, supervision, and attitude they have performed successfully. Work frees the retarded from idleness. Social and economic security is obtained, all of which result in dignity, with society profiting from the investment by the productivity and economic contribution of the retarded.

REFERENCES

American Personnel and Guidance Association. *Guidepost.* Washington, D.C., February 26, 1976, p. 10.

Bolanovich, D. J., Drought, N. E., and Stewart, D. A.: Full employment for the mentally retarded, St. Louis, 1972, The Jewish Employment and Vocational Service.

Browning, P. L.: Mental retardation, rehabilitation and counseling, Springfield, Ill., 1974, Charles C Thomas, Publisher.

Cohen, J. S.: An analysis of vocational failures of mental retardates placed in the community after a period of institutionalization, Am. J. Ment. Defic. **65:**371-375, 1960.

Cohen, J. S.: Employer attitudes toward hiring mentally retarded individuals, Am. J. Ment. Defic. **67:**705-706, 1963.

Collman, R. D., and Newlyn, D.: Employment success of mentally dull and intellectually normal ex-pupils in England, Am. J. Ment. Defic. **61:**484-490, 1957.

Conley, R. W.: The economics of mental retardation, Baltimore, 1973, The Johns Hopkins University Press.

Cowan, L., and Goldman, M.: The selection of the mentally deficient for vocational training and the effect of this training on vocational success, J. Consult. Psychol. **23:**78-84, 1959.

Daniels, L. K., editor: Vocational rehabilitation of the mentally retarded, Springfield, Ill., 1974, Charles C Thomas, Publisher.

Deardon, H.: The efforts of institutions to meet the problem of job finding, Am. J. Ment. Defic. **56:**295-307, 1951.

Ferguson, T., and Kerr, A. W.: After histories of boys educated in special schools for mentally handicapped children, Scot. Med. J. 31-38, 1958.

Gitlow, A. L.: New approaches to employment of the mentally retarded. In Minutes of annual meeting of president's committee on employment of the handicapped, Washington, D.C., May 2-3, 1968, p. 31.

Hartlage, L. C.: Factors affecting employer receptivity toward the mentally retarded, Am. J. Ment. Defic. **70:**108-113, 1965.

Huber, W. G., and Sofonenko, A. Z.: Factors contributing to the vocational success or non-success of the institutionalized retarded, Training School Bull. **60:**43-51, 1963.

Jackson, R. N.: Employment adjustment of educable mentally handicapped ex-pupils in Scotland, Am. J. Ment. Defic. **72:**924-930, 1968.

Kantner, H. M.: The identification of elements which contribute to occupational success and failure of adults classified as educable mentally retarded, unpublished doctoral dissertation, Arizona State University, 1969.

Kolstoe, O. P.: An examination of some characteristics which discriminate between employed and not-employed mentally retarded males, Am. J. Ment. Defic. **66:**472-482, 1961.

Kruger, D. H.: Trends in service employment: implications for the educable mentally retarded, Except. Child. **29:**167-172, 1963.

National Association for Retarded Children. Mary Switzer, Employer of the Year award. Washington, D.C., 1966.

National Association for Retarded Children. Employer Spotlight, Sky Chef, Inc. *Newsletter.* Washington, D.C., July 1967, p. 3.

O'Brien, M.: A vocational study of a group of institutionalized persons, Am. J. Ment. Defic. **57:**56-62, 1952.

O'Connor, N.: Defectives working in the community, Am. J. Ment. Defic. **59:**173-180, 1954.

Oswald, H. W.: A national follow-up study of mental retardates employed by the federal government: final report, The Department of Vocational Rehabilitation, Washington, D.C., 1968.

Peckham, R. H.: Problems in job adjustment of the mentally retarded, Am. J. Ment. Defic. **56:**448-453, 1951.

Phelps, W. R.: Attitudes related to the employment of the mentally retarded, Am. J. Ment. Defic. **69:**575-585, 1965.

Porter, R. B., and Milazzo, T. C.: A comparison of mentally retarded adults who attended special classes with those who attended regular classes, Except. Child. **24:**410-412, 1958.

Posner, B.: Special report, The President's Committee for Employment of the Handicapped, Washington, D.C., August 1968.

President's Committee on Employment of the Handicapped. Why we hire the mentally retarded, Special report, Washington, D.C., January 1968.

Robinson, R. G., and Pasewark, R.: Behavior in intellectual deficit, Am. J. Ment. Defic. **55:**598-607, 1951.

Sali, J., and Amir, M.: Personal factors influencing the retarded person's success at work: a report from Israel, Am. J. Ment. Defic. **76:**42-47, 1970.

Schumacher, F. A., and Townsell, J. C.: Training mentally retarded for employment, Rehabilitation Record, 1:24-29, 1960.

Sleith, W.: What a mentally retarded worker can do, Supervisory Management Magazine, January 1966.

Strickland, C. G.: Job training placement for retarded youth, Except. Child. 1964, 31:83-86, 1964.

Tarjan, G., Dingham, H. F., Eyman, R., and Brown, S. J.: Effectiveness of hospital release programs, Am. J. Ment. Defic. 64:609-617, 1960.

U.S. Civil Service Commission: Employment of the mentally retarded, by W. B. Irons, Federal Personnel Manual System. Letter Number 339-4, Washington, D.C., December 13, 1963.

U.S. Department of Health, Education and Welfare: Statistical history: federal-state program of vocational rehabilitation (1920-1969), Division of Statistics and Studies, Rehabilitative Services Administration, Social and Rehabilitation Service, Washington, D.C., June 1970.

U.S. Department of Health, Education and Welfare: Mental retardation and the law: a report on status of current court cases, Office of Mental Retardation Coordination, Washington, D.C., October 1973.

Voelker, P.: The public school system, Vocational Training Rehabil. Except. Child., Langhorne, Pa., 1957, The Woods Schools, p. 94.

Wall Street Journal: Howard Johnson is joining program to hire retarded, September 1966.

Warren, S. L.: Problems in the placement and follow-up of the mentally retarded, Am. J. Ment. Defic. 59:408-412, 1955.

Wolfbein, S. F.: Education and training for full employment, New York, 1967, Columbia University Press.

Wolfensberger, W.: Vocational preparation and occupation. In Baumeister, A. A., editor: Mental retardation: appraisal, education, and rehabilitation, Chicago, 1967, Aldine Publishing Co., pp. 232-273.

Wolfensberger, W.: The principle of normalization in human services, Toronto, 1972, National Institute on Mental Retardation.

CHAPTER 30

A vocational delivery system for the mildly retarded

HARRY P. BLUHM
University of Utah

It is estimated that there are 6.1 million retarded persons in the United States. Approximately 2.4 million of these individuals are children and young people under 21 years of age. According to conservative estimates, three-fourths of these individuals could become self-supporting and another 10% to 15% partially self-supporting as adults if appropriate education and training are given to them.

To attain these expectations, delivery systems must be implemented to enable the retarded citizen to become employed either competitively or under sheltered conditions. My purpose is to discuss a vocational delivery system that is aimed primarily at the competitive employment market. This system consists of two phases, a prevocational or educational phase and a vocational or work-oriented phase. The components of each phase are diagrammed in Fig. 1.

THE PREVOCATIONAL PHASE

The prevocational phase is educationally based and incorporates several fundamental aspects of occupational training. This phase generally commences at the junior high school level and is maintained in the initial senior high curriculum. It precedes the vocational phase, which begins in the upper grades of high school and may continue at the postsecondary school level. Curriculum considerations provide for the development of functional academic skills, exploratory experiences pertaining to the world of work, and the attainment of personal-social and home-living skills needed to function in society.

Functional academic skills

The purpose of academics, according to Syden (1962), is to provide retarded individuals with information and experiences that should assist them in meeting daily problems, finding their place in the economic world, and giving them an understanding of their responsibilities as citizens. Basic skills would be taught in reading, language, and number concepts during the elementary years with the emphasis taking a decidedly vocational direction during the junior and senior high school years.

Reading. Baroff (1974) suggests that a secondary reading skills program with the primary focus on protection and information is necessary. The ability to read safety and warning signs are primary examples of the protection emphasis. Reading for information includes the functional use of catalogs, telephone directories, maps, classified ads, magazines, television and movie listings, etc.

Language. The primary focus of language instruction is oral expression or the effective

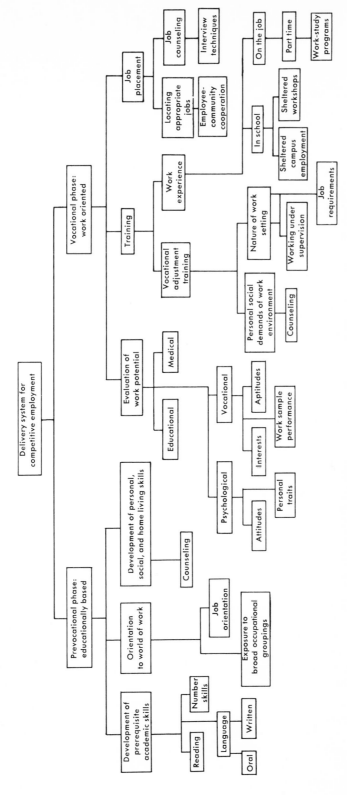

Fig. 1. A vocational delivery system for the mildly retarded individual.

use of expressive language (Martens, 1950). Listening for comprehension, carrying on conversations, talking on the telephone, and being able to ask and answer questions are all critical to the development of basic communication structures. A degree of writing proficiency should also be attained by retarded individuals, permitting them to write legibly and accurately in either print or cursive form. They should develop experience in completing various printed forms and in writing personal and business letters.

Number skills. The basic skills in arithmetic would essentially be delimited to addition and subtraction, although multiplication, short division, and simple fractions are also relevant concepts of the arithmetic curricula for this population. The ability to read time tables and schedules and to employ common units of measures must be emphasized in order to ensure job survival.

The application of number skills to the activities of daily living becomes essential. Thus retarded individuals must develop the skill of using coins and bills of all denominations and must learn about budgeting, banking, credit buying, insurance, taxes, and wage and payroll deductions.

Summary. Although functional academic skills are accented in the retarded individual's educational program, literature in this area has suggested that the absence of functional reading and number skills does not seriously limit the employment of retarded individuals in unskilled work. Dinger (1961) indicates that almost one-half (47%) of the jobs engaged in by employed retarded individuals required no more than counting, and 10% of the jobs required no number skills at all. Approximately 69% of the jobs required no more writing than signing a paycheck or application form. Additionally, 67% of the jobs required only the reading of single words (word recognition), and 33% required no reading at all. These findings suggest that at the junior and senior high school levels the educational experience should not be limited totally to academic training but should also include prevocational and vocational experiences as well (Baroff, 1974).

Orientation to the world of work

Special education teachers and/or school counselors have the responsibility of orienting retarded individuals to the world of work. Vocational guidance deals with the matters of occupational choice, preparation, placement, and adjustment on the job (London, 1973). Typically, vocational guidance regarding career choice is initiated during the latter part of the adolescent years. However, during junior high school retarded individuals are generally introduced to the world of work through simulated and on-the-job exploratory experiences. They learn about various occupations, participate in industrial tours or field trips, and experience certain jobs through in-school work situations.

Specifically, classroom experiences for the retarded individual would involve learning about the opportunities and requirements of service, clerical, agricultural, skilled, semiskilled, and unskilled occupations. These seem to be the job areas in which most retarded persons find employment. The percentage of retarded individuals employed in given job areas is reported to be: service (30%), clerical (12%), agricultural (5.9%), skilled (5.4%), semiskilled (19.3%), unskilled (21.2%), and family worker (6.2%) (President's Committee on Employment of the Handicapped, 1963).

It is also highly recommended that parents of the retarded be involved in this orientation. This permits both parties to obtain information regarding the opportunities available, facts about entry requirements, working conditions, duties performed, health hazards encountered, and the rate of pay for each of the studied occupations.

Field trips. The field trip experience provides the retarded individual with firsthand information regarding alternative career choices. The individual becomes aware of working conditions and worker requirements through this direct observation method (London, 1973). These field trips, organized as part of the orientation process, include visits to laundries, medical centers, hotels, restaurants, large retail stores, meat packing plants, and large farms or dairies. It is important to note that the use of audiovisual media and specialized guest speakers is an effective alternative when personal direct observation is not possible.

Simulated work experiences. The in-school simulated work experience provides another means of orienting retarded individuals to occupational alternatives. These simulated experiences coordinate the interests and capabilities of the retarded individual to the requirements of the work setting. Common junior high experiences include school lunch, custodial, shop, school office, and library clerical jobs. The in-school work placement program at the senior high level provides specific preparatory training experiences prior to on-the-job training.

Personal-social and home-living skills. The retarded individual must possess the requisite personal-social and home-living skills in order to function independently in society and become engaged in productive work experiences. Throughout the junior and senior high school levels, instructional objectives should focus on assisting retarded individuals to: (1) become aware of themselves, their strengths, and their limitations; (2) develop good health and nutritional practices; (3) become aware of and maintain appropriate dress and grooming; (4) get along with others—adults, the opposite sex, and the same sex peers; and (5) develop home economic skills (Baroff, 1974).

Retarded individuals who are experiencing poor peer relationships, feeling of inadequacy, and a tendency toward self-depreciation may need counseling services. When a counseling service is available the counselor should seek to provide a much more friendly, accepting, and supportive learning situation

than would be required for nonretarded individuals with these same feelings (Thorne, 1960).

THE VOCATIONAL PHASE

The primary purpose of the vocational phase is preparation of the retarded individual for placement in the world of work. The components of this phase, including the evaluation of work potential, job training, and placement, have their roots in the trait and factor vocational theory (Shertzer and Stone, 1968; Zaccaria, 1970). This theory provides for the following steps:

1. The traits of the retarded individual are to be assessed by psychological tests and other evaluative tools. This permits the retarded individual and those who work with him or her to obtain a clear understanding of the individual's attitudes, abilities, interests, ambitions, resources, and limitations.
2. An assessment is obtained regarding the requirements and conditions for success, advantages, compensation, and the prospects of alternative occupational opportunities as they relate to the retarded individual.
3. The counselor (school and/or rehabilitation), the special education teacher, or the vocational coordinator seeks to match the retarded individual to the job with the greatest opportunity for success.

The relationship between the components of the vocational phase and the steps associated with the trait and factor theory is shown in Fig. 2. Burrow (1964) suggests that the match between the job and the individual is the culmination of the entire job development process. The retarded individual's pros-

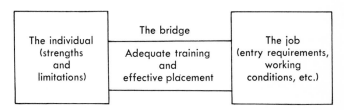

Fig. 2. Matching the individual and the job.

pects for job stability are not good if the match is not made on a completely selective basis.

Evaluation of work potential

The purpose of evaluating the work potential of retarded individuals is to determine what type of work they can do or can be trained to do. This requires identifying the specific abilities or assets they may possess. The evaluation should be comprehensive in order to examine the retarded individual's intellectual abilities, academic achievement, manual skills, personality traits, vocational interests, etc. (Patterson, 1964; Katz, 1968; Kolstoe, 1960).

Instruments used to collect these data include standardized tests, attitude scales, vocational adjustment scales, checklists, rating scales, personal-social inventories, performance scales, interest inventories, and work samples. A basic concern regarding the use of these instruments is their reliability and validity. One problem with standardized tests is that they have not been normed on mentally retarded individuals, thus making their reliability and validity questionable with this population (Walthall and Love, 1974; Katz, 1968).

Personality inventories have been of little use with the retarded since it is unclear whether they tap the characteristics important to job success. The utilization of work samples for evaluative purposes has also been questioned because of the lack of a specified criteria and a low correlation with job requirements (Patterson, 1964). However, direct observations by trained personnel are essential. They are useful in providing information on the retarded individual's vocational interests, attitudes, and work habits.

It is essential that only skilled personnel be included in the comprehensive evaluation. The team approach involving psychologists, physicians, social workers, educational specialists, and rehabilitation counselors is highly recommended (Katz, 1968). The evaluation may be conducted by public schools, sheltered workshops, or rehabilitation agencies. It may last from several weeks to 1 or 2 years, depending upon the problems presented by the retarded individual (Bolanovich, 1972). The evaluation of the retarded individual's work potential should be considered as a process of gathering, interpreting, analyzing, and synthesizing all vocationally significant data (Malikin and Rusalem, 1969).

Training

The employability of the retarded individual is dependent upon the successful development of vocational skills in combination with desired personal-social skills. This goal is attained through vocational adjustment training and work experiences. Personal-social factors have been recognized as the most important determinant of the retarded individual's employability (Syden, 1962; Deno, 1966). Vocational adjustment training serves to assist the individual in becoming dependable and emotionally mature. Additionally, work experiences enable the retarded individual to practice job skills in a protective environment under the supervision of an employer and school official.

Work adjustment training. Work adjustment training is work rather than education oriented (Daniels, 1974). It may be given without any specific job in mind, but generally occurs when the retarded individual is obtaining job training in an on-campus or community job.

The purpose of work adjustment training is for the retarded individual to experience actual work situations under the guidance of a work supervisor and counselor. During such training retarded individuals are oriented to the personal-social demands of the work environment and to the nature of work settings. They are taught courteousness, cleanliness, punctuality, cooperation, tolerance toward pressures of meetings and deadlines, and the need to work harmoniously with other employees, to stick to given work tasks, and to take responsibility for work assigned (Davis, 1959; Stahlecker, 1964; Daniels, 1974; Bolanovich, 1972).

The counselor conducting the training can assist the retarded individual in learning appropriate behaviors and eliminating those that are undesirable. Individual or group counseling may be utilized depending upon the situation or problem that exists. Two techniques, role playing and behavior modification, have been found to be very effective in a variety of these counseling situations. Role playing is effective in providing retarded individuals the opportunity of confronting interpersonal problems in a simulated and sheltered environment. Behavior modification focuses upon specific behaviorally defined problems incorporated within a system of consistent feedback. This facilitates the monitoring of client progress within a designated program structure (Halpern and Berard, 1974).

Counselors and sheltered workshop foremen may monitor or assess the work adjustment behavior by using one of several vocational adjustment scales (Daniels, 1972; Bitter and Bolanovich, 1970). The scales purport to measure job readiness but may be limited by interrater variations and the lack of empirical data correlating measured behavior to rehabilitation needs (Bitter and Bolanovich, 1970).

Work experience. Erickson (1947) defines work experience as

. . . a means and method in the program of the school by which the learner actually produces goods or renders useful service through participation in socially desirable activities in the community under real conditions. [p. 355]

Successful in-school work experiences should precede out-of-school vocational encounters. These in-school work experiences may be obtained through sheltered campus employment and sheltered workshops. Out-of-school experiences result from student participation in work-study programs.

Work experience serves as a valuable testing ground for practicing related job skills under the supervision of school officials. The retarded individuals are in a protective environment where they may learn by trial and error with no fear of losing the job. The practical experience they obtain serves to help them develop work confidence (Stahlecker, 1964; Kokaska, 1964; Burdett, 1963). Addi-

tionally, school officials have the advantage of observing the retarded individual's work attitude and response to supervision. Deficits that are noted can be incorporated into the vocational adjustment program. A disadvantage of sheltered on-campus work experiences is that the supervising personnel, including custodians and cafeteria workers, may look at the retarded individual as merely a helper and thus fail to instruct or supervise (Hickman, 1967).

The sheltered workshop program has two basic functions: (1) to train retarded individuals for employment in competitive jobs, and (2) to provide a terminal employment opportunity for retarded adults who cannot succeed in competitive employment conditions (Wallin, 1960; Bolanovich, 1972). As a rehabilitative facility, the sheltered workshop seeks to prepare mildly retarded individuals for unsheltered employment through the molding of attitudes, vocational training, and achievement of social skills (Zaetz, 1971; Conley, 1973).

On-the-job training of retarded individuals between the ages of 17 and 21 years is facilitated through the establishment of work-study programs. Generally, individuals participating in work-study programs are considered to be emotionally stable and socially mature. Physically, they should be able to perform the job requirements and not represent a danger to themselves or their fellow workers (Shawn, 1964).

The responsibility for work-study programs is shared by the local school district and community agencies. School officials must identify employers within the community that have jobs suited to the needs and limitations of the retarded client. Vocational rehabilitation offices and state employment agencies should assist in this process. Once identified, employers must be willing to assume responsibility for training the retarded individual and orienting current employees to the exceptional needs of the retarded client. Retarded individuals must also accept responsibility. They must be willing to work cooperatively with their fellow employees and supervisory personnel. Retarded individuals who participate in work study programs profit by (1) learning the characteristics of a particular job, (2) knowing what the job requirements are, (3) receiving assistance in job interviewing, (4) understanding the purpose of wage deductions and various fringe benefits, and (5) acquiring an identity as responsible and productive workers (Daniels, 1974).

Job placement. Job placement is the culminating activity of the delivery system for competitive employment. It consists of matching the right person to the right job. Job placement brings the employer, school or rehabilitative counselor, and the retarded client together. Burrow (1964) outlines several steps a counselor should follow in securing employment for the retarded individual in a competitive labor market. First, the counselor seeks to identify employers with jobs available that meet the skill requirements of the retarded client. The counselor then discusses with the employer the needs, capabilities, and limitations of the retarded client. When the employer and counselor are reasonably sure that the client matches the job, the retarded individual is brought in for a formal job interview. Role playing of the job interview should have been previously conducted in order to prepare the retarded individual for this situation. Once the job has been secured the counselor is obligated to conduct follow-up assessment on the retarded individual's job performance. The previously discussed delivery system will be successful if the retarded individual, through continual employment in the labor force, attains the expected goal of self-sufficiency.

REFERENCES

Baroff, G. A.: Mental retardation: nature, cause, and management, New York, 1974, Halsted Press.

Bitter, J. A., and Bolanovich, D. J.: WARF: a scale for measuring job readiness behaviors, Am. J. Ment. Defic. **74**: 616-621, 1970.

Bolanovich, D. J., Drought, N. E., and Stewart, D. A.: Full employment for the mentally retarded, St. Louis, 1972, The Jewish Employment and Vocational Service.

Burdett, A. D.: An examination of selected prevocational techniques utilized in programs for the mentally retarded, Ment. Retard. **1**: 230-237, 1963.

Burrow, W. H.: Job development: a problem in interpersonal dynamics training, Training School Bull. **61**: 12-20, 1964.

Conley, R. W.: The economics of mental retardation, Baltimore, 1973, The Johns Hopkins University Press.

Daniels, L. K.: An experimental edition of a rating scale of vocational adjustment for the mentally retarded, Training School Bull. **69**: 92-98, 1972.

Daniels, L. K., editor: Vocational rehabilitation of the mentally retarded, Springfield, Ill., 1974, Charles C Thomas, Publisher.

Davis, D. A.: Counseling the mentally retarded, Vocational Guidance Quarterly **7**: 184-188, 1959.

Deno, E.: Vocational preparation of the retarded during school years. In Michael, S. G. D., editor: New vocational pathways for the mentally retarded, Washington, D.C., 1966, American Personnel and Guidance Association, pp. 20-29.

Dinger, J. C.: Post-school adjustment of former educable retarded pupils, Except. Child. **27**: 353-356, 1961.

Erickson, C. E.: A basic text for guidance workers, New York, 1947, Prentice-Hall, Inc.

Halpern, A. S., and Berard, W. R.: Counseling the mentally retarded: a review for practice. In Browning, P. L., editor: Mental retardation: rehabilitation and counseling, Springfield, Ill., 1974, Charles C Thomas, Publisher, pp. 269-289.

Hickman, L. H., Jr.: A foundation for the preparation of the educable child for the world of work, Training School Bull. **64**: 39-44, 1967.

Katz, E.: The retarded adult in the community, Springfield, Ill., 1968, Charles C Thomas, Publisher.

Kokaska, C.: In-school work experience: a tool for community adjustment, Ment. Retard. **2:** 365-367, 1964.

Kolstoe, O. P.: The employment evaluation and training program, Am. J. Ment. Defic. **65:** 17-31, 1960.

London, H. H.: Principles and techniques of vocational guidance, Columbus, 1973, Charles E. Merrill Publishing Co.

Malikin, D., and Rusalem, H.: Vocational rehabilitation of the disabled: an overview, New York, 1969, New York University Press.

Martens, E.: Curriculum experiences for the educable mentally retarded. Curriculum adjustment for the mentally retarded, Washington, D.C., 1950, U.S. Government Printing Office. In Rothstein, J. H., editor: Mental retardation: reading and resources, New York, 1961, Holt, Rinehart & Winston, pp. 231-239.

Patterson, C. H.: Methods of assessing the vocational adjustment potential of the mentally handicapped, Training School Bull. **61:** 129-152, 1964.

President's Committee on Employment of the Handicapped: guide to job placement of the mentally retarded, Washington, D.C., 1963, U.S. Government Printing Office.

Shawn, B.: Review of a work-experience program, Ment. Retard. **2:** 360-364, 1964.

Shertzer, B., and Stone, S. C.: Fundamentals of counseling, Boston, 1968, Houghton Mifflin Co.

Stahlecker, L. V.: School work programs for the slow learners, Clearing House **38:** 299-301, 1964.

Syden, M.: Preparation for work: an aspect of the secondary school's curriculum for mentally retarded youth, Except. Child. **28:** 325-331, 1962.

Thorne, F. C.: Tutorial counseling with mental defectives, J. Clin. Psychol. **16:** 73-79, 1960.

Wallin, J. E. W.: Sheltered workshops for older adolescents and adults, Training School Bull. **57:** 24-30, 1960.

Walthall, J. E., and Love, H. D.: Habilitation of the mentally retarded individual, Springfield, Ill., 1974, Charles C Thomas, Publisher.

Zaccaria, J.: Theories of occupational choice and vocational development, Boston, 1970, Houghton Mifflin Co.

Zaetz, J. L.: Organization of sheltered workshop programs for the mentally retarded adult, Springfield, Ill., 1971, Charles C Thomas, Publisher.

CHAPTER 31

Vocational evaluation:
special education's responsibility

DONN BROLIN

University of Missouri at Columbia

ABSTRACT: *Many educable mentally retarded persons continue to lead a marginal life after school despite higher potentials. Schools can and should provide more relevant vocationally oriented programs to help eliminate the barriers formerly encountered by the mentally retarded after they leave school. Initiating vocational evaluation programs in the school is recommended and the components of the process are described. A model for operating a vocational evaluation and placement program is suggested.*

The majority of persons who are labeled as educable mentally retarded could achieve higher levels of personal, social, and vocational functioning if they had better educational and vocational opportunities. Too many retarded persons are not learning to live and work successfully in our society.

One reason is a lack of public understanding about the ability of the educable mentally retarded. Most of these students are not significantly brain damaged or otherwise medically disabled and have many positive abilities that can be converted to vocational assets. However, there is still a tendency to place the mentally retarded in routine, repetitive, simple, and low paying jobs even though many could perform successfully in more highly skilled and highly paid occupations (Kokaska, 1971; Oswald, 1968).

Another reason is the lack of appropriate educational and vocational programs in the

secondary schools. Many professionals believe that too much emphasis is placed on academic instruction and too little on the development of socio-occupational competence (Goldstein, 1969). This criticism is being leveled against special education in secondary schools even though there has been a greater emphasis on vocational programing in the secondary schools in the last decade. Work experience has been incorporated into the high school curriculum, often with the cooperation of the state rehabilitation agency, employment service, and sheltered workshops. These work study programs have had the benefit of getting the agencies involved in the vocational problems of the educable retarded students before graduation, but yet they have not worked as efficiently as was hoped.

Communication problems, in many cases, have existed between the secondary school and the rehabilitation agency, resulting in sporadic services and inadequate continuity of service (Hammerlynck & Espeseth, 1969).

Reprinted from Education and Training of the Mentally Retarded 8:12-17, 1973, with permission.

224

The same has been true of the relationship between the school and the employment service. In a recent study, Colorado State Employment Service counselors indicated that they did not feel it was their responsibility to find employment for the mentally retarded; moreover, 38 percent of the counselors surveyed said that they often did not have any working relationship with special classroom programs for these students (Smith, 1970).

Sheltered workshops have provided vocational evaluation, training, and placement services for many of these students, thereby relieving participating schools of vocational responsibilities. But again the help provided by the workshops often has not met the needs of the students. Often workshop personnel are not well trained in mental retardation and are neither aware of the student's background nor are able to observe his functioning over a long period of time. Consequently, the students have not been able to receive the individual and specialized assistance they need. In addition, the performance of many educable retarded students has been lower than their actual potential because they have not yet reached a certain level of vocational maturity, motivation, and experience.

Giving the responsibility for vocational evaluation and training of these students to rehabilitation agencies, employment services, and sheltered workshops will not totally solve the problems. These agencies have many types of vocationally handicapped clients to serve and cannot be expected to train their already overloaded staff to deal effectively with all the vocational problems of the educable retarded student. Some secondary schools have provided vocational evaluation for their students, but this usually has not been done in any systematic way.

Up to this point the extent and quality of vocational programing for these students has depended primarily upon the individual teacher's inclination, ingenuity, training, vocational experience, and the like. Some teachers have developed good vocational programs; others have not, placing students in jobs with the hope that some vocational

skills and interests will develop. Schools can and should be providing better programs to help eliminate the educational and vocational barriers that the retarded student encounters.

The secondary school program must assume a larger responsibility for the vocational development of its educable retarded students by initiating a vocational evaluation program as an integral part of its curriculum. This is consistent with the recent statement by US Commissioner of Education, Sidney P. Marland (1972) who listed career education for the handicapped as one of the nation's primary educational needs.

THE VOCATIONAL EVALUATION PROCEDURE

Vocational evaluation, according to Gellman (1968), is concerned with the prognosis of whether a person can work, what kind, and what types of training are needed. Although there are varying opinions on how to do this, it is my opinion that vocational evaluation should consist of the following components: clinical assessment, work evaluation, work adjustment, and on-the-job tryout.

Clinical assessment

There are four types of clinical assessment: medical, social, educational, and psychological.

Medical assessment. This assessment involves evaluating the individual's physical capacity, general health, brain damage, vision, hearing, speech, perceptual motor functioning, coordination, dexterity, and any suspected or evident anomalies precluding optimal health and physical functioning. In addition to pointing out limitations to vocational functioning, a medical assessment should indicate whether treatment can modify or remedy some or all of the limitations and this information should be used for vocational planning.

Social assessment. This assessment involves evaluating the educable retarded student's family relationship, social skills, interpersonal relationships, care of his personal needs, and ability to use leisure time. For example, it has been found that the parents have a significant influence on the student's eventual vocational outcome (Brolin, 1969). Moreover, lack of appropriate social skills, rather than inability to do the job, is the major reason for loss of employment.

Educational assessment. This assessment involves evaluating the student's academic ability for job placement. Many jobs do not require a high academic level but a certain academic level is needed for care for one's everyday affairs. Proper educational assessment could assist in preventing a mildly retarded student from being placed in an unchallenging position and in becoming underemployed.

Psychological assessment. This assessment at its best involves evaluating the educable retarded student's verbal skills, performance skills, special interests and knowledge, and the like. In the past, psychological assessment has focused on IQ scores despite their insignificance in determining the individual's vocational potential. The psychologist can be of real help in assessing the individual's skills and in pinpointing intellectual and personality strengths and weaknesses for eventual vocational programing.

Work evaluation. The second component, work evaluation, in the vocational evaluation procedure consists of: intake and other counseling interviews; interest, dexterity, and other standardized vocational tests; work and job samples; and situational assessment.

Interviews. These are extremely important in the work evaluation process, for they can provide essential information on the interests, needs, knowledge, and personality of the student.

Standardized testing. This testing should be used with caution. The tests are often inappropriate for educable mentally retarded students because of the verbal ability required and/or the norm groups used. While there have been attempts to develop less verbal measures, such as *Standardization of the Vocational Interest Sophistication Assessment* (VISA), (Parnicky, Kahn, & Burdett, 1968), *The Geist Picture Interest Inventory,*

(Giest, 1959), and the new *Reading-Free Vocational Interest Inventory*, the validity of all these measures is questionable and any interest test should be used with care. The *Purdue Pegboard* (Tobias & Gorelick, 1960), is perhaps the best fine finger dexterity test to use. The *General Aptitude Test Battery* (GATB), (US Department of Labor, 1966), should be used with caution despite a recent study in Minnesota (Lofquist, Dawis, & Weiss, 1970) concluding that it is appropriate.

Work and job samples. These are becoming increasingly important components of the work evaluation process and range from simple to complex operations. Work samples are simulated tasks or activities but do not actually replicate a specific job whereas a job sample is a model or replication of an actual job or part of a job that exists in industry. Both are set up like a testing procedure where there are definite instructions, standards, time and/or units performed requirements, and hopefully norms on which to compare the individual's performance with other groups. They do not consist merely of giving individuals work and seeing how they do on it.

Unlike standardized tests, however, work and job samples have these advantages: (a) they are more like jobs than tests are; (b) they are more motivating, less anxiety producing, and more appropriate than tests for persons with cultural and language difficulties; (c) they may sample actual operations of a job, and (d) they provide better evidence for the prospective employer of the types of abilities the client has.

The disadvantages most frequently cited of work and job samples are: (a) many clients may not take work samples related to jobs that they do not like; (b) it is difficult to develop enough representative job samples to cover all the major occupations; (c) they are expensive and time consuming to develop; and (d) there is still much subjective evaluation in the use of work and job samples. *The Dictionary of Occupational Titles* (DOT), (US Department of Labor, 1965), is valuable in conducting job analyses which is a first step in developing work and job samples.

Situational assessment. This assessment is the typical technique used by sheltered workshops and is oriented toward simulating actual working conditions. Instead of focusing on specific work skills, as in the work or job sample, the situational assessment focuses on general work habits and behaviors. The client usually works on subcontracted, production assembly work that is fairly simple. Clients are systematically observed and rated on their work personality and their behaviors are compared to behaviors deemed necessary to secure employment.

Work adjustment

The third component work adjustment, of the vocational evaluation procedure is particularly helpful for the educable retarded student who is inexperienced and unmotivated. The work adjustment program is planned individually for each student and concentrates on his particular deficiencies that have been delineated in the work evaluation period. The work adjustment program helps the student develop adequate physical tolerances, change work behaviors, and acquire new vocational related information and experiences.

There are several different kinds of work adjustment techniques. One is a simulated work experience setting that provides work activities and that emphasizes productivity. Another is individual and group counseling. A third, and perhaps the most effective with many retarded individuals, is behavior modification in which operant conditioning focuses on reinforcement to control and shape behavior. The goal in the behavior modification approach is to alter the client's work environment so that appropriate behaviors are learned and maintained and inappropriate behaviors extinguished. After a period of work adjustment, a more realistic assessment of the educable retarded student's vocational strengths, weaknesses, and potentials can be made.

On-the-job tryouts

The final component of the vocational evaluation process, on-the-job tryouts, pro-vides perhaps the only realistic assessment of the client's abilities. On-the-job try-outs should be separate from work evaluation because the former gives the student the opportunity to perform an actual job under the supervision of industrial and business personnel. Prerequisite to a relevant decision about the job tryout is the conducting of a job analysis, focusing on a description of the work to be performed and on the required characteristics of the worker.

Job analysis takes into consideration what the worker does, how he does it, why he does it, and the skill involved in doing it. When the student is engaged in the on-the-job tryout, the job analyst can observe him at the place of work and give whatever training and instruction is needed before making a final judgment as to the student's potential for that type of work. Neff (1970) has stated that perhaps "the site of the vocational evaluator ought to be in the work place itself [p. 29]." If the vocational evaluator has done his job, the student should be ready for the on-the-job experience and should do well. The on-the-job tryout should reflect the actual vocational capacities of the student, provided that the evaluation and adjustment that preceded it was adequate.

The above comprises the vocational evaluation process. It appears that special education teachers must have the competencies of a social worker, psychologist, counselor, evaluator, and placement specialist if vocational evaluation is their responsibility. This may well be true, but someone has to conduct and coordinate the vocational evaluation and it is going to have to be the teacher if the students are to be served adequately. Other resources should be utilized if they are available and appropriate.

A VOCATIONAL EVALUATION MODEL

To make sense out of the mass of vocational evaluation data collected on students, there must be some systematic framework or model from which the teacher can operate so appropriate evaluation, adjustment, and placement techniques can be employed. One

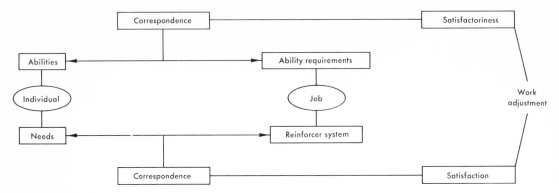

Fig. 1. Minnesota Theory of Work Adjustment.

that could be useful is the *Minnesota Theory of Work Adjustment* (Dawis, 1967). This theory is concerned with placing the individual on an appropriate job and is based on the assumption that work adjustment depends on the correspondence between the individual's work personality and the work environment.

The individual's work personality is made up of his abilities and needs, and the work environment consists of the abilities required for satisfactory work performance and the needs that can be satisfied by the job reinforcer system. This can be depicted as seen in Fig. 1.

When the individual's abilities correspond to the abilities required to do the job, there is *satisfactoriness*. When the individual's needs correspond to the job reinforcer system, there is satisfaction, that is, the individual is happy with what he is doing. There are well designed followup questionnaires to assess these two areas. If there is both satisfactoriness (the individual can do the job) and satisfaction (the individual is happy about his job), there is work adjustment and job stability (Dawis, 1967).

To measure the various components in the model, the following can be used:

- Abilities. These can be measured by work samples, situational assessment, on-the-job tryouts, GATB, *Purdue Pegboard*, and other vocational aptitude tests and clinical assessments.
- Ability requirements. These can be measured by the DOT, job analysis, *Guide to*

Jobs for the Mentally Retarded, (Peterson & Jones, 1964) and *Occupational Adjustment Patterns*. (US Department of Labor, 1962).

- Needs. These can be measured by the *Minnesota Importance Questionnaire* (MIQ) (Lofquist, Dawis & Weiss, 1970), interest inventories, personality measures, expressed needs, and past history.
- Reinforcer system. These can be measured by the DOT, job analysis, and *Occupational Reinforcer Patterns* (ORPs), (Borgen, Weiss, Tinsley, Dawis, & Lofquist, 1968).

The *Minnesota Theory of Work Adjustment* provides a systematic framework for operating a vocational evaluation and placement program. It is a way to obtain information about work personalities, abilities, needs, and work environments to find the correspondence between all these factors that will lead to successful work adjustment.

A successful and effective vocational evaluation program can be designed within the school structure and be complemented by an appropriate community job site experience. By using the techniques described above, the secondary special education teacher will be able to enhance the opportunities for our mentally retarded citizens and truly provide a career education.

REFERENCES

Borgen, F., Weiss, D., Tinsley, H., Dawis, R., & Lofquist, L. The measurement of Occupational Reinforcer Patterns. *Minnesota Studies in Vocational Rehabilitation*, 1968.

Brolin, D. E. The implementation of recommendations from an evaluation center for the mentally retarded and an analysis of variables related to client outcome. Unpublished doctoral dissertation, University of Wisconsin, 1969.

Dawis, R. The Minnesota studies in vocational rehabilitation. *Rehabilitation Counseling Bulletin*, 1967, **11**, 1-10.

Geist, H. *Geist Picture Interest Inventory*. Berkeley: Southern Universities Press, 1959.

Gellman, W. The principles of vocational evaluation. *Rehabilitation Literature*, 1968, **29**, 98-102.

Goldstein, H. Construction of a social learning curriculum. *Focus on Exceptional Children*, 1969, **1**, 1-10.

Hammerlynck, L. A., & Espeseth, V. K. Dual specialist: Vocational rehabilitation counselor and teacher of the mentally retarded. *Mental Retardation*, 1969, **7**, 49-50.

Kokaska, C. The need for economic security for the mentally retarded. In Brolin, D., & Thomas, B. (Eds.), *Preparing teachers of secondary level educable mentally retarded: Proposal for a new model*. Menomonie, Wisconsin: Stout State University, 1971, pp. 18-21.

Lofquist, L., Dawis, R., & Weiss, D. *Assessing the work personalities of mentally retarded adults*. Minneapolis: University of Minnesota, 1970.

Marland, S. Career education 300 days later. *American Vocational Journal*, 1972, **47**, (2), 14-17.

Neff, W. Vocational Assessment - theory and models. *Journal of Rehabilitation*, 1970 **36**(1), 27-29.

Oswald, H. *A national follow-up study of mental retardates employed by the federal government*. Grant RD-2425-6, Washington, D.C.: Department of Vocational Rehabilitation, 1968.

Parnicky, J., Kahn, H. & Burdett, A. *Standardization of the Vocational Interest and Sophistication Assessment (VISA): A reading free test for retardates*. Bordentown, N.J.: Johnstone Training and Research Center, 1968.

Peterson, R., & Jones, E. *Guide to jobs for the mentally retarded*. Pittsburgh: American Institute for Research, 1964.

Smith, G. The mentally retarded: Is the public employment service prepared to serve them? *Mental Retardation*, 1970, **8**, 26-29.

Tobias, J. & Gorelick, J. The effectiveness of the *Purdue Pegboard* in evaluating the work potential of retarded adults. *Training School Bulletin*, 1960, **57**, 94-104.

US Department of Labor. *Dictionary of occupational titles*. (3rd ed.) 1965.

US Department of Labor, United States Employment Service. *General Aptitude Test Battery*. Washington: USGPO, 1966.

US Department of Labor, *Guide to the use of the General Aptitude Test Battery*. Section II: Norms; Occupational Aptitude Pattern Structure, 1962.

SECTION SEVEN

Discussion questions

1. What do you see as the most significant problems confronting mentally retarded individuals seeking employment? Attitudes? Training? Economics? In what ways could steps be taken to reduce these difficulties?

2. Is competitive employment a reasonable concept for mentally retarded individuals? Why or why not? Would your views be altered if you found yourself in competition with a retarded person for employment?

3. Do vocational *issues* such as training, placement, and evaluation differ for retarded and nonretarded individuals? What should the public schools be doing in this regard for both segments of the population?

PHYSICAL AND RECREATIONAL EDUCATION

The differences between retarded and nonretarded individuals have traditionally been characterized by the retarded child's inability to function in an academically oriented curriculum. This emphasis upon academics has resulted in a considerable amount of controversy regarding programs that focus upon physical development as it relates to the educational and social growth of the retarded child. Many educators suggest that the role of physical education has been relegated to a secondary position in the schools with little, if any, consistency in program structure for this population.

The present section focuses upon three basic philosophical positions regarding physical education and recreational programming for the mentally retarded. These statements reflect a diversification of viewpoints relating to the specified role of physical education for this population. Additionally, the section will review the current status of physical education programs for the retarded, including administrative factors, facilities, teaching styles, and evaluation techniques.

The value of physical education programs may be viewed from several perspectives. However, prior to establishing the overall value of these programs it is imperative to identify the specific goals of a physical education curriculum. This delineation of goals is the basis for the current controversy surrounding physical education and recreational programming considerations. The first article in this series views physical education as a direct correlate to the child's future progress in educational and social endeavors. Peter G. Kramer cites the limited success that academically oriented programs have had with the mentally retarded child and attributes this to the child's lack of necessary readiness skills to progress in academic areas. Kramer's basic premise is that the retarded child must have a sequenced and consistent motor background, or a structure upon which to build future learning experiences will be absent. The discussion revolves around the role of physical education as a foundational discipline that will assist the child in developing a greater attention span and improved social skills. The author directly correlates physical education programming with improved vocational readiness and productivity.

The next article in this series questions the generalization characteristics of physical education programs for the retarded. Peter Valletutti and Florence Christoplos would agree that physical education for the mentally retarded has been grossly neglected by educators. However, they criticize the "generalization" concept of physical education as mere "wishful thinking." These authors suggest that any at-

tempt to generalize progress in a specific area such as physical education to another area (academics) simply serves to confuse the issues. Physical education should be viewed as valuable for its own sake. A proposal is made to redefine the goals of physical education and recreational programs to a more realistic perspective. Physical educators need to investigate, task analyze, and empirically validate a curricular structure for this population utilizing defined goals within the framework of a discipline.

Eleanor Coleman's article also supports a research emphasis in the development and implementation of physical education programs. She visualizes a new and expanding role for the physical educator in a comprehensive program for the retarded individual. This role is enhanced by effective research efforts within the discipline. The nature of these investigative efforts should not, however, be one of a continual defensive posture. The emphasis has been upon discreditation of earlier theories, and these investigations have basically focused upon "difference" questions. She suggests that there is a need to establish the relationship between physical education and related disciplines in order to more effectively meet the functional requirements of the individual.

The primary theme within each article in this series is the development of an appropriate curricular structure for physical education programs geared to the retarded individual. It is generally accepted that independence is the basic goal of educational and social programs for this population. Therefore, it is the responsibility of education to prepare these individuals for community roles. However, a recent trend in many physical education and recreation programs has been to segregate them from community-oriented physical education and recreation opportunities. The final article in this section reviews the current status of physical education programs for the handicapped. Walter F. Ersing surveys schools, community agencies, and institutions in order to assess the current impact of instructional programs for this population. Several conclusions are drawn and recommendations made regarding the present status and future needs of physical education for the mentally retarded and physically handicapped.

CHAPTER 32

The way they see it

Three basic philosophic positions regarding physical education and recreational programming for the mentally retarded are presented in the following articles.

The physical educator . . .

PETER G. KRAMER

Director of Physical Education
Golden Hills Academy, Ocala, Florida

Much time and effort have been devoted to educating and training the mentally retarded. Different systems have been advanced and various methods advocated for teaching them to read, to write, and to solve simple arithmetic problems. The emphasis has not really been solely upon intellectual development as claimed, but upon academic development and achievement. For the mentally retarded, academic success is often limited; often, emphasis upon academic activities is too great and begun much too early. Many young and low-level retardates are not mature enough—mentally, emotionally, or physically—to benefit from an academic program, especially during the early portions of their schooling. In many cases, mentally retarded children lack preschool experiences and readiness skills necessary to succeed and progress in academic activities. It seems strange that the task of educating the mentally retarded has not become a major concern of physical educators. Physical educators, through adapted and individualized programs, can help the

Reprinted from *The Best of Challenge,* 1971, published by the American Association for Health, Physical Education and Recreation, with permission.

retarded develop motor patterns, attain social skills, and acquire vocational abilities to help them secure functional positions in the community.

Motor development connotes improved control over one's body and involves related progress in learning associated with such control. Associated learnings are related to space, size, direction, distance, speed, intensity, shape, etc. A great deal of early learning and experience is basic to more sophisticated learning and is derived through motor activities and their associated learnings. Mentally retarded children whose motor development is slow and in many cases faulty are deprived of associated learnings which form the foundation of experiences needed for future intellectual progress.

According to Newell Kephart, there are three stages in human development: motor generalization, perceptual generalization, and symbolic generalization.

The stage of motor generalization begins with the development of balance and posture. During this stage an infant begins to develop concepts of body awareness as he becomes aware of gravity and how it must be overcome to move segments of the body; this also helps him develop an awareness of space. The infant's world consists of objects within his reach; objects beyond his reach are beyond comprehension.

The second stage of motor learning involves contact with objects. The child touches and manipulates them; he attempts to move them, bites and tastes them, and watches others to see how they react to them. Through contact, manipulation, and observation, the child develops background knowledge and information about objects prior to verbalization about them. No one tells a normal child what a chair is; he knows this through his past experience.

Locomotion is the third stage in motor development. It commences with crawling and creeping, advances to walking and running, and proceeds to the more complicated skipping, leaping, and prancing. The infant learns about the world beyond his crib; he learns of distance, size, shape, and other relationships—but, at this stage, learning is entirely through movement and motor acts.

After the child has acquired certain motor generalizations, he possesses the basic abilities to develop perceptual generalizations and ultimately symbolic generalizations. However, if the child does not have the motor background, he has no foundation on which to build future learning. Attempting to further educate the individual with inadequate motor experience is much like trying to explain the difference between red and orange to a blind child.

Physical education and classroom teachers should refer back to the stages of motor development in remedial programs to construct a better foundation on which future learning can be based. Emphasis should be placed on developing basic motor patterns: unilateral, where one segment of the body is moved; bilateral, where limbs on opposite sides of the body are moved in the same way and at the same time; cross pattern, where a lower segment on one side and an upper segment on the other side are moved simultaneously; and axial, where body parts are moved in a twisting manner. Complex or coordinated movements are a composite of two or more of the simpler motor patterns. Running, jumping, climbing, tumbling, throwing, and catching, presented in a logical progression, are of great value in promoting the development of motor generalizations.

Jean Piaget felt that social development in children was directly related to their level and degree of play development. Piaget divided play into six categories: adult initiated, where the child reacts and responds to an adult; self-initiated, where the child plays by himself with no other children present; parallel play, where a number of children share the same area but play independently; cooperative play, where members of a group work together to achieve a common goal; games of low organization, such as tag; and games of high organization, including team sports and activities.

Each level of play can represent another degree of social development. When a child reaches the stage of parallel play, he must respect other children as human beings and not just as objects. While playing in a sandbox, a child may manipulate his cars and trucks in any way he sees fit, but he must respect the rights and privileges of other children. When the child takes part in games of low organization, he must be prepared to follow certain rules; these rules can be replaced later by the laws, folkways, and mores of society. When the child participates in games of high organization, he must work with others for the common goal and good of the group.

Vocational skills help the mentally retarded to perform specific tasks and work as productive members of society. Physical educators can assist the retarded to develop a greater attention span and improved manipulative skills which will promote their vocational readiness and productivity.

Attention span is relatively short in most children and especially so in the mentally retarded when they are not interested, motivated, or challenged. Active participation in physical education activities can provide enjoyment and fun for retarded participants and at the same time help them improve their ability to follow directions and see a task through from beginning to end.

Manipulative skills are dependent on hand-eye coordination and perception which begin to develop during the period of motor generalization. Physical educators can help the mentally retarded develop manipulative skills through craft activities, stringing beads, arranging puzzle segments, and through activities such as jacks. These activities help the individual to improve his hand-eye coordination and aid in developing coordination and perceptual skills.

The modern comprehensive physical education program must provide more than enjoyment for the mentally retarded. Although fun and pleasure are important elements and cannot be minimized, physical education programs should be designed to develop the whole person, so that the mentally retarded may fulfill their potential and reach higher levels of function.

Wishful thinking . . .

PETER VALLETUTTI
Director of Special Education
Coppin State College, Baltimore, Maryland

FLORENCE CHRISTOPLOS
Associate Professor of Physical Education,
Coppin State College, Baltimore, Maryland

A number of reports about apparent beneficial and differential effects of physical education on the mentally retarded have been published recently in professional journals. Two generalizations seem to reflect the professional consensus:

1. Mentally retarded children score below the norms for the general population on tests of motor skills.
2. Mentally retarded children improve their psychomotor proficiency through training.

In addition, it is generally accepted that physical education training of the mentally retarded has been neglected by many educators.

Implicit in much of the literature but rarely explicitly noted is the elementary axiom supported by most educational research, that children learn that which we teach them. If specific motor skills or physical fitness activities are taught, then that is the area in which progress can be expected. If directionality, fine motor coordination, laterality, or self-confidence in play are taught, then these are the behaviors in which improvement can be expected.

When educators attempt to generalize progress in a specific area to other areas such as academics, abstract thinking, verbal ability, and/or personal and social adjustment, they manifest confused and wishful thinking. Physical education is somehow expected to affect a series of intervening variables and to have predictable positive influence on such far-removed behaviors as reading.

Teaching is usually viewed more as an art than as a skill. The effects of this art are mysterious and unpredictable. In educational circles, it is not unusual to find the belief that training procedures, such as physical education, will have magical effects. For this reason, educational panaceas have a bandwagon effect on educators, allowing them to continue along, trusting that good intentions will lead to miracles.

Instead of asking for or expecting miracles, educators would do well to settle for more modest and realistic goals. In physical education, a healthy body over which the child has reasonably good control and which the child enjoys using, are appropriate goals. Although verbal support may be given to these noncognitive goals, the literature reflects a latent ambivalence, in that many of the studies find it necessary to establish correlations between psychomotor and nonpsychomotor behaviors in order to justify physical education. Teachers apparently must discover or identify an intellectual *raison d'être* for everything they do. A cultural bias within education has, it would seem, addled the minds of investigators in this area.

As long as physical education is secondary to nonpsychomotor goals and as long as physical education is predominantly a motivational technique employed by teachers for *more important* achievements. then, logically, progress in cognitive and effective areas may not be attributed to psychomotor achievements. The pleasure in physical education activities may become associated with concurrent nonphysical education activities or may even permeate other areas of the curriculum. The growth in these other areas may be a product of the transference of motivational factors, rather than of skill transference or improved neurological organization.

On the other hand, if physical education is valued for its own sake, then research should take the direction of empirically validating a sequential program for the achievement of specifically defined goals in health, strength, endurance, agility, coordination, etc. By using a task analysis programing approach, the error of making illogical generalizations can be avoided. A more intensely analyzed program, applicable to all children, can then be developed. If the task is analyzed, and not just the child, professionals then assure their responsibility for achieving behaviorally identified goals. The alternative is likely to be the watering down of the physical education curriculum for the mentally retarded, a familiar danger to special educators.

A task analysis programing approach is not only empirically but theoretically sound. Some have reported that the mentally retarded perform at the same rate as the normal, once adequate attention to relevant stimuli is achieved. This meshes well with the argument for establishing clear and specific goals. By using the task analysis approach, the teacher is more purposefully directed toward the goals set for the child. Therefore, he should be better able to focus the attention of the child himself on those behaviors which are necessary for the attainment of the goal. Irrelevant and unimportant activities in the attainment of these goals may then be eliminated. For example, what is the specific goal set for the retarded child when we teach a skill such as crawling when he is already able to walk? The direct relevance of crawling to improved neurological organization and thus to reading is too obscure for most teachers. How then can we expect this purpose to be perceived by the child? The importance of perceived purpose for achieving motivation is generally accepted. Vague purposes lead to a buckshot curriculum.

A changing role . . .

ELEANOR COLEMAN

Supervisor, Girls' Physical Education,
Duval County, Jacksonville, Florida

Much attention has been given to the value of physical education as it relates to the mentally retarded, and advocates are emerging who sometimes project physical education as the ultimate medium for their education. Through research and activity programs for the retarded, physical education is attaining a new high status in education. Real or imagined intellectual barriers are crumbling. As a physical educator, I am delighted with the new-found acceptance of physical education by our academic colleagues. In the past, any attempt to communicate with the physically unenlightened has been difficult and has rendered an intellectual approach the only road to communication. That is now changed, largely due to research dealing with the retarded, as well as to an increasing awareness of the importance of physical fitness for everyone.

The prospect of the continued acceptance of our present status is viewed with some apprehension—what's that thing about thin ice? As a proponent of activity programs for the retarded, I view research in almost the same perspective as the missile program— for every missile, there is an antimissile, and for every antimissile, an antimissile missile. Some studies seem to be motivated by the desire to discredit previous studies. There appears to be an insidious concentration on disproving theories and methods which have experienced relative success. Following the establishment of discreditation, the earlier theorists feel a need to defend their findings, often in obscurities which detract from the original value.

There should be no inference that physical educators are the only culprits involved in such negative attempts toward progress. There are those who endorse music as the major motivator for the retarded, and those who, conversely, demand its complete elimination, as an inhibitor to progress!

It is all very confusing to the teacher who, until the last few years, evaluated physical education in terms of increased levels of physical performance and the sound of little children's laughter where before there was none. There were those who correlated and integrated physical education with other subjects with no great clamor. No fantastic claims were made—it just appeared to be an acceptable teaching procedure.

Research in the area of physical education as it relates to the education of the retarded should not be discouraged. In fact, valid experimentation should be expanded to include the normal child. Future research may disprove some claims which have been made, or it may reflect similar beneficial correlations within the normal range of intelligence.

As an exponent of physical education who holds the highest expectations for its contribution to human development, I decry the Doubting Thomases who, despite optimistic findings, relegate physical education to its traditional role of contributing only to the most obvious outcomes of fitness and skill. Those who are involved in teaching ask only that valid, scientific research be conducted. It is time to cease recognizing hypotheses as principles; to stop attempting to apply deductive reasoning to empirical studies.

If there is anything the teacher of the retarded has learned it is *patience* and *hope*. He shall remain patient and hopeful. He shall continue to progress, preferably with valid research which can provide positive direction; or he shall continue on his own path, not dealing in isolated alternatives but in the assimilation of the most promising reasonable aspects of available information.

It must not be imagined that those at the grass roots are jumping on bandwagons or pinning their hopes to a star. They are not so disposed. They recognize the possibility that the range of basic interests and talents of the retarded is no smaller than that of normal children—simpler, yes, but not smaller. Until they are presented with substantial evidence of *the* program to pursue, they shall continue to offer a variety of programs and stimuli. They support anything which brings hope to the parent and progress for the child.

Fear not that the teacher will accept prescribed elixirs. Any observable bandwagon phenomenon lies not with the teacher but with those involved in research. Teachers face the future with optimism that out of all research shall emerge increased hope for the retarded. Who shall accept the premise that that which has not been scientifically established is not possible?

There is much more that could be said. As the children play, perhaps they will laugh and have fun—or could this apparent reaction be overcompensation for their inner apathy and rejection of activity? Are they merely registering a conditioned response? Maybe today I should use operant conditioning! (Lots of mothers and coaches use it, but have never named it!)

If nothing else, the vocabulary of special education and physical education has created a nice, new, academic aura, except for *creeping* and *crawling*—and even Webster contributes to that confusion.

One final request to those engaged in research—please hire interpreters! I fear that the little knowledge that filters down through this unscientifically oriented mind can be a dangerous thing!

CHAPTER 33

The nature of physical education programming for the mentally retarded and physically handicapped

WALTER F. ERSING
Ohio State University

It is generally recognized that physical education programs for children with mental retardation and/or a physical handicap have developed and expanded during the 1960's and early 1970's. The growth in programming for this type of child is undoubtedly the result of the joint effort by professional organizations, private institutions, and agencies of the federal government.

Although a cursory review of the evidence available relative to this development seems to indicate a significant increase in programming for such children, there appears to be relatively little substantive and organized data as to the exact nature or content of existing physical education programs for the mentally retarded and physically handicapped. Furthermore, it was felt that the availability of such information would serve to provide valuable impact in modifying present instructional programs for the handicapped but also serve to guide the content of professional preparation programs.

To achieve this purpose, a national survey

Reprinted from The Journal of Health, Physical Education and Recreation, Feb., 1974, with permission.

Walter F. Ersing is an associate professor of physical education and project director, Bureau of Education for the Handicapped Professional Preparation Grant, Ohio State University, Columbus, Ohio 43210.

was conducted in 1971-1972 among schools, agencies, and institutions with physical education programs for the handicapped. The survey was conducted as part of a Planning Grant, Bureau of Education for the Handicapped, Office of Education, H.E.W. Two hundred fifty-eight institutions, schools, and/or agencies in 50 states conducting physical education programs were surveyed, of which 129 (50%) replied, representing 35 states. Of those responding to the survey, four categories of schools were evident—schools from public school systems, state institutions, private and/or parochial schools, and county public schools.

Seven different kinds of categorical disabilities within the schools and institutions surveyed were identified—mentally retarded (educable and trainable), blind, deaf, orthopedically handicapped, minimal brain dysfunction, emotionally disturbed, and cardiac impairment.

The study examined several dimensions of physical education programs being offered to children with handicaps. One of the areas studied was the administrative factors, including such items as class size, time allotted, number per week, class groupings, and staff qualifications. Another item investigated was the type of activities offered in the curriculum either daily, daily in a specific season, occasionally, or not at all. Other factors examined were the type of teaching styles, evaluation tools, extracurricular activity programs, and kind of facilities used for physical education programming for the handicapped.

Several conclusions can be drawn from the responses obtained from the sampling of 129 institutions. Among the conclusions of relevance to those involved in program development for the handicapped or in professional preparation programs, the following may be of interest:

1. The opportunity for adequate and controlled development of physical and motor abilities of the developmentally disabled seems limited in view of the time per class and number of times per week for adapted physical education classes. This is evident in view of the findings that over 50% (or a mean of 87%) of the institutions surveyed reported offering physical education at least one time per week and that over 50% (or a mean of 65%) reported having a range of 15 to 20 minutes for adapted physical education.

2. The size of the physical education class does not appear to be as critical a factor in determining the effectiveness of these classes. This conclusion is based on the findings that the number of students assigned to each physical education class was in the range of 11 to 20 students per class for all levels except preschool. An even lower range, 0 to 10, was reported as the most popular for the preschool level.

3. Categorical grouping based on the type of disability tends to be the most prevalent approach in placing children within adapted physical education classes. Evidence to this conclusion can be found in the results indicating that 91 institutions (70%) reported using a homogeneous grouping of children with similar disabilities in adapted physical education classes. Sex categorization did not seem to be a factor since 72% (91 institutions) reported their class as being coeducational.

4. There appears to be a substantial need for physical educators with specialized training in teaching the mentally retarded and physically handicapped in view of the finding that only 17% of the teachers of physical education were professionally prepared within adapted physical education or corrective therapy. In addition, it should be noted that although 78 (35%) of the teachers reported by the institutions had professional training in physical education, the remaining 108 (48%) of the teachers were individuals with professional backgrounds from other areas—special education, therapeutic recreation, lay specialist, and physical therapy. It was evident that many institutions employed teachers of adapted physical education whose credentials were from different fields. The study did not attempt to determine the quality of the programs offered by the teachers from various types of professional backgrounds, however.

5. The distribution of responses relative to the type of activities offered in the adapted physical education program tended to identify certain groupings. The activities which appeared most popular on a daily basis were fundamental movements, fundamental nonlocomotive, body image, manipulative skill, perceptual motor, and physical fitness. The activities offered daily during a specific season were stunts and tumbling, high organizational games, track and field, jumping, singing-folk games, team sports, low organizational games, and creative rhythms. Clearly identified as the type of activities tending not to be offered in programs were dance, dual sports, aquatics, and gymnastics. Three other activities, balance, posture education, and close order drill, tend to be offered only occasionally in programs.

One may conclude from these results that programs for the developmentally disabled could be expanded by adding to or including more frequently the activities of dance, dual sports, and balance tasks. Since the lack of facilities or equipment is not a primary factor for the inclusion of these activities in adapted physical education programs, greater emphasis on the knowledge and skills to teach such activities within professional preparation programs along with in-service workshops would facilitate the inclusion of these activities in programs. Though the lack of a facility or equipment could restrict the expansion of swimming and gymnastics within programs, similar training seems to be needed in both of these areas as well.

6. Of the eight styles of teaching ranked by frequency of use, one may conclude that the command teaching style, which is a formal, dictatorial, teacher-centered approach, is the most commonly used for all types of developmental disabilities. The creative or totally exploratory approach was clearly identified as the style not favored in teaching the developmentally disabled. Evidence seems to support the judicious use of guided discovery and small group styles as appropriate in select situations.

7. The emphasis in assessing motor performance of the developmentally disabled is primarily in the areas of physical fitness and perceptual motor assessment. The three tests mentioned most frequently were the AAHPER Kennedy Fitness Test, the President's Council Fitness Test, and Kephart's Perceptual Motor Survey. In view of the limited use of developmental, sport, skill, strength, cardiovascular, and motor ability tests, there appears to be a need for increasing the awareness of the tests presently available in these areas and the development of these tests with performance scores established as normal for the given developmental disability category.

8. Though recreational swimming and special sports days were included in programs of 50% of the institutions surveyed, the availability of other extracurricular physical activities was generally limited. Approximately one-third (37%) or less of the institutions offered programs in intramural sports, camping, recreational activities, and interscholastic sport. Judging from this pattern of responses, it seems evident that the developmentally disabled are not exposed generally to programs of adapted physical education which are broad in scope and rich in opportunities for participation at various performance levels. Though the state institutions appear to have a higher percentage of

involvement in extracurricular programming than any other type of institution, the existence of such programs is generally limited.

9. Outdoor playgrounds, gymnasiums, and/or multi-purpose rooms were available in a majority of the institutions. Though initially one may conclude that the lack of facilities does not seem to be a major factor in restricting programs, the study was not able to determine the size of the facilities or the number of students served in the facilities. Both of these factors, along with the availability of staff to implement programs, are crucial elements to weigh before arriving at any such conclusion.

10. An examination of the type of community facilities used by the institutions reveals that no one type of community facility is used by more than 15% of the institutions. This seems to suggest that greater use of opportunities for activity within the community could be developed and thus stimulate program expansion.

In view of the data available and the conclusions drawn from this study, one recognizes that several challenging problems exist in physical education programs for the handicapped. Foremost among the problems seems to be the need for more physical educators with specialized training to provide developmental and instructional physical activity programs for the handicapped. Creating interest in teaching the handicapped among those students presently in physical education and the availability of adequate professional preparation programs to train those interested will be a continued challenge for the profession. Other problems needing attention are the need for more time for regular participation in physical activity programs and the expansion of the kind of physical activities offered the handicapped child within existing and new programs. These are but a sample of the problems evident. Solutions to those problems identified as well as others implied in the findings remain to be attacked with the energies and resources available to, and within, the profession.

Discussion questions

1. The first three articles in this section presented three contrasting philosophical positions regarding physical education and recreation programming for the retarded. Discuss each position as it relates to the value of physical education programming for this population. Are there differing viewpoints as to what should be the role of physical education in the child's overall curriculum? In what ways are these authors in basic philosophical agreement?

2. Why is it important to delineate the goals of a physical education curriculum for the retarded? Discuss some of the problems and controversies that have been generated because goals have not been clearly stated and sequenced.

3. Discuss the current status of physical education programming in the schools according to Ersing. Relate your response to each of the following areas: integrated programming, specialized personnel, types of activities offered, and the kind of facilities available. Do your experiences in the schools corroborate the results of Ersing's investigation? What are some of the recommendations you would make to improve physical education services for the handicapped?

AUTHOR INDEX

SUBJECT INDEX